CRIMINOLOGICAL THEORIES

THEORIES

UNDERSTANDING CRIME IN AMERICA

SECOND EDITION

James F. Anderson

Professor of Criminal Justice
East Carolina University
Greenville, North Carolina

JONES & BARTLETT
LEARNING

World Headquarters
Jones & Bartlett Learning
5 Wall Street
Burlington, MA 01803
978-443-5000
info@jblearning.com
www.jblearning.com

Jones & Bartlett Learning books and products are available through most bookstores and online booksellers. To contact Jones & Bartlett Learning directly, call 800-832-0034, fax 978-443-8000, or visit our website, www.jblearning.com.

Substantial discounts on bulk quantities of Jones & Bartlett Learning publications are available to corporations, professional associations, and other qualified organizations. For details and specific discount information, contact the special sales department at Jones & Bartlett Learning via the above contact information or send an email to specialsales@jblearning.com.

Production Credits
Executive Publisher: Kimberly Brophy
Executive Acquisitions Editor: Bill Larkin
Editorial Assistant: Audrey Schwinn
Associate Production Editor: Rebekah Linga
Marketing Manager: Lindsay White
Manufacturing and Inventory Control Supervisor: Amy Bacus
Composition: Cenveo Publisher Services
Cover Design: Kristin E. Parker
Rights and Permissions Coordinator: Ashley Dos Santos
Cover and Title Page Images: Top: © vs148/ShutterStock, Inc.; Bottom: © DrHitch/ShutterStock, Inc.
Printing and Binding: Edwards Brothers Malloy
Cover Printing: Edwards Brothers Malloy

Library of Congress Cataloging-in-Publication Data
Anderson, James F.
  Criminological theories: understanding crime in America/James F. Anderson. — Second edition.
    pages cm
  Revised edition of the author's Criminological theories, first published in 2002.
  Includes bibliographical references and index.
  ISBN 978-1-4496-8187-6 (pbk) — ISBN 1-4496-8187-5 (pbk)
  1. Criminology—United States. 2. Crime—United States.
  3. Crime—United States—Sociological aspects. I. Title.
  HV6022.U6A53 2015
  364.973—dc23
                                      2014008741
6048

Printed in the United States of America
18 17 16 15 14   10 9 8 7 6 5 4 3 2 1

DEDICATION

This book is dedicated to the memory of
Jerald C. Burns who was my teacher, mentor, and friend.

CONTENTS

PREFACE

This book has been written for several purposes. The first is to present plausible explanation of crime causation. The second is to foster a greater appreciation of criminological theory. The third is to get students to think critically about the social reality we call crime. To this end, the second edition of *Criminological Theories: Understanding Crime in America* is an updated version of the original book that was published in the summer of 2002. It contains current research findings as well as updated statistics on the crime rate and new developments in criminological theory to clarify and strengthen arguments made throughout the book.

This edition features major revisions while maintaining its vital core from the previous version. The organization of the work will guide students through criminological theory in a historically correct manner. For example, in the first edition of the text, the first section focused on Chapters 1, 2, and 3. These chapters have been rewritten to include contemporary illustrations of crime, research findings, and updated statistical data. The second section of the book, which included Chapters 4 and 5, addressed Classical Theory and Positivistic Criminology, respectively. Substantial revisions were also made to these chapters with discussions on the reemergence of choice theory, general deterrence theory, specific deterrence theory, and profiles of noted criminologists who contributed to the development and expansion of these criminological traditions. Moreover, Chapter 5 formerly titled, "Positivistic Criminology," has been renamed "Trait Theories" to reflect its new content.

In the first edition of the book, the third section was devoted to social structural theories. Each theory in this criminological tradition was given special attention within individual chapters. Consequently, there were separate chapters devoted to the Chicago School, Anomie, Strain, and Cultural Deviance Theories. However, in the second edition, all structural theories are presented in one chapter. Chapter 6 is titled, "Social Structural Theories: Emphasis on the Social Structure." In this chapter, several additions have been made that include discussions of the size and growth of the underclass, child poverty, and minority groups and poverty, as well as an examination of Steven Messner and Richard Rosenfeld's Institutional Anomie Theory. This chapter includes James W. Messerschmidt's Structured Action Theory and how social settings and one's place in the social structure influences behavior. This chapter also contains several profiles of noted criminologists who contributed to the development and growth of this criminological tradition.

Extensive changes were also made to Chapter 7. In the first edition, the fourth section presented social processing theories with each theory in this tradition given special attention by appearing as a single chapter. As such, separate chapters were devoted to social learning theories, social control theories, and labeling theories. In the second edition, all social processing theories are combined and presented in one chapter. Chapter 7 is titled, "Social Processing Theories: Emphasis on Socialization." It provides several additions that include discussions of family relations, peer relationships, educational experiences, and religion. Moreover, this chapter explores life course theory as well as theory integration and its variations.

Chapter 8 has also been revised and restructured. In the first edition, the fifth section of the book addressed social conflict theories and theory integration with each theory given special treatment. However, in the second edition, these theories are preceded by a discussion of the newly emerged Occupy Movement followed by several fundamental changes to the first edition. First, the section on theory integration has been substantially revised, shortened, and moved to Chapter 7. Second, several relatively new conflict theories have been analyzed and added to the discussion. Some of the new theories include: cultural criminology, green criminology, power threat theory, as well as the latest developments in power–control theory.

In closing, the book predicts what criminological theory will likely address in the future. Predictions range from placing more emphasis on preventing domestic terrorism to implementing restorative justice models to addressing cyber-crime, and the influence that grant awarding agencies have on setting the research agendas in both criminology and criminal justice, especially with respect to how they may invariably determine what is important to research. Nevertheless, while the criminological theories in this book are presented in a historically correct manner, instructors may choose to present chapters to reflect their teaching needs.

James F. Anderson

ACKNOWLEDGMENTS

I am grateful to those students and colleagues who communicated with me about their reactions to *Criminological Theories: Understanding Crime in America* and to the reviewers who provided invaluable criticisms about the first edition and clear instructions on improving the second. In response to their suggestions, extensive efforts were placed on updating and expanding, as well as sharpening the focus of many arguments presented throughout the book. Some of those who provided insightful comments, suggestions, and encouragement to the second manuscript were Adam Langsam, Northeastern State University; Francis P. Reddington, University of Central Missouri; David Spinner, University of Maryland-Eastern Shores; and Vic Bumphus, University of Tennessee-Chattanooga. Among those who were instrumental in the second edition, I would like to offer my deepest appreciation to the faculty, staff, and students in the Department of Criminal Justice at East Carolina University. Without their support, this book would not have been completed. I would also like to express appreciation to Gregg Barak, Eastern Michigan University, and Christina J. Johns (retired), Florida A&M University who introduced me to criminological theory.

The author and publisher would also like to thank the following individuals for their valuable input in the development of this text.

Kevin Barnes-Ceeney
John Jay College of Criminal Justice

Brian B. Boutwell
Sam Houston State University

Ellen G. Cohn
Florida International University

Mary Beth Finn
Herzing University

Suzanne M. Godboldt
Missouri Western State University

John P. Gray
Faulkner University

Lisa M. Graziano
California State University, Los Angeles

Lisa Landis
University of South Florida

Kathryn Morgan
University of Alabama at Birmingham

Billye Janiece Nipper
Embry-Riddle Aeronautical University

Michael Parker
Hartnell College

Mary E. Pyle
Tyler Junior College

Michael Raymond
New Hampshire Technical Institute–Concord's Community College

Beverly Ross
California University of Pennsylvania

Melissa M. Walbridge
Florida State University

Jason B. Waller
Tyler Junior College

INTRODUCTION

The Crime Problem in America

Despite the release of recent statistics from the U.S. Department of Justice (2013) indicating that the number of violent crimes, including murder, rape, and robbery, have fallen for the fifth consecutive year, the general public still harbors fear of crime. As such, crime is still among the top concerns in America. This insecurity is largely influenced by nearly everyone in America knowing someone who has been the victim of some type of violence or suffered an economic victimization, such as theft and burglary. Because crime and violence are so pervasive in America, no one truly enjoys immunity or is completely safe from crime. This concern is revealed by the number of neighborhood crime watch programs, gun purchases, people enrolled in self-defense training, and citizens willing to work hand-in-hand with law enforcement to keep their neighborhoods crime-free (Masters et al., 2011). Despite this reality, much fear of crime might be unfounded and artificially manipulated by the mass media and politicians (Surette, 2007; Barak, 1994; Elias, 1986). For example, media critics argue that newspapers, television, and movies glorify and sensationalize personal tragedies to sell papers, boost ratings, or generate huge profits. They also claim that the more controversial the act of violence, the better. For example, critics contend that crime stories with a class or racial element tend to attract more interest, ignite greater social passion, and have a polarizing effect on the public (Surette, 2007). Moreover, politicians typically campaign on issues such as law and order, reducing the crime problem, and "getting tough" on violent offenders. In fact, politicians are particularly known for exaggerating crime statistics during election season to show the public that the incumbent has been ineffective at keeping the community safe, and thus advance their own political ambitions. This often occurs even if no crime problem exists. Therefore, the fear of crime is very likely to be greater than the actual threat.

An irony about crime and victimization is that those who fear crime the most are those least likely to be victimized, while those who fear crime the least are those who disproportionately appear in crime victimization statistics (Siegel, 2012). For example, consider elderly citizens. They make up a very small segment of the population, but yet they are the most fearful of crime. They account for the smallest number of victimizations with respect to violent crime. In contrast, consider teenagers and young adults who seemingly enjoy a carefree existence, yet they are those who are most likely to be the victims and perpetrators of violent crime. In fact, statistics reveal that teenagers between the ages of 13 and 17 make up 6% of the U.S. population, but account for 30% of index crime arrests. Some criminologists believe that the victimization and offending disparity that exists between the elderly and young adults is because of the lifestyles of younger versus older Americans (Siegel, 2012). Teenagers in the United States, unlike their counterparts in other nations, live in a culture that encourages permissiveness, self-expression, and experimentation, and glorifies violence while discouraging moral values, such as marriage, religion, honesty, and being drug-free. Some contend that this is why America has the dubious distinction of having the highest prison incarceration rates in the civilized world and arguably the most violent and troubled children (Bennett, Dilulio, and Walters, 1996).

Young Americans have open access to computers, the Internet, and social networking. They frequent places where the criminal element congregates (i.e., online chat rooms, bars, parks, schools, and parking lots). They drink (some even experiment with drugs) and associate with others who are usually in the same age category who might also drink and possibly engage in drug use. Some carry firearms for intimidation, crime, or self-protection. Some young adults even associate with others who have violent and troubled histories. Again, consider the elderly, who have very different lifestyles. They do not typically frequent public places where younger Americans congregate (i.e., online chat rooms, bars, parks, schools, and parking lots). They do not associate with high-risk peers who engage in intimidation or commit violent crime. Perhaps the factor that best explains why the elderly face fewer victimization risks is that they tend to stay inside at night (Siegel, 2012). Statistics reveal that crime peak hours are from 6:00 p.m. to 6:00 a.m. While this does not affect the number of elderly people who are burglarized, it does mean that their chances of being robbed, assaulted, or killed are greatly reduced. The difference between the victimization rates of younger and older Americans can be attributed to the fact that younger people have lifestyles that are conducive to violence and crime.

National Youth Survey—An important instrument used to collect data on adolescents. It allows researchers to test integrated sociological and psychological theory.

While self-report surveys or studies can be conducted by independent researchers, there is one major self-report survey: the **National Youth Survey (NYS)**. The survey was started in 1976. It is a single formal entity that is cited in reference to juvenile delinquency and juvenile crime. It uses a national sample of youth between the ages of 11 and 17. Researchers use self-report surveys or studies to measure adult offending.

Also interesting is the way that rates vary for men and women. All sources of crime data—including the Uniform Crime Reports (UCR), National Crime Victimization Survey (NCVS), and self-report surveys (SRSs)—report that men commit more crimes than their female counterparts, but the rate of women offending has been on the rise in recent years (Brown, Esbensen, and Geis, 2007; Siegel, 2012). This includes crimes of violence and crimes related to property and drugs. (Drug-related crime now accounts for 45% of arrests for women.) Statistics reveal that the number of women in prison is growing faster than that of any other demographic group. Still, women account for only 15% of violent crime and 28% of property crime. Some criminologists argue that women's lesser participation in crime can be explained by the way they are socialized and their lack of access to opportunities to commit crime. In fact, some feminist scholars contend that when women are provided complete equality in the economic market, their participation in crime will almost equal that of their male counterparts. Neither has yet been realized. Statistics also reveal that women are victimized less frequently than men, but are more likely to be injured during violent encounters. After being victimized, women are more likely to change their lifestyles to prevent continued or future victimizations. This is not the case with men, since they face greater amounts of victimization and commit more crime than their female counterparts. After victimizations, men rarely make changes to their routines and are very difficult to treat because many refuse to accept or attend counseling to help them cope with the aftermath of being victimized (Siegel, 2012; Stanko and Hobdell, 1993).

Unlike women who have been the victims of crime, male victims are more likely to blame their attacker, question their masculinity, and sometimes refuse to discuss how they feel about being a crime victim. Criminal justice experts argue that men may have lifestyles that actually increase their victimization risk. Research reveals that men are more likely to be victimized by a stranger, while women are likely to be hurt, injured, or even killed by someone they know or with whom they share an intimate relationship. Women typically face violence at the hands of a relative, ex-boyfriend, spouse, estranged husband, or acquaintance. Women are victimized in a number of ways that include, but are not limited to, date rape, spouse abuse, domestic violence, prostitution, pornography, and deception over the Internet and through social media networks. Despite this, some scholars argue that women are reluctant to participate in the criminal justice process, because they could face a second victimization at the hands of the justice machinery by police, lawyers on cross-examination, or judge and jury.

Those who study criminology examine a number of areas that range from crime, to victims, to causes, and how society responds to offenders who inflict harm on other members of society. Students interested in criminology must be able to understand the social reality we refer to as crime as well as legal definitions of crime (Barkan, 2012; Anderson and Slate, 2011). Hence, crime is defined as any act of commission or omission of a law forbidding or commanding such behavior. This refers to two categories of behaviors. First, the law requires that people abstain from committing behaviors such as stealing, raping, and killing others. Second, the law demands that people participate in behaviors such as paying one's annual income tax and getting one's driving license renewed.

A crime of omission stems from a failure to take action where there is a legal or contractual obligation to do so. For example, lifeguards, parents, spouses, and doctors have a legal obligation to assist others even when they have feelings of indifference. Consider the lifeguard who witnesses a drowning swimmer fighting for his or her life, but does nothing. He can be charged with failing to help, because of his legal obligation to assist swimmers and save lives. Similarly, a parent can be charged and punished in cases stemming from neglect of a child. Furthermore, because marriage is contractual, a spouse who does not assist the other in a life-threatening situation can be charged with failure to assist if it is determined that death occurred because of the omission of indifference. Doctors can also be sued or imprisoned if they fail to treat patients with serious medical needs. A failure to abstain from some acts or engage in others will mean that one is legally responsible for either course of action. Notwithstanding, when a crime is committed, the offender is punished by the state and not the victim.

mala in se—Crimes that are inherently evil by their nature, such as murder, rape, and robbery.

mala prohibita—Crimes that offend the sensibility of some people's morality. They are crimes because statutes are in place to prevent them. Such crimes include prostitution, drug sales, drug use, and gambling.

In the United States, crimes are mostly viewed as either **mala in se** or **mala prohibita**. The distinctions between these crimes are glaring. For example, mala in se crimes are offenses that are inherently wrong, or evil in and of themselves. There is usually a consensus among people about the seriousness of these actions and a shared disdain for offenders who engage in them. These crimes offend the morality of the society. Mala in se crimes include such acts as murder, rape, child molestation, or forcibly taking someone's property. Conversely, mala prohibita crimes are actions that are not evil in and of themselves, but are considered criminal because state statutes have been passed to prohibit these actions. Mala prohibita crimes are often referred to as public order crimes (Anderson and Slate, 2011). They typically include acts of prostitution, pornography, drug use, and gambling. Such actions create controversy because there is not a consensus among people about the danger they pose to society. They are also commonly referred to as victimless crimes because willing participants engage in the behavior. (In most cases, a participant exchanges money for a desired commodity or service.) As such, some argue that there is no "real" victim. When these actions come to the attention of law enforcement and the court system, some people accuse the government of attempting to legislate public morality instead of enforce laws against "real" crime. The government counters that it is not legislating morality, but rather, it is regulating behavior that usually comes with adverse health consequences. Notwithstanding, a perpetrator's action is not a crime unless there is a law that prohibits the behavior. Therefore, it is possible for some actions (while morally disdainful), not to be considered a crime because they do not violate any existing law. Consider a contemporary and controversial argument that is instructive in this regard. Marijuana use is viewed by some as dangerous because they see it as a gateway drug that leads to the use of more serious drugs. However, some segments of the population openly condone smoking it for recreational use (Siegel, 2012). The issue is complicated by the fact that recently, some states have made it legal for individuals to use specified amounts of marijuana for medicinal purposes (Masters et al., 2011).

Criminology examines several types of crime that range from street crime to elite crime. Street crimes include actions such as murder, rape, theft, robbery, burglary, larceny, auto theft, arson, and hate crimes. These are referred to as index crimes. Crime sources reveal that people who make up the poor underclass in society disproportionately commit these types of crime. In response to these acts, the criminal justice system spends billions of dollars annually on preventing, apprehending, and punishing the offenders who perpetrate these crimes (Siegel, 2012; Barkan, 2012). However, some criminologists argue that white-collar, organized, computer, corporate, political, governmental, medical, and healthcare offenders commit the most serious crimes. These crimes often require education and social status. These crimes are those committed by the criminal elite. Critical criminologists argue that they contribute to more widespread human suffering, injuries, and financial devastation than street crime. Unfortunately, these offenses typically go undetected and unreported (Barkan, 2012). In fact, crimes committed by the criminal elite are not addressed with the same seriousness and vigor as index crimes, but instead are typically left to the enforcement of regulatory agencies, special taskforces, and special prosecutors who rarely operate with the same degree of urgency. The efforts of these agencies pale in comparison to the thousands of police agencies charged with preventing index crime. As such, some critical scholars charge that society has a limited understanding of what constitutes real crime and victimization.

Figure 1 presents the big crime pie. The pie is a distribution of the totality of criminality that is committed annually in the United States. In addition to including the index crimes, it lists crimes that largely go undetected and unreported in many of the crime and victimization indexes. The big crime pie illustrates criminal behavior that includes white collar, organized, corporate, political, computer, governmental, and medical crimes. This diagram does not attempt to justify, excuse, or diminish the seriousness of index crime. Instead, it seeks to reveal other types of crimes that are arguably more dangerous and cause greater human suffering both financially as well as physically. Yet, its perpetrators are not known to the general public or its victims since they rarely are held criminally responsible for their actions.

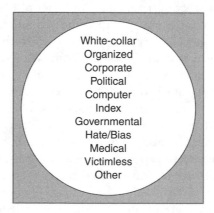

Figure 1 The Big Crime Pie

Criminology is the scientific study of the origin, causation, nature, and extent of crimes. The study of crime also entails an examination of how society reacts and responds to crime (Reid, 2012; Siegel, 2012; Barkan, 2012). For example, do public policies emerge from the efforts of criminologists? Do their research findings impact crime control and justice education policies? Criminologists are set apart from the lay public, because they are trained to use science to study deviant and criminal behavior. When criminologists undertake the study of crime, they do so using objectivity and the scientific method. Objectivity frees criminologists from biases. While conducting research, criminologists set aside personal assumptions about behavior and enter into a value-free exercise. When criminologists employ the scientific method, they generate hypotheses, engage in data collection, formulate theories, and test the validity of those theories. Criminologists rely on several methods of data gathering when engaging in research that includes, but is not limited to, attitudinal surveys, experimental designs, longitudinal designs, observational studies, use of existing data, and unobtrusive methods (Hagan, 2012). Sometimes criminologists may even use triangulated measures to examine a phenomenon, combining three or more forms of data collection (Hagan, 2012). Multiple methods serve to increase the validity and accuracy of the investigation. They allow criminologists to assert with confidence that they truly understand the social reality that we call crime. The scientific method is not an exercise known by all and is, in fact, quite esoteric. People in the lay public readily accept inaccurate views about crime causation. Some believe that offenders engage in crime because they are demonically possessed, born bad, poorly socialized, or simply morally depraved. By using the scientific method, criminologists are able to make accurate assertions about the nature of crime and its consequences, instead of relying on reports from the news media, popularly held views, or personal biases about the nature of crime and offenders who commit such behaviors.

An essential goal of criminology is to identify, describe, explain, predict, and control deviant and criminal behavior (Hagan, 2012). This must be the primary goal of the discipline so as to reduce human misery, suffering, and pain. By determining crime causation, criminologists can assist society in developing strategies to help at-risk individuals and possibly deter them and others from a life of crime. Criminologists can also be instrumental in influencing policies that are designed to react to those who have committed crimes and others who could potentially commit crime. This task is not as easy as some might think. For example, crime statistics are mainly collected by the UCR, NCVS, and SRS. These sources overwhelmingly agree on where crime and victimization occur. The patterns and trends are fairly consistent with respect to when, where, and who is more likely to commit index crime (not the other varieties of crime presented in Figure 1). Criminologists and criminal justice scholars should be able to make accurate predictions about the crime rate from year to year by examining the trends and patterns associated with crime (Siegel, 2012). However, crime is so complex that it is sometimes difficult to isolate where crime will occur next. Crime has a freakish nature and sometimes occurs randomly. Another troubling aspect about studying and explaining crime is the question of why, with the human suffering and misery it causes, people freely engage in such behavior. Consider a few recent examples of crime that have intrigued social observers of criminal behavior.

On Valentine's Day 2008, Steven Phillip Kazmierczak, a former graduate sociology student at Northern Illinois University, entered a large lecture classroom and opened fire on more than 160 students. He murdered six students and wounded 20 others (Nizza, 2008). It was later discovered that he was an exceptional student who had received a dean's award for being an academic standout. In fact, former faculty, students, and staff later reported that on reflection, there were no indicators that he was troubled or disturbed. Later, the university president stated that Kazmierczak had a very good academic record and there were no signs or indicators of impending trouble.

December 14, 2012, marks what is considered the worst school massacre in American history, next to the Columbine High School shooting that occurred in Littleton, Colorado, in 1999. In Newtown, Connecticut, a troubled teenager, Adam Lanza, killed his mother that morning and subsequently entered an unsuspecting and unprotected elementary school, Sandy Hook Elementary, at approximately 9:40 a.m. with three guns, including a .223 caliber rifle, and shot indiscriminately, killing 20 children and six teachers who tried to shield them. This crime shocked the nation and reignited debates over mental health and gun control.

In 2013, it was discovered that Ariel Castro, a 52-year-old former school bus driver, had held Michelle Knight, Amanda Berry, and Gina DeJesus captive in the basement of his home for more than 10 years. He pled guilty to nearly 1,000 charges of rape, kidnapping, and sexual abuse, as well as aggravated murder charges under a fetal homicide law for causing one of the women to miscarry.

In 2011, Casey Anthony was acquitted by a Florida jury in the murder of her daughter, Caylee Marie Anthony, who had disappeared before she was eventually reported missing and found dead. The case was perplexing to many Americans because Casey never reported that Caylee was missing. However, she was convicted of lying to police officers. In the end, Florida lawmakers' efforts to strengthen laws on reporting missing children led to "Caylee's Law," which makes failing to report a missing child an act of reckless disregard for the child's safety.

On April 15, 2013, two bombs were set off near the finish line of the Boston Marathon, killing three people and injuring 260 others. Local, state, and federal law enforcement led a massive effort to apprehend two suspects, Dzhokar Tsarnaev and his brother, Tamerlan. Tamerlan was killed during a shootout with the police, but Dzhokar was arrested and accused of planting and setting off the pair of bombs. The prosecutor in this case claimed that Dzhokhar and his brother were also responsible for the death of Sean Collier, a police officer at the Massachusetts Institute of Technology, during the manhunt. Despite knowing the crime was recorded on surveillance video and the police were able to track the offenders from the crime scene, Dzhokhar has pleaded not guilty. On January 30, 2014, Attorney General Eric Holder authorized Federal prosecutors in Boston to seek the death penalty in the marathon bombing. Currently, it is unknown whether Dzhokhar's defense lawyers will attempt to negotiate a plea of no trial in exchange for a sentence of life in prison without the possibility of parole. The trial has been scheduled to start in November.

In 2011, it was discovered that Penn State's former assistant football coach Jerry Sandusky had been sexually abusing children for years. He was eventually sentenced to serve at least 30 years in prison. The university itself paid a heavy price after it was revealed that others were aware of Sandusky's behavior, including his supervisor, who failed to take immediate actions to have him questioned, arrested, or terminated from the Penn State football program. In fact, investigators reported that there may have been a massive cover-up by university officials to hide the abuse in order to avoid any possible embarrassment to the university and its sports program. Former head coach Joe Paterno was ultimately fired, and a class action lawsuit was filed against the university naming several officials (Paterno, former president Graham Spanier, and others) as parties, alleging that they are liable for endangering the welfare of children because they had knowledge of the sexual abuse allegations of Sandusky, but failed to take action against him. The National Collegiate Athletic Association also handed down several penalties against Penn State, including a $60 million fine (which will be used to fund educational programs in Pennsylvania on child abuse prevention) and the loss of football scholarships.

The untimely death of the "King of Pop," Michael Jackson, in 2009 also stunned the nation. What was more shocking was the manner in which he died. It was revealed that he had accidentally died at the hands of his personal physician, Dr. Conrad Murray, who told everyone during his criminal trial that because Michael Jackson was in a lot of pain and had difficulty sleeping, he had prescribed him painkillers and sleeping aids, but Michael had become addicted to pain medications. However, it was discovered that Dr. Murray had used the surgical anesthetic propofol, which is what ultimately led to Jackson's death. During the trial, medical experts testified that they had never heard of anyone using propofol outside of an operating room because of the danger it posed to a patient's respiratory system. They also indicated that when it is used by a surgeon, it requires the assistance of nurses, doctors, and heart and lung monitors. Before sentencing Dr. Murray, the judge claimed that because of greed and incompetence, Dr. Murray caused Jackson's death by giving him an overdose of a drug that caused cardiac arrest. He was subsequently sentenced to four years in jail. A wrongful death suit was initiated by Jackson's mother.

These crimes illustrate the types of issues that criminologists examine. Criminologists must ask hard questions, such as: Are some offenders merely pleasure seekers who have disregard for others? Are some offenders born criminals who lack moral and mental development? Do other offenders commit crime because they are economically disadvantaged? Do some offenders commit crime to support their lifestyle? Do some offenders commit crime to increase their wealth? Do some offenders learn criminal behavior from associates, a violent culture, or the media? Could the answer to the search for criminal motivation lie in a combination of these? This text attempts to make sense of these possibilities by isolating crime causation and offers strategies to prevent crime and improve the human condition.

The definition of crime is found in the criminal law, or state penal code, created by legislative bodies (Anderson and Slate, 2011). One criticism of the law is that it is biased in favor of wealthy people. For example, some criminologists argue that the criminal law disproportionately targets behaviors that are common to people with little social, economic, or political power, while crimes committed by people in positions of power rarely come to the attention of the criminal justice system (Siegel, 2012; Barkan, 2012). For example, medical doctors, corporate offenders, politicians, government, and white-collar offenders rarely receive media attention, and if they do, they are seldom referred to as offenders, let alone prosecuted. Their crimes are policed by regulatory agencies, which are not noted for moving with the same speed as criminal justice actors. In a departure from this pattern, the tobacco industry came under increasing attention in the 1990s. This could not have been imagined decades earlier.

Though the study of crime emerged during the 18th century, the field of criminology continues to benefit greatly from the contributions that are currently being made. This is especially seen in the areas of processing, structural, and conflict theories and also from newly emerging feminist scholarship that has called for a "gender-aware" criminology that has embraced the use of masculinity to explain crime variations. As stated previously, while criminology is the scientific study of crime and criminal behavior, it also examines its nature and extent. In addition, it focuses on how society reacts and responds to crime and criminals. For example, when crime rates increase, does society respond by creating conservative policies that "get tough" on offenders by mandating severe punishment, such as long prison sentences, or does society seek alternatives to traditional incarceration by diverting less serious offenders from a career path in crime by offering community corrections or restorative justice programs?

While some people in the lay public (without benefit of scientific research) have argued that "demonic forces" have caused criminals to engage in criminal behavior, structural and conflict criminologists would argue that adverse life circumstances, such as poverty and feelings of hopelessness, may induce or entice some offenders into thinking their environment and economic situation is never going to get better, and therefore the only logical recourse is to commit a crime for economic gain. Conversely, others have argued that for some offenders, family structure or the way it functions is so dysfunctional that they cannot avoid a life of crime. Perhaps the lack of educational attainment almost guarantees participation in crime, or maybe poor judgment influences the selection of inappropriate peers. Conceivably, poverty and negative environmental forces provide some with abundant access to drugs and other mind-altering substances. While these views have been perpetuated by some customs and traditions, they also have a sociohistorical context. The mass media is also responsible for disseminating erroneous beliefs about the origins of criminal behavior. Only those who study crime can offer valid and informed assessments of crime causation and its nature.

In the United States, billions of dollars are spent each year to combat the crime problem. Resources are allocated separately to every component of the criminal justice system. These include police, courts, and corrections. In addition, money is spent on recruiting and training personnel in each of these areas. It is estimated that there are more than 17,000 police organizations in the United States (Masters et al., 2011). Money is spent on providing these agencies with the technology, manpower, and equipment needed to apprehend offenders and bring them to justice. The corrections system also commands overwhelming resources. For example, to date, there are more than two million offenders in places of confinement. At the same time, there are more than four million offenders under some form of community supervision, serving time on parole or probation.

In addition, the victims of crime endure a tremendous amount of pain and suffering after their initial victimization. Victimization surveys report that some victims spend years receiving physical and psychological therapy. Sometimes they need medication and medical devices after sustaining debilitating injuries. Many Americans lose money after having to stay home from work to heal from devastating injuries. The fear of crime is so acute that many Americans invest in home security devices to ensure their safety. Some with the financial resources move to gated communities.

Why study crime and criminal behavior? Crime is a social reality that all of us must confront. Nearly everyone knows someone who has committed or been the victim of a crime. Statistics indicate that all Americans, at some point in their lives, will be the victim of either a violent or a property crime. Therefore, we should study crime because it involves everyone. Perhaps some more important reasons are to: improve the human condition by creating crime-prevention strategies; eliminate or reduce crime-producing factors for criminals; learn how not to be a crime victim; learn how to identify, describe, explain, predict, and control criminal behavior; determine if crime prevention strategies are effective; and, if they are discovered to be ineffective, create new ones. The study of crime is critical because it reveals, through patterns and trends reported each year, if the crime rate is actually increasing or decreasing. Perhaps more important, it indicates whether crime-prevention strategies are meeting their goals of reducing crime. If, after examining crime rates for a reasonable amount of time, we discover that the rates are increasing, we would probably do well to focus our crime-prevention efforts and resources in another area. Therefore, criminologists should embrace the study of crime as an attempt to alleviate human suffering and to reduce the costs of crime. This can be achieved only when criminologists examine the totality of criminality committed by offenders in the lower class, as well as by criminal elites. This is the challenge that confronts criminologists and students of justice.

References

Anderson, P. R., and Slate, R. N. (2011). *The Decision-Making Network: An Introduction to Criminal Justice*. Durham, NC: Carolina Academic Press.

Barak, G. (1994). *Media, Process, and the Social Construction of Crime: Studies in Newsmaking Criminology*. New York, NY: Garland.

Barkan, S. E. (2012). *Criminology: A Sociological Understanding* (5th ed.). Upper Saddle River, NJ: Pearson-Prentice Hall.

Bennett, W. J., Dilulio, J., and Walters, J. P. (1996). *Body Count: Moral Poverty . . . and How to Win America's War Against Crime and Drugs.* New York, NY: Simon & Schuster.

Brown, S. E., Esbensen, F. A., and Geis, G. (2007). *Criminology: Explaining Crime and Its Context* (6th ed.). Newark, NJ: Anderson.

Del Carmen, R. V. (1995). *Criminal Procedures: Law and Practice* (3rd ed.). Pacific Grove, CA: Brooks/ Cole.

Elias, R. (1986). *The Politics of Victimization: Victims, Victimology, and Human Rights.* New York, NY: Oxford University Press.

Hagan, F. E. (2012). *Essentials of Research Methods in Criminal Justice and Criminology* (3rd ed.). Upper Saddle River, NJ: Pearson/Prentice-Hall.

Masters, R. E., Way, L. B., Gerstenfeld, P. B., Muscat, B. T., Hooper, M., Dussich, J. P., . . . Skrapec, C. A. (2011). *Criminal Justice Realities and Challenges.* New York, NY: McGraw-Hill.

Reid, S. T. (2012). *Crime and Criminology* (13th ed.). New York, NY: Oxford University Press.

Sanders, W. B. (1994). *Gangbangs and Drive-bys: Grounded Culture and Juvenile Gang Violence.* Hawthorne, NY: Aldine De Gruyter.

Siegel, L. J. (2012). *Criminology* (11th ed.). Belmont, CA: Wadsworth Cengage Learning.

Stanko, E., and Hobdell, E. (1993). Assault on Men, Masculinity, and Male Victimization. *British Journal of Criminology, 33,* 400–415.

Surette, R. (2007). *Media, Crime, and Criminal Justice: Images, Realities, and Policies.* Belmont, CA: Wadsworth.

U.S. Department of Justice. (2013). *National Crime Victimization Survey.* Bureau of Justice Statistics. Washington, DC. U.S. Government Printing Office.

Waldman, M. (1990). *Who Robbed America? Citizen's Guide to the Savings and Loan Scandal.* New York, NY: Random House.

Chapter 1

What Is Theory?

Chapter Outline

theory—A speculation about how phenomena, behavior, or processes are caused and what takes place after the cause is determined.

What Is Theory?

A **theory** is an objective, educated guess about a set of assumptions. Scholars argue that theories provide plausible explanations for reality (Maxfield & Babbie, 2012; Hagan, 2012). In the study of crime, theories have several functions. They enable researchers to identify, describe, explain, predict, and control for problems found in deviant and criminal behavior. By applying theories, researchers are able to identify social facts as they occur in their natural environment. Theories can describe conditions that precipitate deviant and criminal behavior. Theories have explanatory powers that allow researchers to discern why some people react the way they do to certain conditions. They enable researchers to understand the motivation of behavior within a given social context, while giving the researcher a frame of reference to isolate behavior. Theories provide researchers with the ability to make predictions regarding what the future could hold for those living under similar or adverse conditions or for other at-risk individuals. Moreover, theories enable researchers to propose and influence public policy so that undesirable behaviors will be controllable. In sum, theories can direct **research** and influence policies created to improve the human condition.

> **research**—An investigation that employs the use of the scientific method. It is considered as a systematic investigation of phenomena, behavior, or processes that relies on empirical data and logical study and analysis.

What Is Good Theory?

Contrary to popular opinion, not all theories are good theories. Hubert Blalock (1979) defines several criteria that make for good theory. He argues that these include **testability** and the ability of the theory to fit the research question. In social science research, testability is essential. Without testing and proving or disproving a theory, researchers cannot make qualified assertions about its predictive powers. In fact, without good theory, scientific researchers would have no claim of intellectual accuracy; their findings would be reduced to claims that are similarly made by the general public with respect to crime and criminal behavior. Moreover, since social researchers engage in the scientific method, their claims of accuracy should be based on research evidence and not mere speculation (Babbie, 1998).

> **testability**—Where research is concerned, one criteria of a good theory is that it must be tested. If it can be tested, it has the potential of making for good theory.

Theories must fit the research question at hand. For instance, researchers would be hard pressed to apply a macro theory (one that addresses the aggregate) to answer a micro-level (individual) research question. An example even more to the point is that one should not use crime theories to explain delinquency. This mistake is often found in criminology. The inverse mistake is also made: theories that have been constructed to explain the behavior of juveniles are used to explain and make predictions about adult criminality. In research, this mistake is referred as an **ecological fallacy**. When such a mistake is made, one has to seriously question whether a misclassified theory can hold up to a particular investigation.

> **ecological fallacy**—A logical error that results when one attempts to make conclusions about individuals based on group data.

Criminological theories attempt to make sense of social phenomena, especially when no previous explanation has been given for the behavior in question. However, many theories cannot be tested, because their ideas are not fully developed or clearly defined (Hagan, 2012). Some theories that highlight this point include conflict, Marxism, differential association, and labeling. For instance, conflict theory argues that crime is a by-product of unequal distributions of wealth and the disparate treatment of the people whom William Julius Wilson refers to as "the truly disadvantaged" (1987). The problem with this general theory is in defining, or **operationalizing**, what is meant by "unequal distributions" and "disparate treatment."

> **operationalize**—The process of defining variables that represent specific concepts, or portions of concepts, that will be collected from the study subjects. Researchers operationalize by imposing their ideas about how a concept should be measured in the study situation.

What is more perplexing and challenging to criminologists is explaining why some individuals who live in poverty, experiencing social, political, and economic inequalities, abstain from crime, while others vigorously pursue criminal ambitions. Differential association theory, developed by Edwin Sutherland, comes short of explaining why some individuals sharing the group's experiences, socializations, values, and definitions do not engage in crime while others do. Edwin Sutherland was also the first to argue that anyone in society regardless of social class could commit crime. Moreover, when outlining this theory, Edwin Sutherland never explained what was meant by definitions favorable to law violations.

The labeling theory argues that if a person acquires a weak self-image after being labeled, he or she will eventually engage in secondary deviance. How does one conceptualize and operationalize a weak self-image? A better question is, at what point does one experience identity transformation into a criminal or social deviant? And how can a researcher test such theories?

What Kinds of Theories Are There?

There are two general **typologies** of theories. Theories can be used for explaining phenomena on both the macro and micro levels. **Macro-level theories** explain larger social occurrences. For example, theories that attribute crime to the social order operate at the macro level in their explanatory powers. They often ask, to what extent does poverty influence crime? Such theories are often called social structure theories. They argue that there is something

> **typologies**—The different types of theories used to explain criminal behavior.
>
> **macro-level theory**—A theoretical explanation that has an extensive explanatory power, and can be used to explain group behavior. Theories that examine poverty and socialization are typically macro in their level of explanation.

in the social order or environment that propels individuals to commit crime. Such an environmental factor could be poverty or a lack of community mechanisms, such as traditional families, leaders, monetary resources, and group cohesion that exert social control. Some macro-level theories include social disorganization, strain, and conflict.

Micro-level theories attempt to explain the causes of crime on a smaller scale. Instead of attributing the origins of crime to the broader society, these theories argue that by examining an individual's group experiences and interactions, crime causation can be discovered. Social

> **micro-level theory**—Theoretical explanation that has very limited explanatory power—for instance, to explain the behavior of a single individual. In the study of crime, micro-level theories are primarily biological and psychological.

learning and social control are theories found on this level. These theories are often referred to as social processing theories, because they look at the process by which one learns and develops criminal behavior patterns. They typically focus on certain groups of people or subcultures. Micro-level theories also examine an individual's social, biological, and psychological makeup. The key difference between macro- and micro-level theories is that macro theories are concerned with the aggregate entities of society, while micro-level theories focus on individuals. Micro-level explanations are most effective when they endeavor to explain behavior on a case-by-case basis, while macro-level theories are generalized to cover larger groups of people.

Levels of Explanation

Each theory is designed with a certain level of explanatory power. These levels of explanation often include the behaviors of individuals, groups, and social classes. It is important that one's theory has the correct explanatory power, because many theories fall short, generalizing about an incorrect level or object. Some theories attribute the cause of crime to social factors, while others maintain that crime is caused by psychological or physical anomalies. Some theories attempt to explain why governments engage in criminality, and yet other theories focus on why individuals commit criminal activities.

The Classification of Theory

Another area of concern in criminological theory is classification. Theoretical classification is a way to group theoretical development into neat packages. However, this practice is not as concise as it could be, since criminological theories are not clearly stated. Two forms of classification, and perhaps the oldest, are the classical and positivist theories. The classical theory emerged during the 18th century. It focused on making legal reforms and humanizing the administration of justice. The positive school emerged a century later, making the individual its primary focus. Positivists argued that offenders engaged in crime and antisocial behavior because they were either physically or psychologically impaired, or suffered from criminogenic environmental influences. Both classical and positive schools of thought served as the genesis of criminological theory.

Processual and structural classification are dichotomous yet intertwined arguments about criminal behavior. Processual classification states that becoming a criminal and committing aberrant behavior is a gradual process whereby one learns and accepts definitions favorable to committing these actions while interacting in personal groups or cliques. Some processual, or social processing, theories are social learning, social control, and labeling theories. This tradition argues that people are socialized into either law-abiding or criminal behavior. And some offenders may persist in a life of crime because of negative societal reactions.

Structural classification contends that negative social forces in the environment, community, or society push offenders in the direction of crime, leaving them little choice in the matter. Structural classification theories argue that the social order is unjust and resources are distributed unequally. In addition, poor segments of the population have inept community controls that make them disorganized. Classical strain theory points out a factor that amplifies the difficulty of the underclass; namely, that the American culture teaches that anyone can live the "American Dream" if one engages in hard work. This is not necessarily the case, however; those in the middle and upper classes already have an advantage in their pursuit of the American Dream. They have avenues to economic opportunities that may be withheld or blocked from members of the lower class, which in turn may cause those in the lower class to feel frustrations that push them toward crime.

Theory-Then-Research versus Research-Then-Theory

Before undertaking a scientific investigation, researchers may want to determine an appropriate methodology or protocol to use. For example, a researcher may ask, should scientific investigations be guided by theory, or should research inform theory? There are two schools of thought where theory and research are concerned. One is advanced by Karl Popper (theory-then-research) and the other by Robert K. Merton (research-then-theory). The general argument is that social scientists operate and exist in two "worlds." These include the world of observation and experience, and the world of ideas, or theories and models. Understanding a systematic connection between these two worlds enhances the goals of the social sciences (Babbie, 1998).

The theory-then-research argument of Popper holds that theory should come first and research should follow. Stated another way, theory should guide research. Popper contends that with this approach, scientific knowledge would advance more rapidly through the development of ideas and attempts at refuting those ideas through empirical observations. He argues that theories can be reached only by intuition that is supported by experience.

Merton, in his counterargument, argues that empirical research goes beyond the passive role of verifying and testing theories. It does more than confirm or refute hypotheses. It shapes the development of theory because it initiates, reformulates, deflects, and clarifies theory. Merton contends that research suggests new problems for theory, calls for new theoretical formulations, and leads to the refinement of existing theories in addition to serving the function of verification (Babbie, 1998).

Despite the two opposing views, there is still no consensus on which should come first, theory or research. The disciplines of criminology and criminal justice have embraced both approaches.

How Do Criminologists Conduct Research?

What most people understand about crime, justice, law, and the criminal justice system is often presented to them by the mass media (Surette, 2013), typically the local news, newspapers, and television programming that is packed with a little information about the justice system and a lot of entertainment. Unfortunately, this is what constitutes the social reality for many Americans. Unlike citizens in the lay public, criminologists are professionally trained to use the scientific method to study crime. This alone gives credibility or believability to the assertions they make about crime and its causation.

validity—The accuracy or exactness of measurement in research investigations.

reliability—A consistent or repeated measure. It allows for replication in research.

In making assertions about crime, criminologists are concerned with validity and reliability. **Validity** is the accuracy of measurement, and **reliability** is the consistency of measurement. Those who study crime must be sure that they are studying exactly what they should and, at the same time, that their research findings yield consistent measures and lend themselves to replication studies. Unfortunately, it is sometimes very difficult to achieve both in research. As such, some scholars may focus on validity or an accurate measurement of the investigation in question, reasoning that to consistently get an invalid measure does nothing to advance the discipline's body of knowledge.

Researchers use many techniques or methodologies to arrive at their conclusions. Techniques include the following: social surveys, longitudinal designs, aggregate data, experimental designs, observational measures, case studies, life history methods, and unobtrusive measures (Champion, 1993; Hagan, 2012). An important fact to remember is that the research question or problem the researcher is attempting to answer will determine the type of methodology that he or she uses in the investigation (Hagan, 2012; Nachmias and Nachmias, 1981). Moreover, some researchers recommend the use of triangulated measures. This practice allows for better control over rival causal factors that may be responsible for the findings or outcome in research. It encourages the use of multiple methods to gain greater control.

Survey Research

Researchers use social surveys to measure attitudes, beliefs, values, orientation, and behavior. There are several types of surveys, including questionnaires, interviews, and telephone calls (Fowler, 1988; Hagan, 2012). Surveys allow criminologists and criminal justicians to get to the "dark" figures of crime. These are figures that are not calculated into official crime statistics. They are the unknown data that often puzzle researchers. Some scholars contend that surveys, especially those that allow respondents to remain anonymous, are very helpful when collecting sensitive data. For example, they can be used to gather respondents' beliefs about other racial and ethnic groups, and other areas and subject matter that researchers may have a difficult time collecting since respondents may be uncomfortable answering questions face-to-face. Surveys can also be used to measure the experiences of respondents, such as their levels of victimization as well as participation in offending behavior. **Survey** research is often referred to as cross-sectional research. This type of research allows researchers to collect data from a **cross-section** of the community, thereby representing the entire community.

survey—An instrument used by social scientists to measure attitudes, behaviors, beliefs, and preferences of respondents.

cross-section—A representation of an entire community or data collected at one point in time.

Unless it is followed up, survey research represents taking a measure at one point in time. Survey data lack predictive power regarding the future behavior of people who are surveyed. For example, if survey research is conducted at a local public high school to measure the students' involvement in drug use, one would assume that the students would represent the entire community. We would expect that the students would have different positions in the economic structure of society. Stated differently, the students would be from different social economic backgrounds. Taken together, they represent the diversity of the entire community. Surveys are also used to measure if racial bias or selective law enforcement exists in official processing that may be apparent in the Uniform Crime Reports (UCR) and the National Incident-Based Reporting System (NIBRS). In fact, many self-report studies of juvenile delinquency reveal that despite social class, juveniles report engaging in similar amounts of behavior, but poor juveniles are more likely to be arrested and receive official processing.

When these data are collected at a single point in time, they indicate the students' level of drug involvement only at the time these data are collected. They do not indicate if students either abstained or continued to use drugs after the survey.

Sampling

Most surveys use sampling techniques after data have been collected. A **sample** can be representative of the population if it is properly collected (Philliber, Schwab, and Sloss, 1980; Hagan, 2012). There are two types of samples: probability and nonprobability. Those samples that use

> **sample**—A smaller number of individuals taken from a population for the purpose of generalizing to the whole. If the sample is conducted in a random fashion, it should reflect the population.

an equal probability of selection method are often preferred and are used to represent the entire population (Champion, 1993; Babbie, 1998; Senese, 1997). This is not the case for nonprobability samples. Frank Hagan (2012) describes the equal probability of selection method (EPSEM). In this method, every element in a targeted population has an equal probability of being selected into the sample. For example, researchers do not always have the time or resources to interview everyone in a targeted population, nor is it necessary to survey the entire population (Hagan, 2012; Maxfield and Babbie, 2012). A randomly selected probability sample allows researchers to make valid inferences about the targeted population. However, if the sample is not selected in a random manner, the findings from the research cannot be inferred to represent a larger population. This places limitations on the study in question. In the study of crime, the two main types of surveys are self-report surveys (in which people self-report their levels of unreported crime) and the National Crime Victimization Survey (in which victims report victimizations that are not calculated into official police reports).

While no research technique is without flaw, there are several criticisms of surveys: (1) respondents often lie about, forget, or even exaggerate their criminal behavior; (2) surveys fail to measure changes that occur within people over time; and (3) research questions may not measure what they are intended to measure. As a result, some researchers argue that surveys should provide open-ended questions instead of closed-ended. They contend that this may be the only way to achieve validity, because items included in closed-ended questions may not truly reflect the respondent's feelings. The respondent is then left to select the response that is most closely related to his or her true feelings.

Researchers also attempt to validate some responses they receive in surveys. Some techniques that they use to determine if reports are accurate are truth scales and outside sources when possible. Because surveys can be unreliable, steps must be taken to enhance their accuracy. For this reason, surveys are believed to be high on reliability but low on validity (Babbie, 1998; Hagan, 2012).

Longitudinal Research

While cross-sectional research provides a single measure at a given point in time, longitudinal research designs entail observing a group of people who share a like characteristic for an extended period of time to measure changes that take place (Hagan, 2012; Agresti and Finlay, 1997). Typically, the group shares characteristics, such as age, race, social class, education, or even birth dates. For example, Marvin Wolfgang, Robert Figlio, and Thorsten Sellin in Philadelphia conducted a longitudinal study on a birth cohort for 18 years, tracking 9,945 boys, and Sheldon and Eleanor Glueck studied the life cycle of delinquency, following the careers of known delinquents (1972). **Longitudinal designs** measure change that occurs within the lives of the subjects of an investigation that may explain a particular outcome. Stated another way, this method is used to determine which events experienced by the subjects caused them to develop into who they are.

longitudinal design—A study that is conducted over time to determine what causes change. These studies typically use a group of subjects who share similar characteristics (a cohort).

While engaged in longitudinal research, criminologists may examine newspapers, hospital records, educational background records, marital records, police records, and death records. Sometimes longitudinal designs rely on a process called retrospective format. It essentially requires taking a group of known offenders and looking back into their early childhood experiences to determine what may have caused their law violations. Researchers may examine the subjects' family relationships, academic failures, alcohol and drug use, or whether they lacked a proper male or female role model. One type of longitudinal design referred to as **time series** involves observing a group of subjects for a while and then giving them a stimuli or treatment and making several more observations at different intervals to determine the effect of the intervention. This technique is used to determine if any changes occur over time and whether the stimulus is responsible.

time series design—A research method that refers to the analysis of a single variable at several successive time periods with a measure taken before treatment and several observations after treatment.

Aggregate Data Research

Aggregate data research relies on official crime reports or any officially collected data—that is, any data that are

aggregate data research—Studies that rely on existing statistics or numbers about social behavior.

collected and kept by governmental agencies (Hagan, 2012; Babbie, 1998). For example, the Federal Bureau of Investigation annually publishes the UCR (also see the NIBRS). Official data are also collected by courts, corrections and juvenile justice departments, and the U.S. Census Bureau, to name a few. These data often provide demographical information (such as race, ethnicity, age, gender) and reveal trends and patterns than can be used to determine whether there are increases or decreases in the numbers of crimes that are reported. These data often reveal the type of offense an arrestee may have committed. Other crime data are collected by the Vera Institute and the National Institute of Justice Council on Juvenile Justice and Delinquency Prevention. Because of the problems associated with collecting these data, they are high on reliability and low on validity. Critics claim that these data should be accepted with caution owing to citizen reporting practices, law enforcement practices, and methodological problems. At the very least, these concerns make us question the accuracy of these data. Aggregate data are perhaps stronger when they are corroborated by other data.

Experimental Research Designs

Social science research utilizes several types of **experimental designs**: classical, Solomon Four, and pre-experimental. These designs entail intervening in the lives of subjects to determine the outcome of an intervention. These studies focus on cause and effect (see Simon, 1978; Champion, 1993; Senese, 1997). Critics charge that there are not enough experimental designs used in criminal justice and criminological research. Perhaps the two most publicized experiments are the Kansas City Police Prevention Patrol Experiment and the Minneapolis Domestic Violence Experiment. In the first experiment, researchers

> **experimental design**—A study that attempts to approximate laboratory conditions. Experiments include two groups, control and experimental. The experimental group is exposed to a treatment, or independent variable, and the control group is not exposed to the treatment; it is used to compare to the experimental group. The purpose of this research is to determine cause and effect.

wanted to determine if routine patrol decreased crime, decreased fear of crime, and increased arrests. This was accomplished by comparing measures of crime, fear, and arrests in several beats by employing the use of reactive patrol, regular patrol, and proactive patrol. The research revealed no difference with regard to crime, fear, and arrest (Larson, 1975). In the second experiment, Sherman and Berk (1984) investigated police response to domestic violence in Minneapolis. In the investigation, police used several approaches to respond to cases of intimate personal violence. They discovered that when police effected an arrest instead of relying on mediation, separation, or a "cooling-off" period, offenders were less likely to reoffend. While engaging in a classical experimental design, researchers must be aware of the elements associated with conducting experiments. They include: the random selection of subjects, control and comparison groups, the experimental condition (treatment or stimuli), and pre- and post-measure. The formula for experimental research is represented in **Table 1.1**.

Theoretically, the classical experimental design uses two samples that are selected from a population. The assumption is that equivalence (E) exists with regard to every element

Table 1.1 The formula for experimental research.

Experimental Group	Control Group
Equivalence (E)	Equivalence (E)
Pre-measure (01)	Pre-measure (01)
Treatment (X)	Placebo (0)
Post-measure (02)	Post-measure (02)

found in the population. That is, subjects taken from the population are similar and can therefore be placed in either group. If this condition is not achieved, the experiment is believed to be contaminated (Hagan, 2012). One group is called the experimental and the other is called the control group. However, to ensure that the two groups are equivalent, the researcher should conduct a premeasure (01) for confirmation to determine if equivalence exists. This takes place with regard to both the experimental and control groups. Later, the experimental group gets the treatment or stimuli (X), while the control group receives the placebo (0). After the experiment runs its course, a post-measure (02) should be taken to determine if the treatment had any effect on the outcome (since experiments are concerned with cause and effect). Within the context of an experiment, the treatment is referred to as the independent variable, and the outcome is the dependent variable. The logic of the experiment assumes that the independent variable is causal. Experimental research is high on validity and reliability.

observational research—A research design whereby the investigator collects data by interacting with the subjects of the research in their natural setting to understand what their experiences mean to them. This approach renders a grounded theory when the research is completed.

Observational Research

Some social scientists view **observational research** as a more valid measure than the other methodologies, but argue that it poses more ethical questions (Senese, 1997). Observational research is typically referred to as field research or qualitative methods. The technique involves spending time in the natural environment of the subjects and interacting with them. This allows researchers to determine how people react in their natural environment and what behaviors mean to those who engage in them (Maxfield and Babbie, 2012; Hagan, 2012). Observational research is a sensitizing approach used to inform the reader about the plight of the subjects under investigation in the research. The technique requires that the researcher not start with a theory, but move toward a grounded theory as the research is being performed. Some of the tools on which this methodology relies are informants, gaining access, tests, rapport, and ethics. The advantages of using this method are: (1) one can observe changes in people over time, (2) the method is fairly inexpensive, and (3) it is high on validity. The negative points are: (1) the method is very time-consuming, (2) researchers cannot control the behaviors of the subjects, (3) there are sometimes problems gaining entry, (4) the research conclusions are tentative, (5) there are problems with generalizations, (6) the method may be low on reliability, and (7) the researcher may face ethical dilemmas. Classical research that has relied on this methodology includes William Foote Whyte's "Street Corner Society," Lord Humphey's "Tearoom Trade," Joseph Styles's "Outsider/Insider," Martinez Jankowski's "Island in the Streets," Elias Anderson's "A Place on the Corner," and Elliot Liebow's "Tallay's Corner." Again, though the research question typically dictates the methodology, some researchers rely on multiple methods to address a research question. This process is known as triangulation, and is believed by some scholars to bring more credibility to the research investigation (Whyte, 1984).

Ethics in Criminological Research

The concept of ethics is very important to criminological research. **Ethics** refers to the standard of conduct used by a given profession or group. Those in a particular profession try to safeguard the reputation of their profession by

> **ethics**—What is morally right or wrong as agreed to by a group or profession.

rigorously adhering to agreed-upon standards of conduct (see Babbie, 1998; Maxfield and Babbie, 2012; Kraska and Neuman, 2012). Sam Souryal (1992) defines ethics as a branch of philosophy that studies what is morally right and wrong or good and bad, as decided on by a group of people. The academic disciplines of criminology and criminal justice have such a code (Hagan, 2012). The purpose of the code is to ensure that the subjects of research are not harmed or injured during or after their participation in research. At the same time, the code ensures that the purpose of research is to advance the understanding of human behavior and social reality. Subjects of research must be protected since they are making a sacrifice by participating in a scientific investigation. In many cases, they have very little to gain economically, and, at best, the only thing that researchers can promise them is that their participation will contribute to positive change in the human condition (Babbie, 1998; Maxfield and Babbie, 2012). If participants are harmed in scientific investigations, others in the general public may refuse to participate in any academic research in the future. Therefore, researchers have established general guidelines with which to approach their investigations: (1) make participation voluntary, (2) never injure participants, (3) protect anonymity and confidentiality, (4) practice full disclosure, and (5) remember ethics when analyzing and reporting the research findings.

Make Participation Voluntary

The history of research conducted in the name of science is saturated with shameful accounts of participants being either forced into or deceived into submitting to scientific investigations that ended in horrific tragedy, with many unknowing subjects used as guinea pigs in biomedical as well as social scientific research (Hagan, 2012). Therefore, researchers should seek informed consent or an agreement of understanding regarding the purpose and consequences associated with the study. For the subjects involved in any research investigation, participation must be voluntary. If participants are forced or coerced into being a part of research, they may be inclined to respond in a manner that they think the investigator expects. For example, if a professor forces her students to complete a survey or questionnaire because they represent a sizable convenience sample or captive audience, the students may feel compelled to respond in a positive manner in an attempt to satisfy the professor. Any response given by the students would be suspect because of the bias built into the student–professor relationship. In an ideal situation, the researcher would get the participants' informed consent, stating that they agree to the conditions and terms of the research investigation. This process makes for bias-free and objective responses from the participants in a given research investigation.

Never Injure Participants

Participants in scientific investigations should never be harmed during or after participating in research. Injuries to participants can go far beyond the physical and psychological; for instance, they could also be responsible for destroying a participant's reputation. Two often cited examples of injuries sustained during research are the Milgram experiment and the Zimbardo prison experiment. The Milgram experiment was premised on the idea that people will continue to obey orders from authority figures even if they know others being adversely affected by what they are doing. In this experiment, a participant was instructed to deliver electric shocks to a person who provided incorrect answers to questions that were being asked of him. The person answering the questions was a member of the research team and was not really being shocked, but this was not known to the subject dispensing the voltages (the only true subject in the investigation). According to the research plan, the more questions the respondent answered incorrectly, the higher the voltage of electricity he or she would receive. This would continue until it was clear that the respondent was either incapacitated or dead. The experiment found that even when it was clear that the respondent was in pain or dead, the participant continued applying electric voltage. As a result of their participation in the experiment, many subjects (those applying the electricity) suffered convulsions and seizures (Milgram, 1963). The true subjects of the investigation were not briefed beforehand that they were participants in an obedience test.

Another prison experiment was conducted at Stanford University. Known as the Zimbardo prison experiment, the study collected a random sample of students to participate in a simulation of a prison setting. The students were selected to serve as either guards or prisoners. After operating for six days, the study was aborted, because the students began taking on the persona of the roles they had been given. Both groups of students went **native**. They experienced an overreaction to research roles that they were assigned. For example, those students who were acting as prison guards started to debase, dehumanize, and treat student-prisoners with contempt. They acted aggressively toward them by swearing, subjecting

native—A term used in observational research that denotes the researcher has lost objectivity and has overidentified with the subjects of the investigation. The term is also used to refer to a subject who has overidentified with his role in a research project.

them to excessive force, and demanding that they do physical exercises as part of their punishment. They also had them simulate homosexual activity. As tension mounted, those in the prisoner group grew depressed and even passive from their brief experience as inmates. Many cried out from the humiliation and were despondent during the experiment, but they did not stage a mass exodus from the simulated prison. They had accepted the role of prisoner and forgot that they were college students participating in a study. They believed that they could not leave until they had "served their sentence" (Zimbardo, 1963). The experiment showed that the social environment (especially an isolated one) can adversely affect one's personality. After the project was terminated, some students received extensive counseling and others left the university. Some scholars believe that these two research projects may have dramatized the need for the development of human subject committees and institutional review boards (Hagan, 2012).

The purpose of human subject committees and institutional review boards (IRBs) is to ensure quality control in research in general, and the safety of research subjects in particular. IRBs are composed of university professors, some of whom are other researchers and scientists, professionals in the community who review proposed research and make a decision regarding its merits, feasibility, risks, and benefits. The board can either approve or disapprove proposed research (Hagan, 2012). IRBs and human subject committees provide oversight and take the steps necessary to safeguard against participants being harmed by any aspect of research. They also require that if human subjects are to be used in research, an informed consent form must accompany the research proposal. Even with such consent, research committees can disapprove any investigation that they deem risky. This is done to protect the subjects of research and to prevent the university from civil liability if any injuries stem from the research investigation.

Protect Anonymity and Confidentiality

As previously stated, in more cases than not, the participants of research rarely have much to gain from social scientist research other than knowing that he or she may be helpful or instrumental in improving the human condition. As such, researchers should make efforts to protect them from harm. One way of doing this is to protect the subjects' anonymity and confidentiality. Many scholars believe that such protection could increase the likelihood that subjects will participate in research investigations (Kraska and Neuman, 2012). Anonymity occurs when the researcher is unable to connect a given response to a particular respondent. Confidentiality is maintained when the researcher is able to connect a given response to the respondent, but promises not to reveal his or her identity (Kraska and Neuman, 2012; Hagan, 2012; Maxfield and Babbie, 2012). Participation in research represents an intrusion into the lives of subjects since it could yield shocking findings and reveal a person's innermost thoughts, secrets, beliefs, and behaviors. Therefore, anonymity and confidentiality must be protected or participants' careers can be forfeited, marriages ruined, and lives shattered. Because of the sensitive nature of some research topics (e.g., alternative lifestyles, early childhood victimizations, drug use, racial views), researchers would do well to protect those who lend themselves to scientific investigations. Failure to do so could mean that participants may be adversely affected by the research process and that the ability of scientists to conduct more research in the future could be drastically compromised (Kraska and Neuman, 2012; Hagan, 2012; Maxfield and Babbie, 2012).

Practice Full Disclosure

Researchers should always practice full disclosure in every aspect of research and at every stage of the research process. The subjects of an investigation should not be deceived, but rather told before they begin the research investigation about: (1) the purpose of the study, (2) how the study is to be conducted, and (3) the use of the research. Subjects should also be informed about the findings of the investigation before they are published. First, subjects should always have a general understanding of the purpose of any investigation in which they choose to participate. They should know what the researcher is trying to measure or determine. Unfortunately, many researchers are reluctant to inform subjects about the objective of the research out of fear that subjects may alter their behavior and act unnatural, thus contaminating the investigation. (This is especially true in qualitative or field research designs.) Second, participants must be aware of each phase of the research. They should know before agreeing to participate in research if there are aspects in which they cannot participate, especially actions that conflict with their ethics or morality. Third, the subjects should know how the findings from research will be used. They should know if the research is being used for political purposes—for example, to justify a policy or to advance a group's ideology. Stated another way, subjects should be told about the intended goals of the research. Fourth, the findings should be revealed to the subjects before they are released to the general public. This is very important, because research and researchers are not infallible. Sometimes, researchers misinterpret events that can easily be made clear by the subjects involved in the investigation. Therefore, to present research findings in an accurate manner, final reports from the investigation should be shared with the participants before they are published and made into public record (Hagan, 2012).

Ethics in Analyzing and Reporting Findings

Another area of research that is highly neglected, yet equally important is analyzing data and reporting the findings. Research data must be objectively interpreted as they are reported or as they are taken from the investigation. Data must be allowed to speak for themselves. Researchers should not take liberties by either fudging the findings or speaking beyond the scope of data. In essence, researchers are not allowed to change or set aside responses that are contrary to what they believe or desire as an outcome of research (Hagan, 2012). However, one huge difference between investigations conducted by researchers in the social sciences and their counterparts in the natural sciences is that a negative finding can have important research implications, especially if it defies conventional wisdom (Hagan, 2012). Researchers should not be reluctant to report negative relationships when they are discovered. Such findings could have the effect of moving criminal justice and criminology into unchartered areas that could facilitate more effective policies, and, at the same time, eliminate spending on programs and policies that are ineffective or those that have not proven helpful in reducing or eliminating crime. Researchers should always report the problems of the data as well as any other problems that may even include the sample selection or subjects who were part of the investigation. More specifically, if the sample is not selected in a randomized manner, it should be reported as such because it has serious implication with regard to generalizations that could be made (Hagan, 2012).

Summary

Unlike lay citizens in the general public whose opinions about crime and justice are socially constructed by television from either the entertainment media or the local news, criminology and criminal justice researchers engage in the process of scientifically finding out about social reality. They conduct research that requires that they engage in the scientific method while using techniques such as experiments, aggregate data, surveys, longitudinal designs, and observational research while adhering to ethical standards of behavior. They often use theories to guide research or allow their research to inform theory in the process of reaching their findings.

In fact, researchers believe that the process is their only claim to intellectual accuracy about the assertions they are able to make about crime and criminal justice reality. Research methodology is very important in any scientific investigation, because it provides the blueprint used in any study from start to finish. If the methodology is flawed, the findings of the research are unreliable and suspect at best.

Methodological problems are typically found in the sample selection, or in how questions or items are constructed and measured. Moreover, problems can be found in the statistical application used to analyze data. For example, if a sample is not selected in a random manner and instead is based on convenience, the research findings could be limited to the subjects used in a given study. At the same time, there are many statistical analyses that should not be used if one lacks a representative sample. Therefore, researchers should speak to any limitations that are found in their investigations.

Limitations do not necessarily mean that the research was conducted poorly; they could signal, however, that the findings are tentative and not generalizable to wider groups and populations. Such reporting could inspire other researchers to replicate the study using a representative sample that could yield more accurate findings.

Discussion Questions

1. What is the fundamental difference in methodological approaches used by researchers who engage in experimental versus participant observation studies?
2. Explain the criteria used to measure whether a theory is considered good and is properly constructed.

3. Is it necessary for criminologists and criminal justicians to be ethical in their pursuit of the truth regarding research knowledge? Give specific examples of areas to avoid while engaging in research investigations.

4. After reading about the different types of research techniques, which do you believe is a more valid way to measure crime and delinquency?

5. What is the implication of selecting a bias sample in any research investigation?

References

Agresti, A., and Finlay, B. (1997). *Statistical Methods for the Social Sciences* (3rd ed.). Upper Saddle River, NJ: Prentice-Hall.

Babbie, E. (1998). *The Practice of Social Research* (8th ed.). Belmont, CA: Wadsworth.

Blalock, H. (1979). *Social Statistics* (2nd ed.). New York, NY: McGraw-Hill.

Champion, D. J. (1993). *Research Methods for Criminal Justice and Criminology*. Englewood Cliff, NJ: Regents/Prentice-Hall.

Fowler, F. J. (1988). *Survey Research Methods: Applied Social Research Methods Series* (Vol. 1). Newbury Park, CA: Sage Publication.

Hagan, F. E. (2012). Essentials of Research Methods in Criminal Justice and Criminology (3rd ed.). Upper Saddle River, New Jersey: Prentice-Hall.

Hagan, F. E. (2013). Research Methods in Criminal Justice and Criminology (9th ed.). Upper Saddle River, New Jersey: Pearson.

Kraska, P. B., and Neuman, W. L. (2012). *Criminal Justice and Criminology Research Methods* (2nd ed.). Upper Saddle River, NJ: Pearson.

Larson, R. (1975). What Happened to Patrol Operations in Kansas City? A Review of the Kansas City Prevention Patrol Experiment. *Journal of Criminal Justice, 3,* 267–97.

Maxfield, M. G., and Babbie, E. R. (2012). *Basics of Research Methods* (3rd ed.). Belmont, CA: Wadsworth.

Milgram, S. (1963). Behavioral Study of Obedience. *Journal of Abnormal Social Psychology, 67,* 371–78.

Nachmias, C., and Nachmias, D. (1981). *Research Methods in the Social Sciences: Alternate Second Edition Without Statistics*. New York, NY: St. Martin's Press.

Philliber, S. G., M. R. Schwab, and Sloss, S. G. (1980). *Social Research: Guides to a Decision-Making Process*. Itasca, IL: F. E. Peacock.

Senese, J. D. (1997). *Applied Research Methods in Criminal Justice*. Chicago: Nelson-Hall.

Sherman, L. W., and Berk, R. A. (1984). *The Minneapolis Domestic Violence Experiment*. Washington, DC: Police Foundation.

Simon, J. L. (1978). *Basic Research Methods in Social Science: The Art of Empirical Investigation* (2nd ed.). New York: Random House.

Souryal, S. S. (1992). *Ethics in Criminal Justice: In Search of the Truth*. Cincinnati, OH: Anderson.

Surette, R. (2013). Media, crime, and criminal justice: Images, realities, and policies. Belmont, CA: Wadsworth Cengage Learning.

Whyte, W. F. (1984). *Learning from the Field: A Guide from Experience*. Newbury Park, CA: Sage.

Wilson, W. J. (1987). The truly disadvantaged. Chicago: University of Chicago Press.

Wolfgang, M., Figlio, R., and Sellin, T. (1972). *Delinquency in a Birth Cohort*. Chicago, IL: University of Chicago Press.

Zimbardo, P. (1963). On the Ethics of Intervention in Human Psychological Research: With Special Reference to the Stanford Prison Study. *Cognition, 22,* 243–46.

Chapter 2

Measuring the Extent of Crime

Chapter Outline

Criminologists, criminal justice experts, policy makers, and citizens alike are concerned about the amount of crime that occurs each year in the United States, but perhaps for different reasons. Criminologists desire to better understand the motivation behind such behavior so that they can develop strategies that might deter crime. Criminal justice experts want to know if existing crime control practices and policies have a positive effect on reducing the crime rate. Policy makers like to monitor the crime rate to determine if resources set aside to fight and prevent crime are monies well spent. If current policies are not accomplishing their goals, then perhaps new policies could be created that are more effective at reducing crime. Concerned citizens typically have safety concerns. Community residents want to feel safe in their homes and to walk down city streets if they so desire. Recent statistics indicate that nearly half of all Americans report that they do not feel safe. People, in general, want to know whether there are increases or decreases in the crime rate.

In the United States, while private researchers and agencies conduct much independent research on crime, the three primary sources for information on national crime rates in general are the Uniform Crime Reports (UCR), self-report surveys, and the National Crime Victimization Survey (although the latter resource is devoted to measuring levels of victimization, it can also be used to determine if crime rates are increasing). These are the leading sources for the criminal statistics upon which conventional criminologists and students of justice rely. Researchers argue that the best measurement of any social phenomenon is to employ several methods to examine the same research question. While

> **triangulation**—A research technique that relies on several methodologies to measure the same subject matter.

these primary sources may seem ideal for examining crime, many scholars argue that they measure different realities. As such, **triangulation** may help researchers to achieve accuracy regarding the total number of crimes that are committed each year.

> **Uniform Crime Reports (UCR)**—An annual publication by the Federal Bureau of Investigation of all reported Part I and Part II index crimes provided by over 17,000 police agencies. Compilation focuses mainly on violent and economic crimes. This source is relied on by many practicing criminal justice experts and criminologists. In 1988, the UCR switched to the National Incident-Based Reporting System.

The Uniform Crime Reports

In the 1920s, a program was created by a committee of the International Association of Chiefs of Police. By the 1930s, the program had developed into the present-day **Uniform Crime Reports** (Barkan, 2012; Gottfredson, 1999). Many practicing criminal justice experts and criminologists view the UCR as the most reliable crime measurement in existence, due to the fact that the UCR is a massive measure of crime that has a vast number of people involved in its process. The UCR is considered the most widely cited source of aggregate criminal statistics.

The process of collecting these data is voluntary. There is nothing that compels state and local police agencies around the country to provide these data to the Federal Bureau of Investigation (FBI). Despite this, the data represent 98% of the U.S. population. If one were to examine almost any article published in any criminal justice or criminology journal, one would easily see the influence of the UCR. The UCR is prepared by the FBI, with over 17,000 police agencies assisting in compiling data. While the UCR contains data on what are referred to as Part I and Part II crimes, its main focus is on Part I crimes, generally referred to as **index crimes**, which

> **index crime**—The eight criminal offenses collected by the Federal Bureau of Investigation to be used in its compilation of the Uniform Crime Reports (UCR). These crimes include homicide, rape, robbery, burglary, aggravated assaults, theft, motor vehicle theft, and arson.

include murder and non-negligent manslaughter, forcible rape, robbery, aggravated assault, burglary, larceny, motor vehicle theft, and arson. Those crimes that are categorized as violent are murder and non-negligent manslaughter, forcible rape, robbery, and aggravated assaults. Property crimes include burglary, larceny, motor vehicle theft, and arson (Barkan, 2012). Part II crimes include simple assaults, fraud, vandalism, sex offenses (except rape), drunkenness, vagrancy, disorderly conduct, drug abuse violations, and violations of liquor laws. The UCR provides definitions of the index crimes as described in the following section.

Part I Crimes

Murder is the unlawful killing of one human being by another. This may include deaths caused by negligence, attempts to kill, assaults to kill, suicides, and accidental deaths. A murder ruled to be a justifiable homicide is excluded from entry. Manslaughter committed by negligence occurs when one accidentally or through gross negligence kills another person.

> **murder**—Intentionally causing the death of another person with malice aforethought or causing the death of another while committing or attempting to commit a crime.

There are several typologies of murder, including mass murder, serial murder, and killing sprees. A mass murder occurs when four or more people are killed at one location. Serial murders occur when several victims are killed at three or more separate locations. While there have been many serial killers, those whose crimes paralyzed their respective cities with fear are among the most notorious murderers. They include John Wayne Gacy, the Zodiac Killer, Ted Bundy, David Berkowitz, Jeffrey Dahmer, Richard Ramirez, Gary Ridgway, and Ed Gein. A killing spree occurs when two or more killings occur at different locations without a break between murders.

Each year in the United States approximately 14,800 murders occur. They typically occur during July and August (but are committed at a higher rate in December and January) by perpetrators between the ages of 20 and 24. Those who are most often victimized are in the same age group. The typical murder weapon of choice is a handgun. Other popular murder weapons include knives, clubs, fists, and blunt objects. Of all index crimes, murder is the least likely to be committed, but the most likely to be cleared by an arrest. The police prioritize serious crime, and when a missing person case arises, the police are usually notified.

Forcible rape is unlawful intercourse with a male or female by force and against his or her will or without legal or factual consent. Statutory rape is excluded (no force is needed when victims are under the age of consent).

> **forcible rape**—Sexual intercourse with a person forcibly and against his or her will. It also refers to assaults or attempts to commit rape by force or threat of force.

There are several types of rape, including statutory, marital, and date rape. Statutory rape involves sexual intercourse with a male or female who is under the age of consent, regardless of whether he or she is a willing partner. Date rape is a growing crime that is receiving greater awareness, especially on many college campuses across the country. This is due in part to a new drug called Rohypnol that has surfaced on almost all campuses. Date rape is usually defined as a planned violent crime that serves to empower the offender rather than to satisfy a sexual desire. Date rape is forced intercourse with a female against her will that occurs within the context of a dating relationship. Marital rape, perhaps the least reported of the three, occurs within the confines of the home between couples contracted to be together. Sometimes it is very difficult establishing that rape occurred, especially when there is a lack of physical evidence proving forced or unwanted participation.

Sexual battery, while not included in the UCR, is defined as wrongful physical conduct with a person without his or her consent that has a sexual purpose. Of all index crimes, rape is the least reported. Some argue that rape is underreported because of the embarrassment that victims face, the social stigma of being raped, and the blaming of the victim that commonly occurs in the criminal justice process.

> **robbery**—The taking or attempt to take from another any goods, monies, items, or anything of value through the use of force, violence, or fear.

Robbery is the unlawful taking or attempted taking of property that is in the immediate possession of another by force or the threat of force.

There are two kinds of robbery, armed and unarmed. Armed robbery occurs when the attacker uses a weapon. Unarmed, or strong-arm, robbery occurs when the attacker uses the threat of violence and intimidation.

Robbery is a personal crime in which a citizen is the target of a predator. In most robberies, a gun is the weapon of choice. However, guns are discharged in only 20% of these encounters. Some experts believe that strong-arm robbery has the potential to be more dangerous than robberies in which weapons are used, because unarmed robbers may have to make good on the threat of physical bodily injury when potential victims are reluctant to hand over their possessions.

> **aggravated assault**—An unlawful attack by one person on another with the intent to inflict severe bodily harm or injury or the attempt or threat of same behavior.

Aggravated assault is the unlawful intentional infliction, or the attempted or threatened infliction, of injury upon an individual. These crimes usually include either the use of a weapon or the victim's need to be hospitalized after the altercation.

Assault is typically categorized in two groups: aggravated and simple. The distinction between them is based on the severity of the offense or the harm sustained during the encounter. Most state penal codes define them as either first-degree or second-degree assaults. In the past, a completed act constituted the separate offense of battery; however, today, most attempted and completed acts are considered assaults.

> **burglary**—Unlawful entry into a building or structure to commit a felony or theft.

Burglary is the unlawful entry of any fixed structure, vehicle, residence, industry, or business with or without force with the intent to commit a felony or larceny.

Burglary can be reported if someone has made an unlawful entry of an unlocked structure, because a breaking and entering has occurred or has been attempted.

Burglary is a property crime. Home burglaries generally take place during the day when owners are at work and property is left unguarded. Burglary has different components, including forcible entry, unlawful entry where no force is used, and attempted forcible entry. Force is not needed for this type of crime to occur. Because stolen goods are quickly pawned or fenced, burglary has a low clearance rate. The most dangerous burglaries occur when occupants are at home during the commission of the crime.

Larceny is the unlawful taking or attempted taking of property of another without force and without deceit with the intent to permanently deprive the owner of the property.

> **larceny**—Unlawful taking and carrying away of the personal property of another with the intent to permanently deprive them of possessions; includes shoplifting, theft of accessories, pocket picking or thefts from motor vehicles.

Another name for larceny is theft. This is the most common of all Part I crimes. Larceny is classified as simple or grand, usually based on the dollar amount of the loss. Simple acts of larceny involve items with a value of $200 or less, while grand larceny refers to items that are valued at more than $200.

With the exception of vehicles, this category of crime includes: theft from motor vehicles, shoplifting, theft of motor vehicle parts and accessories, theft from buildings, bicycle thefts, pocket-picking/purse-snatching, and theft from coin-operated machines. The most common larceny is the theft of motor vehicle parts, such as cell phones, tires, wheels, stereos, Xbox, PlayStation, iPods, MP3 players, digital cameras, Wii, headphones, radar detectors, and citizen band radios.

Motor vehicle theft is the unlawful taking or attempted taking of a self-propelled road vehicle owned by another with the intent to deprive the owner of temporary or permanent use of the vehicle.

> **motor vehicle theft**—Stealing or attempting to steal an automobile or any other mode of transportation that is powered by gasoline or diesel fuel such as trucks, buses, snowmobile, or motor cycles.

Because of the insurance claims that must be completed, this category of crime has a very high reporting rate. Despite this, motor vehicle thefts have a very low clearance rate. Some attribute this to the quickness with which motor vehicles are disassembled and sold.

Carjacking, in which a driver is forced from a vehicle, usually at gunpoint, is an area of concern because it involves an element of danger. The category of motor vehicle theft extends only to road vehicles. As such, the theft of trains, planes, boats, construction equipment, and farm machinery does not fall in this category of crime, but rather is included in the larceny category.

Arson is the unlawful, willful, or malicious burning or attempted burning of property with or without intent to defraud.

> **arson**—Any intentional, malicious burning or attempt to burn with the purpose to defraud a house, building, motor vehicle, aircraft, or the personal property of another.

Property typically included in this category are houses, storage units, buildings, and manufacturing facilities. Fires of unknown origin are excluded from this statistic. Arson is believed to be committed by offenders consumed with resentment and anger, those seeking to file an insurance claim, an isolated few who are pyromaniacs, and offenders who destroy evidence connecting them to another crime. Because fire departments are responsible for determining how fires are started, arson is believed to be among the least reported of the index crimes. Reports from fire investigations are not submitted to the FBI.

Part II Crimes

While these crimes are less serious than Part I crimes, Part II crimes account for the majority of crimes that police officers across the nation respond to each year. They are defined as follows:

Simple assaults are actual and attempted assaults that do not involve the use of a weapon. They do not result in serious injury.

Forgery and counterfeiting involve making and altering or being in possession of forged or counterfeited materials with the intent to distribute and defraud.

Fraud involves obtaining property or money by deceptive or dishonest means or under false pretenses.

Embezzlement is the misappropriation of money or property under someone's control or trust.

Stolen property offenses involve buying, receiving, or possessing items or materials that are stolen, as well as attempts at stealing such property.

Vandalism is the intentional destruction of public or private property of another without permission from the owner.

Weapons offenses involve violating regulations and laws regarding using, carrying, possessing, furnishing, and manufacturing of deadly weapons.

Prostitution and commercialized vice refers to acts related to sex offenses such as money exchanged for sex and procuring sexual acts.

Sex offenses include statutory rape and acts against common decency.

Drug offenses include the unlawful possession, sale, distribution, growing, and manufacturing of an illegal substance.

Gambling involves wagering money or valuable items on an event or competition without certainty of the outcome.

Offenses against the family and children include the neglect, desertion, nonsupport, and abuse of family and children.

Driving under the influence refers to operation of a motor vehicle while being over the legal limits of alcoholic influence.

Liquor law offenses are violations of local and state laws governing liquor.

Drunkenness is the state of being consumed with intoxication by alcohol.

Disorderly conduct is behavior that breaches the peace.

Vagrancy is begging, loitering, and the like.

All other offenses is a term referring to all violations of local and state laws.

Curfew and loitering laws apply to those who are not in the age of majority.

Runaways is a term applied to those under the age of 18 who have absconded from parental or custodial authority.

• Data taken from the UCR provide information on the number and individual characteristics of arrestees for Part I and Part II crimes. Essentially, the UCR gives information on the geographical and the demographical distributions of crime that are reported each year in the United States. These data reveal the types and amounts of crime that occur in each region of the country. They also present a picture of what offenders look like by including the race, age, and gender of arrestees. They reveal where crime is saturated and where it is least likely to occur. With this information, one can easily view the patterns and trends that are associated with crime, allowing for valid predictions on what the future holds for crime in America.

When compiling the data for the UCR, the FBI has the benefit of having police agencies report the number of index crimes that occur monthly. Thus, the UCR contains crimes known to police and local law enforcement. In totaling the number of reported crimes, unfounded or false complaints are not reported; rather, police submit to the FBI the "actual offenses known." Crimes are generally cleared in two ways. First, crimes are cleared by arrests. When this occurs, the suspect is taken into custody to answer charges against him or her. In the United States, only about 21.4% of all reported crimes are cleared by an arrest. Second, crimes are cleared by exceptional means. When this occurs, the suspect is believed either to have committed suicide, to have been killed, or to have fled the country to avoid criminal prosecution. Violent crimes are more likely to be cleared than crimes that are defined as less serious. More resources and attention are given to serious crime. When computing the crime rate for a particular jurisdiction, the FBI takes the total number of crimes, divides it by the population for that jurisdiction, and multiplies that number by 100,000. The formula is given below:

$$\frac{\text{Number of Crimes} \times 100{,}000}{\text{Population}}$$

Criticisms of the UCR

While many people believe that the UCR is the most reliable measure of crime in the United States (arguably because of the number of agencies behind it), it is not without its share of critics. Some experts argue that, despite the number of people who participate in this compilation of aggregate criminal statistics, it has three problem areas that challenge its validity: a lack of reporting by citizens, problems with law enforcement practices, and methodological problems. In an attempt to address these problems, changes have been made to the UCR, producing the National Incident-Based Reporting System (NIBRS). Before discussing the changes to the UCR, we address each of the three areas of criticism.

A Lack of Reporting by Citizens

Obviously, if citizens do not report the commission of a crime, that crime cannot possibly figure into the number of crimes committed for a given year. This lack of reporting adds to what are known as the **"dark figures" of crime** or

"dark figures" of crime—Crimes that are hidden from official statistics because they are unreported.

missing crime data. In fact, some surveys indicate that the UCR is only half correct, since half of all crimes go unreported. There are a number of reasons why citizens may choose not to report a criminal violation, but some of the most common are: (1) people do not have insurance, (2) victims fear reprisal, (3) victimization is viewed as a private matter, (4) nothing could be done about the victimization, and (5) the victimization was not important enough to warrant law enforcement intervention.

First, many people who are victimized lack insurance and do not report economic violations, believing that no economic return will occur. They simply count their losses and keep moving.

Second, some victims never report their victimization because they fear retaliation from their attacker. Many victims of rape and domestic violence never report their misfortune out of fear that they will be confronted once again by the attacker. Crime is usually committed by people who are known to the victim. Perpetrators are typically family members, a spouse, an estranged husband or boyfriend, or others with whom victims share intimate relationships.

Third, some people view victimization as a private matter. Of all victims, this group could be potentially the most dangerous since in many cases, they intend to right the wrong perpetrated against them. They could easily turn toward vigilantism.

Fourth, some victims believe that nothing can be done about the crime. This group may fail to report the crime because it occurred long before it was discovered. They may feel that the trail is too cold and the criminal is long gone.

Fifth, the UCR has been criticized because some people do not see their victimization as being serious enough to require the assistance of police. This group of victims is perhaps more apathetic than the others. In addition to the problems associated with citizens' lack of reporting, the validity of the UCR may be challenged based on police officers' behavior.

Law Enforcement Practices

With the large number of police agencies participating in one yearly data compilation, several things can go wrong. The UCR has been criticized because of the ways in which law enforcement agencies record and report crime, their different definitions of the index crimes, allegations of tampering with data, and questions of efficiency and professionalism. Other factors also add to the dark figures of crime.

First, consistency of measurement can be lost if police agencies experience structural changes that cause an increase in the crime rate. For example, a shift from decentralized to centralized reporting can cause the crime rate to skyrocket. Some attribute this increased crime rate to greater accountability within police departments to record and report crime. With a decentralized structure, accountability is typically lost. Therefore, when police agencies move toward centralization, there is more accountability. This does not suggest that more crimes are being committed. However, it may suggest that the police are doing a better job of measuring and recording crime.

Second, the UCR is questioned because the different police agencies that submit crime data to the FBI sometimes have different definitions for index crimes. For example, some states count only completed acts of rape in the rape category. Other states may include rapes, attempted rapes, and sexual assaults in the rape category. This makes it difficult to accurately determine the overall number of rapes across states. The same principle holds true for other crimes.

Third, allegations have surfaced that some police agencies manipulate their criminal statistics to present their department in either a positive or negative light. This strategy is used when a police agency wishes to demonstrate a need for more resources, such as vehicles, computers, salaries, or manpower. In contrast, in areas that attract tourists, police may downplay the crime rate so as not to frighten potential vacationers. For example, some police agencies have been accused of downgrading burglaries as minor trespasses.

Fourth, statistics indicate that when police agencies modernize and professionalize their departments, crime rates tend to increase. Some attribute this to better qualified officers who are not willing to look the other way when crimes are committed. Moreover, some feel that computer records of crime are more accurate than those taken manually. As such, it may appear that the crime rate is increasing.

Methodological Concerns of the UCR

Another area of the UCR that has received its share of criticism is the methodology used to collect these data. Traditionally, the UCR has been criticized for: (1) not including federal crimes, (2) not having all police agencies participate, (3) using estimates to calculate the total numbers of crimes, (4) counting only the most serious crime when an offender engages in multiple criminal acts, (5) sometimes recording only one crime when the same crime is committed multiple times by an offender, (6) including uncompleted acts with completed ones, and (7) not accounting for the fact that the FBI has a different definition of crime than some local police agencies.

First, only index crimes appear in this compilation of crime statistics. Critics argue that it represents a class bias because it fails to measure the crimes of white-collar, corporate, and other people in positions of respectability. Second, there is nothing that compels police agencies to submit crime reports to the FBI. If agencies choose not to participate, the crime rates in these areas go unknown. Third, since not all police agencies report their crime rates, there are huge gaps of missing crime data. Therefore, the UCR cannot be an accurate measurement of crime. Fourth, using estimates of the crime rate, the FBI typically rounds the numbers and reports averages and percentages. Thus, it is very difficult to pinpoint the exact numbers of law violations. Fifth, if an offender engages in multiple violations in the course of one incident, only the most serious offense is counted. For example, if an offender breaks and enters a home, steals property, assaults the children, rapes the wife, and kills the husband, only the murder is included in the UCR. There is no official record indicating the other crimes were committed. Sixth, if a person frequents a club and decides to rob everyone in attendance, it is listed in the UCR as one robbery, even if he or she robs 30 people. Seventh, the attempted commission of crimes is often included in the statistics with completed crimes. Finally, the FBI's definition of crime is sometimes inconsistent with that of many local law enforcement agencies.

The National Incident-Based Reporting System

In 1977, the International Association of Chiefs of Police and the National Sheriffs Association called for major changes to correct problems found in the UCR (Hagan, 2012). As such, the **National Incident-Based Reporting System** (NIBRS) was created in the late 1980s. Under this system, each law enforcement agency is charged with reporting on each criminal incident and on each arrest. The South Carolina Law Enforcement Division was the first agency to use this proposed system.

> **National Incident-Based Reporting System (NIBRS)**—A crime index created to address the many shortcomings found in the UCR. It includes traditional index crimes, firearms violations, public order crimes, and information on the relationships between victims and offenders.

The NIBRS uses 52 data elements to describe victims, offenders, arrestees, and circumstances of a crime. It also provides detailed information on each crime that is reported. It makes the distinction between incomplete and completed crimes and expands the definition of crime to include more criminal behavior. It also collects data provided by federal law enforcement agencies. NIBRS collects data on more than 22 Group A offenses, which include homicide, arson, assault offenses, burglary/breaking and entering, destruction of property, fraud offenses, larceny/theft offenses, motor vehicle theft, robbery, sex offenses forcible, sex offenses nonforcible, weapons violations, bribery, counterfeiting/forgery, drug and narcotic offenses, extortion/blackmail, prostitution, gambling, pornography, embezzlement, and kidnapping/abduction.

Moreover, NIBRS separates data collection into two levels: Level I and Level II. Level I covers all law enforcement agencies and require basic Group A incident-based data on the 22 categories. Level II includes an additional 11 lesser Group B offenses, which include writing bad checks, curfew/loitering/vagrancy violations, disorderly conduct, driving under the influence, drunkenness, family offenses, nonviolent offenses, liquor law violations, peeping tom offenses, runaway offenses, trespass of real property, and others (Hagan, 2012).

Recently, the NIBRS has begun to include statistics on hate and bias crimes. These crimes are committed against people solely because of their race or ethnicity, religion, or sexual preference. Other bias crimes are committed against the elderly and women. Despite its promise to address the criticisms of the UCR, the NIBRS has been implemented in only 26 states (none having major cities), with 12 other states in the process of testing NIBRS participation. Even in those states that have implemented the NIBRS, not every police agency has embraced collecting crime data in a manner consistent with NIBRS (Gaines, Kaune, and Miller, 2000). As of 2004, 5,271 law enforcement agencies submitted NIBRS data to the UCR program. These data represent 20% of the U.S. population and 16% of the crime statistics collected in the UCR program.

Self-Report Surveys

Self-report surveys (SRSs) are used to help measure the true nature and extent of crime. SRSs are not used to replace the UCR, but instead they are used to supplement official crime reports. SRSs are designed to help get to the "dark figures" of crime. Dark figures are those crimes that are hidden from official detection. SRSs were created because of the many problems associated with the UCR. Self-report surveys allow researchers to measure respondents' personality, attitudes, values, and criminal behavior. Participants are asked to report any law violations that they committed, but were not reported to police. Self-report surveys are most often used when the groups to be studied are already in juvenile or adult correctional facilities. One of the most common surveys used

> **self-report surveys**—A type of research disproportionately conducted by independent researchers. These studies involve asking people to what extent have they violated the law without it having been reported. These surveys help get to the "dark figures" of crime. Conducting this type of research requires interviewing people, such as offenders, inmates, prisoners, judges, prosecutors, thieves, and prostitutes. These surveys allow researchers to measure the association between social variables (e.g., education, family structure, income) and crime.

in criminal justice research is conducted by the Drug Use Forecasting (DUF) program. DUF collects information on the drug histories of new arrestees shortly after the booking process (Gaines, Kaune, and Miller, 2000). These surveys are administered three different ways: through interviews, telephone calls, and questionnaires. While much survey research is conducted by official agencies, private researchers usually conduct the majority of this type of research.

Because self-report research is of a highly personal nature, participants have to be given assurance that their privacy will be safeguarded. Researchers often promise to protect participants' confidentiality and safeguard their anonymity. It is believed that the researcher's academic credentials will convince subjects to participate in research investigations. The subjects of survey research include those arrested and sent to jails and prisons, and juveniles in middle and high schools. Other subjects of surveys are judges, prosecutors, and agents of the criminal justice system. Survey research may attempt to measure their attitudes about criminals, and in many cases about other aspects of their jobs.

Surveys, unlike official statistics, are used to test theories, measure attitudes about crime, and compute the associations among delinquency, crime, and social variables. Social variables include income, educational attainment, employment, family structure, and family function. These data help to indicate whether a person has embarked on a life of delinquency or crime because he or she lived in poverty, had limited education, lacked a job, was from a dysfunctional family, or had been reared in a household where conflict and discord were common. Surveys also allow for an evaluation of criminal behavior that cuts across race, gender, and class lines. This research serves to disprove or confirm that class bias or selective law enforcement exists in the criminal justice system. For example, if every person in all economic classes reports similar amounts of crime, yet the criminal justice system incarcerates and punishes some to a greater extent than others, the system could have a built-in class bias.

Criticisms of SRSs

Like the UCR, SRSs are not without limitations and criticisms. SRSs are overwhelmingly given to students, especially those attending middle and high schools, along with students enrolled in college (Hagan, 2012). For this reason, they typically focus on trivial matters, such as truancy, smoking, and stealing an item that costs less than five dollars. Collective bodies of students are ideal for survey research since they represent a captive audience that should be in attendance and ready to participate. Another criticism is that it may be unreasonable to expect offenders to be completely honest about their past behavior when they have nothing to gain from providing such information. SRSs have also been accused of collecting data from people who exaggerate, forget, or become confused about what is being asked of them. Finally, it is difficult to determine the behavior of chronic offenders and persistent drug users because these groups rarely tell the truth about their deviant behavior and law violations. Some also argue that chronic offenders are probably among those students with the greatest number of absences. In fact, they may be absent on many of the days when researchers visit schools to conduct research. In addition, students who use drugs have a difficult time quitting, and it may be impossible to predict their future behavior.

Ways to Check the Accuracy of SRSs

Validating Against Police Reports

Because SRSs typically focus on people who are not known for their honesty and integrity, the information that they provide must be validated. However, this may be difficult since surveys were created because of weaknesses found in official crime statistics. Thus, it may be impossible to compare self-reported accounts of criminal behavior with police records, but when possible, official statistics can substantiate or contradict self-reports. While there are a number of techniques researchers can use to validate self-reported deviance and crime, they typically rely on strategies such as: (1) comparing law-abiding groups with known offenders, (2) using **peer informants**, and (3) employing test–retest methods.

> **peer informants**—Refers to a technique used in self-report surveys or studies to validate claims.

The Known Group Method

In this process, researchers can compare a known group of offenders with a comparable group of individuals who do not have a record of crime or delinquent behavior to determine which group is more delinquent or criminal. Naturally, the researcher anticipates that the research will reveal those with criminal records to be more delinquent or criminal, but sometimes it finds that those who appear to be law-abiding are, in fact, just as delinquent or criminal. They have managed to elude the "arms of justice." Some scholars contend that the latter group may be from families of relative affluence, while those with criminal records are commonly from disadvantaged backgrounds. They are those who are more likely to receive a disproportionate amount of processing from the criminal justice system.

Peer Informants

When feasible, researchers can contact close friends and associates of respondents to validate reported claims of delinquency and crime. Though seldom used, the technique allows researchers to corroborate reported incidences of a measured behavior, especially when a disproportionate amount of activity or serious crime is reported by someone who is relatively young (Hagan, 2012). Researchers believe that in middle and high school settings, unlike in college settings, close friends are typically aware of the activities in which their friends have engaged. Because teenagers may share their experiences with peers and close friends to boost their popularity, researchers find use of peer informants to be a valuable tool to either confirm or dismiss reported behavior given by respondents in survey research. After contacting the friends and associates of a respondent who has reported excessive criminal behavior, a researcher may be inclined to exclude the responses from the research investigation if there is no corroboration from those friends, thus indicating that the respondent may have embellished his or her activities.

The Test–Retest Method

Another strategy used to validate responses given by a participant in survey research is the test–retest method. It is arguably the best and most effective measure to validate reported behavior. The technique requires that the researcher give the respondent the same instrument (survey) shortly after he or she has completed the initial survey. If the survey responses are valid, the respondent should provide the exact same responses. If the respondent provides too many inconsistencies on the second measure, his or her survey should not be included (i.e., in the final data compilation), because the respondent was dishonest. To include such a survey in the final analysis of the research would impede the discovery of the truth about the research question. In the end, the researcher may have to decide on an acceptable amount of inaccuracy or inconsistency to allow from respondents.

While the aforementioned strategies are typically used to validate self-reported data, several other techniques bear mentioning, especially those that include comparing self-reported data with official data, lie scales, and measures of internal consistency in self-report surveys. When feasible, researchers should attempt to compare reported claims of behavior with official records. Since the disproportionate amount of self-reported research targets students from captive audiences, these data will typically come from schools and colleges (or from police departments in isolated cases). However, because of privacy rights, researchers may face an insurmountable task when trying to ascertain these data. Moreover, since self-reported data are an attempt to measure unknown and unreported activities, there may not be an existing record of the behavior. The inclusions of lie scales, also referred to as "truth scales," along with measures of internal consistency in surveys assist researchers in collecting valid data and thereby avoiding socially desirable responses that respondents are inclined to provide in research investigations (Hagan, 2012).

> **National Crime Victimization Survey**—Survey used to supplement the Uniform Crime Reports by helping to arrive at an accurate measure of the nature and extent of crime and victimization.

The National Crime Victimization Survey

The first **National Crime Victimization Survey** was conducted in 1966. During this time, it was discovered that victimization rates were higher than initially expected. Many people were aware that large numbers of crimes went unreported and underreported. Because of this, efforts were made to gather data on the nature and extent of crime. The survey, created to supplement the UCR, was first called the National Crime Survey and later renamed the National Crime Victimization Survey (NCVS). It is conducted by the U.S. Census Bureau in cooperation with the Bureau of Justice Statistics and the U.S. Department of Justice. The NCVS is used to measure levels of personal and household victimization as well as determine the "dark figures" of crime, the rates of crime that are unknown due to a lack of reporting. More specifically, the NCVS measurement of personal crimes includes rape and sexual attack, robbery, aggravated and simple assault, and purse-snatching/pocket-picking. Its measurement of property crimes includes burglary, theft, motor vehicle theft, and vandalism (Bureau of Justice Statistics, 2010). Data are obtained each year from a national survey of about 77,200 households taken from a stratified multistage cluster sample of 134,000 people. Residents who are interviewed are usually ages 12 and older (Bureau of Justice Statistics, 2007). These households remain in the sample for three years.

While being surveyed, respondents are first asked a set of screening questions to determine if they were victimized during the six months prior to the interview. They are also asked to report any crimes committed against the household such as a burglary or motor vehicle theft. Respondents are asked whether they have been victimized in the past six months with respect to aggravated or simple assault, rape, sexual assault, robbery, burglary, or larceny. Crimes such as homicide and arson are not included in the survey. The NCVS includes discussions on the context of crimes, including the type of crime, time of day, month, the setting, characteristics of the offender (race, ethnicity, age, gender, and income), and the victims' relationship with the offenders. Residents are also asked if the crime was reported to police and reasons for reporting or not reporting, about consequences of the victimization, if the offender used a weapon, and whether he or she was under the influence of drugs or alcohol. The NCVS has a completion rate of 95% (Bureau of Justice Statistics, 2007). The NCVS also allows for explanations of increases and decreases in the crime rate. Moreover, it allows researchers to create and test victimization theories that explain and offer the social context behind levels of victimization. Several popular theories of victimization include routine activity theory and deviant place theory. The more controversial theories are: lifestyle theory, victim precipitation, and victim precipitation and rape (Siegel, 2009).

Criticisms of the NCVS

While the NCVS provides information that is very important to the study of crime, it too, has its share of problems and criticisms. First, victims tend to overreport their victimizations. Some believe that this is caused by a misinterpretation of events. For example, if victims misplace or lose items, they may report them in the survey as having been stolen. Second, victims of sexual crimes do not always report them. In fact, many victims of rape consciously decide not to report the matter because they are fearful of the reprisal and stigma that are often attached to being raped or sexually assaulted. Respondents sometimes forget about minor victimizations. Third, the respondents of the survey are not questioned about family members' involvement in crime. Another concern is that the researcher does not ask the respondent any questions about his or her involvement in criminal activity. It may be that the resident who is being interviewed is a criminal offender. Fourth, the NCVS does not attempt to record victimizations caused by white-collar, corporate, or governmental crime. Without the inclusion of these crimes and victimizations, we cannot get a complete picture of the crime rate, nor can we fully measure all victimizations that occur each year.

The Comparability of the UCR, SRS, and NCVS

Some researchers argue that it is impossible to use all three data sources at the same time to measure the crime problem because they focus on different units of analysis. They argue that the UCR measures reported levels of crime and the SRS measures actual crimes, while the NCVS measures levels of victimization. Therefore, they have different units of analysis. Despite this valid point, these crime statistics are more comparable than many may believe. For example, if crime rates increase or decrease, it should be indicated in each of these data sources. The UCR, SRS, and NCVS are in agreement about the personal characteristics of serious criminal offenders and where and when crime takes place. They all agree that crimes are disproportionately saturated in urban areas, occurring at nighttime, and during the summer months. With regard to property and violent crime, the UCR reveals substantial increases during the 1960s and 1970s. More specifically, it shows that property crimes increased from less than 2,000 per 100,000 population to more than 5,000 per 100,000 by 1980. The property crime rate remained at a high level until the early 1990s. During that time, it began to slowly decline to approximately 3,000 per 100,000 population. Scholars argue that the amount of property crimes may have decreased for the same reasons (e.g., changes in drug use, shifts in economic conditions, changes in the age composition of the population, changes in policing and sentencing practices, and others) as the rate of violent crime. In fact, the UCR reports that from 2000 to 2011, the number of violent and property crimes declined (Federal Bureau of Investigation, 2012).

The NCVS reports that the victimization rate for property crime has fallen drastically from more than 500 victimizations per 1,000 households to 200 per 1,000 households for the early 1970s into the early 2000s. An important point to observe is that in the 1980s, the UCR reported that the property crime rate remained at a high level, while the NCVS showed that the rate of household property victimization experienced a steady decline. The inconsistency may reveal that both citizens and police were reporting a greater number of household victimizations (Bureau of Justice Statistics, 2010). The UCR and NCVS agree that the rate of property crime dropped significantly during the 1990s and early 2000s. Self-report trends indicate a far greater number of criminals than official statistics and that offenders engage in a "mixed bag" of crime and deviance (Barkan, 2000 2001 in endnote). What is important to remember about the three data sources is that, unlike the UCR, which generates a crime rate based on individuals in the population, the NCVS is based on households, while self-report surveys disproportionately target captive audiences of juveniles and measure delinquency.

When criminologists study crime using the UCR, SRS, and NCVS, they find patterns with respect to geography (region), communities, people, climate, and seasons. Criminologists also research temporal and ecological factors associated with crime, finding, for instance, that more crimes occur during the summer months, with the exceptions of murder and robbery, which occur more often in December and January. Population density is also related to crime. The majority of crimes occur in urban areas rather than in suburban or rural areas (Siegel, 2000, 2009). Some argue that areas where diversity abounds and people live in close physical proximity to each other may promote the occasion of crime. Also, in highly populated areas, people who commit crimes can quickly become anonymous. In rural areas with small populations, communities are close-knit and people generally know one another, making anonymity almost impossible. The primary data sources provide information on the regional distribution of crime. They report that the majority of violence and crime occurs in urban areas in the southern and western United States.

While the UCR, SRS, and NCVS indicate that index crimes are given more attention in the criminal justice system, it is believed by many that these crimes pale in comparison to crimes committed by people who are wealthy, powerful, and hold positions of respectability. These types of crime include organized, white-collar and corporate, political and governmental, and healthcare crime. Though these crimes have long resulted in more deaths and injuries than the index crimes, there are no established data collection methods or agencies devoted solely to compiling yearly statistics on victimizations perpetrated by these criminal elites. These crimes are typically made known when an independent researcher investigates them and reports the findings to the academic community. In this situation, one cannot be sure about the extent to which the information will be disseminated to others. Another way these crimes are exposed is when concerned citizens report them to their local attorney general or the U.S. Attorney General, who then takes action that makes the local and national news. From all accounts, it does not appear that independent research foundations or the **National Institute of Justice** (the research arm of the U.S. Department of Justice) has an interest in awarding grants to researchers studying

National Institute of Justice—The research component of the U.S. Department of Justice concerned with funding criminal justice projects and investigations of the elements of the justice system such as police, courts, corrections, and juvenile justice.

crimes committed by criminal elites. Again, crimes committed by the criminal elite take a greater toll on society in terms of social harm, injuries, and human life. Consider, for example, the recent devastation caused by the collapse of the U.S. economy and, arguably, the world financial crisis perpetrated by key players on Wall Street. According to Gregg Barak (2012), the federal government's lack of action in holding Wall Street bankers, mortgage lenders, and associated fraudsters criminally responsible for their involvement in fraudulent behavior reveals institutionalized crime and the contradictions of how law and punishment is unequally applied when confronted by power and wealth. As of early 2014, not a single offender has been charged, arrested, or held criminally responsible for any wrongdoing that affected millions of Main Street victims.

Neglected Areas of Crime

The aforementioned data sources are primarily used to collect data on index crimes or street crimes and juvenile delinquency. Despite this, some scholars (Barkan, 2012; Reiman and Leighton, 2010; Elias, 1986; Beirne and Messerschmidt, 1991) argue that other types of crime that are committed each year appear to go largely ignored or neglected because they do not receive the same amount of attention and resources from the law enforcement community as those crimes discussed at the beginning of the chapter—namely, Type I and Type II crimes. Despite this, many criminologists believe that these crimes may actually produce greater social harm and injury than street crime. While these crimes are less publicized, they are present and often devastating to victims. They include organized crime, white-collar and corporate crime, political and governmental crime, and healthcare crime.

Organized Crime

Organized crime is defined as those illegal activities that are connected with the management and coordination of extortion and vices, such as illegal drugs, gambling, pornography, prostitution, and usury (Block and Chambliss, 1981). Organized crime is believed by many experts to have developed in the early 1920s, at which time it was committed mainly by immigrants who recognized the large amounts of money that could be made in the United States. It was often romanticized as a hierarchical Italian-dominated structure with 24 ruling families (Albanese, 1982). While this myth may have been perpetuated by television series like *The Sopranos* as well as movies such as *The Godfather* series, *Goodfellas, A Bronx Tale, The Untouchables, Carlito's Way, Sugar Hill, Hoodlums,* and others, experts argue that this mythology led to a conspiracy theory that later included other minority groups such as Asians (Albanese, 1982; Kappeler and Potter, 2005). The myth ignores the existence of organized crime before Italians immigrated to the United States. It also ignores the root causes of organized crime—namely, poverty, discrimination, and peoples' willingness to

> **organized crime**—Criminal structures that are involved in the management and coordination of providing illegal goods and services that are desired by many people in society. Such goods and services may include pornography, gambling, prostitution, drugs, and highinterest loans.

defray the cost of goods and services, along with politicians', legitimate businesses', and governmental officials' willingness to participate in illegal activities (Barkan, 2012).

Today, the global nature of organized crime is widely recognized. In fact, a modern-day type of organized crime that is fast becoming a global problem is human trafficking—essentially slavery (Wilson, Walsh, and Kleuber, 2006; Winterdyk and Reichel, 2010). The United Nations (2005) estimates that each year, four million people, including men, women, and children, are the victims of transnational human trafficking (Aguilar-Millan, Foltz, Jackson, and Oberg, 2008). More specifically, experts estimate that approximately 70% of trafficking victims are women and girls and up to 30% are minors. The United Nations (2005) states that there are several forms of trafficking in persons ranging from prostitution, forced labor, and slavery, to the murder of people for the primary purpose of removing and selling their body organs to be sold for a profit (Winterdyk and Reichel, 2010).

Organized crime is committed by persons of almost every nationality or ethnic group (Lyman and Potter, 2011). Some view organized crime as structures of individuals and groups who enter into illegal associations for the purpose of generating profits through illegal means, protecting their illegal activities through graft and corruption (Lyman and Potter, 2011). Larry Gaines, Michael Kaune, and Roger Miller (2000) argue that organized crime functions to satisfy the public's demand for illegal goods and services, such as pornography, firearms, credit card scams, drugs, gambling, and counterfeiting. Furthermore, Gaines and colleagues contend that it is very difficult to completely rid society of organized crime, because it is deeply embedded in the nation's culture, and many of its operations mirror legitimate business. Experts argue that the only way to rid society of the supply is to eliminate the demand for these goods and services (Lyman and Potter, 2011). At the same time, Americans continue to glamorize organize crime in its depictions of crime families that traffic in humans, firearms, and drugs. This is revealed through Hollywood's fascination with the mafia and other powerful crime organizations.

> **white-collar crime**—Typically associated with people in positions of respectability in society who take advantage of their social class positions by engaging in crime. The term was initially coined by Edwin Sutherland in 1939 when he argued that crimes committed "in the suites" are just as worthy of sociological attention as crimes committed on the streets. Commonly referred to as corporate crime.
>
> **corporate crime**—Crime committed by people in positions of respectability in the course of their occupation. Corporate crime is also referred to as white-collar crime. Some examples of corporate crime are price fixing, fraudulent stock manipulation, insider trading, and the establishment of junk bonds. The purpose of such crime is usually to advance one's personal fortune or the company of one's employment.

White-Collar and Corporate Crime

In a general sense, **white-collar** and **corporate crimes** are similar and can be defined as crime committed by persons of higher socioeconomic status in the course of their business, occupation, or profession (Sutherland, 1949). John Conklin (2001) argues that the definition of white-collar crime has been expanded to include any illegal act that is punishable by criminal sanction that is committed by a person or corporation with high social standing. In fact, Neal Shover and Jennifer Scroggins (2009) contend that the name *organizational crime* is preferred over *corporate* *crime* because it suggests that crimes can be committed by and on behalf of organizations that are big and small. Thus, the scope of organizational crime includes large corporations as well as blue-collar businesses such as automotive repair shops.

Conklin contends that the majority of white-collar crime is punishable under the criminal law. The reality, he argues, is that most acts are punished under regulatory law. White-collar or corporate crime occurs when industries knowingly release onto unsuspecting consumers defective products that cause injury and/or death. Stocks and securities fraud and theft are considered white-collar crime (Conklin, 2001), as are deceptive advertising and price-fixing.

An example of one of the biggest security fraud cases in American history was tried in criminal court in 2009. More specifically, Bernard "Bernie" Madoff, former Wall Street stock broker and investment adviser, was arrested, charged, and found guilty of securities fraud, investment adviser fraud, mail fraud, wire fraud, money laundering, making false statements to the Securities and Exchange Commission, perjury, and stealing employee benefits. In court, Madoff pleaded guilty to 17 federal felonies and admitted to turning his business into a massive **Ponzi scheme** that defrauded thousands of investors out of an estimated $65 billion. In June 2009, he was sentenced to 150 years in prison, the maximum punishment that the law would allow. He was also made to forfeit $17 billion of his personal assets. Madoff will be remembered as the most notorious white collar criminal in American history (Henriques, 2009; Rashbaum and Henriques, 2009).

> **Ponzi scheme**—A fraudulent investment that pays returns to investors from existing or new capital that comes from new investors instead of from monies earned by the individual or institution.

Other examples of such crimes are unsafe working conditions, tax fraud, antitrust violations, environmental law violations, and industrial espionage. An employee's embezzling from a company is another example of white-collar crime. In general, experts view white-collar crime as any illegal means used by a person or business to gain a personal or business advantage (Gaines, Kaune, and Miller, 2000). The U.S. Department of Commerce estimates that white-collar crime costs corporate America $40 billion yearly (Brian, 1998). Steven Chermak (1995) argues that reports of white-collar and corporate crime are unlikely to make headline news because many businesses support newspapers and television stations with the money they spend on advertisements and commercials. As such, the news media may avoid stories on white-collar and corporate crimes to avoid alienating their sponsors.

Political and Governmental Crime

Political and governmental crimes are believed to be widespread, and no nation is exempted from engaging in such practices. These crimes are defined as unlawful or

> **political crime**—Illegal activities that can be committed on the city, county, state, and national levels. When they occur on the state level, they may entail state corruption and repression. When they are committed on the international level, they may entail violating an international law or even domestic actions perpetrated against a nation's own people, such as genocide. Also referred to as governmental crime.
>
> **governmental crime**—Also referred to as state crime consists of central political insitutions of a given society. Its major institutions of the government: the legal system, the military, police, management of public health, and administrative branches.

unethical actions conducted by state officials and state agencies in violation of domestic or international law where victimizations occur domestically or internationally (Beirne and Messerschmidt, 1991). Therefore, political crimes can be committed domestically, as well as internationally, by a nation's government. Piers Beirne and James Messerschmidt argue that domestic political crimes are committed by the state in two areas. First, state corruption is the illegal or unethical use of state authority for personal or political gain. Second, state repression occurs when the state uses its authority and power to repress domestic political dissent. State corruption can exist at the city, county, state, and national levels. While state corruption comes in many varieties, the most common types of state corruption include: (1) political bribery (accepting money for introducing special legislation or voting a specific way), (2) political kickbacks (voting in favor of a government contract), (3) election fraud (illegal voting, false registration, stuffing ballot boxes), and (4) corrupt campaign practices (politicians granting favors to those who contribute large sums of money to their campaigns).

In a recent case in Detroit, Michigan, for example, former mayor Kwame Kilpatrick was convicted and found guilty of corruption charges that included two dozen offenses that ranged from racketeering conspiracy, to bribery, to tax crime. State witnesses alleged that Kilpatrick accepted kickbacks, rigged contracts, and lived far beyond his means. The state's star witness testified that over the course of several meetings in the mayor's office, she gave him more than $200,000 as his personal cut of political donations. Furthermore, the Internal Revenue Service claimed that Kilpatrick spent $840,000 beyond his salary. The former mayor is expected to spend more than 28 years in prison for his crimes (White, 2013).

Another form of political crime that has become widespread in the United States in recent years is voter suppression. Voter suppression occurs when efforts are made to illegally influence the outcome of an election by preventing or obstructing citizens from voting in the democratic process (Welsh, 2012). During the presidency of Barack Obama, political scientists, as well as pollsters and concerned citizens in many key states such as Florida, Ohio, and Pennsylvania, have accused members of the Republican Party of engaging in this political crime designed to prevent voters from exercising their constitutional right to vote. More specifically, Democrats argue that conservatives in general, but Tea Party members in particular, associated with the organization True the Vote have challenged voters' eligibility in communities with high minority populations by using a number of illegal tactics to prevent them from voting. These measures range from sending potential voters automated calls with inaccurate information about polling sites and closing times, to rolling back early voting, to asking voters for identification outside of polling places. Critics argue that these measures are commonly used in minority areas with the sole purpose of intimidating potential voters (Welsh, 2012).

State repression may be used against those whom the government has labeled as "subversive." They may become the targets of both state and federal law enforcement investigations. When one thinks of political repression, one quickly thinks of counterintelligence programs (COINTELPRO). The FBI and the Central Intelligence Agency (CIA) have engaged in many illegal activities that relate to political repression in the name of counter-intelligence. Historically, those who have been the targets of COINTELPRO have included educational institutions, organized labor, youth groups, black groups, governmental affairs, the military, and industry (Beirne and Messerschmidt, 1991).

 Another form of political crime occurs when a nation's state commits criminal behavior against another nation. This type of behavior is referred to as international crime and has serious implications for the allies of the country that has come under attack. President Harry Truman signed into law the National Security Act, which made the CIA and the National Security Council (NSC) responsible for gathering foreign intelligence and transmitting this information directly to the White House. The NSC was to serve as a civilian advisory group to the President on domestic, foreign, and military policies that relate to national security. Both the CIA and the NSC have routinely violated the National Security Act and other U.S. laws, particularly the Neutrality Act, which prohibits the providing of weapons or military assistance to any foreign country with which the United States is at peace.

Shortly after the attacks of September 11, 2001, President George W. Bush issued a resolution to Congress entitled "Authorization for Use of Military Force." With its approval, American troops invaded Afghanistan, and the Taliban were forcefully driven from power in the country (Haas, 2012, 2013). However, critics of American aggression charged that for a war to be in accord with the Charter of the United Nations (UN), the UN Security Council must give approval. President Bush did not seek approval to engage in war with Afghanistan from the Security Council, and therefore, these critics believe that the war was entered into illegally under international law. Though the Security Council eventually approved of the military force that was already present inside Afghanistan by giving the force a mission to maintain stability in both countries, critics still view the act as a blatant violation of international law. Moreover, many believe that the United States committed war crimes in Afghanistan, such as attacking defenseless targets, bombing the neutral country of Pakistan, and engaging in indiscriminate attacks on civilians via drones. Critics argue that this misconduct has claimed the lives of thousands of civilians who were in areas where war was being waged. The Bush administration was eventually charged with an estimated 269 war crimes (Haas, 2012, 2013).

On June 10, 2008, Congressmen Dennis Kucinich and Robert Wexler introduced 35 articles of impeachment against President George W. Bush, accusing him of violating international law by knowingly misleading the American public into war. More specifically, the articles addressed the case made for war (prevention of terrorism in general, and a search for weapons of mass destruction that never existed in particular), treatment of prisoners of war, and spying on and wiretapping U.S. citizens. Although the House of Representatives voted 251 to 166 to refer the matter to the Judiciary Committee, nothing came of the matter.

 Another shocking political crime, genocide, occurs when a nation engages in the extermination of its people or the people of another nation's state. Such practices were conducted under the reign of Adolf Hitler in Germany, under Pol Pot and the Khmer Rouge in Cambodia, and by the Hutus on the Tutsis in Rwanda.

> **healthcare crime**—A catchall phrase for any crime committed by medical doctors and others associated with the medical profession in the course of their occupation. Such crimes include ordering unnecessary surgery and prescriptions, defrauding insurance companies to advance one's wealth, or diluting a patient's medication.

Healthcare Industry Crimes

Research reveals that healthcare providers often engage in an abundance of crimes that go largely unreported, referred to as **healthcare crime**. For example, Stephen Rosoff, Henry Pontell, and Robert Tillman (2010) report that each year, physicians, pharmacists, medical equipment companies, nursing home, medical testing laboratories, home healthcare providers, medical billing services, and ambulance services commit an estimated $100 billion of healthcare fraud.

They argue that this occurs for a number of reasons that include: this type of work is private and complex, there is no one providing oversight or policing these professionals because they are self-regulated, and patients and clients are unaware if their bills are accurate and reflect needed procedures and proscribed medications that will treat their illnesses. These factors combined make it difficult to detect this type of fraud. Similarly, William Cohen (1994) finds that patients and clients are often billed for many services that they never receive, and in many cases, their clients are subjected to inferior products, inflated charges, and false prescriptions, and are unnecessarily sent to several doctors for medical visits.

It is also estimated that each year many Americans are subjected to unnecessary surgery and drug prescriptions at the hands of doctors and others in the healthcare industry (Inlander, Levin, and Weiner, 1988). Some sources estimate that each year as many as 10,000 victims die as a result of unnecessary prescriptions, and 16,000 die due to unnecessary surgery (Elias, 1986; Reiman and Leighton, 2010). James Coleman (2006) observes that an overwhelming number of operations are performed on patients with private insurance compared with the number performed on those belonging to prepaid health plans. He suggests that private insurance companies allow surgeons to collect higher fees for their operations than the set salary they receive from prepaid plans.

Unfortunately, many actions committed against patients go unchecked because the medical profession regulates its own behavior through the American Medical Association (AMA). Stated another way, doctors are policing other doctors, and they protect their own. Experts believe that many patients are placed in harm's way, since they could be under the medical care of someone who has had a number of complaints filed against him or her about the quality of medical attention provided. In *Medicine on Trial*, Charles Inlander, Lowell Levin, and Ed Weiner (1988) argue that the AMA protects the licenses of some doctors who suffer from drug addiction and incompetence, allowing them to practice medicine on the unsuspecting public. Moreover, due to doctor incompetence, 43 million Americans are misdiagnosed and are provided unneeded treatment for conditions they do not have. Despite the undeniable harm that can come from incompetence in the healthcare industry, such behaviors are not viewed as criminal.

Again, it is elite offenders who commit organized, corporate, political, and healthcare industry crimes. These offenders receive far less attention than street-level criminals. This is ironic, because elite crimes can be more devastating to the general public and inflict more human suffering and pain. Society should take greater steps toward holding elite offenders accountable for their illegal behavior. At the same time, criminal justice and criminology scholars should increase their efforts to create a uniform crime report of elite criminal behavior—because if we are to truly study crime, it should be examined in its totality and not selectively. Failure to make such changes could leave the lives and financial savings of many Americans in great jeopardy.

Summary

When it comes to measuring the nature and extent of the crime problem, criminologists and criminal justicians use a number of sources to collect these data. For example, they often rely on official data referred to as the Uniform Crime Reports. These data are collected by more than 17,000 police agencies each year and given to the FBI to be used as measures of the amounts of reported crime. These data can be used to assess whether the crime rate is increasing or decreasing. However, because of the problems associated with the UCR, efforts have been made to correct them with the implementation of the National Incident-Based Reporting System.

Moreover, researchers also use surveys to address the shortcomings that are commonly found in official data. The UCR contains only data on reported levels of crime; it is not a complete or an accurate measure of all crime. Surveys supplement the UCR and the NIBRS with information that is missing from official statistics, helping to uncover missing data or the "dark figures" of crime. These are the unreported crimes that occur each year.

Some experts believe that official data give conservative estimates of crime, while surveys provide liberal numbers of crime because they typically reveal that officially reported data provide only about half of what respondents report in surveys. The two main types of surveys used in criminal justice and criminological studies are the National Crime Victimization Survey and self-report surveys that focus on levels of victimization and self-reported criminal activity, respectively.

Despite the differences found among the UCR, NCVS, and SRSs, they share many similarities regarding information such as time, place, and settings of crime. They can also reveal personal characteristics of arrestees, victims, and the actual perpetrators of crime. While the vast amount of research is conducted on street crime, other areas of crime are neglected by the broader law enforcement community. They include organized, white-collar and corporate, political and governmental crimes, as well as crimes committed by the healthcare industry. Many scholars feel that studying these types of crime is very important because they arguably cause more social harm and injury to more Americans than do street crimes.

Discussion Questions

1. What are some major concerns of using official crime statistics such as the Uniform Crime Reports?

2. What can survey data tell us about the level of reported crime?

3. What are some efforts that were created to supplement the use of official data?

4. Name several concerns associated with the National Incident-Based Reporting System.

5. What are major criticisms facing the use of self-reported surveys?

References

Aguilar-Millan, S., Foltz, J. E., Jackson, J., and Oberg, A. (2008, November–December). Global Crime Case: The Modern Slave Trade. *The Futurist*.

Albanese, J. S. (1982). What Lockheed and LaCosta Nostra Have in Common: The Effect of Ideology on Criminal Justice Policy. *Crime and Delinquency, 28*, 211–32.

Barak, G. (2012). *Theft of a Nation: Wall Street Looting and Federal Regulatory Colluding* (Issues Crime and Justice). Lanham, MD: Rowman & Littlefield.

Barkan, S.E. (2000). "Household crowding and aggregate crime rates." *Journal of Crime and Justice, 23*:47–64.

Barkan, S. E. (2001). *Criminology: A Sociological Understanding* (2nd ed.). Upper Saddle River, NJ: Prentice-Hall.

Barkan, S. E. (2012). *Criminology: A Sociological Understanding* (5th ed.). Upper Saddle River, NJ: Prentice-Hall.

Beirne, P., and Messerschmidt, J. (1991). *Criminology*. New York, NY: Harcourt Brace Jovanovich.

Block, A., and Chambliss, W. J. (1981). *Organizing Crime*. New York, NY: Elsevier.

Brian, D. (1998, April 25). Beating Bolder Corporate Crooks. *Fortune*, 193.

Bureau of Justice Statistics. (2007). *National Crime Victimization Survey, Criminal Victimization, 2006*. Office of Justice Programs. Washington, DC: U.S. Department of Justice

Bureau of Justice Statistics. (2010). *National Crime Victimization Survey, Criminal Victimization, 2009*. Office of Justice Programs. Washington, DC: U.S. Department of Justice.

Chermak, S. M. (1995). *Victims in the News: Crime and the American News Media*. Boulder, CO: Westview.

Cohen, W. (1994). *Gaming the Health Care System: Billions of Dollars Lost to Fraud and Abuse Each Year*. Washington, DC: Senate Special Committee on Aging.

Coleman, J. W. (2006). *The Criminal Elite: Understanding White-Collar Crime*. New York, NY: Worth.

Conklin, J. E. (2001). *Criminology* (7th ed.). Needham Heights, MA: Allyn & Bacon.

Federal Bureau of Investigation (2012). "Crime in the United States," Uniform Crime Report: Washington, DC: U.S. Department of Justice.

Elias, R. (1986). *The Politics of Victimization: Victims, Victimology, and Human Rights*. New York, NY: Oxford University Press.

Gaines, L., Kaune, M., and Miller, R. L. (2000). *Criminal Justice in Action*. Belmont, CA: Wadsworth Thomson Learning.

Gottfredson, D. M. (1999). *Exploring Criminal Justice: An Introduction*. Los Angeles, CA: Roxbury.

Haas, M. (2012, April 15). America's Continuing War Crimes Quagmire. http://www.uswarcrimes.com.

Haas, M. (2013, February 16). The Asymmetric War on Al-Qaeda. http://www.uswarcrimes.com.

Hagan, F.E. (2012). Essentials of Research Methods in Criminal Justice and Criminology (3rd ed.). Upper Saddle River, New Jersey: Prentice-Hall.

Henriques, D. B. (2009, June 29). Madoff Is Sentenced to 150 Years for Ponzi Scheme. *New York Times*.

Inlander, C. B., Levin, L. S., and Weiner, E. (1988). *Medicine on Trial: The Appalling Story of Ineptitude, Malfeasance, Neglect, and Arrogance*. New York, NY: Prentice-Hall.

Kappeler, V. E., and Potter, G. (2005). *The Mythology of Crime and Criminal Justice*. Prospect Heights, IL: Waveland.

Lyman, M. D., and Potter, G. W. (2011). *Organized Crime*. Upper Saddle River, NJ: Prentice-Hall.

Rashbaum, W. K., and Henriques, D. B. (2009, March 10). Madoff to Plead Guilty: Charges Carry a Life Sentence. *New York Times*.

Reiman, J., and Leighton, P. (2010). *The Rich Get Richer and the Poor Get Prison: Ideology, Class, and Criminal Justice*. Upper Saddle River, NJ: Prentice-Hall.

Rosoff, S. M., Pontell, H. N., and Tillman, R. (2010). *Profit Without Honor: White Collar Crime and the Looting of America*. Upper Saddle River, NJ: Prentice-Hall.Shover, N., and Scroggins, J. (2009). Organizational Crime. In *The Oxford Handbook of Crime and Public Policy*, ed. Michael Tonry (pp. 273–303). New York, NY: Oxford University Press.

Siegel, L. (2000). *Criminology* (7th ed.). Belmont, CA: Wadsworth/Thomson Learning.

Siegel, L. (2009). *Criminology* (11th ed.). Belmont, CA: Wadsworth/Thomson Learning.

Sutherland, E. (1949). *White Collar Crime*. New York, NY: Holt, Rinehart, and Winston.

Uniform Crime Reports. (1994). *Crime in the United States*. Washington, DC: Department of Justice, Federal Bureau of Investigation.

United Nations (2005). *Conference of the Parties to the United Nations Convention Against Transnational Organized Crime*. Second session. Vienna, October 10–21.

U.S. Department of Justice, Bureau of Justice Statistics. (1993). *National Crime Victimization Survey*. Washington, DC: Government Printing Office.

Welsh, T. (2012, November 6). Is Voter Suppression a Real Problem? Reports from Swing States Show Irregularities with the Voting Process Both Before and After Election Day. *U.S. News & World Report*.

White, E. (2013, March 14). *Ex-Mayor Heads to Prison: Kwame Kilpatrick of Detroit convicted*. Associated Press.

Wilson, D. G., Walsh, W. F., and Kleuber, S. (2006). Trafficking in Human Beings: Training and Services Among U.S. Law Enforcement Agencies. *Police Practice and Research, 7*(2), 149–60.

Winterdyk, J., and Reichel, P. (2010). Introduction to Special Issue Human Trafficking: Issues and Perspectives. *European Journal of Criminology, 7*(1), 5–10.

Chapter 3
Crime Victimizations

© vs148/ShutterStock, Inc.

Chapter Outline

- Why Study Crime Victims?
- Victimization Theories
- Helping Crime Victims
- Strategies to Prevent Criminal Victimizations
- Summary
- Discussion Questions

Why Study Crime Victims?

victim—Any person who has sustained an injurious action at the hands of another or an object.

Several decades ago, many people, including criminal justice scholars and sociologists, discounted the importance of the **victim's** role in the criminal justice process and the criminal episode. Unfortunately, victims were seen or thought of as people who were simply in the wrong place at the wrong time (Siegel, 2012). This sentiment is echoed by the very name given to the American system of justice, or the place where victims go to seek justice after being victimized. One could argue that if society was genuinely concerned about the plight of victims, the system would be named the victims justice system, rather than the criminal justice system, thus giving the appearance that victims are of primary importance. Critics of the justice system argue that society does more to safeguard the rights of suspects and criminal defendants than to attend to the needs and interests of crime victims (Fattah, 1986). The basis for this can be seen in the Bill of Rights, or the first 10 amendments (Elias, 1986), which were designed to ensure that the rights of the individual will not be infringed by government officials (Anderson and Thompson, 2007; Alder, Mueller, and Laufer, 2012).

Victimization is widespread in the United States. In fact, statistics show that each year, more than 30,000 people are killed by guns in the form of murder, suicide, or an unintentional fatality. Moreover, each day 85 deaths and hundreds of nonfatal injuries occur (Hoyert and Xu, 2012). Recent reports reveal that no one in society is completely isolated, protected, or immune from being a crime victim. Experts warn that while there are patterns associated with victimization (Hoyert and Xu, 2012), it can occur randomly, without warning, and have devastating consequences, including injury and death to unsuspecting people and the general community. For example, on January 18, 2011, U.S. Representative Gabrielle Giffords and 18 others were shot by Jared Lee Loughner as they gathered at a meeting called "Congress on Your Corner" in the parking lot of a Safeway store in Casas Adobes, Arizona. As a result of the shooting, six people were killed, including a district court chief judge, a staff member, and a 9-year-old girl, Christina-Taylor Green. Representative Giffords was shot in the head and is believed to have sustained injuries that will affect her for the rest of her life. Loughner, the gunman, was arrested at the crime scene. He was later diagnosed with paranoid schizophrenia.

Another shocking and disturbing act of violence occurred in Newtown, Connecticut, a relatively small southern New England town. On December 14, 2012, a gunman wearing black fatigues and a military vest stormed into Sandy Hook Elementary School and opened fire, claiming the lives of 26 people. Among those killed were 20 children and 6 adults, including teachers, a principal, and the school psychologist. The shooter was later identified as 20-year-old Adam Lanza, who is reported to have taken his own life. In a follow-up investigation, law enforcement authorities discovered that prior to the deadly shooting at Sandy Hook, Lanza had brutally killed his mother by shooting her in the face. This massacre shocked both the national and the international community because most of the victims were children, all first graders. Reporters, community residents, and family members of the victims remarked that these victims were among the most innocent in society. In the aftermath of this deadly shooting, the small community of Newtown still searches for healing and answers.

The Newtown shooting is the second deadliest school shooting reported in American history next to the tragedy that occurred on April 16, 2007, at Virginia Tech in Blacksburg, Virginia, when an undergraduate student, Seung Hui Cho, killed 32 fellow students before turning the gun on himself. In both tragedies, the shooters were believed to suffer from a mental disorder. Another example that speaks to the random nature of victimization occurred at a movie theater in Aurora, Colorado, on July 20, 2012. James Eagan Holmes, a doctoral student at the University of Colorado, attended the opening of a midnight screening of the movie *The Dark Knight Rises*. Reports reveal that upon Holmes's initial entrance into the theater he sat in the front row, where he watched the first 20 minutes of the movie. Afterward, he quickly left from an exit door that he kept opened. He went to his car, which he had parked near the exit. He changed clothes, got several guns, including a 12-gauge Remington 870 Express Tactical shotgun, and reentered the theater through the exit door. This time, he was dressed in tactical clothing, set off tear gas grenades, and opened fire into the crowded theater, killing 12 people and injuring 58 others. He was later arrested outside of the theater.

In the wake of these atrocities in which the perpetrators used high-caliber weapons, there has been renewed interest in the gun control debate, especially with regard to restricting access to semiautomatic weapons (Mozaffarian, Hemenway, and Ludwig, 2013). President Barack Obama and a majority of U.S. citizens, both Republicans and Democrats, have called for a ban on rapid-fire assault weapons, piercing bullets, and high-capacity ammunition clips, as well the implementation of waiting periods for firearm purchases and universal background checks for all gun sales and transfers (Mozaffarian, Hemenway, and Ludwig, 2013, p. 551). The goal of new gun control measures is not to deny citizens the right to possess a firearm, but rather to prevent those with mental health issues, those with a criminal record, and those who commit violence against women from having access to firearms. While polls reveal that the majority of Americans favor legislation requiring a background check before anyone can purchase a firearm, the matter has not been voted on by the U.S. Congress. Therefore, it is unknown at this time whether public sentiments will translate into legislation designed to prevent similar atrocities in the future.

Though victimization is widespread in the United States, efforts are made to keep an accurate account of what transpires. This is typically done through survey research. In fact, the leading survey on victimization (the National Crime Victimization Survey, or NCVS) reports that during 2010, residents in the United States who are age 12 or older experienced 18.7 million violent and property crimes victimizations. In some cases, reports were made to the police, and in other cases no reports were filed with local law enforcement in the respective jurisdictions. (Fifty percent of violent victimizations and nearly 40% of property crimes were reported to the police in 2010. This level of reporting has remained stable in the NCVS over the past 10 years). The Bureau of Justice Statistics reports that this represents a decrease in the reported level of victimizations that occurred in 2009, when an estimated 20.1 victimizations occurred. Of the total number of victimizations, 3.8 million were classified as violent victimizations, 1.4 million were serious violent victimizations, 14.8 million were property victimizations, and 138,000 were personal thefts. The report also reveals that victimization in the United States declined by nearly 34% between 2001 and 2010 (Truman, 2011).

While the NCVS offers the numbers and rates of victimization, it also suggests that there are trends and patterns associated with crime, which are revealed via surveys. The data also suggest that crime and victimization, though they could occur anywhere, are disproportionately found in certain places among certain people. This, for many people, may suggest that victimization could be determined by where one lives, since victim surveys reveal personal and ecological factors associated with crime and its victims, dependent on characteristics such as race/ethnicity, age, and household income. For example, the NCVS reports that in 2010, the violent victimization and aggravated assault rate was higher for black non-Hispanics (20.8 per 1,000) and Hispanics (15.6 per 1,00) compared with whites (13.6 per 1,000). At the same time, Asians and Pacific Islanders had the lowest rates of violent victimizations (6.3 per 1,000). The survey also reported that for persons of two or more races, 52.6 per 1,000 were victims of violent crime—a rate higher than that for any other racial or ethnic category, with the exception of American Indians and Alaskan Natives (Truman, 2011).

The NCVS also reports on the importance of age and associated levels of victimization. People age 25 or older experience less victimization than people in younger age categories. People ages 18 to 20 reported the highest rate of robbery (5.9 per 1,000), compared with people between the ages of 12 and 14 (0.7 per 1,000), while people ages 25 or older reported being robbed at a rate of 2.5 to .06 per 1,000. This was marginally higher than people in the age category of 15 to 17 (2.7 per 1,000) (Truman, 2011).

The NCVS also examines ecological factors that may explain rates of victimization, especially income and neighborhood. The NCVS reports that more low-income households experienced property crimes. More specifically, lower-income households accounted for higher rates of property crimes compared with all other households. Those households that were categorized as lower income reported an annual income of less than $7,500. They experienced a higher overall property victimization rate (168.7 per 1,000 households), compared with households with a reported annual income of $75,000 or more (119.3 per 1,000). Residents living in households in the lowest income category experienced a burglary rate of 44.4 per 1,000, compared with a rate that was more than twice as high for those who reported an earned yearly income of $75,000 or more (20.8 per 1,000) (Truman, 2011). Surprisingly, households whose income was either unreported or unknown had the lowest rates of property victimizations (98.3 per 1,000) and property theft (74.8 per 1,000) compared with other households. The NCVS reveals a stable rate of higher property crime for larger households than for smaller households in 2010. Moreover, the rate of property crime was higher for larger households. Residents living in households with more than six or more people experienced more property crime, property theft, and burglaries than smaller households (Truman, 2011).

NCVS data often force us to take a closer look at victims, their characteristics and surroundings, and examine why victimization is patterned with regard to personal and ecological factors. We also ask, what constitutes victimization? Where the latter is concerned, we most often define someone as a victim when he or she has suffered an injurious action at the hands of another. In the United States, the prospect of facing victimization is great, and research reveals that young children are just as likely to face repeat victimization as older youths (Finkelhor, Turner, and Ormrod, 2006).

Twenty-five percent of all Americans will experience violence three or more times in their lifetimes. Ninety-nine percent of all Americans will experience theft, and 87 percent will be victimized by theft three or more times (Siegel, 2000). What accounts for such high levels of victimization? Are victims simply in the wrong place at the wrong time, or do they influence the occasion of crime by their own action or inaction? Can crime victims tell us more about crime than we already know? Can they complete the part of the crime picture referred to as the "dark figures" of crime? Should we study crime victims? What can they tell us about crime and offenders? Can they help us create typologies of victims? Can they inform others on what steps to take to avoid being victimized? These questions are of interest to those who study crime victims. Criminologists who focus on crime victims are referred to as **victimologists**.

> **victimologist**—A professional trained to use the scientific method to study crime victims. Victimologists study crime victims to create typologies of victimization, to examine trends and patterns associated with victimization, and to determine how society reacts and responds to the victims of crime. By studying crime victims, they can assess whether crime rates are increasing or decreasing.

Why should we be concerned about the victims of crime? Statistics provided by the Uniform Crime Reports (UCR), self-report surveys (SRSs), and the NCVS reveal that crime and victimization are yearly occurrences, and, simply put, they are natural. These surveys indicate personal and ecological factors associated with crime (Weiner and Wolfgang, 1989). They also agree on when and where crime takes place. All three sources indicate that crime and victimization occur disproportionately in urban areas and that those in the lower class are disproportionately the offenders, as well as the victims, of crime. Unfortunately, if nothing is done to alleviate the problems of victimization, future generations of lower-class people will experience the same victimization that proliferates in many lower-class neighborhoods today. While crime statistics show that victimization is saturated in central city areas, no one, irrespective of social class, is immune from being a crime victim. Society should be concerned about victimization, because victimization is pervasive, expensive, and inevitable.

Victimization Theories

Some scholars believe that crime victims are central to the study of crime and victimization. Early victimologists, such as Hans Von Hentig, Stephen Schafer, and Marvin Wolfgang, argued that to a large extent, victims either were responsible for their own victimization or shared a relationship with those who victimized them (Siegel, 2000). Several theories are used to explain victimization. As one quickly discovers, these theories do not show any sympathy toward those who have faced criminal victimization, but instead are critical of the victims' role in the crime. In fact, these theories may even suggest that the victims themselves are ultimately responsible for what happens to them. Critics of victimization theories argue that such theories are guilty of victim blaming since they offer very little in the area of creating strategies that focus on offenders' behavior rather than victims' behavior. The most popular victimization theories include: victim precipitation (active and passive), victim precipitation and rape, lifestyle theory, routine activity theory, the equivalent group hypothesis, and the proximity hypothesis. A **hypothesis** is a tentative theory that predicts a relationship that exists between variables. More specifically, it states the expected relationship between an independent variable and a dependent variable.

Victim Precipitation Theory

Sometimes when innocent people are victimized by crime, some in the general public ponder their role or involvement in the criminal episode. For example, they typically ask, what was the victim doing in the area or neighborhood where the crime was committed? Others, in contrast, may react with concern or compassion for the victims, reasoning that they may simply have been in the wrong place at the wrong time. Nevertheless, **victim precipitation theory** (VPT) offers two explanations for criminal victimizations, active and passive precipitation. **Active precipitation theory** (APT) advances the argument that victimization occurs when the victim is the first to initiate a course of action that leads to him or her being victimized. More specifically, active precipitation occurs when the victim is the first to use words that may initiate a physical altercation, act provocatively, or use threatening language, and suffers violence or death as a result of such action. For example, victimization is said to be precipitated if a victim is killed in a bar-room brawl that the victim initiated. APT does not posit that victims get what they deserve. It does, however, suggest that the behavior of victims can determine whether they are responsible for the final outcome. APT can be understood within the context of road rage—for example, a motorist may be provoked to anger because another motorist cuts in front of him or her on the road without signaling a change of lane, and responds to the slight by accosting the speedster with threats. The speedster goes on the offensive by physically assaulting or even killing the motorist. Victimologists examining the crime would be convinced that the victim's action invariably led to the crime.

In contrast, **passive precipitation theory** (PPT) is more elusive than APT. It contends that victims can unknowingly cause their victimization by threatening or encroaching on the power of a group of people. According to PPT, if people engage in social, political, or economic protests and are met with violence by those unwilling to share their power base, the victims have passively precipitated their victimization. Aggressive action by a victim is not needed where PPT is concerned. According to the

> **victim precipitation theory**—A theory on victimization that argues that victims are responsible and may even cause the harm that they receive by the way they act. The theory argues that if victims act in an aggressive manner by attacking first with physical action, threats, or fighting words, they are believed responsible if someone reacts to their initial behavior.

> **active precipitation theory**—A victimization theory that holds that victims of crime are often responsible for the injury or harm they sustain because they are usually the instigator of an event that ends in their victimization. The theory suggests that victims often initiate crime by being the first to either use an insult, rebuke, or physical violence that ends in them becoming a victim.

> **passive precipitation theory**—A controversial victimization theory that contends that one can sustain victimization after he or she unknowingly becomes a threat to another's power base. The theory is used to explain rape in the workplace and social, political, and economic situations where the victims unknowingly are perceived as a threat from their attackers.

theory, people who seek marriage equality (same-sex marriage), seek legal immigration status, or illegally cross the borders into the United States could unknowingly offend the power base of those with opposing views and suffer victimization as a consequence.

A controversial issue that has been linked to VPT is rape. Some scholars argue that date or acquaintance rape can be viewed as being precipitated by the victim if the victim either acted or dressed in a sexually provocative or suggestive manner that caused the attacker to believe that the person was advertising for sex. Again, victimization theories do not postulate that people deserve to be sexually assaulted. Rather, the theories focus on the behavior of the victims prior to the criminal episode (Warshaw, 1988; Finkelhor and Yllo, 1985).

Lifestyle Theory

The **lifestyle theory** of victimization argues that some people's behavior patterns and lifestyles place them in harm's way. It is believed that those who frequent clubs, taverns, parks, and other public places and consume large quantities of alcohol and use illicit drugs are more likely to be the victims of crime than those who confine themselves to the home or make conscious decisions to stay out of public places. Furthermore, a person's chance of becoming a crime victim is accelerated if he or she is single or unmarried and has friends with the same social status. This is based on the belief that single persons have

> **lifestyle theory**—A victimization theory that posits that some people have certain behavior patterns and lifestyles that increase the likelihood that they will become the victims of crime. They are typically those who frequent public places where the criminal element is found—usually places where alcohol is used. The risk of victimization is increased if a person frequents public places during crime peak hours.

lifestyles that take them out of the home during peak crime hours. Moreover, the friends of single people could be part of the criminal element and unintentionally expose them to dangerous situations.

Other groups that have high-risk lifestyles are children and homeless populations. Juveniles run the risk of coming into contact with danger because they frequent public places, such as schools, where a disproportionate number of crimes are committed. Deborah Prothrow-Stith (1991) argues that children expelled from school also face a greater chance of being the victims of crime because they lack the verbal skills necessary to peacefully resolve conflict and are more inclined to seek a nonpeaceful resolution to settle arguments. Similarly, homeless populations are often the victims of crime because they are constantly exposed to the general public in open spaces, and are therefore targeted by predators. Recently, a number of reported incidents of violent attacks have surfaced revealing that the homeless are subject to violent attacks (typically with baseball bats) in the community as well as on college campuses. For example, a teen was sentenced to life in the beating of two men and in the death of Jacques Pierre, a homeless man, targeted because he was sleeping on a bench (Alanez, 2006). The crime, which occurred at the Las Olas Boulevard campus of Florida Atlantic University, was captured by video surveillance cameras.

Routine Activity Theory

routine activity theory—Theory introduced by Lawrence Cohen and Marcus Felson, who argued that victimization is greater when there is an availability of suitable targets, an absence of capable guardians, and motivated offenders. These elements, they contend, will not guarantee that crime will occur, but they will increase its likelihood.

Of all victimization theories, **routine activity theory** (RAT) is the most tested and referenced, and enjoys the most acclaim. Introduced by Lawrence Cohen and Marcus Felson (1979), RAT has three main components: (1) the availability of suitable targets, (2) the absence of capable guardians, and (3) a group of motivated offenders. According to the theory, these three components do not guarantee that a crime will be committed, but instead they increase the likelihood that a predatory crime will occur. RAT postulates that economic and property crimes are more likely to occur in homes or apartments that contain easy-to-sell goods such as televisions, stereos, and computers. Furthermore, these crimes are more likely to occur if there is an absence of capable guardianship to prevent intruders from successfully engaging in crime. For example, crime might be higher in areas where police protection is ineffective or where police officers engage in reactive rather than proactive policing strategies. The last component of RAT concerns motivated offenders. It argues that unsupervised teenagers who are unemployed and out of school, especially during the summer months, may prey on the innocent if property is left unguarded by a person or an alarm system.

A major focus of RAT is on eliminating the opportunity for the commission of crime. Advocates of the theory also believe that situational crime prevention strategies can be used to address crimes motivated by victims' routine activities. For example, some strategies may include target hardening techniques such as installing burglar bars, surveillance cameras, and alarm systems; carving serial numbers on personal property; and creating neighborhood watch programs. These efforts go far in crime prevention and may even reduce potential gain from successful crime. This is especially true in cases where people engrave their initials on electronic appliances so that they are difficult to fence.

Equivalent Group Hypothesis

equivalent group hypothesis—A theory of victimization that argues that victims and offenders are essentially the same, since many offenders were once the victim of crime.

Victimologists sometimes argue that victims of crime can themselves become predators. They refer to this condition as the **equivalent group hypothesis**. This hypothesis states that a person can be both a victim and an offender. Research shows that many people who are criminal offenders have also experienced high rates of victimization. This is especially true for sexual offenders and many teenagers in public schools (Towers, 1996; Wallace, 1998). Today, some research supports the belief that many children who have been the subject of bullying either fight back for self-preservation or bully others.

Research also supports the contention that after being frustrated over their victimization, some people may engage in violence to seek revenge, to regain their possessions, or to advocate social control (Wilson, 1990). The latter group of victims is considered more dangerous since they may cross the line and become vigilantes by acting as judge, jury, and executioner. The case of Bernhard Goetz captures this point in realistic terms. The Goetz case, which became known as the "Subway Vigilante" case, occurred after Goetz shot and seriously wounded four young African American males he believed intended to harm him on December 22, 1984. The case was sensational, as well as controversial, since he was subsequently found not guilty of attempted murder or assault, but guilty only of being in possession of an illegal firearm. Some experts believe that Goetz was convicted of a lesser offense because New Yorkers were disgusted with the high crime rates that plagued the city during the 1980s. Others argued that the verdict highlighted the state of race relations in the city at the time.

Proximity Hypothesis

Victimologists believe that in poor areas where there are high levels of unemployment, unsupervised teenagers, and availability of alcohol, drugs, and firearms, one can also expect to see a correspondingly high crime rate. They also advance the **proximity hypothesis,** also known as the deviant place theory. It contends that many people experience high levels of victimization not necessarily because of what they do, but because of where they live. For example, in criminogenic communities, crime and deviance abound. Typically, the people in these communities share similar backgrounds and circumstances with their victimizers.

> **proximity hypothesis**—A victimization theory that argues that if people live in criminogenic communities, they face a greater chance of being the victim of crime than others who live in a crime-free neighborhood. The theory posits that even if a person practiced a law-abiding and healthy lifestyle in such an area, there would be no guarantee that he or she would not experience victimization. Victimization may be an inevitable consequence of living among the criminal element.

Victimization is viewed as unavoidable for residents living in these areas. Since the victim and offender live in close proximity to each other, the offender can easily determine when the victim is more vulnerable to crime. For example, the offender may be able to learn the routine activities or whereabouts of a potential target by observing his or her daily schedule. As such, even if one adopted a puritanical lifestyle, he or she could easily become the victim of a property or violent crime. Experts argue that in high crime areas, victimization is common because of the presence of drugs, prostitution, fencing, and easy access to handguns. Crime and victimization is common in areas where communities often lack social controls that would make it difficult for criminals to openly engage in such behavior. In disorganized communities, one often hears of drug deals gone bad, or gangs exchanging open fire with rivals, robbers, or law enforcement officers. Unfortunately, many innocent residents meet an untimely demise because of stray bullets and the continuing use of firearms (Sanders, 1994).

While victimization may be unavoidable for people who reside in criminogenic areas, they can avoid being crime victims to some degree by not going outside during peak crime hours or saving enough money to move out of these socially disorganized areas. Some critics of this position argue that because these residents are typically the working poor and the elderly, the suggestion of them moving to an area of the city that affords them a better quality of life is unrealistic and insensitive.

Helping Crime Victims

Both official crime statistics and victimization surveys reveal that many people in the United States are negatively impacted by crime and victimizations. Some experts even suggest that those among us who are the most likely to be affected by crime can ill afford to be its victims, owing to a lack of resources needed to defray the cost of returning them to their pre-victimization status. The same experts argue that this may be contingent on the type of injury that one experiences. For example, with adequate resources, property can be replaced. With medical treatment and counseling, some physical and psychological injuries can be treated and healed. However, homicide victimizations close the door on any treatment efforts for victims themselves. Despite this, surviving family members may benefit from receiving therapy sessions to help cope with the loss of a family member, relative, or friend. Nevertheless, because victimization is pervasive, expensive, and inevitable, caring for the victims of crime is the responsibility of everyone in society. Since victimization is so widespread and varied, delivering the help that victims need takes a community-wide initiative. For example, the needs of rape victims are different from those of domestic violence victims or victims who may have lost everything in their home because of arson. The care that victims need cannot be successfully provided by a single person or agency; it takes a united effort from all community residents with respect to volunteering time, money, clothes, and other services. The most common services that are provided to crime victims are: (1) explaining the court process, (2) making referrals, (3) providing a court escort, (4) helping with compensation applications, (5) educating the general public, (6) assisting with employers, (7) providing transportation to court, (8) providing crisis intervention, (9) providing child-care services, and (10) allowing victims impact statements at trial (Ginsburg, 1994).

Explaining the Court Process

A lack of knowledge about the justice system may discourage some people from getting involved in the process. Therefore, explaining the court process is a program to assist the victim-turned-witness in a criminal prosecution. Many experts believe that the cooperation and participation of victims can help bring an offender to justice if the victim-turned-witness can give compelling testimony in court identifying the offender. It is believed that the image in court of a victim confronting the accused and saying, "the person who caused my victimization is sitting across from me," is convincing to a sympathetic jury. Because of this, efforts are made to inform victims-turned-witnesses of their vital role in the criminal justice process. Again, some experts believe that a lack of knowledge about the justice process causes confusion and emotional stress, which often discourages victim-turned-witness participation. As such, explaining the court process can help to ensure a successful criminal prosecution. These programs are specifically designed to provide victims-turned-witnesses with information about their rights while emphasizing the importance of their participation (Ginsburg, 1994).

Making Referrals

Referral programs are created to assist victims with their immediate needs. These may include quick and easy access to food, clothing, shelter, transportation, and medical assistance, as well as financial assistance. Referral programs consist of: (1) assessing the victims' needs, (2) locating the appropriate agency and making arrangements for the victim to receive needed services, and (3) conducting follow-up contact with the service providers to determine whether the victim's needs were met. Again, it is important to note that because victims have different needs, providing and delivering these services requires the participation of the entire community (Ginsburg, 1994).

Providing Court Escort

In the past, providing an escort to court meant simply assisting with transportation so that the victim could testify against the accused. Many victims' advocacy agencies realized that this was not enough. Today, providing an escort to court also means accompanying the victim-turned-witness to court and providing moral support while explaining and interpreting the court proceedings. Victims' advocates discovered that sometimes it takes great fortitude to appear in court before a judge and jury and testify against one's attacker. Moral support is needed to console the victim and encourage participation in the justice process. Escort services are especially appropriate for victims-turned-witnesses who are elderly, physically disabled, children, sexual assault victims, or domestic violence victims—all of whom may be reluctant to leave home out of fear of retaliation by a defendant on bail or the friends or family of the defendant (Ginsburg, 1994).

Helping with Compensation Application

Perhaps the single most important programs that assist crime victims are those that help defray the cost of criminal victimization. Each state allocates a specified amount of money to assist the victims of crime. For example, Alaska allocates an estimated $40,000 per person, while some states, such as Georgia, provide as little as $1,000 as their maximum award (Ginsburg, 1994). It is the duty of prosecutors in each state to inform victims of the availability of state funds set aside to assist them. However, if a victim refuses to file charges or participate in the criminal prosecution of the defendant, the funds may not be forthcoming (Elias, 1986).

Some victims' advocacy groups (e.g., Mothers Against Drunk Driving) argue that victims may suffer from undue financial insecurity and loss because they do not know about

victim compensation—One of many programs designed to assist the victims of crime. Applications for victim compensation are given to the victim-turned-witness to a crime to help reimburse or defray the cost of victimization sustained during a criminal episode of violence. In most states, the amount of money one can receive is contingent on the amount available in the state reserve. Typically, it is the job of the local prosecutor to inform the victim-turned-witness about victim compensation applications.

the existence of **victim compensation** programs, or because they are unable to correctly complete and submit a compensation claim. Critics charge that when victims make mistakes on their application or fail to complete it in its entirety, no effort is made to contact the victim about omissions and errors. As a result, compensation is not provided (Ginsburg, 1994).

The logic of victim compensation programs is that victims can apply for and receive state-administered funds reimbursing them for injuries sustained during a crime if they lack insurance that will cover incurred damages. Compensation may be provided for medical bills, lost wages, loss of future earnings, and psychological treatment (in some states). Compensation can also be made to dependents of victims who died as a result of a crime. For example, monies may be provided for burial expenses, loss of support, and damage to property (e.g., doors, locks, windows, or security devices). Again, many people are unaware of the existence of victim compensation programs and suffer needlessly (Ginsburg, 1994; Siegel, 2000).

Educating the General Public

Programs that are used to educate the general public tend overwhelmingly to focus on acquainting the public with agencies that offer help and information to victims-turned-witnesses. These programs may target victims of domestic violence, child abuse (physical or sexual), or rape. Such programs encourage citizens to (1) report crime, (2) assist in the prosecution of criminal offenders, and (3) be willing to participate in the court process to bring the defendant to justice. Public education programs strive to make the public aware of (1) existing programs and services, (2) the issues with which victims-turned-witnesses are confronted, and (3) the ways in which traumatic crime affects victims. Public education programs also provide information on crime prevention and self-defense (Ginsburg, 1994).

Assisting with Employers

Some victims are reluctant to participate in the justice process because they fear it may be too time-consuming. They weigh the thought of participation against the prospect of losing money by having to take time off from work to participate in the criminal justice process. The victim-turned-witness may also be concerned about negative reactions from an unsympathetic employer. Some individuals may have to be absent from work because of physical and psychological injuries sustained during a criminal episode. Police officers' ongoing or follow-up investigations may also interrupt the daily routines of crime victims. Because of these concerns, programs have been created that contact employers, persuading them to allow the victim to participate in the trial process. Even when contact is made with employers, these efforts do not always meet with success (Ginsburg, 1994).

Providing Transportation to Court

Because events may conspire to make court appearances inconvenient, efforts have been made to reduce or alleviate potential problems faced by victims-turned-witnesses. Victim advocates recognize that transportation costs, difficulty in finding parking near the courthouse, and difficulty in locating the correct building may cause late arrivals or non-appearances. Providing victims with transportation has served to negate these potential hindrances to their participation in the justice process.

Victims with their own transportation have been given incentives to participate in the process. For example, some are reimbursed for gas mileage and provided reserved parking at or near the courthouse. Volunteers, police agencies, and local social service agencies have also provided alternative sources of transportation as a part of such programs. In isolated cases, taxi companies donate free services to elderly and physically disabled victims (Ginsburg, 1994).

Providing Crisis Intervention

Crisis intervention programs are designed to assist victims in their time of greatest need. The main methods of delivering these services include: (1) via phone/hotline, (2) via phone and in person, (3) in person only, (4) at the crime scene, (5) through home visits, and (6) at the hospital. Victims of rape and/or domestic violence, those experiencing the death of a loved one, or others who are suicidal are in need of crisis intervention. The biggest challenge to crisis intervention programs may be in providing services to everyone who is in need of immediate help. Certain populations of crime victims, such as the elderly, the physically disabled, the socially isolated, and those lacking transportation, may pose a serious challenge, because they will not get the help they need unless crisis intervention providers are willing to visit their homes. This can be problematic since most agencies are understaffed because not enough people volunteer, and most programs do not make home visits due to a lack of liability insurance (Ginsburg, 1994).

> **crisis intervention**—One of the services provided to the victims of crime. It is the immediate help or assistance that victims need to help them get through their criminal victimization. Crimes such as domestic violence and rape typically require crisis intervention programs.

Providing Child-Care Service

Providing child care is of primary concern to victims-turned-witnesses who have children. At best, such programs make short-term arrangements to provide child-care services while the victim-turned-witness is either in consultation with the prosecutor or participating in court. Children may be placed in a day care center or provided with an in-house babysitter for the time that the victim is at trial. Special programs have also been created to meet the needs of children who have been either the victim of or witness to a violent crime.

victim impact statements—A device used to garner greater participation of victims or surviving family members in the criminal justice process. In some cases, statements are written by victims and submitted to a judge as part of the investigation before sentence is imposed on the defendant. In others, victims or their surviving family members are allowed to stand before the judge and jury and speak to how the victimization affected the lives of family members. Yet in others, victims sometimes appear before parole hearings to discuss the impact of their victimization. This is believed to affect the board's decision to release the petitioner. To some, the process is heavily weighted against the accused. To others, it allows the victims a sense of closure.

Such programs may be necessary when a child witnesses violence by one parent against another or is the victim of physical or sexual assault. The child may need extensive counseling by a trained professional (Ginsburg, 1994).

Allowing Victim Impact Statements

Victim impact statements are considered by defense attorneys to be controversial. They allow the victim to address the court and provide testimony about how the victimization has affected the victim, in particular, and the victim's family, in general. The majority of impact statements are written and submitted to a judge before he or she imposes sentence on the offender. Defense attorneys criticize this process because they believe it helps to sway a judge's decision and adversely affects the outcome of the case. Prosecutors, on the other hand, favor the process because it offers compelling evidence to the judge and jury about how serious and traumatic the criminal victimization has been on the victim and family members.

Other experts argue that victim impact statements can be therapeutic for surviving victims and family members because it helps them bring closure to the criminal episode. It brings the victim into the criminal justice process and allows the victim to have his or her day in court. It is estimated that 33 states allow this process (Ginsburg, 1994). In many states, victims or surviving family members are also allowed to submit impact statements to and appear before parole board hearings that make decisions about whether an offender should be released back into society.

Strategies to Prevent Criminal Victimizations

While the police are charged with preventing and fighting crime in America, the responsibility of reducing crime falls on every person and his or her respective community. Police officers cannot be everywhere at all times. Therefore, it is incumbent upon community residents to combine their efforts to prevent crime and levels of victimization. The reality of crime prevention is that law enforcement officers alone cannot successfully prevent crime. In fact, the overwhelming amount of police officers' time is spent following up on citizens' reports and complaints. In short, most police work is reactive instead of taking proactive efforts to reduce or eliminate crime. Again, if society is to see substantial reductions in the crime rate, it would do well to get involved in efforts to "weed out" the criminal element. Some helpful strategies may include: (1) creating neighborhood anticrime campaigns for self-protection, (2) developing cleanup programs, (3) creating partnerships with law enforcement, (4) implementing school prevention programs, (5) controlling the availability of guns, and (6) creating a comprehensive family policy.

Neighborhood Anticrime Campaigns for Self-Protection

Communities with crime problems should create or implement **neighborhood anticrime campaigns** for self-protection. In doing so, residents can make efforts to reduce the level of fear and intimidation found within these communities. Moreover, such efforts have been found to reduce criminal activity and move the community toward crime prevention. Anticrime campaigns include neighborhood and block watches that immediately signal to potential lawbreakers that a community is protected from criminal activity and its residents are watching for any suspicious activity. Research suggests that communities with signs that reveal residents are watching for suspicious-looking people tend to have lower levels of community fear. Unfortunately, the same research indicates that these are typically communities that need watch programs the least. In socially disorganized areas that have an abundance of crime, one rarely finds residents who will unite and create neighborhood anticrime campaigns. Anticrime campaigns should also provide increased lighting in dimly lit areas and deadbolt locks and other security devices where guardianship is lacking.

> **neighborhood anticrime campaigns**—These are initiatives used by community residents across the country to take an active role in reducing crime and fear. These programs encourage citizens to report suspicious behavior to local law enforcement and not take enforcement matters into their own hands. Such programs work better when they are part of a comprehensive effort to transcend the quality of life for community residents.

Cleanup Programs

Cleanup programs can be very helpful in socially disorganized communities. The objective behind cleanup programs is to rid neighborhoods of dilapidated property and abandoned buildings covered with graffiti. George Kelling and James Q. Wilson (1982) introduced what they referred to as a "broken windows theory." The theory postulates that in communities that are not properly kept and suffer from deterioration, places such as abandoned houses are used for drug sales and acts of prostitution. If residents do not care enough about ridding their neighborhood of such properties, it signals to criminals, deviants, and others that it is okay to engage in illegal activities there. When this occurs, the quality of life declines and fear becomes more pronounced. In essence, a failure to clean up one's community may signal to the criminal element that community residents do not care enough about the plight of the area and vicariously invite crime.

Partnerships with Law Enforcement

Since crime prevention is a community-wide effort, citizens should form partnerships with police agencies. It is believed that no one knows more about the needs and problems of the community than its residents. They can be instrumental in helping officers improve the quality of life in the community. Residents can assist officers by providing them with profile information on suspicious people or those whom they witness engaging in criminal behavior. They can also aid the police in apprehending fugitives from justice by providing information leading to the whereabouts of such suspects. At the same time, citizens should never attempt to apprehend criminals on their own, because they are not properly trained to do so and the criminal suspect could be armed and dangerous. Police should apply both proactive and reactive strategies to reduce crime. Proactively, police can take steps toward crime prevention by becoming familiar with community residents. It is hoped that through these interactions officers will develop a trusting relationship with those whom they are sworn to serve and protect. If residents trust officers, they will be inclined to provide them with valuable information about crime in the community that will help efforts to improve the quality of life for everyone in the community (Thurman and McGarrell, 1997).

School Violence Prevention Programs

Prothrow-Stith (1991) argues that young inner-city males are at risk of becoming involved in gang violence in public schools; however, they are not alone. She contends that high school dropouts are at a greater risk of violence because they exercise physical aggression to resolve disputes rather than search for peaceful resolutions. She argues that many dropouts are found in local juvenile detention facilities or adult prisons. She believes that education is one strategy to deter violence. She contends that education entails reaching teenagers both in and out of school to teach them to manage anger and peacefully resolve conflict.

Other strategies to alleviate violence in school include removing graffiti, banning gang attire and symbols, creating and enforcing school safety policies, and forming violence resistance curricula (Crime and Violence Prevention Center, 1994). First, removing graffiti alerts gangs that they are not welcome. More important, it signals that students are safe from being crime victims. This eliminates the need for students to arm themselves for self-protection. Second, policies prohibiting gang attire and symbols reduce the possibility of gang warfare in public schools. This strategy serves the twin effect of reducing random violence and reducing the attraction of joining a gang. Third, safety policies ensure the physical well-being of students. Such policies are needed to prevent children from bringing guns to school (Murray, 1994). Fourth, violence resistance curricula can socialize youths into believing that violence and crime are unacceptable ways to resolve problems. Though these lessons are learned at school, it is hoped that they would be applied in the communities where children live. These policies advocate a weapons-free environment.

Controlling Gun Availability

The Centers for Disease Control and Prevention (CDC) (1994) contends that if communities are to reduce the number of guns, they must reformulate the gun control debate. The CDC contends that although there is disagreement regarding the issue of gun control, nearly everyone agrees that guns are dangerous and cause the deaths of thousands each year. Therefore, those who advocate reform should change the issue from "gun control" to "preventing firearm injuries." This paradigm shift addresses criminals, children, homes, and communities with guns. Communities can intervene in the proliferation of guns by: (1) making owners liable for damage done by guns, (2) placing metal detectors in schools,

(3) facilitating safety education, (4) implementing waiting periods, and (5) investing in buy-back programs (Murray, 1994). The latter programs have proven to be successful in removing many guns from the streets that may otherwise have been used in the commission of property, as well as personal, crime (Siegel, 2000).

Creating a Comprehensive Family Policy

Family members must get involved in the lives of teenagers to guide them in the direction of morality. Failure to take such action could mean more violence and crime in inner-city areas (Bennett, Dilulio, and Walters, 1996). The majority of violent offenders are found among people who make up the working and underclass. They are those stricken by poverty and social disorganization. They come from families that are the recipients of inadequate welfare programs and have poor family structures (Wilson, 1987, 1996). Prothrow-Stith (1991) contends that unless the United States follows the paths of other developed nations by providing every child with a minimal standard of care, many more poor minorities will become predators or victims of random violence. She argues that what is needed is a comprehensive family policy that provides all families with (1) universal health care, (2) subsidized high-quality child care, (3) nutritional services for poor children, (4) universal preschool for children who are educationally at risk, (5) after-school programs for the children of working parents, and (6) schools that provide educational, social, and recreational activities. In short, Prothrow-Stith challenges the United States to invest in its youth by providing them the essentials needed to become productive citizens. If this investment is not made, it may become necessary to prepare for more crime and higher rates of criminal victimizations.

Summary

Studying crime victims is very important to under-standing the magnitude of the crime problem in America. This specialized area of criminology is often referred to as **victimology**. Studying the victims of crime allows us to have a better understanding of the criminal episode through the eyes of the victims. Who could be better to study since they were there at the crime scene? Victims are in a unique position to provide details of the crime, offender, place, time, and personal characteristics of the offender that may otherwise not be discovered. Scholars believe that getting the victim's perspective on crime adds to our understanding of the relationship that often exists between victims and offenders.

> **victimology**—The scientific study of crime victims and the dynamics that exist between victims and offenders. The discipline is also concerned with victim typologies, victimization theories as well as victims experiences in the criminal justice system.

While crimes are often committed by strangers, emerging evidence suggests that many crimes are committed by someone known to the victim. Theories of **victimization** such as the routine activity theory, active and passive precipitation theories, the equivalent group hypothesis, and the proximity theory allow us to place the crime and victimization

> **victimization**—The process by which people get victimized.

into the proper context. They also help us to make valid predictions about the future of crime, offenders, and victims. Because victimization is widespread, varied, and expensive, the community and society must create programs to meet the needs of the victims of crime.

Caring for crime victims can be expensive because some of them may require long-term treatment and therapy, while others may only need help for the short term. While crime is inevitable, there are efforts that people and communities can engage in to reduce their chances of being crime victims. Some efforts may include creating cleanup programs, implementing school prevention programs, controlling the availability of firearms, partnering with law enforcement, and creating neighborhood anticrime campaigns.

Discussion Questions

1. What can we learn from crime victims?
2. What is the difference between active and passive victim precipitation theory?
3. What can we learn from the equivalent group hypothesis?
4. How can treating crime victims be an expensive undertaking?
5. What are some effective crime prevention strategies?

References

Adler, F., Mueller, G. O., and Laufer, W. S. (2012). *Criminal Justice: An Introduction* (6th ed.). New York, NY: McGraw-Hill.

Alanez, T. (2006, October 24). Plantation Teen Gets Life in Prison for Beating Death of Homeless Man. (*Broward County, Florida*) *SunSentinel*.

Anderson, J. F., and Thompson, B. (2007). *American Criminal Procedures*. Durham, North Carolina: Carolina Academic Press.

Bennett, W. J., Dilulio, J. J., and Walters, J. P. (1996). *Body Count: Moral Poverty . . . And How to Win America's War Against Crime and Drugs*. New York, NY: Simon & Schuster.

Centers for Disease Control and Prevention, National Center for Injury Prevention and Control. (1994). *Violence Prevention: Integrating Public Health and Criminal Justice*. Washington, DC: U.S. Health and Human Services, Public Health Service.

Cohen, L., and Felson, M. (1979). Social Change and Crime Rate Trends: A Routine Activities Approach. *American Sociological Review, 44,* 588–608.

Crime and Violence Prevention Center. (1994). *Gangs: A Community Response*. California Attorney General's Office. Available at http://www.paramountcity.com/download.cfm?ID=1124.

Elias, R. (1986). *The Politics of Victimization: Victims, Victimology, and Human Rights*. New York, NY: Oxford University Press.

Fattah, E. (1986). *From Crime Policy to Victim Policy: Reorienting the Justice System*. New York, NY: St. Martin's Press.

Finkelhor, D., Turner, H., and Ormrod, R. (2006). Kid's Stuff: The Nature and Impact of Peer and Sibling Violence on Younger and Older Children. *Child Abuse and Neglect, 30*(1), 1401–21.

Finkelhor, D., and Yllo, K. (1985). *License to Rape: Sexual Abuse of Wives*. New York, NY: Free Press.

Ginsburg, W. L. (1994). *Victims' Rights: The Complete Guide to Crime Victim Compensation*. Clearwater, FL: Sphinx Publishing.

Hoyert, D. L., and Xu, J. (2012). Deaths: Preliminary Data for 2011. *National Vital Statistics Reports, 61*(6), 1–65.

Kelling, G. L, and Wilson, J. Q. (1982, March). Police and Neighborhood Safety: Broken Windows. *Atlantic Monthly*, 29–38.

Mozaffarian, D. M., Hemenway, D., and Ludwig, D. S. (2013). Curbing Gun Violence: Lessons from Public Health Successes. *JAMA, 309*(6), 551–52.

Murray, J. M. (1994). *50 Things You Can Do About Guns*. San Francisco, CA: Robert D. Reed.

Prothrow-Stith, D. (1991). *Deadly Consequences: How Violence Is Destroying Our Teenage Population and a Plan to Begin Solving the Problem*. New York, NY: Harper Perennial.

Sanders, W. (1994). *Gangbangs and Drive-bys: Grounded Culture and Juvenile Gang Violence*. New York, NY: Aldine De Gruyter Press.

Siegel, L. (2000). *Criminology* (7th ed.). Belmont, CA: Wadsworth/Thomson Learning.

Siegel, L. (2012). *Criminology* (11th ed.). Belmont, CA: Wadsworth/Cengage Learning.

Thurman, Q. C., and McGarrell, E. F. (1997). *Community Policing: In a Rural Setting*. Cincinnati, OH: Anderson.

Tower, C. C. (1996). *Child Abuse and Neglect* (3rd ed.). Boston, MA: Allyn and Bacon.

Truman, J. L. (2011). *Criminal Victimization, 2010*. National Crime Victimization Survey. Washington, DC: Bureau of Justice Statistics.

Wallace, H. (1998). *Victimology: Legal, Psychological, and Social Perspectives*. Boston, MA: Allyn and Bacon.

Warshaw, R. (1988). *I Never Called It Rape: The Ms. Report on Recognizing, Fighting, and Surviving Date and Acquaintance Rape*. New York, NY: Harper & Row.

Weiner, N. A., and Wolfgang, M. E. (Eds.) (1989). *Violent Crime, Violent Criminals*. Newbury Park, CA: Sage.

Wilson, A. N. (1990). *Black-on-Black Violence: The Psychodynamics of Black Self-Annihilation in Service of White Domination*. New York, NY: Afikan World Infosystems.

Wilson, J. W. (1987). *The Truly Disadvantaged: The Inner City, the Underclass, and Public Policy*. Chicago, IL: University of Chicago Press.

Wilson, J. W. (1996). *When Work Disappears: The World of the Urban Poor*. New York, NY: Alfred A. Knopf.

Chapter 4

The Classical School of Thought

Chapter Outline

- The Development of Rational Choice Theory
- A Critical Analysis of the Classical Period
- Classical Theory Revisited in the 1970s
- Summary
- Shortcomings of the Theories
- Discussion Questions

In 2009, Bernard "Bernie" Madoff, an American success story, quickly faded into the annals of shame when his involvement in crime that spanned decades was revealed to the public. In a case of American greed gone awry, federal prosecutors charged and convicted Madoff of creating a massive Ponzi scheme that defrauded investors out of more than $65 billion. During the investigation, Federal Bureau of Investigation (FBI) agents discovered that the fraud began as early as the 1970s and went undetected for decades despite previous investigations into Madoff Securities by the U.S. Securities and Exchange Commission (SEC). Unfortunately, some of Madoff's investors were financially ruined as a consequence of the deception. Many people believe that this is the biggest case of white-collar crime in American history. Madoff received a 150-year prison sentence, the maximum punishment he could have received.

It takes intelligence and knowledge of the stock market to manipulate and deceive all actors involved in this crime. For example, how was Madoff able to hide this financial fraud and stock market manipulation from other members of Wall Street? How was he able to deceive his investors for so long? How was he able to conceal his criminal behavior from the SEC for decades? How did his Wall Street investment firm remain one of the top businesses for so long when other firms met with routine failure? Many would argue that it took keen intelligence and understanding of the market to successfully engage in this level of manipulation for so long. Madoff's action suggests that he made a conscious decision for a very long time to withhold the truth about the realities of the financial market from his investment partners, family, and investors. More specifically, his actions reveal detailed planning and decision making designed to maximize profits for himself, as well as investors, even if it meant engaging in fraudulent behavior as well as violating regulatory laws governing securities and investments.

Some criminologists argue that this example of white-collar crime, like other crimes, such as street-level crime involving robbery or fencing stolen goods, occurs when an offender makes a rational decision to engage in illegal behavior. The decision to engage in crime could be based on a number of reasons that may include greed, revenge, anger, need for excitement, stimulation, or boredom. However, some criminologists believe that the final decision to engage in a crime is contingent on how a potential offender weighs the advantages and disadvantages associated with committing the criminal act. He or she may consider the ease or the amount of difficulty associated with successfully committing the crime versus the prospect of being captured and punished. If the benefits or gains from committing the crime outweigh the chances of the offender being caught and punished, he or she may decide to commit the crime.

- A rapist may target elderly, young, or married women who he believes will be too embarrassed to report the crime.
- A student sitting in the back of a classroom may decide to cheat after discovering that her professor never walks to the back of the classroom during examinations.
- A bully may direct his anger at passive, antisocial, or socially isolated classmates who lack confidence and friends.
- A drug dealer may quickly reason that he can make large sums of money selling drugs if the community is afraid to report such activity to law enforcement.

Some still question if all crime is a product of deliberate planning and using available information before deciding whether to engage in criminal behavior. For example, it seems logical that stock manipulation, fraud, and organized crime such as human trafficking and firearm smuggling require a high level of management and coordination, but even crimes such as robbery, burglary, and selling stolen goods reveal elements of planning and decision making. Predatory offenders often observe the routine activities of potential victims before they decide to commit crime. Before some rapists engage in the act, they stalk their victims and selectively choose those they believe will not strongly resist. They often target college students and young adults. They rarely select potential victims who are leaving gun firing ranges or self-defense classes. The same is true of serial killers. They are known to select those who are arguably the most vulnerable among us, including children, runaways, homeless, women, prostitutes, gay men, and the elderly. Some experts argue that serial killers select those who are disproportionately ignored by police. They rarely select men leaving weight-lifting classes or firing ranges. To some, this reveals that offenders are methodical about their selection of a suitable target. Some criminologists believe that all crime, no matter how destructive, senseless, or impulsive it seems, is carried out after the offender thinks it through and makes a decision to execute the behavior. Such criminologists are referred to as **rational choice** theorists.

> **rational choice**—The theory that offenders engage in crime with knowledge of the law and an awareness of the prospect of punishment. They weigh the advantages and disadvantages before they engage in criminal behavior. If they feel that they can successfully engage in crime without apprehension, they will do so.

The Development of Rational Choice Theory

Prior to the emergence of the classical period of criminological thinking, Europe believed that **demonic possession** was an explanation for crime, deviance, and other social maladies (Erikson, 1966; Pleck, 1987). Commentaries argue that during this time, Europe had no records of the Roman **Twelve Tables**, the **Ten Commandments**, or the **Code of Hammurabi**. The people who lived during medieval times were the victims of superstition and believed in the supernatural. For example, during the **Middle Ages**, which lasted from the 14th to the 17th centuries, many people were accused of witchery even though there was no compelling evidence connecting the accused to satanic influences. Many women were charged with participating in witchery for not complying with the prevailing social norms, which were based on submitting to the will of and being subservient to their male counterparts (Pleck, 1987). Women who deviated from traditional roles were considered an aberration with the ability to contaminate virtuous women and disrupt the social order. Therefore, troublemakers were punished and sacrificed for the good of the community. Unfortunately, when people were accused of being witches or demons, family members rarely came forward to defend their innocence since they feared reprisal from the existing social structure, especially the authorities, who had the power

> **demonic possession**—The state of being controlled by evil forces or the devil and his angels. During the Middle Ages, this was thought to be common among social deviants, sinners, and adulterers. Those who were labeled as being demonically possessed were typically put to death through trial by ordeal.
>
> **Twelve Tables**—Also referred to as the Roman Twelve Tables. This set of laws is believed to have provided noble Romans with their rights.
>
> **Ten Commandments**—Mosaic code given to the Israelites by God as instructions by which to live.
>
> **Code of Hammurabi**—A biblical code that is commonly referred to as the lex talons, or "an eye for an eye and a tooth for a tooth." Though this code is controversial, many believe that it serves the interests of equal justice or equality of the law.
>
> **Middle Ages**—Referred to as the Dark Ages by some because it is believed that during this period, there were no contributions made in the arts and sciences. The period extended from the 14th through the 17th centuries.

trial by ordeal—A trial used by "courts" during the Middle Ages. Offenders accused of being witches or demonically possessed were challenged to prove their innocence by showing that God would intervene on their behalf. Ordeals, such as walking on water and holding burning coal, allowed that opportunity. If an offender failed at the ordeal, he or she would be put to death.

to label them in a like manner. When people were accused of demonic possession, they were not secretly punished, but instead were subjected to a **trial by ordeal**. Historians contend that these trials were provided to give an overt semblance of fairness, while the covert reason for them was to exert social control and to invoke fear within a given community.

From Superstition to Philosophy

Historical evidence indicates that during the Middle Ages, when the harvest was poor and crops were not plentiful, people believed God was punishing their community for moral and religious transgressions. Religious leaders and wealthy citizens started witch hunts by accusing those poorer than themselves of engaging in witchcraft and secretly following Satan. By all accounts, this was a profitable enterprise for the clergy and the aristocracy. For example, when the church or the aristocracy brought claims of witchery against an individual or an entire family, they were able to claim ownership of the property that belonged to the accused. Despite this, when someone was accused, he or she was provided an opportunity to prove his or her innocence. Trials by ordeal afforded the accused one last chance in the presence of the community to prove that he or she was not possessed with the power of Satan and to show himself or herself as a true believer in God. The reason for having such trials was not to demonstrate that God would naturally intervene on behalf of a Christian to save him or her from imminent death. Instead, these trials served to generate group conformity and social control, and to invoke fear, since the outcome was always death in a manner that shocked everyone who witnessed these public executions (Erikson, 1966; Pleck, 1987).

Figure 4.1 reveals the early explanation of antisocial behavior, such as deviant and criminal behavior during the Middle Ages. It illustrates the belief that antisocial behaviors were caused by demonic possession and temptation. Offenders were seen as agents of the devil and demonic forces.

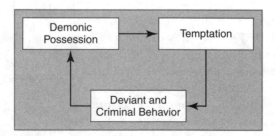

Figure 4.1 Early Explanations of Antisocial Behavior

During trials by ordeal, the accused would be forced to complete a task that would require divine intervention to prove an intact relationship with God. These trials included walking on water, holding burning coal, or having to endure large stones placed on one's body without drowning or being crushed to death. If the accused was successful, charges were sometimes dropped since it was believed that God had come to the person's defense. Other times, passing the trial successfully confirmed demonic possession, since only a person of supernatural power could have withstood such an impossible task. In cases where God failed to intervene, the consequence naturally was death. The methods of execution were just as barbaric as the trials by ordeal. For example, it was not uncommon for those accused of witchcraft, a religious violation, or a breach of social norms to be (1) drawn and quartered, (2) tarred and feathered, (3) boiled, (4) burned at the stake, (5) decapitated, (6) amputated, or (7) subject to at least one of 300 other methods of death. Another punishment that was commonly meted out was being attached to a whipping post or a hitching post for public humiliation. In some cases, people were banished from communal life. During the period of 1575 to 1590, there were 100,000 people executed in Europe for practicing witchery, while hundreds of thousands of others were punished and tortured for the sake of conformity and preserving the existing social arrangement, most notably religious extremism (Erikson, 1966; Pleck, 1987).

In 1757, Robert Damiens unsuccessfully tried to assassinate King Louis XV. He was sentenced to death. Michel Foucault (1976) provides an example of the savagery and barbarism of the time:

> On March 1757, Damiens was burned alive. Flesh was pulled from his legs, thighs, arms, and breasts. Left thigh? Horses were harnessed at his thighs and arms where he was drawn and quartered. Though his limbs were torn off, he was still alive

This example reveals that **punishment** in the period that preceded classical criminology was dominated by barbarism and a misguided understanding of religion. Again, many social commentators contend that religion was not misunderstood by the ruling elite (clergy and aristocracy), but rather it was used as a mechanism to maintain control of the existing social arrangement, to profit economically, and to exploit those who were true believers in God.

Development of Classical Criminology

The **Age of Enlightenment**, or Reason, started as early as the 1500s and lasted until the late 1700s. Enlightened thinkers advanced the scientific view of the world. Thinkers from this period assumed that humans could understand the world through science by reasoning and

punishment—Just deserts for engaging in law-violative behavior. There are many ways to punish offenders, such as incarceration, rehabilitation, retribution, and deterrence.

Age of Enlightenment—Often referred to as the Renaissance. It was a period of intellectual movement and growth, occurring between the 14th and 17th centuries and flourishing in western Europe. The age encouraged the growth of skepticism and free thought, and there were major contributions made in the arts and sciences.

> **classical criminology**—The branch of criminological theory considered to be the genesis of the study of crime. This school was instrumental in advancing the idea that criminals were not motivated by demonic or satanic forces, but they engage in crime after exercising free will and a rational thinking process.

making observations. Enlightened thinkers rejected the belief that the natural order was ordained by God. The term **classical criminology** is something of a misnomer, since the study of crime did not develop until the emergence of the positivistic school. Despite this, criminological inquiry is reported to have started in the 18th century. Those who pioneered the classical school were philosophers. They were concerned about the ethics and morality of the justice system, since many of the traditions of the Middle Ages were still widespread.

> **Beccaria, Cesare**—One of the founders of the classical school of criminology. He advocated major overhauls to the administration of justice and the use of punishment (only) if it had a deterrent effect.
>
> **Bentham, Jeremy**—One of the founders of the classical school of criminology; he thought that crime could be deterred only if punishment is great enough to offset the desire to continue crime, and is swift, certain, and severe.

Cesare Beccaria and Jeremy Bentham

Cesare Beccaria (1738–1794) and **Jeremy Bentham** (1748–1832) pioneered the classical school of criminology. After closely examining the state of justice in Europe, Beccaria published a book entitled *On Crimes and Punishments*, in which he challenged the rights of the state to punish crime. Beccaria and Bentham advocated sweeping changes and reforms to be made on a system-wide level. For example, during this period it was not uncommon for people to be illegally detained and taken away without notice to their families regarding their whereabouts. Moreover, offenders were routinely tortured and forced to confess to crimes that they did not commit. Trials were held in secret places where hearsay evidence was admitted without affording the accused the right to cross-examine the party bringing the accusation. Beccaria and Bentham wanted the administration of justice to be compassionate and humane, both of which qualities were absent from the process. Because of their early efforts, they are considered to be the founders of criminology.

Beccaria and Bentham were vocal about the brutality that existed in the justice machinery. As stated earlier, many of the barbaric practices that were common during medieval times were still in place. For example, there were hundreds of crimes that an offender could commit for which the punishment would be a sentence of death. Reformers argued that the law should be codified and crimes should be written so that the people could be made aware of law violations and their punishments. They wanted the justice system to be based on principles of fairness and to be a protector of human dignity. They called for policies that made the justice system fair and humane. They also observed that the conditions found in jails and prisons were insufferable and these places were not suitable for human occupancy. They advocated reforms for places of confinement.

Some scholars contend that justice was elusive for some. It was widely believed that judges were partial to the aristocracy, but viewed the poor with contempt. Many thought that justice was purchased by the wealthy. However, in very rare instances, members of the aristocracy were accused of crime. It was believed that they could pay judges to dismiss charges against them or have judges appointed to preside over their case. Because of this, Beccaria and Bentham wanted to limit the power of judges, many of whom they suspected were corrupt. They opposed the arbitrary and capricious nature of the criminal justice system. Classical scholars reasoned that since the government derives its power from the social contract, and the social contract exists because of the will of the people, the people are responsible for the existence of organized government. Since each man essentially has one voice or vote that he gives to the government, every man should be treated equal under the law regardless of social class position (Bentham, 1789/1948).

Beccaria and Bentham based the need to reform the criminal justice system on the social contract. The social contract establishes organized government or the state (armies, bureaucracies, police, courts, prisons) for the purpose of reconciling the differences of members of the society. It was believed that the social contract required each person to give up a small amount of freedom so that the state could regulate the smooth function of behavior of the entire populace. The social contract allows for an impartial body to correct and resolve the differences of those who would otherwise be at odds, or even in conflict, with one another. One of the reasons for the social contract was to prevent family feuds, which were common at the time. In fact, it was not uncommon for family feuds to extend from generation to generation, with countless numbers of people killed because of previous wrongs committed against the opposing family. The social contract eliminated unnecessary killings and individual harm by naming the state as the injured party, making offenses perpetrated by individuals into offenses against the state (Masters and Masters, 1978). Although the social contract has egalitarian overtones, many think its existence is owed to protecting the interests of an emerging middle class. This is believed true because with the new middle class also came notions of the accumulation of property, criminal laws, police, courts, prisons, and armies. It appeared that the formal laws and elements of social control disproportionately protected private property.

The Classical School on Crime and Punishment

The classical school advocated that the rule of law be written down and that people bear responsibility for their actions. It also advanced the idea that individuals engage in crime because of **free will**, rational choice, and hedonism. According to this position, crime provides pleasure to criminals, and the more they engage in crime, the more pleasure they derive from such activity. It presupposes that offenders make rational and logical decisions to engage in crime before actually carrying out the behavior. This school of thought contends that criminals are not guided by demonic possession, temptation, or even poverty, but rather engage in crime because it brings pleasure. Moreover, criminals will continue to engage in crime as long as such behavior continues to bring satisfaction. On the other hand, if any activity brings

> **free will**—The ability to choose a course of action without external influences. For example, where crime is concerned, it means that the offender voluntarily chooses to engage in crime on his or her own accord.

criminals displeasure, they will avoid re-engaging in that behavior. Therefore, classical scholars reasoned that the best way to prevent criminal behavior is to apply enough pain to offset any pleasure an offender receives from committing crime (Bentham, 1830).

Classical criminologists saw punishment as evil, but postulated that it was a necessary evil used for the regulation of a civil society. Bentham believed it was necessary to prevent greater evil from being inflicted. It was needed because not everyone respects the rights and freedom of others. Despite this, they cautioned that excessive punishment puts the state in the position of oppressor. Therefore, only the amount of punishment to prevent the continuation of crime was needed. Classical theoreticians insisted that the purposes of punishment were incapacitation, retribution, rehabilitation, and restitution. They argued that when punishment is meted out, its only purpose should be to deter offenders and others who could potentially engage in crime. To this end, they argued that punishment should remove the offender's desire to re-engage in crime. At the same time, people in the social audience who are aware of this punishment will also be deterred from engaging in crime out of fear that they will meet the same fate. This is referred to as **general deterrence**. Beccaria felt that punishment would be effective only if it were meted out in a swift, certain, and severe manner. Otherwise, law violators and potential offenders would not be convinced of society's intolerance of law violations.

> **general deterrence**—Action used by the justice system to prevent potential offenders from engaging in crime. For example, it is hoped that the spread of information about an offender receiving punishment for having committed a crime will have a deterrent effect on others.

Classical scholars wanted the punishment to fit the crime. They contended that only the amount of punishment necessary to prevent the incidence from reoccurring should be used. The classical school also introduced **proportionate sentencing**. As mentioned earlier, there were hundreds of crimes that carried a sentence of death. Burglary and robbery were such crimes. There were mounting concerns that if an offender committed burglary and was seen by a witness who could identify him to authorities, he would have no reason not to kill those who could testify against him at trial. The classical school advocated proportionate sentencing so that the punishment could reflect the amount of social harm incurred. The punishment should be only what was necessary to restore social balance.

> **proportionate sentencing**—A punishment in the form of a sentence given by a judge or magistrate that is equal to the gravity or the social injury of the crime.

Figure 4.2 shows the classical explanation that criminal behavior was caused by free will, choice, or hedonism. Participation in antisocial behavior was not believed to require all three. Classical scholars largely ignored excuses or rationales provided by offenders. One of the cornerstones of this school of thought is that it does not place a tremendous amount of emphasis on the causation of crime. Instead, it focuses on getting offenders to accept responsibility for their behavior (Beccaria, 1764/1963; Bentham, 1830).

Some reforms that occurred during the classical movement included seeing criminals as people who possessed free will and rationality instead of being demonically possessed. Again, individuals were seen as capable of discerning the advantages and disadvantages of crime before engaging in unlawful behavior. Criminals were viewed as cold and

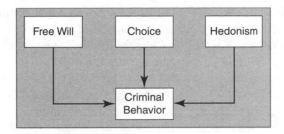

Figure 4.2 Classical Criminology Explanation of Crime

calculating; if the benefits of committing the crime outweighed the possible punishment, they would favor committing the crime. Bentham argued that human behavior is based on hedonism, that humans naturally desire to maximize pleasure and avoid pain.

Classical philosophers integrated utilitarian principles of the greatest good for the greatest number in nearly all of their practices. According to these scholars, both the law and punishment should serve the good of those under the rule of law by protecting the rights of every member of society. They argued that since the government derived its power from the people, the government was responsible for ensuring that the people were free from both domestic and nondomestic threats. Frank Williams and Marilyn McShane (1993) contend that the 18th century witnessed the emergence of (1) civil rights, (2) due process of law, (3) rules of evidence and testimony, (4) determinate sentencing, and (5) theories of specific and general deterrence—all of which have influenced the present-day American systems of jurisprudence and criminal justice.

A Critical Analysis of the Classical Period

An interesting question is why these reforms occurred in the 18th century. During this period, the time was ripe for major social, political, economic, and legal changes. History indicates that the old aristocracy was confronted with claims that there were many contra-dictions and inequalities in the social system. For instance, there were disparities in the treatment of the nobility and those in the **"dangerous" classes**. At the same time, a new middle class emerged from the profits of mercantilism that came with the age of industrialization. Traditional concepts of property and ownership were also being disrupted and displaced. Raymond Michalowski (1985) in his book *Order, Law, and Crime* reveals that during the industrial revolu-tion, radical changes were made in the European social structure. He postulates that during this period, property owners, for the first time, began claiming sole ownership of land. They fenced off property that previously had been open to everyone for fishing, hunting, collecting firewood, and living. Common people were abruptly denied those resources which they had come to look upon as their birthright. These radical changes drastically frustrated

"dangerous" classes—Those who were not part of the aristocracy and who were disproportionately pau-pers. Traditionally, poor people, especially those who are criminals, were considered as belonging to the "dangerous" classes.

the relations between the aristocracy and the common people. The common people came to resent and question the legitimacy of the power structure of the upper class.

Influenced by the Roman Catholic Church, the judicial system underwent major changes. Commentators argue that the law was used to maintain an unequal social structure by controlling and repressing those in the "dangerous" classes. The law was used at the whim of judicial officials. This was especially true since many crimes were not codified. The law was used in an arbitrary, capricious, and sometimes abusive manner. The use of torture was common for defendants in the lower class, as were long sentences. Those in the upper class, if their behavior ever came to the attention of the judicial system, were known to use their social status to influence the judicial outcome. What is even more indicative of the legal inequality of that time is the overwhelming number of laws applied to those in the lower class, while only few applied to the aristocracy.

The legacy of the classical period is that it fought to reform the administration of justice by making it humane and respectful of individuals' rights. The moral philosophers who pioneered classical criminology called for equal treatment and due process for everyone subjected to the system. This included the rich as well as the poor. Because of the capricious tactics that were being used by officials in the judicial system, the classical scholars demanded that limitations be placed on the power of judges. They called for determinate sentencing to prevent inconsistencies in sentencing and codification of the laws so that people could be aware of behaviors that were defined as criminal. Determinate sentencing is concerned with placing a limited or fixed period on a sentence. The classical school of thought singlehandedly replaced demonic possession and temptation with individual responsibility as the cause of criminal behavior. Contributions of the classical school were: arguments of free will, criminals as rational beings, utilitarianism, civil rights, due process of law, rules of evidence, determinate sentencing, and **deterrence** (Williams and McShane, 1993).

> **deterrence**—Actions used to prevent crime from occurring by threatening the potential offender with punishment. Deterrence usually has two forms: general and specific. Some experts argue that the criminal justice system acts as a threat system and some do not commit crime because they fear being apprehended and punished.

Classical Theory Revisited in the 1970s

Neoclassical Theories

The classical theory provides evidence that the more things change, the more they stay the same. It emerged in the 18th century, faded, and then resurfaced in the mid-1970s. Despite many criminological advances (e.g., theories of strain, social disorganization, social learning, social control, labeling, and conflict), classical theory reemerged under a new name and once again dominated the way society viewed and processed criminal offenders. Classical theory in the 1970s was referred to as neoclassical theory, which included choice theory and deterrence theory. Rational choice theory makes the assumption that potential offenders choose whether to commit crime after carefully applying the knowledge they possess about potential offenders and targets before deciding whether to commit a crime. It also assumes that they may have general or specific knowledge about the capabilities of local law enforcement or a community's ability to prevent a crime from occurring. Offenders consider the risks and rewards that are likely to be attached to engaging in the behavior. If they believe that rewards can be gained, they will likely commit the crime. However, if they reason that local law enforcement is aggressive and effective, they will abstain from committing the crime in that jurisdiction, reasoning that it is simply too risky to chance being caught, arrested, and punished.

While choice theory is rooted in the aforementioned classical theory, it is also influenced by economic models of rational decision making and others (McCarthy, 2002). For example, Gary Becker, an economist, published research arguing that choosing to commit a crime is similar to a consumer making a decision to purchase a product. More specifically, Becker (1968) created a model that postulated that prior to committing a crime, potential offenders must decide whether the expected utility or monetary value of committing the crime exceeds the expected utility of not engaging in the crime. They make a rational decision to commit the crime. Conversely, they reason that if the expected utility of not engaging in crime exceeds the expected utility of engaging in crime, they will not commit the offense. To Becker, potential offenders consider several factors, including: (1) whether they have any legitimate opportunities to earn money, (2) the amount of legitimate money they can earn, (3) the amount of money they can gain from the criminal act, (4) the likelihood of being arrested for the criminal offense, and (5) the likelihood of punishment following an arrest. Becker argued that offenders are also like consumers in that customers use any available information before deciding how they will spend their money. The decision they make can later prove to be a good or poor one, but consumers make decisions after calculating the potential benefits and costs associated with their decision. According to Becker, offenders operate in a like manner. If they are aware that law enforcement efforts are aggressive in one area of a city, potential offenders may decide to commit crime in areas were law enforcement is inept or ineffective.

Derek Cornish and Ronald Clarke also advanced the rational choice theory. However, unlike previous rational choice theories, their approach focused on offenders committing specific crimes under specific circumstances. In other words, they addressed a neglected area of the rational choice approach: the actual decision-making process of offenders. Their theory considers that potential offenders engage in crime because of the benefits attached to such behavior, but they take the investigation beyond that by also focusing on conditions needed for specific crimes to occur. In doing so, they place emphasis on the role of crime opportunities and how they contribute to crime causation (Clarke and Cornish, 2001).

Unlike Becker, they argue that money is not the only factor that an offender weighs before engaging in crime, but rather some potential offenders are also motivated by the prospect of excitement, fun, and the prestige associated with being successful in committing the crime. Clarke and Cornish argue that offenders do not always collect and deliberate on information important to their decision to commit crime. Instead, offenders act with limited rationality, since their decisions to engage in crime are not always perfectly planned or executed. Sometimes, they elude detection and capture, and other times they are apprehended and punished. Clarke and Cornish (2001) provide distinctions between involvement and event decisions. Despite this, they focus on the five stages of event decisions: (1) preparing to commit a crime, (2) selecting a target, (3) committing the crime, (4) escaping, and (5) aftermath of the crime. The involvement decisions have three stages: (1) committing crime for the first time (initiation), (2) continuing to commit crime (habituation), and (3) ceasing to commit crime (desistance). They argue that to fully understand crime, one must understand all factors that influence the decision to engage in the behavior.

The explanations provided by Clarke and Cornish have contributed greatly to our understanding of event decisions. As stated earlier, this was a neglected area of rational choice theory. With the addition of their research, the theory focuses on two related concepts: situational factors and opportunities. Situational factors are primarily focused on the immediate physical setting, such as street lighting and the presence or absence of alarms and surveillance cameras, and opportunities that may or may not exist for offenders to commit a crime with or without fear of capture or negative consequence. In the end, Clarke and Cornish's contribution to the rational choice theory postulates that offenders are not dissimilar from law-abiding people in that need, temptation, and opportunity could induce an otherwise law-abiding person to commit a crime.

Deterrence Theory

Another neoclassical explanation rooted in early classical theory, most notably in the works of Thomas Hobbes, Cesare Beccaria, and Jeremy Bentham, is referred to as deterrence theory. There are two types of deterrence theory: general and specific. General deterrence occurs when people decide not to violate the law because they are afraid of legal punishment. More specifically, general deterrence is designed to send a message to the general population. For example, when someone is punished for committing a crime, it is to serve as a reminder or example to the public that if they commit similar behavior, they too will be punished. General deterrence theory holds that crime rates are influenced and determined by the threat of criminal punishments. For example, if people are fearful of being apprehended and punished, they will not commit crime. As such, one should expect to see low crime rates where there are effective crime-fighting law enforcement personnel, and in those areas where crime rates are high, one can expect that police efforts are ineffective. Hence, to the extent that people are afraid of being apprehended and punished for committing crime, they will not violate the law. However, if offenders are unafraid of being caught and punished, the theory provides that crimes are very likely to occur. Because of this, some commentators have argued that in order to be effective, the criminal justice system must always function as a threat system.

Whether punishment can have a deterrent effect is contingent on whether it is meted out in a swift, certain, and severe manner. If a crime is committed and the offender is not caught, then the elements associated with deterrence are not achieved. Conversely, if a crime is committed and the offender is quickly apprehended and punished, according to deterrence theorists, the action may serve as a deterrent to offenders. With today's technology, law enforcement is more advanced, thus increasing the certainty of apprehension, especially with regard to surveillance and DNA testing and other physical trace evidence. Experts argue that even minor punishment can deter crime. For example, shopping centers and parking lots are saturated with cameras that record and monitor the movement of shoppers. Because most people are aware that they can be identified, they are less likely to engage in criminal behavior.

Specific deterrence occurs when an already punished offender decides not to reoffend because he does not want to face legal consequence again. It is not designed to send a message to the general public since it is individualized. Those who subscribe to specific deterrence believe that

> **specific deterrence**—Action used by the criminal justice system to prevent a punished offender from recidivating or re-engaging in crime.

severe punishment will convince offenders not to recidivate by re-engaging in crime. Proponents of specific deterrence believe that the state must apply enough pain to make the offender forgo his desire to reoffend. For example, a shoplifter who is arrested and receives a sentence of five years in prison, and upon release must stand in front of the establishment where the crime was committed holding a poster that reads that he was incarcerated for stealing, may be deterred from stealing in the future.

Which element of deterrence is most important? For example, is a swift or fast apprehension more important than the certainty of punishment (perception), or is the threat of a severe sentence alone enough to convince potential offenders that crime is not worth the effort? Deterrence theorists argue that the certainty of punishment is more compelling and has a greater impact on the decision to commit a crime compared with quick apprehension and severe punishment. These theorists hold that the certainty of punishment or believing one will be caught serves as a deterrent to crime. The other elements have less impact. For example, most research on deterrence has focused on certainty and severity of punishment—namely, the likelihood of being arrested and the use of incarceration—to determine if they deliver deterrence.

The differences between classical and neoclassical, or choice, theory are twofold. First, choice theory emphasizes that the fear of punishment can be an effective deterrent to crime because the threat of punishment alone is enough to deter criminal behavior. Moreover, this position holds that offenders make rational and conscious decisions to engage in crime. Choice theory contends that offenders weigh the advantages and disadvantages associated with crime and then consider the possibility of apprehension. The second and major difference between classical and neoclassical criminology, according to Robert Bohm and Keith Haley (1999), is the assumption of free will. The neoclassical school argues that factors such as insanity can inhibit the exercise of free will. Furthermore, mitigating circumstances surrounding a crime can explain diminished capacity for rational decision-making. Despite this, the main assumption of neoclassical theory is that offenders are not negatively affected by their environment, are not the victims of a dysfunctional childhood, and do not commit crimes out of economic necessity. Rather, offenders are people who seek out those in the population who are weak and victimize them when the opportunity presents itself.

In the late 1980s, many states in America managed their increasing criminal populations and crime rates by implementing strict sentencing guidelines that included mandatory sentencing, "three strikes" policies, and the death penalty. Some correctional experts believe that these efforts, along with other factors, led to the decline in the crime rate in the 1990s, but at what cost? Many states have abolished the use of parole. Offenders are staying in prison for longer periods of time, which contributes to overcrowding and expense. Strict sentencing guidelines, such as "three strikes" laws, are used on offenders who have not engaged in serious or violent crime. When these offenders faced their second or third felony, they typically received a sentence of life without the possibility of parole or at least a very long prison sentence (Gaines, Kaune, and Miller, 2000). This added to an already geriatric prison population because offenders are spending longer periods of time in prison. The results of research on the deterrent effects of "three strikes" laws reveal that they have no discernible deterrent effect on criminal behavior. Despite the decline in the crime rate in the 1990s, violent crime rates dropped at a higher rate in states that did not enact "three strikes" laws than in those states that implemented them (Ehlers, Schiraldi, and Ziedenberg, 2004).

Some criminologists ask, why did choice theory reemerge in the 1970s? As previously mentioned, criminological theory had undergone a tremendous amount of growth since its inception in the 18th century. Many scholars attribute the resurrection of classical theory, now called choice theory, to the social, political, and economic events that occurred in the 1970s. More specifically, the 1960s had been a time of civil unrest and protests in many of the nation's streets, crime was widespread, and the divide between the rich and poor was very pronounced. The nation also witnessed the disparate treatment of cultural and ethnic minorities and people labeled unconventional. During this time, the government and the social structure were blamed for the plight of the nation. Despite this, more salient events of the time included positivistic theories coming under attack for failing to isolate crime-producing factors. President Lyndon B. Johnson's Great Society effort had invested hundreds of millions of dollars to fight the "war on poverty" and to make the nation more inclusive of the diversity that reflected the fabric of the American society (Cammisa, 1998). These efforts (largely influenced by positivistic theories) were ineffective in changing the social conditions with which the poor had to contend. Critics of positivistic theory charged that criminologists failed to demonstrate that social class, broken homes, school failures, or mental defects were associated with crime. Conservative criminology charged that the plight of the poor had much to do with individual responsibility and very little to do with adverse social conditions. This shift may have also revealed the competing goals of rehabilitation and punishment.

Also sparking the development of choice theory was research conducted by leading experts in the area of criminal justice policy that found that rehabilitation of known offenders did not work. For example, Robert Martinson (a leading correctional expert) and his colleagues conducted evaluation research to determine whether offenders would recidivate (re-engage in crime) after being released from programs designed to allow for their successful reintegration back into society. After examining 231 programs, they could not find any that had an appreciable effect on rehabilitating offenders. When this report was published, it dealt a "death blow" to human service and rehabilitation in general, and to corrections and positivistic criminology in particular. Many in the criminal justice system interpreted the report to mean that nothing worked to rehabilitate offenders and prevent them from engaging in criminal activities upon their release. Many people, including offenders, practitioners, and scholars, were disillusioned over the findings (Cullen, Fisher, & Applegate, 2000).

The mid-1970s also saw serious riots in places of confinement. Perhaps none captured the attention of Americans more than the riot at the Attica Correctional Facility in upstate New York, where several inmates were seriously injured or killed, along with prison guards (killed at the hands of state troopers). In addition, the crime rate was steadily increasing in America. At the same time, several scholars published documents that criticized "coddling" criminal offenders. Chief among them was James Q. Wilson's work *Thinking About Crime* (1979). In this book, Wilson argues that there will always be people among us who are willing to engage in crime and violate the rights and safety of others. He argues that criminals are rational people who plan their crimes, fear punishment, and deserve to be punished for their misdeeds. Wilson also argues that it is not the responsibility of the government to give everyone a job or a house, or to remove them from poverty. However, even if the government engaged in such practices, Wilson contends, some people would still find excuses to engage in criminal behavior. Because of this, society must create ways to reduce the opportunities offenders have to engage in crime and punish those who do, which might deter potential offenders. In *Beyond Probation*, Charles Murray and Louis Cox (1979) argued that programs that emphasize punishment would be more effective at preventing future criminal behaviors than those with treatment and rehabilitation components. Because of the social and political climates, politicians and policy makers embraced these conservative ideas. These events in total made Americans more fearful of crime and criminals. As a result, some contend that the time and circumstances were ripe for a paradigm shift from a liberal approach of dealing with offenders to a conservative approach. Therefore, choice theory seemed a likely direction in which to move to restore the social order and, at the same time, make individuals more accountable and responsible for their behavior.

Summary

While considered the first school of criminological theory, classical criminology emphasized that reforms needed to be made to the administration of justice mainly because of the many abuses that were carried over from the Middle Ages. In fact, criminal justice historians report that in Europe, as late as the 18th century, those accused of committing social deviance and crime were commonly tortured, abducted, forced to confess to crimes, and denied basic human rights. Philosophers such as Cesare Beccaria and Jeremy Bentham, influenced by the changing times, worked to humanize the administration of justice. Because of their efforts, they are considered to be the founders of criminology.

> **utilitarianism**—A concept that refers to the greatest good for the greatest number of people. In criminal justice, the utilitarian purpose of the system is to protect the broader society from offenders who prey on lawabiding citizens.

While using principles of **utilitarianism** and the social contract, they challenged the state's right to punish. They worked to normalize fairness and justice for the poor as well as the wealthy. They worked to codify laws and advance the need for sweeping reforms to be made to the justice system in general, but to the prison systems in particular.

The classical school of criminology introduced general ideas of deterrence theory and asserted that crime and deviance were not caused by demonic or spiritual possession, but rather, offenders freely engaged in a rational thinking process while weighing the benefits to be gained from their involvement in crime. They discussed how punishment was a necessary evil that should be used only to prevent some greater evil from being inflicted on society.

There were also several themes that emerged from the classical movement, one of which was punishment proportionate to the degree of crime seriousness inflicted by offenders. The school also ushered in the development of neoclassical theories such as rational choice and deterrence theories. While the classical school's popularity faded at the beginning of the positivistic movement, classical theory experienced a resurgence in the 1970s that continues to influence the current-day criminal justice system.

Shortcomings of the Theories

1. Classical theory and rational choice theory do not consider social problems such as poverty as a cause of crime.

2. Classical theory is a misnomer since this early period did not focus on crime causation. In fact, many criminologists argue that the classical school of thought is not considered the beginning of criminological theory because its primary focus was on making reforms to the administration of justice and holding offenders accountable for their actions.

3. Classical explanations were too simplistic and mainly limited to free will, rational thinking, and hedonism.

4. Rational choice theories do not address reasons why offenders engage in crime, but rather they focus on eliminating the opportunities that offenders have to engage in criminal activity.

Discussion Questions

1. Who were the major philosophers who influenced classical criminology?

2. What were some common explanations given to explain deviant and criminal behavior?

3. Why did Cesare Beccaria and Jeremy Bentham reform the European administration of justice?

4. What were some of the barbaric ways used for accused criminals to prove their innocence?

5. What are the differences between classical and neoclassical theory?

6. Why did the neoclassical theories emerge in the 1970s?

References

Beccaria, C. (1764/1963). *On Crimes and Punishments*. Trans. Henry Paolucci. Indianapolis, IN: Bobbs-Merrill.

Becker, G. S. (1968). Crime and Punishment: An Economic Approach. *Journal of Political Economy, 76*, 169–217.

Bentham, J. (1830). *The Rationale of Punishment*. London: Robert Heward.

Bentham, J. (1789/1948). *An Introduction to the Principles of Morals and Legislation* [1789]. New York, NY: Kegan Paul.

Bohm, R., and Haley, K. N. (1999). *Introduction to Criminal Justice*. New York, NY: Glencoe/McGraw-Hill.

Cammisa, A. M. (1998). *From Rhetoric to Reform?: Welfare Policy in American Politics*. Oxford: Westview Press.

Clarke, R. V., and Cornish, D. B. (2001). Rational Choice. In Paternoster, R., and Bachman, R. (Eds.), *Explaining Criminals and Crime* (pp. 23–42). Los Angeles, CA: Roxbury.

Cullen, F. T., Fisher, B. S., and Applegate, B. K. 2000. *Public Opinion About Punishment and Corrections.* In M. Tonry (Ed.), *Crime and Justice: A Review of Research* (pp. 1 70). Chicago, IL: University of Chicago Press.

Ehlers, S., Schiraldi, V., and Ziedenberg, J. (2004). *Still Striking Out: Ten Years of California's Three Strikes Laws*. Washington, DC: Justice Policy Institute.

Erikson, K. T. (1966). *Wayward Puritans: A Study in the Sociology of Deviance*. New York, NY: John Wiley & Sons.

Foucault, M. (1976). *Discipline and Punishment: The Birth of the Prison*. London: Allen Lane.

Gaines, L., Kaune, M., and Miller, R. L. (2000). *Criminal Justice in Action*. Belmont, CA: Wadsworth/Thomson Learning.

Masters, R. D., and Masters, J. R. (1978). *Jean-Jacques Rousseau: On the Social Contract with Geneva Manuscript and Political Economy*. New York, NY: St. Martin's Press.

McCarthy, B. (2002). New Economics of Sociological Criminology. *Annual Review of Sociology, 28*, 417–42.

Michalowski, R. J. (1985). *Order, Law, and Crime: An Introduction to Criminology*. New York, NY: Random House.

Murray, C., and Cox, L. (1979). *Beyond Probation*. Beverly Hills, CA: Sage.

Pleck, E. (1987). *Domestic Tyranny: The Making of American Social Policy Against Family Violence from Colonial Times to the Present*. Oxford: Oxford University Press.

Williams, F. P., and McShane, M. D. (1993). *Criminology Theory: Selected Readings*. Cincinnati, OH: Anderson.

Wilson, J. Q. (1979). *Thinking About Crime*. New York, NY: Vintage Books.

Chapter 5

Trait Theories

Chapter Outline

The relatively recent massacre that occurred at Virginia Polytechnic University (commonly called "Virginia Tech" or VT) is well documented. On Monday, April 16, 2007, Seung-Hui Cho unleashed a degree of violence on his fellow students that is the deadliest school shooting in American history. The tragedy claimed the lives of 32 people, including five professors. Afterward, reports surfaced that there were early warning signs of an imminent disaster, but nothing was done to prevent the atrocity from occurring. Fellow classmates and Cho's creative writing professor later recounted it was obvious that Cho suffered from a disturbed personality (Golden, 2007), as revealed in samples of his writing that he had read to his classmates. On one occasion, his writings were so troubling that his professor reported the matter to one university official. On another occasion, Cho read an essay to his class that was so disturbing, some of the students skipped the next class session. His writings would later be described as dark and providing a glimpse into his personality that went completely ignored. Little did his classmates and professors know that Cho's personality disorder had been diagnosed and he had been a patient at a mental hospital.

Because of privacy rights, his mental health status was never revealed to the university. Students who knew Cho claimed that he was a loner who had a very difficult time assimilating and connecting with other students at the university. He was isolated from others. After Cho murdered the 32 students and professors, he committed suicide (Golden, 2007; Herring, 2009). This case is similar to another campus shooting that occurred at Northern Illinois University (NIU) on February 14, 2008. Steven Phillip Kazmierczak, a former graduate sociology student at NIU and a former patient at a psychiatric center, entered a large lecture classroom at Cole Hall and opened fire on more than 160 students who were in attendance, murdering six students and wounding 20 others (Nizza, 2008). It was later discovered that he was an exceptional student who had received a dean's award for being an academic standout. In fact, former faculty, students, and staff later reported that on reflection, there were no indicators that he was troubled or disturbed. The president of NIU later remarked that Kazmierczak had a very good academic record and there were no signs or indicators of any impending trouble.

After the shootings, investigations found that Kazmierczak was believed to have stopped taking his psychiatric medication, which may have accounted for his erratic behavior. His girlfriend later confirmed that he had been prescribed Xanax, Ambien, and Prozac by his psychiatrist, but at some point, he stopped taking the recommended dosages (Boudreau and Scott, 2008). At the time of this tragedy, he was enrolled at the University of Illinois at Urbana–Champaign as a graduate student in social work. In fact, he was so accomplished that he, along with two other graduate students, and a professor had published a peer-reviewed article in an academic journal. After opening fire on the students, Kazmierczak turned the weapon on himself and committed suicide (Nizza, 2008). Similar to the Cho case, the university was not made aware of Kazmierczak's mental health history. In the aftermath of both of these deadly school shootings, many colleges and universities across the nation responded by implementing "lockdown" policies on their respective campuses to prevent similar atrocities from occurring when there is a report or citing of a gunman on campus.

One simply does not expect mass shootings to occur on American college or university campuses. When crimes such as these are committed, students, family members, university officials, and the lay public may ask, why did they occur? This is especially the case when they appear to be as senseless and involve as many people as the tragedies that occurred at VT and NIU. These kinds of crime appear to lack a real motive, or a target that has infuriated a shooter to the point where he or she is willing to endanger the lives of others to get to the object of their rage. For example, at the time of the attack, were Cho and Kazmierczak angry at all of the students enrolled at their respective colleges? Did they have a personal dispute with any student who was murdered or wounded? Is committing suicide after engaging in acts of mass terror a normal response to life's problems? Many criminologists would argue that the answer to these questions is probably no. In fact, they would likely argue that this type of sporadic violence is rooted in or attributed to declining mental health, or some type of physical abnormality. After investigations into these murder-suicides, it was revealed that both gunmen suffered from poor mental health or had stopped taking medication to address a psychological disorder. They were also under stress, and in the case of Kazmierczak, no one close to him ever imagined that his behavior would manifest in the mass terror that unfolded on the NIU campus.

The idea of motivated offenders engaging in criminal behavior because they are either mentally impaired or suffer from a biological condition is nothing new to criminologists. Experts even suggest that in recent times, the media have done much to desensitize the general public to the idea of offenders engaging in behaviors that can only be explained by accepting that in some cases, offenders have clearly gone mad. The news media typically report crime stories that are freakish, if not bizarre, sometimes reporting on cannibal flesh-eating offenders, or murderers who cook their victims. Two reports illustrate this point. First, in Sacramento, 29-year-old Ka Yang was arrested and charged in the death of her six-week-old daughter, whom she cooked in her microwave oven. While shocking, three similar microwave crimes (including two that resulted in murder) also occurred in Ohio, Texas, and Virginia (Thompson, 2013). Second, according to reports from the Miami–Dade County Medical Examiner Department, a Florida man, Rudy Eugene, was shot and killed by police officers after he chewed off the face of a homeless man (Martinez, 2012). Moreover, Hollywood's depiction of murderers in movies such as *American Psycho*, *Misery*, *Silence of the Lambs*, *Disturbia*, *Obsession*, *Children of the Corn*, *I Know What You Did Last Summer*, and the *Scream* franchise have made the reality of disturbed murderers an acceptable and believable explanation as to why some people engage in violent behavior (Siegel, 2012).

Foundations of Trait Theories

Unlike the philosophers who created classical criminology, those who advocated positivism were scientists. Because of their initial efforts to determine crime causation rather than emphasizing the rule of law, they arguably constitute the first school of criminological thought. The positive school emerged in the 19th century, essentially replacing classical criminology as the dominant school of thought and rejecting the critical philosophy of the Age of Enlightenment. Despite this, many elements of the classical school remain an established presence in the administration of justice. The move toward positive thinking emerged for several reasons. First, after 100 years of treating the motivation of crime as free will, choice, and hedonism, the crime rate continued to increase. More specifically, the classical approach largely ignored poverty and other factors that may have explained why destitute people committed economic crime. Therefore, scholars began searching for alternative reasons to explain the behavior of criminals.

Second, science transformed society, in general, but it moved the study of human behavior from the metaphysical to empirical observation, in particular. As a result, scientists began applying the **scientific method** to study many problems that challenged the human condition, and crime was not an exception. Unlike their counterparts of the classical tradition, **positivists** attributed crime and deviant behavior to factors such as having a biological impairment, being mentally deficient, or being the product of poor environmental conditions. They argued that these factors were crime producing. They reasoned that crime is primarily caused by internal and external factors that have nothing to do with a rational or conscious decision to engage in crime. Instead, they viewed offenders as individuals who are different from law-abiding people biologically, psychologically, and socially. They argued that criminals are predetermined to commit crime: they are essentially thrust into crime because of circumstances beyond their control. For this reason, positivists, unlike classical scholars, advocated treatment and rehabilitation instead of punishment. This allowed them the opportunity to study offenders who suffered from circumstances over which they had no control.

scientific method—An objective strategy used by natural and social scientists to conduct research. The process entails formulating a hypothesis, collecting data, creating theories, and testing the validity of theories in order to disprove them.

positivists—Criminologists who attribute crime causation to internal and external forces such as biology, psychology, and the social environment.

From Philosophy to Science

sociology—The study of society and what transpires when people interact with each other. It also encompasses the study of the origins and development of social institutions.

Comte, August—Considered, with Émile Durkheim, to be the founder of sociology.

Under positivism, **sociology** was developed as a unique way to study society and the evolutionary changes that evolved in the 19th century. **August Comte** (the founder of sociology) argued that the thinkers of the Enlightenment movement had done much to reform the old system of justice, but had not gone far enough. He reasoned that though it had been instrumental in moving society forward, the period of Enlightenment was passé and, in some ways, even obstructive. Comte also advanced the idea of applying the scientific method to study crime. Before the age of science, any inquiry about the cause of crime was limited to either superstition or philosophy. The scientific approach moved crime from the abstract to the empirical (Barkan, 2012). By applying science to the study of crime, it required that an objective study of crime be based on creating hypothesis, gathering data, creating theories, and testing the validity of the theories in an attempt to disprove them. Because of this, scholars agree that the age of positivism represents the beginning of the study of crime causation. This approach seemed a likely outcome since during this time many advances and discoveries were made in physiology, medicine, psychology, and psychiatry (Barkan, 2012).

Unlike the philosophers who studied crime in the 18th century, those who embarked upon this endeavor in the 19th century were scientists who brought to bear on this task the rigors of research methodology. Essentially, these scientists were advancing the credibility of their respective disciplines, but at the same time, they were studying crime by using objectivity and the scientific method. Social scientists believed that by being objective, they removed any personal biases that they may have had about the research they conducted. By using the scientific method and promoting rigorous methodology, they gave credibility to their work, allowing others the opportunity to replicate their findings (Barkan, 2012).

The Positivistic School on Crime Causation

Early positivists thought that crime was caused by biological, psychological, or environmental factors that the offender could not control. They thought offenders engaged in crime because they were either biologically flawed or psychologically impaired, or lived in environments or communities that were saturated with crime. Therefore, they viewed criminals as being predisposed to a life of crime. These scientists argued that offenders exercised no rational choice, free will, or drive toward hedonism, but rather were the victims of determinism. Positivists thought that criminals were predestined to be criminals, because they were essentially different from people who obeyed the law. Criminals were viewed by early positivists as inferior to law-abiding citizens. Because of their inherent inferiority or sickness, positivists argued that offenders should not be punished for their law violations, because they did not freely decide to engage in crime and lacked the power to resist the temptations of crime. Positivists argued that treatment and rehabilitation are the most appropriate ways to respond to crime. Some early positivists advocated isolating and "sterilizing" offenders. This process was considered necessary in order to prevent criminals from procreating and passing criminogenic genes to their offspring (Hooton, 1940; Dugdale, 1877).

Figure 5.1 represents the first efforts of **positivistic criminology**. It presents that criminal behavior is a function of biological, psychological, and social environmental

positivistic criminology—The branch of criminology that began in the 19th century and extended into the 1950s. This school of thought rejected the arguments of free will and rational choice and embraced arguments of biological and psychological determinism. It held that criminals are predestined to be criminals. The school rejected punishing offenders and advocated rehabilitation and treatment.

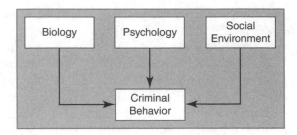

Figure 5.1 Positivistic Explanations to Crime

factors. This model shows that criminal behavior can be a function of one's biological predisposition to engage in criminal behavior, or that some commit crime for psychological reasons or due to a mental defect. The last area highlights the impact of the social environment, positing that offenders may commit criminal behavior because they learned criminogenic behaviors from their interactions with others.

> **Darwin, Charles**—An English naturalist who lived from 1809 to 1882. His work discussing the evolution of man was instrumental in influencing the early biological work of the positivistic school.

The Influence of Evolution on the Study of Crime

Charles Darwin's theory of evolution was widely disseminated in academia, and those who pioneered the positivist movement were influenced by his writings. Darwin argued that mankind was the product of years of evolution and not of creation. Social Darwinists believed in the "struggle to survive," the "survival of the fittest," and "natural selection." It was a social theory that opposed equal treatment and programs designed to help the unfortunate. It argued that such programs would promote and reward the lazy, shiftless, and immoral, and at the same time, retard individual and economic development (Lilly, Cullen, and Ball, 1989). Those positivists who believed criminals were different from law-abiding citizens quickly embraced **Darwinism**. Again, positivists were scientists who only believed in what could be empirically measured and tested, and since religion or the existence of God could not be empirically proven, they opted for Darwinian views, calling religion mere speculation. The earliest form of positivism focused on **phrenology**. Crime and biological explanations have been linked since the 19th century to the early works of phrenologists, who argued that criminals were biologically different from other individuals in society.

> **Darwinism**—The theory that argues that species are derived by descent through the natural selection of those best adapted to survive in the struggle of existence.

> **phrenology**—One of the first branches of positivistic theories, it examined the shape and size of the human skull as an indicator of propensity to commit crime.

Franz Joseph Gall: Phrenology (1758–1828)

Phrenology was one of the first sciences, devoted to studying the relationship between a person's character and the morphology of the skull. It attempted to link the identification of features such as bumps on a person's head to aspects of the human personality and character. Phrenology postulated that each function had its organ seat in the brain, and externally, one could see them on the skull. For example, the theory argued that a bump on an offender's skull could explain his involvement in criminal behavior (Wolfgang, 1973). Popularized by German physician **Franz Joseph Gall**, it advanced the belief that moral and intellectual features were innate. In fact, in his book entitled

> **Gall, Franz**—An early phrenologist who advocated that people with unusually shaped skulls have a propensity to engage in criminal behavior.

The Anatomy and Physiology of the Nervous System in General and the Brain, in Particular, Gall argued that the brain is the organ that controls every human propensity, sentiment, and facility. He went on to argue that the way the head is formed represents the form of the brain, and it reflects the relative development of the brain. In his work on phrenology, Gall visited prisons, hospitals, and mental asylums, where he measured the skulls of inmates and patients. Of special interest to Gall were individuals with oddly shaped heads. He eventually introduced a system of 27 different facilities that he believed could be diagnosed by measuring specific parts of the human head. Furthermore, he created a chart that isolated the areas of the skull that he believed were linked to specific personality traits and characteristics. In the end, Gall's research was attacked for a lack of scientific rigor. Despite this, his work in phrenology enjoyed popularity

> **Spurzheim, Johann Gaspar**—One of the earlier positivists who advocated the tradition of phrenology.

in the 1880s and early 1900s and continued to influence thinkers of this period. Gall and his contemporary **Johann Gaspar Spurzheim** (1776–1832) coauthored several works in the area of phrenology—namely, *Phrenology in Connection with the study of Physiognomy* (1826), which stimulated more interest in phrenology that spread throughout the United Kingdom and the United States. In their work, they argued that the shape of the head could reveal if one had a propensity to become a criminal. They also closely examined the lumps and bumps and bone structure of offenders to identify who would likely engage in crime.

Though today this kind of research seems overly simplistic and methodologically flawed, it nonetheless demonstrates early attempts to use science to explain crime because it relied on empirical observations and measurements. Phrenology led to the start of positive criminology, which would be expanded by scholars such as Cesare Lombroso, Charles Buckman Goring, Earnest A. Hooton, and William Herbert Sheldon.

> **Lombroso, Cesare**—Considered to be the father of criminology. An Italian physician and professor of psychiatry at the University of Turin, he studied the cadavers of criminals in order to determine scientifically whether they were different physically from people with more conventional behaviors and attitudes. Lombrosian theory can be outlined in two simple steps. First, Lombroso believed that serious criminal conduct was inherited: criminals were compelled to commit criminal acts. Second, Lombroso asserted that born criminals were atavistic throwbacks from primitive times.

Cesare Lombroso: Atavism (1835–1909)

Cesare Lombroso, an early positivist, is credited as the father of criminology because his work shifted the discipline from its legal emphasis on crime to the scientific study of criminals. He wrote several books and perhaps is best known for his works entitled *The Criminal Man* (1876) and

Crime, Its Causes and Its Remedies (1899). In these works, he advanced discussions of biology and crime and argued that offenders were different from other individuals. More specifically, he postulated the existence of physical characteristics and the innate tendency of some individuals to engage in sociopathic and criminal behavior. In fact, he believed that some features of criminals were readily identifiable. For example, these included unusual skull sizes and asymmetric facial features such as large jaws. He also discussed other body parts and how they could lead individuals to commit crime (Wolfgang, 1973). Lombroso's work was influenced by Darwin's discussion of the evolutionary processes.

Lombroso was an Italian physician who held several positions, such as professor of psychiatry, criminal anthropologist, and director of a mental asylum. He routinely measured criminals' body parts, and conducted autopsies on several criminal offenders. During these autopsies, he made striking discoveries. Lombroso found that some prisoners had features and characteristics that were similar to those of primitive man. Lombroso referred to this condition as stigmata or **atavistic anomaly** (Wolfgang, 1973). He advanced the idea that some individuals were "born" criminals who were throwbacks to primitive beasts or earlier man, such as the Neanderthal. He argued that they had not developed beyond the primitive stage of human evolution. In keeping with the dictates of Darwin, Lombroso advanced the belief that these were individuals who had not fully evolved to keep pace with a progressive and advancing society. While focusing on the relationship between criminal psychology and physical or constitutional defects, he reasoned that criminals were moral and mental degenerates (Wolfgang, 1973; Lombroso-Ferrero, 1911).

> **atavistic anomaly**—A condition discussed by Cesare Lombroso; refers to the idea that offenders are biologically different from law-abiding people.

> **Ferri, Enrico**—A theoretician who asserted that free will had no place in criminological theory; he believed crime was caused by three factors: anthropological, physical, and social.

> **Garofalo, Rafael**—A contemporary of Cesare Lombroso and Enrico Ferri who also advocated the early tradition of a biological basis to criminal behavior. He further argued that criminals should be sterilized.

With the help of contemporaries such as **Enrico Ferri** and **Raffaele Garofalo**, Lombroso created other types of criminal profiles. Ferri and Garofalo were not as convinced as Lombroso about the existence of a born criminal, but instead saw other factors that influenced crime. Some of these were population density, climate, season, and alcohol. They helped Lombroso expand his discussions on crime to include typologies such as insane criminals, criminoloids, criminals of passion, and born criminals (Garofalo, 1885/1914). More specifically, insane criminals were described as idiots, alcoholics, epileptics, and imbeciles. Criminoloids were individuals who engaged in crime when the opportunity presented itself. Criminals of passion were individuals who killed out of love or anger, or for honor, and born criminals were those who suffered from stigmata or an atavistic anomaly. Some early positivists advocated that criminals should be sterilized, put to death, or transported to remote places to prevent them from transmitting criminogenic genes to the next generation. These theories were eventually discredited because of methodological weaknesses, but not before creating a biocriminological legacy that still exists today (Jacoby, 1979; Barkan, 2012; Siegel, 2012).

Crime and its Biological Nexus

Though today, most criminologists reject the idea that biology alone causes crime, there are two studies that have puzzled criminologists: the **Juke family** and the **Kallikak family** (Dugdale, 1877). Richard Dugdale researched the Juke family tree back 200 years and found that 140 family members had served time in prison. Many believed that the Jukes were able to transmit criminal genes from one generation to the next. On the other hand, Henry Goddard (1914) reported his investigation of the Kallikaks. He concluded that one man fathered two families, one criminal and the other law-abiding. It was discovered that each family had a different social environment. It was argued that crime may be a function of nurture instead of

> **Juke family**—A family studied by Robert Dugdale; he believed this family showed that heredity is a source of criminal conduct.
>
> **Kallikak family**—The fictitious name of a family studied by Henry Goddard in the early 1900s. He was quite impressed with Sir Francis Galton's assertions that intelligence was hereditary. From this line of thinking he contended that delinquency was also transmitted through lines of heredity. In this text, published in 1912, the author asserted that his analysis showed that heredity could be a cause of criminal behavior.

nature. Though biological explanations, considered politically incorrect, are not favored in contemporary times, studies do embrace biology and the social environment.

Early Theories of Biological Positivism

Charles Buckman Goring (1870–1919)

In 1913, Charles Buckman Goring, an English psychiatrist who worked with prisoners, challenged Lombroso's atavistic anomaly theory. Using techniques of physical anthropology and statistical analysis, Goring spent 12 years examining 96 traits of more than 3,000 prisoners and nonprisoners. He tested propositions of the positive school of criminology and advanced the scientific foundation of constructing scientific criminology (Driver, 1957). Goring made many contributions to criminology that included advancing the use of statistics in research and using age as a variable to explain crime. He was one of the first researchers to argue that prisons were not adequate places to reform criminals, and he used vital statistics in his study of crime. Despite this, Goring is best known for examining offender traits such as distance between the eyes, head circumstance, weight, and cephalic index. His research also focused on hair and eye color, defective hearing, left-handedness, and other characteristics he believed distinguished offenders from others. While comparing criminals and noncriminals, Goring concluded that there were positive differences between age, stature, and intelligence. He found criminals to be inferior to the general population in stature and weight. More specifically, Goring wrote that violent offenders were stronger and more constitutionally sound, and thieves and burglars were physically weaker compared with the general population (Driver, 1957).

While using statistics, Goring measured criminality by temperament, temper, faculty, conduct (while imprisoned), suicidal tendency (by suicide attempts), and insane diathesis (Driver, 1957). He discovered that offenders who committed fraud were egoistical, and violent offenders had violent tempers, lack of faculty, and insane and suicidal tendencies. He reported that other differences between criminals were dependent on their level of intelligence. He found a high association between crime and defective intelligence. He believed that English criminals were selected by physical constitution, mental constitution, and defective intelligence (Driver, 1957). In his book entitled *The English Convict: A Statistical Study* (1913), Goring repudiated Lombroso's thesis on the born criminal, arguing that the atavistic anomaly did not exist. As a result of Goring's finding, Lombroso's work was discredited in Europe as well as America.

Earnest Albert Hooton (1887–1954)

Hooton, Earnest Albert—A Harvard University physical anthropologist who asserted that criminals were organically inferior and that crime was a result of physiological conditions inherent in the criminal.

In 1939, **Earnest Albert Hooton**, an American anthropologist and Harvard professor, studied body types and how they influenced personality traits. Hooton argued that criminals were physically inferiors to others. In his book entitled *The Asymmetrical Character of Human Evolution* (1925), he argued that human development had not been uniform for everyone—some traits had developed differently for certain segments of the people, and they are common in modern races (Hooton, 1926). Hooton accepted Lombroso's thesis of the born criminal and embraced the idea that criminals held identifiable physical characteristics. Hooton believed that there were general physical attributes that distinguished the races. However, he rejected the contention that biological characteristics could determine personality or propensity to engage in crime (Hooton, 1940). In his research, Hooton measured the physical characteristics of 13,873 criminals from 10 states and compared them with a control group of 3,203 noncriminals. He measured physical characteristics such as weight, height, head length, nose height, and ear length. He also examined age, religion, education, offense committed, marital status, IQ, eye color, moles, tattooing, and race. According to Hooton, criminals had low foreheads, crooked noses, narrow jaws, small ears, long necks, and stooped shoulders. Because of this, he concluded that criminals were "organically inferior" to law-abiding people, and the cause of their criminal behavior was due to biological differences (Hooton, 1939). Stated differently, he believed that deviant or criminal behavior was caused by physical inferiority. He argued that criminals were beyond the scope of rehabilitation, and the only viable method of social control was segregation or elimination (Hooton, 1940). Hooton's research also faced the same criticisms as other biological criminologists—namely, that his work was methodologically flawed.

Body Typologies

William Herbert Sheldon (1898–1977)

Sheldon, William Herbert—An American psychologist and naturalist who developed the field of somatology and its relationship to delinquent and criminal behavior.

In 1949, **William Herbert Sheldon**, a psychologist, became the first American researcher to examine the relationship between body type and delinquent behavior. His research was in the area of human personality traits. Sheldon's work symbolized the association between physique, personality, and crime. He believed the physical makeup of humans had biological foundations. Sheldon's research compared 200 male delinquents in an institution with a control group of 4,000 male college students. Sheldon found that compared with the students, the delinquents were disproportionately mesomorphs (Sheldon, 1949). He argued that his research supported the contention that one's personality and propensity to engage in delinquency were affected by body shape. From this thesis, Sheldon created the theory of somatology, which classifies body shapes as endomorphs, mesomorphs, and ectomorphs. In his work entitled *The Varieties of Delinquent Youth* (1949), he argues that offenders with the endomorph body shape were relatively heavy, with short arms and legs. These offenders were likely to have extroverted personalities and be noncriminal, but they would engage in occasional delinquency. **Mesomorph** offenders were muscular with an athletic build. They would be likely to engage in violent and aggressive behavior such as crime. Ectomorphs were thin and introverted offenders who were overly sensitive. Of these body types, Sheldon thought that mesomorphs were more likely to engage in delinquency and crime. Sheldon's research was attacked for a lack of methodological rigor.

> **mesomorph**—One of the three body types developed by William Sheldon. Sheldon believed in somatotyping and that criminals displayed body builds that made them more prone to criminal behavior. The mesomorph was described as a muscular and aggressive type. This individual was assertive and confident in his exploits.

Chromosome Studies

While some researchers have rejected the notion that body type can influence delinquency and crime, others have embraced research linking chromosomal makeup to personality traits and criminal behavior. Each person has 46 chromosomes found in the cell nucleus that carry genes. In human beings, gender is determined by one of the 23 pairs of inherited chromosomes. For example, a female receives an X chromosome from each parent; a male receives an X from his mother and a Y from his father. But defects in the production of eggs or sperm result in certain genetic anomalies, of which one type is the XYY male, who receives two Y chromosomes from his father (Jacobs et al., 1965). Some criminologists believe that the extra Y chromosome leads to criminal behavior. For example, Patricia Jacobs and associates found a disproportionate number of male inmates at a maximum security state mental hospital in Scotland with an extra Y chromosome. Their report raised the possibility of the presence of the XYY chromosome as a genetic correlate of criminality. Jacobs's research, along with other studies, found that the frequency of XYY males in the general population is about one per 1,000. However, in correctional institutions, the frequency of XYY males is about 10 to 20 times greater, with 1–2% having this trait (Jacobs et al., 1965).

Chromosomal studies are considered limited because they may apply only to a small number of offenders. Moreover, Jacobs's theory excludes offenders under six feet in height, because of the low incidence of XYY males of short and medium height. The theory gained widespread popularity when Richard Speck, who had committed mass murder, was reported to carry the XYY chromosome. However, these reports were later determined to be false. The XYY theory is considered speculative at best, since it has not been proven that genetic differences translate into behavioral differences (Craft, 1985).

Twin Studies: Monozygotic Versus Dizygotic

Most critics argue that if there is a biological relationship to crime, it should reveal itself in the behavior of twins. Since most twins are reared in the same household and exposed to the same set of social conditions, determining whether their behavior is a result of biological, sociological, or psychological conditions would be difficult. Biocriminologists have tried to overcome this dilemma by comparing identical (monozygotic or MZ) twins with fraternal (dizygotic or DZ) twins of the same sex. MZ twins are genetically identical, while DZ twins have only half their genes in common. Biocriminologists contend that studies of identical twins support a genetic basis for crime. For example, earlier studies conducted on the criminal behavior of twins detected a significant relationship between MZ twins and a much lower association between DZ twins. Sarnoff Mednick and Karl Christiansen (1977) report that in studies conducted between 1929 and 1961, 60% of MZ twins shared criminal behavior patterns (if one twin was criminal, so was the other), while only 30% of DZ twins were similarly related. These findings may be viewed as evidence that a genetic basis for criminality exists. Moreover, Christiansen examined a sample of 4,000 male twins and found that 52% of the MZ twins engaged in similar behavior, compared with 22% of the DZ twins.

Despite this finding, other research findings remain inconclusive (Mednick and Christiansen, 1977). David Rowe (1986) reports that where delinquency is concerned, non-twin siblings resemble each other to the same extent as twins. Other research has found that twins separated shortly after birth show signs of similar criminal activity. Does this support a genetic basis for crime? Critics charge that these twins are probably adopted into similar environments several months after birth, and sometimes by relatives who allow the twins to interact with each other. The efforts of twin studies to connect **genetics** with crime remain inconclusive and speculative at best (Siegel, 2012).

> **genetics**—In criminology, the idea that crime is inheritable and can be transmitted to families. The most famous studies used to demonstrate this line of thinking involve two families, the Jukes and the Kallikaks, who were believed to perpetuate criminality via the inheritance of genes.

Adoption Studies

In other attempts to measure whether biological or genetic makeup influences criminality, biocriminologists have examined the behavior of non-twins adopted by different families. This research is premised on the notion of whether the criminality of the biological parents will determine whether the offspring will also engage in criminal behavior. The logic behind this approach is to remove children from the environment of their criminal biological parent to exclude the effects of the environment. If the adopted children of criminal parents are placed in noncriminal environments and they do not engage in crime, crime could be a function of the social environment, or nurture, instead of nature.

The results of adoption studies have been that children with criminal parents typically engage in crime. Several studies indicate that a relationship may exist between biological parents' behavior and the behavior of their children, even when their contact has been infrequent. Barry Hutchings and Sarnoff Mednick (1977) analyzed 1,145 male adoptees born in Copenhagen, Denmark, between 1927 and 1941. Of these, 185 had criminal records. After following up on 143 of the criminal adoptees and matching them with a control group of 143 noncriminal adoptees, it was discovered that the criminality of the biological father was a strong predictor of the child's criminal behavior. Moreover, researchers found that when both the biological and the adoptive fathers were criminal, the probability that the youth would engage in criminal behavior greatly increased (Rowe, 1986).

Neurochemical Mechanisms

In recent years, researchers have examined the impact that neurochemical mechanisms such as hormones and neurotransmitters have on behavior. Hormones are molecules that regulate growth, sexual activity, and emotions. There is evidence that suggests an association between testosterone (male hormone) and estrogen (female hormone) levels on aggressive or criminal behavior (Schauss, 1981). Neurotransmitters are chemicals that are released by nerve cells that transmit messages between the nerve cell receptors (Barkan, 2012). If messages from the central nervous system are not received by other parts of the body, it could cause aggressive and criminal behavior. While controversial, another hormonal explanation that has been used to explain why some women have engaged in crime is premenstrual syndrome or PMS (Barkan, 2012; Siegel, 2012). Researchers arguing this position hold that when women experience PMS, their emotional condition can make them violently aggressive. This research has been discredited as methodologically flawed (Katz and Chambliss, 1995).

Research shows that the relationship between human aggression and testosterone is inconclusive (Wallman, 1999). The neurotransmitter serotonin is a chemical released by nerve cells that transmit signals. It regulates pain perception and normal or abnormal behavior. It also affects body temperature, sleep, and blood pressure. Serotonin levels are influenced by antidepressants that block the uptake of neurotransmitters. When this happens, the brain and body do not get the messages sent from neurotransmitters, and the outcome could mean an individual may respond with aggressive behavior (Schauss, 1981). In animal studies, low levels of serotonin have been linked with high levels of aggression. However, many studies of humans find that violent offenders have low levels of serotonin (Moffitt et al., 1998). Experts agree that the link between serotonin and violent behavior is interesting, but the evidence from research supporting the contention is absent from the literature (Wallman, 1999).

Diet and Nutrition

Some criminologists believe that diet and nutrition play a major role in aggressive and criminal behavior. They argue that brain cells require proper feeding in order to function properly. If the brain is deprived of proper nutrition, the body becomes filled with pollutants. For example, experts argue that a deprivation of sugar, vitamin deficiencies, lead pollution, and food allergies can convert a normal brain into a criminal mind (Schauss, 1981). Researchers who point to the relationships between diet and crime argue that ordinary food, or the lack thereof, can alter the mind much like alcohol or drugs, unleashing criminal behavior (Schauss, 1981). Kenneth Moyer (1976) contends that allergic reactions to foods may be a factor associated with criminal behavior. Allergic reactions to food may directly affect the body's nervous system by causing non-inflammatory swelling of the brain that could trigger aggression, which could lead to crime. Despite studies in this area that typically compare the eating habits of juvenile offenders and non-offending groups, most experts find that these studies suffer from methodological problems that render any conclusions tentative at best, since they lack proper sample sizes, spurious findings, and ambiguity in defining "offending" (Curran and Renzetti, 2001).

Psychological Trait Theories

On a quiet Colorado night, a young man entered a packed movie theater to attend the showing of a long-anticipated movie, *The Dark Knight Rises*. The theater was full of people who had been waiting for what was billed as one of the best movies of the year. Several minutes into the movie, the young man exited the theater for a few minutes, but returned dressed in black tactical clothing, wearing a gas mask, and brandishing several weapons. He went ignored since many of the moviegoers were also wearing costumes. Some thought he was joking, and others believed he was part of the festivities for the opening night of the movie. He threw two gas grenades into the audience and then opened fire with a semiautomatic weapon, killing 12 people and wounding 58 others. Several minutes later, the gunman attempted to leave from the same exit that he had used earlier, but was apprehended by police officers who later found other weapons in his car. While searching his apartment, police found it rigged with explosives. It also contained a number of firearms, including semiautomatic weapons. Arresting officers reported that the gunman had dyed his hair red and called himself "The Joker." What would make a person attend a movie theater with the intent to inflict fatal violence on others? Would a normal person commit such a horrendous act of violence? Some experts believe that only those who are truly disturbed have the mindset or capacity to carry out this type of harm.

Positive criminology also looked to psychology to explain deviant and criminal behavior. Psychology offers important explanation regarding why a few individuals rather than groups participate in certain types of social behavior. Researchers who hold to psychological theory argue that criminals engage in crime because they are psychologically impaired or different from law-abiding people. Like biological explanations, psychology offers invaluable understanding of individual behavior and discounts aggregate behavior. At the same time, psychological explanation largely ignores social and structural problems that could lead some offenders into a life of deviant and criminal behavior. Some of the earlier psychological research applied psychoanalytic theory and examined relationships between moral development and crime, and between intelligence and crime.

Psychoanalytic Theory

Psychoanalytic theory argues that mental disorders are caused by internal disturbances developed in early childhood, brought on by poor interactions between parents and children. Psychoanalytic theory was introduced by **Sigmund Freud**. Though Freud never said much about crime, his analysis of mental disorders has been used to explain crime and delinquency.

> **Freud, Sigmund**—The originator of the psychoanalytic perspective. Freud asserted that most human behavior is motivated by unconscious thoughts and memories.

According to Freud, mental disorders arise from a conflict between society and instinctive needs of the individual. The personality is divided into three parts: the id, ego, and the superego. Freud argued that the **id** is present at birth. It represents the instinctive or impulsive drives that demand immediate gratification. The ego develops

> **id**—A Freudian concept designed to explain that part of the personality from which urges and desires emanate. It is concerned with primitive instinctual desires and demands for immediate gratification.

later, and it is the rational part of the personality that indicates whether something is right or wrong. Later, the superego develops, and it is the internationalization of society's moral code. The superego is also the individual conscience that leads one to feel ashamed and embarrassed. Experts argue that these parts of the personality are developed by the age of 5.

Freud believed that because people are naturally pleasure seekers, many are likely to engage in antisocial or prohibitive behavior. As such, he believed the ego and superego are responsible for restraining the id. Therefore, if the superego is too weak to control the id's impulsiveness, crime and delinquency might be an inevitable outcome. Many believe the three parts of the personality must exist in harmony, or problems will likely occur. What is more interesting is the fact that feelings of guilt and embarrassment can occur if the superego is too strong. Those who follow in the tradition of psychoanalytic theory view crime as being caused by the conflict between society and the instinctive needs of the individual (Freud, 1966). More specifically, they see a disconnection between the individual and society that stems from early childhood experiences and later manifest in behavior. However, many fail to see the connection between crime and poor mental health since the majority of offenders are, by all accounts, mentally healthy individuals (Bernard, Snipes, and Gerould, 2009).

Moral Development and Crime

Some scholars argue that people who engage in crime and delinquency are not as morally developed as law-abiding people (Bennett, Dilulio, and Walters, 1996). The reasoning behind this is that if they were as moral as others, they would not engage in actions that cause harm, injury, and death. This way of thinking is not new. In fact, theorists have considered the connection between moral and mental development and criminal behavior for centuries (Nye, 1996). For example, Jean Piaget argued that psychologists have always been concerned with the moral and mental development of children. Piaget argued that not all children make it through the different stages of healthy development.

Unfortunately, some children never complete the cycle or progression, and for them, crime and delinquency may be a consequence. Piaget reasoned that all children should experience four stages of mental development: sensorimotor, preoperational, concrete operations, and formal operations. In the sensorimotor stage, which lasts until the child is 2 years old, he or she learns the immediate environment and the use of reflexes. The preoperational stage occurs when the child is between the ages of 2 and 7. At this time, the child learns languages and how to draw and use other skills. The concrete operations stage takes place when the child is between the ages of 7 and 11. The child learns to think logically and also to use problem-solving techniques. The last stage, the formal operations stage, occurs when the child is between the ages of 11 and 15. During this time, the child learns abstract ideas. To Piaget, the lack of mental and moral development could lead to aggressive and criminal behavior. Stated another way, Piaget argued that some people who engage in crime and delinquent activities do so because they have not developed morally.

Developing the Theory of Moral Development

Lawrence Kohlberg, a psychologist, followed in the same tradition as Piaget, arguing that a lack of moral and mental development could contribute to crime and other antisocial behavior. However, Kohlberg's theory is somewhat different. For example, while Piaget concentrated on the progression of moral development, Kohlberg focused on the stages of development that would lead to the ability to tell the difference between right and wrong and making ethical decisions under complex circumstances. He argued that individuals pass through several stages of moral learning in order to make ethical decisions. According to Kohlberg's *Theory of Moral Development*, every individual experiences three stages: early stage, later stage, and final stage.

First, in the early stage of moral development, individuals learn moral reasoning that is solely related to punishment. Kohlberg believed that if punishment followed a certain behavior, individuals may avoid the behavior not because it is morally wrong to do so, but because it brings punishment. He argued that most criminals never progress beyond the early stage of moral development. The later stage of moral development occurs when adolescents realize that parents and societal rules are worth obeying, not only to avoid punishment, but because they are designed to achieve a higher objective for the good of the community. In following parental and societal rules, youths learn that others will respect them for complying with expected behaviors.

In Kohlberg's final stage, one understands that a universal morality supersedes the laws of society. This stage occurs during late adolescence and early adulthood, though Kohlberg argued that few ever reach it. In it, individuals obey rules or laws for the sake of complying with a "higher law." This stage of development can make those who reach it violate the law in some cases, especially when they perceive that the law is unfair. For example, many people objected to the Jim Crow laws that were used to promote and sustain divisiveness in many southern states in the 1950s and 1960s; such people could be said to have reached this final stage of moral development, which led them to protest these laws that they knew to be morally unjust. While Kohlberg's theory was an extension of the theory of moral development, it argued that not everyone in a society makes it through all the stages of moral development. Unfortunately, some people never move beyond the early stages and do not develop a moral conscience. These people will engage in a life of crime if they believe they will not be punished.

Intelligence and Crime Studies

For a long time, researchers attributed crime to the low intelligence (IQ) of offenders. Intelligence addresses an individual's ability to reason clearly, solve problems, comprehend, think in the abstract, learn from experience, and solve complex problems (Siegel, 2012). Many people believe that delinquents and criminals are intellectually inferior and are more likely than intelligent people to engage in crime. In fact, before the 1930s, the association between crime and IQ enjoyed widespread attention in academia. This was largely due to the low IQs found among prisoners and juveniles in correctional institutions. Consequently, offenders in these institutions were routinely used to measure IQs and test theories related to crime. After this period, however, interest in this type of research plummeted, largely because of its lack of methodological rigors until the 1970s, when research on intelligence and crime was revisited (Hirschi and Hindelang, 1977).

Researchers once again began asking if there is a relationship between one's level of intelligence and the propensity to engage in crime. A research study found that IQ is a more important factor than race and socioeconomic class when predicting crime and delinquency (Hirschi and Hindelang, 1977). While rejecting the argument that class bias exists in IQ tests, the researchers focused on the similarities found in criminals and noncriminals, especially as they relate to racial and socioeconomic categories. Despite this, are crimes committed by people who are less intelligent than those who are law-abiding? Does low intelligence drive some offenders to a life of crime?

These are important questions with serious policy implications. For example, if those among us with low intelligence are the only people to engage in crime, maybe the crime problem can be corrected through effective educational campaigns designed to remove the veil of ignorance that covers culturally and economically challenged communities. However, if crime is not a product of low intelligence and can, therefore, be found in other communities, maybe researchers should look elsewhere for criminogenic factors. The question of whether there is a relationship between intelligence and crime is a valid one, since crime statistics in the United States reveal that a disproportionate number of those who are arrested for crime are educationally weaker. Official statistics indicate that offenders in jails and prisons around the country have the equivalent of a 10th-grade education. Thus, the question becomes one of whether offenders commit crimes because of low intelligence, or because they have no marketable skills and have trouble finding legitimate employment (Tunnell, 2000). And, if a lack of intelligence causes crime, what explains crimes committed by educated people in positions of respectability, such as corporate, white-collar, healthcare, and governmental crime?

Why does research on intelligence and crime focus solely on the crimes committed by people who are poor and disenfranchised? Notwithstanding, there has been much research that has examined this relationship. For example, James Wilson and Richard Herrnstein's (1985) research finds support for the contention that parents can transmit personality traits and capacities to children. The researchers argue that while no one believes there are "crime genes," there are two major attributes that have a heritable base and that appear to influence criminal behavior. These are intelligence and temperament (makeup). Wilson and Herrnstein argue that hundreds of studies have found that the more genes people share, the more likely they are to resemble each other intellectually and temperamentally.

Researchers have long attributed crime to low intelligence (see Goring, 1913; Goddard, 1914; Eysenck, 1977; Herrnstein, 1983), arguing that offenders perform worse on standardized tests than noncriminals. Furthermore, Sheldon Glueck and Eleanor Glueck (1950) and Donald West and David Farrington (1973) argue that traits predicting involvement in crime are low intelligence, high activity level, and adventurousness. Likewise, Travis Gottfredson and Michael Hirschi (1990) argue that individuals with limited scholastic aptitude are likely to have less favorable long-term prospects, which can result in criminal behavior. Other studies (Hirschi and Hindelang, 1977; Wilson and Herrnstein, 1985) suggest that IQ is a stronger predictor of delinquency than either race or social class, and that the low intelligence found among minority populations is the major reason they commit more street crimes than their white counterparts. These research studies surmise that lower intelligence is linked to a lower ability to engage in moral reasoning and to resist immediate gratification. Therefore, IQ could increase the likelihood of criminal offending.

Some criminologists have discounted these correlations for various reasons (Nisbett, 2009). Some scholars have suggested that the correlation can be explained by the association between low socioeconomic status and crime. They contend that low socioeconomic status, rather than low IQ, may cause crime. They also question whether IQ tests accurately measure intelligence for the populations that are at greater risk for breaking the law. The low scores of offenders may be caused by the lack of cultural and economic resources that alienate inner-city residents from societal values, and not by low intelligence. Finally, it is important to recognize that the offenders who are a part of crime studies have been caught; perhaps those criminals who are able to avoid detection and apprehension have higher IQs.

Some people worry that any claim that biological factors may influence criminality is tantamount to saying that the higher crime rate of minorities compared with Caucasian Americans has a genetic basis. But no serious scholarship free from methodological problems exists that indicates such a conclusion (Nisbett, 2009; Herrnstein and Murray, 1994). Stated another way, in contemporary society, there are no definitive studies reporting that intelligence alone causes crime. In fact, studies reveal that previous IQ research was saturated with flaws and questions, and controversy still remains as to whether IQ tests measure intelligence or reflect white middle-class experiences. Some critics of this research argue that a cultural bias exists and that such tests may only reveal poor schooling, which enhances the chances of crime (Wilson and Herrnstein, 1985). However, current IQ studies are more carefully designed, but still disproportionately rely on samples of incarcerated adults and juveniles. Therefore, any meaningful discussions of IQ and crime must include an examination of personal as well as social factors that could influence crime and delinquency.

Crime and Human Nature

Wilson and Herrnstein (1985) argue that a link exists between an individual's decision to commit crime and biosocial factors such as low intelligence, mesomorph body type, having a criminal father, impulsivity, and having an autonomic nervous system that may drive one to commit crime. They contend the presence of these traits alone will not guarantee that a person will become a criminal; however, those who have them will be more likely to react to these stimuli by choosing crime over noncriminal behavior in certain situations. By considering social factors that could influence crime, Wilson and Herrnstein have moved the discussion beyond biology and intelligence as sole reasons to explain crime. For example, they argue that being reared in a destructive family environment, school failure, and associating with a deviant teenage subculture also have a powerful influence on criminality.

Race, IQ, and Crime

Similar to early findings on IQ and crime, contemporary research also suggests racial and ethnic differences exist in offending behavior. Studies have shown that minority groups are more likely to engage in delinquency and crime compared with their white counterparts. A number of studies support differential offending patterns across race, ethnicity, and IQ. For example, Richard Herrnstein and Charles Murray (1994) report that African Americans commit more street crimes than whites, and they have differential intelligence scores that are about 10 to 15 points lower than those of whites. Some experts believe the higher degree of participation in crime found among African Americans can naturally be attributed to lower intelligence.

If we accept that lower intelligence influences differential offending rates, many questions would still be left unanswered. For example, why do males disproportionately engage in crime compared with females? Why does crime differ with respect to time, season, and weather? Why is crime unequally distributed regionally, as revealed by every source of data collection, including the Uniform Crime Reports (UCR), the National Crime Victimization Survey (NCVS), and self-report surveys (SRSs)? Because this research is controversial, many researchers have a difficult time readily accepting such studies as valid measures of crime, reasoning that they discount social factors that may influence crime. If we accept the race, IQ, and crime nexus, there is little need to address the social inequities or structural problems that may influence and reduce crime. Hence, we must be cautious in this area.

Problems with Biological Research

Researchers in general, but criminologists in particular, have taken great care not to rush to judgment by quickly establishing a link between crime and biology. To do so would essentially endorse the notion that certain segments of the population have criminogenic genes and tendencies that may drive them to a life of crime and delinquency. Stated another way, to draw this conclusion would be tantamount to agreeing that there are people in society who are biologically different from their law-abiding counterparts and that these people commit crimes not because they choose to, but because they are who they are. This position would negate any responsibility attached to the behaviors they commit. Moreover, the biological explanation for crime would have devastating effects on groups of offenders, especially those who are most often represented in official crime statistics and arrests. While criminologists are hopeful about the potential that biological research holds, many of its past problems remain unresolved. For example, critics of the biology, crime, and research nexus have brought up the issues of: (1) diversity of types of crime, (2) group rate differences, (3) methodological flaws, and (4) social policy implications.

Diversity of Types of Crime

If we believe in the existence of a relationship between biology and crime, it presupposes that everyone who commits a crime is biologically different from their law-abiding counterpart. Since biocriminologists argue that all criminals are predisposed to crime, this would require that social scientists remain objective and vigilant in their study of offenders. Thus, they must closely examine all offenders, including those who engage in index, white-collar, corporate, organized, computer, governmental, political, and health-care crimes, to determine if they have biological differences from nonoffenders. There should be no differential treatment given to any group of offenders. Unfortunately, most research that supports a link between biology and crime has examined the behaviors only of offenders who engage in index or violent crimes. This is revealed in research that relies on samples of inmates in jails, prisons, and juvenile detention centers. While these offenders and their crimes are scrutinized and studied, little if any effort is made at linking the criminals involved in other types of crime with biological analysis. In fact, such research is absent from criminological analysis. To suggest that biology can explain or predict crime without examining all types of crime is irresponsible and arguably ignores the true sources or causes of crime and delinquency.

Group Rate Differences

As mentioned earlier, the criminal justice system devotes an overwhelming amount of attention to crimes committed by certain segments of the population. To some, it may appear that crime reporting is treated in a disparate manner. For example, the major crime reports, such as the UCR, SRSs, and the NCVS, indicate that poor segments of the community and population are responsible for a disproportionate number of index crimes committed on a yearly basis. One could infer from these data that poor people commit more crime than other segments in society. Critics often argue that an abundance of law enforcement resources are devoted to collecting UCR data, and fewer resources are devoted to detecting and preventing crimes committed by offenders from other segments of society (Barkan, 2012). Despite this, minority communities are not relegated to the lower class. Instead, minority communities are found in the upper and middle, as well as the lower, classes. Researchers who use the crime rates of the poor to infer that they describe all minorities without considering social class differences make an ecological fallacy.

Methodological Flaws

As a general rule, mistakes made in data collection affect the findings in a study. Studies that fail to adhere to the rigors of scientific research produce findings that are invalid. Typically, methodological problems can be found in how a study population is targeted, sampling selection, and data analysis. For example, most biocriminological research since the 19th century has been compromised due to methodological problems, especially where sampling is concerned. Researchers have overrelied on sampling offenders in juvenile detention facilities as well as adult correctional institutions. Moreover, these researchers have also consistently failed to use or provide a representative control group. As revealed, earlier biocriminological research failed to use comparison groups in experimental designs. In many cases, biological research has somehow advanced in the name of science, but in many cases, it has typically relied on convenience or nonrepresentative samples that failed to approximate the population. Therefore, any research conclusions derived from such studies should be accepted with caution since they lack the methodological rigors needed to make valid inferences or generalizations to the broader population.

Social Policy Implications

If we believe that certain individuals engage in crime for biological reasons, how does society prevent criminal behavior? One viable, though extreme, strategy is to isolate or sterilize (castrate) criminal offenders, or subject them to medical procedures designed to change them from being criminal to law-abiding. Such practices may be the only way to either contain or remove the criminogenic genes that could otherwise be transmitted to other generations. These extreme practices could be the basis for calling for eugenics. This same ideology proved dangerous in Nazi Germany in World War II when German citizens with mental retardation and physical disabilities were sterilized to prevent them from producing what many scientists and leaders argued were inferior offspring. At the same time, the need to have "perfect" people manifested in the extermination of millions of Jews, Gypsies, homosexuals, and others because they were viewed as biologically different. In the United States, segregation was based on perceived biological differences and resulted in unequal treatment and the denial of due process rights to many Americans of color (Mangels, 2000). Furthermore, at least 64,000 Americans were sterilized between 1911 and 1930 in efforts to control alcoholism, criminality, and sodomy (Lilly, Cullen, and Ball, 1989).

Similar to the past, contemporary biocriminological research focuses solely on crimes committed by marginal groups in general and street crime in particular. Ignored in these analyses are crimes committed by offenders with wealth, power, and influence. Critics argue that from such a practice, a one-sided, distorted picture of crime and criminals emerges that excludes white-collar and corporate offenders, but paints the face of biological inferiority on the poor and disadvantaged members of society. Such neglect on the part of criminologists who are disproportionately white and middle-class gives the impression of classism as well as racism (Mangels, 2000). Unfortunately, some scholars believe that such neglect has led to racial profiling in contemporary times, whereby blacks, Latinos, and other minorities are singled out by police officers for questioning even when the officers lack probable cause to believe that the suspects have engaged in any wrongdoing. Those who still view merit in biological research have crafted their discussion so as not to rely on biology alone, but now include a discussion of the social environment. They advocate sociobiological explanations of crime.

Summary

The roots of trait theories date back to the 19th century, beginning with the contributions of the positivistic school of criminology. Inspired by the scientific method, this school emphasized that the cause of delinquency and crime was attributed to biology, psychology, and the social environment. More important, however, is that for the first time, science was used to measure deviant and criminal behavior. The first positivists used phrenology to explain criminal behavior, eventually leading to Lombroso's work on the atavistic anomaly. Though Lombroso's work on the "born criminal" was later dismissed, other researchers continued to advance the biology and crime movement. Their research was accepted in European countries as well as the United States.

While today most criminologists reject the idea of biology as the sole cause of crime, some biocriminologists examine biology and other factors that include, but are not limited to, diet and nutrition, neurochemical mechanisms, social environment, temperament, and intelligence. These researchers argue that to reduce crime, society must change the offender. They place little consideration on the social factors that may produce crime and delinquency.

Psychological explanations in the 19th century argued that offenders were mentally flawed or diseased of the mind. Some early explanations came from psychoanalytic theory, which believed that psychological problems occurred because of conflict between a child and his or her parents. Others claimed that offenders lacked proper moral development or had low intelligence. The last area addressed by early positivists was the social environment and its impact on the decision to engage in crime and delinquency.

Simply put, environmental factors, including social forces that individuals are confronted with in their immediate surroundings or community, can influence one's behavior. However, biological and psychological studies have historically suffered from methodological flaws that have rendered their finding suspicious, so any results from these studies should be accepted with caution.

Shortcomings of the Theories

1. Positivistic explanations do not consider offender choice and instead hold that people are predestined to be criminals.

2. Early positivism suffered from a lack of methodological rigor, including the use of small samples and no comparison groups.

3. Early positivistic research led to negative or even dangerous policy recommendations that included segregation, institutionalization, and sterilization to prevent criminals from reproducing or procreating inferior offspring.

4. Since biocriminological explanations are reserved for street crime instead of white-collar or corporate crime, they appear to be racially and culturally insensitive.

Discussion Questions

1. Which body type in William Sheldon's somatology is more likely to engage in crime?

2. What is the relationship between heredity and crime?

3. What is the relationship between IQ, delinquency, and crime?

4. What is the most important element found in the psychoanalytic theory?

5. How do neurochemical mechanisms explain behavior that can lead to violent and aggressive behavior?

6. What are the methodological problems found in biological and psychological research?

References

Barkan, S. E. (2012). *Criminology: A Sociological Understanding* (5th ed.). New York, NY: Prentice-Hall.

Bennett, W., Dilulio, J., and Walters, J. (1996). *Body Count: Moral Poverty and How to Win America's War Against Crime and Drugs*. New York, NY: Simon & Schuster.

Bernard, T. J., Snipes, J. B., and Gerould, A. L. (2009). *Vold's Theoretical Criminology*. New York, NY: Oxford University Press.

Boudreau, A., and Scott, Z. (2008, February 20). Girlfriend: Shooter Was Taking Cocktail of Three Drugs. *CNN.com*. Available at http://www.cnn.com/2008/CRIME/02/20/shooter.girlfriend /index.html?iref=topnews.

Craft, M. (1985). The Current Status of X-Y and X-Y Syndromes: A Review of Treatment Implications. In F. H. Marsh and J. Katz (Eds.), *Biology, Crime and Ethics: A Study of Biological Explanation for Criminal Behavior* (pp. 113–15). Cincinnati, OH: Anderson.

Curran, D. J., and Renzetti, C. M. (2001). *Theories of Crime*. Boston, MA: Allyn and Bacon.

Driver, E. D. (1957). Pioneers in Criminology XIV: Charles Buckman Goring. *Journal of Criminal Law and Criminology, 47*(5), 1–12.

Dugdale, R. L. (1877). *The Jukes*. New York, NY: Putnam.

Eysenck, H. (1977). *Crime and Personality* (Rev. ed.). London: Paladin.

Ferri, E. (1881/1917). *Criminal Sociology*. Trans. Joseph Killey and John Lisle. Boston, MA: Little, Brown.

Freud, A. (1966). *The Ego and the Mechanisms of Defense* (Rev. ed.). New York, NY: International Universities Press.

Garofalo, R. (1885/1914). *Criminology*. Trans. Robert W. Millar. Boston, MA: Little, Brown.

Glueck, S., and Glueck, E. (1950). *Unraveling Juvenile Delinquency*. Cambridge, MA: Harvard University Press.

Goddard, H. H. (1914). *Feeble-Mindedness: Its Causes and Consequences*. New York, NY: Macmillan.

Golden, D. (2007, August 20). From Disturbed High Schooler to College Killer. *Wall Street Journal*. Available at http://online.wsj.com/news/articles/SB118756463647202374.

Goring, C. (1913). *The English Convict* (Rev. ed.). London: His Majesty's Stationery Office.

Gottfredson, M., and Hirschi, T. (1990). *A General Theory of Crime*. Stanford, CA: Stanford University Press.

Herring, C. (2009, December 5). Report Faults Virginia Tech in Shooting. *Wall Street Journal*.

Herrnstein, R. (1983). Some Criminogenic Traits of Offenders. In J. Q. Wilson (Ed.), *Crime and Public Policy* (pp. 31–52). San Francisco, CA: Institute for Contemporary Studies.

Herrnstein, R., and Murray, C. (1994). *The Bell Curve: Intelligence and Class Structure in American Life*. New York: Free Press.

Hirschi, T., and Hindelang, M. L. (1977). Intelligence and Delinquency: A Revisionist View. *American Sociological Review, 42,* 571–87.

Hooton, E. A. (1926). Methods of Racial Analysis. *Science, 63*(1621), 75–81.

Hooton, E. A. (1939). *Crime and the Man*. Cambridge, MA: Harvard University Press.

Hooton, E. A. (1940). *Why Men Behave Like Apes and Vice Versa*. Princeton, NJ: Princeton University Press.

Hutchings, B., and Mednick, S. (1977). Criminality in Adoptees and Their Adoptive and Biological Parents: A Pilot Study. In S. Mednick and K. O. Christiansen (Eds.), *Biosocial Basis of Criminal Behavior* (pp. 127–43). New York, NY: Gardner.

Jacobs, P. A., Brunton, M., Melville, M. M., Brittain, R. P., and McClemert, W. F. (1965). Aggressive Behavior, Mental Subnormality and the X-Y Males. *Nature, 208,* 1351–52.

Jacoby, J. E. (1979). *Classics of Criminology*. Prospect Heights, IL: Waveland Press.

Katz, J., and Chambliss, W. J. (1995). Biology and Crime. In J. F. Sheley (Ed.), *Criminology: A Contemporary Handbook* (pp. 275–303). Belmont, CA: Wadsworth.

Lilly, J. R., Cullen, F. T., and Ball, R. A. (1989). *Criminological Theory: Context and Consequences*. Newbury Park, CA: Sage.

Lombroso, C. (1911). *Criminal Man*. Montclair, NJ: Patterson-Smith.

Lombroso-Ferrero, G. (1911). *Criminal Man, According to the Classification of Cesare Lombroso*. New York, NY: G. P. Putnam's Sons.

Mangels, N. J. (2000). Latent Biases in Biocriminological Research. *Justice Professional, 18,* 105–23.

Martinez, M. (2012, June 27). Tests in Cannibalism Case: Zombie-Like Attacker Used Pot, Not "Bath Salts." *CNN.com*. Available at http://www.cnn.com/2012/06/27/us/florida-cannibal-attack.

Mednick, S. A., and Christiansen, K. O. (1977). *Biosocial Bases in Criminal Behavior*. New York, NY: Gardner Press.

Moffitt, T. E., Brammer, G. L., Caspi, A., Fawcett, J.P.,Raleigh, `M., Yuwiler, A., and Silva, P.A. (1998). "Whole Blood Serotonin Relates to Violence in Epidemiological Study." *Biological Psychiatry, 43*:447–457.

Moyer, K. E. (1976). *The Psychology of Aggression*. New York, NY: Harper & Row.

Nisbett, R. E. (2009). *Intelligence and How to Get It: Why Schools and Cultures Count*. New York, NY: W. W. Norton.

Nizza, M. (2008, February 15). Gunman Was Once "Revered" on Campus. *New York Times*. Available at http://www.nytimes.com/2008/02/15/us/15cnd-shoot.html?_r=0.

Nye, R. D. (1996). *Three Psychologies: Perspectives from Freud, Skinner, and Rogers*. New York, NY: Brooks/Cole.

Rowe, D. C. (1986). Genetics and Environmental Components of Antisocial Behaviors: A Study of 265 Twin Pairs. *Criminology, 24,* 513–32.

Schauss, A. (1981). *Diet, Crime and Delinquency: A New Breakthrough to Crime Control.* Berkeley, CA: Parker House.

Sheldon, W. (1949). *The Varieties of Delinquent Youth.* New York, NY: Harper and Row.

Siegel, L. (2000). *Criminology* (7th ed.). Belmont, CA: Wadsworth/Thompson Learning.

Siegel, L. (2012). *Criminology* (11th ed.). Belmont, CA: Wadsworth/Thompson Learning.

Thompson, D. (2013, May 28). Baby Killed in Microwave: Ka Yang, California Woman, Arrested. *HuffingtonPost.com.* Available at http://www.huffingtonpost.com/2011/06/22/baby-killed-in-microwave-_n_882167.html.

Tunnell, K. D. (2000). *Living Off Crime.* Chicago, IL: Burnham.

Wallman, J. (1999). Serotonin and Impulsive Aggression: Not So Fast. *HFG Review, 3,* 21–24.

West, D., and Farrington, D. (1973). *Who Becomes Delinquent?* London: Heinemann.

Wilson, J. Q., and Herrnstein, R. L. (1985). *Crime and Human Nature: The Definitive Study of the Causes of Crime.* New York, NY: Simon and Schuster.

Wolfgang, M. E. (1973). Cesare Lombroso (1835–1909). In H. Mannheim (Ed.), *Pioneers in Criminology* (2nd ed.) (pp. 232–91). Montclair, NJ: Patterson-Smith.

Chapter 6

Social Structure Theories: Emphasis on the Social Structure

Chapter Outline

- Development of Sociological Criminology
- Socioeconomic Structure and Crime
- Social Structure Theories
- The American Dream and Strain Theory
- Subcultural (Cultural Deviance) Theories
- Differential Opportunity Theory
- Summary
- Shortcomings of the Theories
- Discussion Questions

gangs—Groups of people with an identifiable organizational structure that come together to pursue their economic interests. They have identifiable colors and symbols, and occupy an area of a city that is referred to as their turf. They typically engage in criminal activities, such as selling drugs, engaging in prostitution, and dealing in stolen merchandise.

A recent report from the National Youth Gang Survey Analysis reveals that gang violence in general, and gang homicides in particular, are on the rise in the United States. In fact, this report finds that between 2007 and 2011, an estimated 1,900 homicides were reported as gang-related, and while **gangs** are found in almost every American city (Egley and Ritz, 2006), gang homicides are significantly concentrated in major cities such as Chicago, Los Angeles, New York, and St. Louis (National Gang Center, 2013). For example, in Chicago, there were about 7,000 more gang-related arrests in 2012 than in 2011. The report goes on to say that many of the arrests were for gang members' involvement in murder (News One for Black America, 2012). Today, experts estimate that there are more than 30,000 gang members in the United States who are heavily armed, extremely dangerous, and typically use semiautomatic weapons to commit crime, engage in violent retaliations against rival gangs, and promote their economic interests in the drug trade. Research also shows that unlike their counterparts, gang members are more likely to use weapons to commit violent crimes (Egley and Ritz, 2006). Research conducted by Klein and Maxson (2006) and the National Gang Intelligence Center (2010) also shows that despite the drug war of the 1980s that resulted in many gang leaders being sent to prison for a long time, the American gang problem has not abated. It remains a major concern for law enforcement officers, politicians, community residents, and academics.

Criminologists are not surprised that gangs emerge and sustain themselves in conditions that are found in impoverished, lower-class, and mostly inner-city areas (Siegel, 2012). In fact, gang members and their recruits are typically from poor, isolated, and single-parent families. They also suffer from a lack of family support and see few, if any, prospects for a bright future. Gangs often provide their members with a level of protection and opportunities that they otherwise would not have, helping them to avoid feelings of helplessness and hopelessness. Like other members of society, poor residents in urban areas desire the "**American Dream**," and gang members believe that the gang and its activities will provide them a chance to acquire the economic materials associated with being successful in America.

> **American Dream**—A term that refers to both a cultural goal and process in American society. As a goal, it is concerned with achieving abundant economic wealth or material goods and services. As a process, it entails being socialized into wanting to achieve un-limited monetary success and believing that it is attainable.

The relationship between the effects of living in a poor social environment and crime is well documented in the criminological literature (Siegel, 2012; Barkan, 2006; Messner and Rosenfeld, 2007; Anderson, 1999). Most criminologists believe that "bad places" rather than "bad people" are responsible for crime and the continuation of such behavior. Criminologists often postulate that because of their station in life, the poor are relegated to living in the worst areas that a city has to offer. The poor also face limited life opportunities and experiences that may require developing different survival skills (Anderson, 1999). They typically lack social support and access to material and economic resources that are readily available to more affluent members of society. This view holds that rather than individual traits accounting for offending behavior, crime and delinquency can be more accurately explained by the negative social forces that may overwhelmingly affect how the poor are reared and socialized. Moreover, some criminologists believe that these social forces are so compelling that they may actually negate some individuals' decision to engage in crime and delinquency (Siegel, 2012; Anderson, 1999). In his book *Code of the Street*, Elijah Anderson (1999) captures the reality best when he writes that life in the inner city is highly regulated by informal acts of respect or deference that residents are able to command from each other. To these residents, respect is essential to helping one negotiate social capital that is used as currency to acquire what one needs when legitimate opportunities are not available. Having respect is status-conferring, provides protection for residents who either do not trust or cannot depend on police for help, and allows one to possess honor on the streets. However, in middle-class areas, residents are typically provided legitimate resources to pursue their goals or to resist the lure of criminal behavior. This is not so in poor areas. Because of this, criminologists argue that we should focus on destructive social forces found in certain areas of the social structure to determine how they influence crime and delinquency.

Development of Sociological Criminology

In addition to studying biological and psychological explanations, 19th-century positivists also examined the social environment for answers to the crime problem. During this period, sociology emerged as an academic discipline providing scientists with the opportunity to study how society in general and social forces in particular could influence behavior. Scholars attributed the emergence of sociology, in part, to the development of science, and the changes that were occurring in society. Some of these included major changes to the mode of production, division of labor, population growth, and other evolutionary changes. More specifically, history shows that in 1700, there were a recorded 600 million people, but by 1800, the population had exploded to 900 million people.

These expansions and population shifts were pronounced in emerging cities that were being transformed by industrialization. Major population shifts occurred in Manchester, England, and Glasgow, Scotland, from 1760 and 1850 that radically changed the social fabric of Manchester from 12,000 people to 400,000 and Glasgow from 30,000 people to 300,000 (Siegel, 2012). These were not the only places that were being affected by evolutionary changes that were occurring. Historians report that during the 19th century, society was being transformed from primarily agricultural to industrialized. Because of this, people were leaving rural areas and migrating to cities in search of factory work. Cities swelled with residents. Positivists seized the opportunity to use science to observe and measure how these changes were impacting behavior.

Adolf Quetelet (1796-1874) and Émile Durkheim (1857-1917)

Adolf Quetelet, a Belgium mathematician, was one of the founders of the Cartographic School of Criminology. He was one of the first people to objectively apply mathematical techniques to explain the impact social forces had on the crime rate. Many scholars credit his early efforts with influencing the current-day Uniform Crime

Quetelet, Adolf—Belgian mathematician who applied mathematics to the study of crime. He examined the role that social forces play in influencing the crime rate. He argued that there is a correlation between crime and season, climate, population density, and alcohol.

Reports (UCR). Quetelet's contribution to crime is well documented. He argued that social forces influence the occasion of crime (Quetelet, 1831/1984). His research focused on the relationships between age, race, gender, and the geographical distribution of crime. He reported that social forces are related to crime. For example, he argued that crime increases and decreases during certain seasons of the year, with more crime occurring during the warmer months. He also drew a relationship between population density and crime (Quetelet, 1831/1984). Much of this information is found in the present-day UCR, and these variables still remain dominant in contemporary research.

> **Durkheim, Émile**—Considered, with August Comte, to be the founder of sociology.

Émile Durkheim (another founder of sociology) made great contributions to the study of crime. He advanced the argument that social forces in the environment cause some people to engage in deviant and criminal behavior. Durkheim argued that when a society experiences rapid social change (brought on by war, recession, or economic growth), the by-product can be crime and deviant behavior. Durkheim drew from his own social experiences. The 19th century was a period of conflict generated by the French Revolution of 1789 and by the rapid industrialization of French society (Lilly, Cullen, and Ball, 1995; Durkheim, 1895/1982). As a result, Durkheim witnessed the transformation of France from a feudal society to one embracing industrial capitalism.

While explaining the evolution of society, Durkheim argued that society is never stable, but is always in a state of evolution. He saw society constantly advancing from the remedial (mechanical) to the advanced (organic). During the evolution from feudalism to capitalism, he witnessed rural farmers uprooting and moving to developing urban areas in search of greater economic opportunities that were promised by industrialization (Durkheim, 1893/1933). Durkheim explained that in rural areas, life was easy. The division of labor was simple, and people were bonded by shared values, customs, and traditions. In these areas, life was regulated by informalities (Siegel, 2000).

> **social solidarity**—That which binds people and communities together.
>
> **mechanical society**—Society characterized by remedial divisions of labor. It is commonly a close-knit community that is not technologically developed and where informalities govern all aspects of social life.
>
> **organic society**—Characterized as being technologically advanced with a sophisticated division or labor. In these types of societies, formal laws and regulations govern all aspects of social life.

To the extent that a particular society is mechanical, its solidarity would come from the pressure of uniformity exerted against diversity. In contrast, urban life was complex. The division of labor was sophisticated, and people needed formal rules and laws to regulate behavior. Furthermore, since there was great diversity in urban areas, people did not share the same beliefs, values, customs, and traditions. The law performed a major role in maintaining the **social solidarity** of each of these two types of societies. For example, in **mechanical societies**, the law functioned to enforce the uniformity of the members of a given social group, and thus was oriented toward repressing any deviation from the group's norms. However, in **organic societies**, the law regulated the interactions of various parts of society and provided restitution in cases of wrongful transactions. As the society evolved toward an organic form, a pathological state called **anomie** could emerge. When this occurred, social maladies, including crime, could be an outcome (Jacoby, 1979).

> **anomie**—A state of normlessness or deregulation brought on by rapid social change. Émile Durkheim used the term to explain how a breakdown or collapse in collective normative behavior could cause deviant and criminal behavior.

Durkheim advanced the idea that crime is a normal occurrence (Durkheim, 1895/1982). For example, population density could cause people to withdraw from social activities and become isolated from others. This low degree of social integration not only could cause crime and delinquency, but it could lead some to commit suicide (Durkheim, 1897/1951). Durkheim called this condition anomie, or deregulation. This condition occurs when people do not know which behaviors are normative or when the collective norms of a society have broken down. Though a given behavior may have been appropriate in one social setting or context (the rural countryside), it does not mean that the same behavior would be appropriate in another context (an urban area). Durkheim argued that when society experiences rapid social changes caused by war, technology, depression, recession, or economic explosion, crime and deviant behaviors are likely to follow. He attributed delinquency, crime, and suicide to social forces or changes within the social structure (Durkheim, 1897/1951). Despite this, he argued that society has to punish law violators to make others aware that law violations are unacceptable behavior. At the same time, he argued that society must reward conforming behavior in order to maintain the existing arrangement; otherwise, there would be no reason or incentive to conform (Jacoby, 1979).

Durkheim, a structural functionalist, argued that crime serves a positive function, except when it is excessive. He argued that crime is good, healthy, and normal for society. According to Durkheim, crime has always been a part of society. In response to the problem of crime, law-abiding people increase their solidarity and join together to fight crime and deviance. Durkheim argued that crime can bring people together and make them recognize the interests they have in common, such as maintaining the existence of a civil society. Crime also serves to demonstrate when the social structure is too rigid. This, Durkheim argued, would always indicate the need for social change. Further, he argued that crime tests the moral tolerance or moral boundaries of society. Crime serves as a measure of what society is willing to accept or reject as morally correct or reprehensible (Jacoby, 1979).

The Chicago School: Toward a Social Ecology of Crime

Before the contributions of the sociologists at the University of Chicago, criminology was largely influenced by the Germans, Italians, and British. The many social problems that resulted from economic growth and expansion in the United States offered American sociologists an opportunity to address the causes of criminal behavior and advance the credibility of sociology as an academic discipline. American criminologists rejected

> **Chicago School**—Sociologists at the University of Chicago who studied crime in the city in its natural environment. They were instrumental in shifting the focus of criminological studies from the Germans and Italians and giving sociology in the United States more credibility by discussing the social ecology of crime. This school successfully moved away from "armchair" theorizing and embarked on the use of statistics and empirical observations by using anthropological techniques.

arguments of biology and feeblemindedness, and instead embraced environmental factors as a major cause of crime and deviant behavior.

The sociologists at the university referred to themselves as the **Chicago School**. They approached the study of crime in a new way by largely relying on methodological techniques that were common to anthropology and applied them to the study of crime. Instead of engaging in armchair theorizing about crime, they left the "ivory tower" of academia. They went into the social environment of the subjects of their studies and interacted with them to discover what crime and deviance actually meant to the participants. In addition, they used case history techniques while conducting some of their studies. This allowed them to examine the subjects for extended periods of time to fully understand the motivation and cause of criminal behavior. These techniques had never been used before in America to study crime and delinquency. The Chicago School created a tradition of study that remains dominant today.

Those who worked in the social sciences during the early 20th century experienced many of the rapid social changes that were reported and discussed by Durkheim. For example, they saw the development of cities, rapid industrialization, mass immigration and migration, the effects of World War I, Prohibition, and the Great Depression. They witnessed how these changes affected the social fabric of life in America. Though these changes were being made in nearly every major city, sociologists at the University of Chicago used that city as their laboratory to find answers to many of the social problems that emerged during this growing period (Lilly, Cullen, and Ball, 1995; Akers, 1994; Williams and McShane, 1998).

Chicago was a typical small rural community until it experienced rapid social changes in the early 1880s. In the process of becoming industrialized, Chicago provided newcomers with an abundance of canal work and inexpensive landownership. Because of this, many unskilled workers moved to Chicago to contribute to its industrial growth. Chicago's small population was drastically expanded from 1898 to 1930 (Williams and McShane, 1998). Immigrants from Europe and black migrants from the southern states (fleeing racial intolerance and violence) flocked to Chicago and transformed the small-town community into a complex city saturated with diversity. In 1880, Chicago had 4,100 residents, and by 1910, it had over two million residents (Lilly, Cullen, and Ball, 1995). However, when industrialization reached its limits and unskilled laborers were replaced by emerging technologies, economic opportunities dissipated. The by-product was that many communities were hit with populations of homeless men and women, and a host of social problems that ranged from inadequate housing and sanitation to juvenile gangs and vice (Siegel, 2000).

Unfortunately, many of the immigrants and migrants who had come to Chicago in search of a better life and greater opportunities found no help or consolation in their time of economic hardship. They had no one to turn to for relief or refuge. As a result, thousands of unemployed people became transients. Many social work organizations and relief programs were created between the 1920s and 1930s to assist the destitute (Whitehead and Lab, 1990; Trojanowicz and Morash, 1987; Cavan, 1969). These programs were pioneered by the middle class and were designed to properly socialize immigrants and migrant children and prevent them from becoming wards of the state. The programs focused specifically on training and rehabilitating those who were homeless and unemployed. While these humanitarian programs emerged to assist paupers, at the same time, slums were saturated with crime and delinquency. Again, these areas were disproportionately populated by poor immigrants and migrants. As a result, the sociologists at the University of Chicago seized the opportunity to study the vast amounts of crime, delinquency, and other social problems that had infiltrated the once small, rural community of Chicago.

The Five Concentric Circles

The Chicago School sociologists capitalized on problems that emerged in the city of Chicago. They tested the assumptions of past theories and formulated new theories regarding crime causation. Under the leadership of sociologists **Robert Park** and **Ernest Burgess**, the university's sociology department advanced the idea of the **social ecology of crime.** Park and Burgess believed that cities do not merely grow at their edges, but expand and radically form their centers in patterns of concentric circles, each moving gradually outward. They proposed a map that contained zones encompassing the entire city. They called the zones the **five concentric circles**. These circles, or zones, were a geographical distribution of every area in the city (Palen, 1981).

Park and Burgess were of the opinion that the five concentric circles model could provide a framework for understanding the root causes of crime (Gibbons, 1979; Pfohl, 1985). They argued that neighborhood organizations were instrumental in preventing or encouraging crime and delinquency (Burgess, 1926; Park, 1936). They examined how cities grow over time and rejected the notion that they grow haphazardly, arguing instead that there are social patterns associated with urban development (Park and Burgess, 1924). Of the two scholars, Burgess maintained that cities grow radically in a series of concentric

Park, Robert—A sociologist who shaped the Chicago School, symbolic interactionism, and much of sociology. He advocated going into the field, or the "real world," and making observations and analyses of social life. This would become the hallmark of the Chicago School. He was also one of the developers of the five concentric circles.

Burgess, Ernest—A sociologist at the University of Chicago who helped to design the five concentric circles.

social ecology—Examines the influence that one's community or neighborhood has on the behavior of crime. The argument is that one's neighborhood and surroundings might propel one into a life of crime.

five concentric circles—A layout of the city of Chicago that divided the community into different sections, as delineated by Robert Park and Ernest Burgess; also referred to as zone maps.

zones or rings (Burgess, 1926; Palen, 1981). He later argued that competition determines how people are distributed within these zones (Burgess, 1926). In a stratified society, a person's social class and the amount of resources he or she has accumulated determine in which area he or she can afford to live. The characteristics of a community are determined by the economic well-being of its residents. Park and Burgess delineated the five concentric circles into zones.

Figure 6.1 shows the five concentric circles. Zone One was labeled the Central Business District (CBD), or loop area. It contained commercial enterprises and provided access to transportation, such as railroads and waterways. It was also the place where one could find the cheapest rental property. This was extremely attractive to newly arrived immigrants and migrants who were destitute. Zones in which it was more expensive to reside were located away from the city and factories (Lilly, Cullen, and Ball, 1995). Despite this, Zone One constantly invaded Zone Two. Zone Two was called the "Zone in Transition." It was the oldest area in town and had existed before industrialized growth began. This zone was an area of concern, because many social problems were found there. The area was characterized by physical deterioration and tenements that were often built next to polluting factories. The quality of residential life was poor in the area, because businesses and factories were constantly built at the expense of any sense of community that may

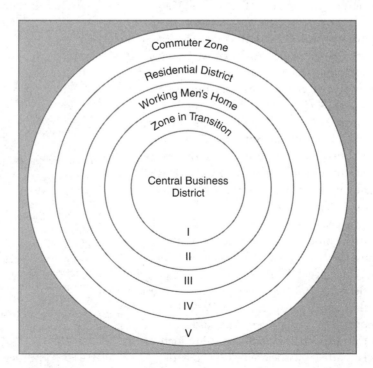

Figure 6.1 The Five Concentric Circles
Data from: Park, R., Burgess, E.W., and McKenzie, R. D. (1925). *The City*. Chicago: University of Chicago Press.

have existed. This occurred because the residents who lived in Zone Two were poor and had no social, political, or economic power to prevent the constant flow of construction. Furthermore, they were too poor to live anywhere else. Scholars contend that since Zone Two was being pushed outward into Zone Three, this led to the displacement of residents. The owners of the businesses and factories did not live in the second zone, but instead many lived in what would be considered by today's standards as the suburbs.

Zone Three was referred to as the "Working Men's Home" and was occupied by those who had saved enough money to escape the deteriorating conditions in the second zone. Zone Four was the Residential District. It was occupied by single-family houses and provided expensive apartments. Zone Five represented the suburban areas and satellite cities. It was referred to as the Commuter Zone. Though on the map each zone appeared to be clearly defined, setting established boundaries, the reality was different since each zone encroached upon or radiated into the other zones. Some contend the zones were characterized by succession, dominance, and invasion into others' territory (Williams and McShane, 1999). This created major concerns, because when one location invaded another, the established relationship that held communities together was destroyed. New residents had not yet established meaningful bonds with older residents, nor had new arrivals been present long enough to invest in the community upkeep. There were also claims that new residents could not identify with the ideas and values shared by older residents. As a result, many communities faced decline because older residents were not willing to establish relationships with new residents, especially if they were seen as inferior. During this time, racial prejudice and discrimination was widespread even among members of the same race and ethnic group (Lilly, Cullen, and Ball, 1995). Discrimination affected mostly the new waves of immigrants and southern blacks. Immigrants, though, had greater mobility than blacks. They could assimilate into the **dominant culture** with relative ease. One by-product of zone movement was that many neighborhoods either lost or never acquired the ability to control their youth.

Culture Conflict

The work of **Thorsten Sellin** on **culture conflict** also influenced the sociologists at the University of Chicago. According to Sellin, there are two types of culture conflict, primary and secondary. Primary conflict occurs when immigrants (and to a lesser degree, migrants) are introduced into a new culture, especially if the new culture conflicts with that to which the new arrivals are accustomed (Sellin, 1938). For example, many Europeans brought with them "old world" traditions and customs that were applicable in their former culture, but were illegal in America. In fact, many came into direct violation with American

dominant culture—The conventional value system of a given society.

Sellin, Thorsten—Contributor to studies on the social ecology of crime who posited the existence of culture conflict. He argued that diversity brings with it different cultural values, traditions, and mores that sometimes clash with those of the dominant culture. He also argued that cultural conflict is primary and secondary in nature, and that it could lead to the formation of gangs.

culture conflict—A state in which people of different cultural backgrounds clash with one another. This typically occurs when one cultural group is subjected to the culture of another group.

law. Sellin provides an example that highlights this point. There were reported instances in which immigrant girls were seduced by American boys and were seen by their parents as tainted or dishonored. Back in the "old world," the honorable way to respond to such a violation would be to kill the seducer. When immigrant fathers applied this practice in America, many could not comprehend that they had violated American law.

Secondary culture conflict occurred when subcultures were created (Sellin, 1938). Subcultures emerged in the form of gangs in the late 1920s (Thrasher, 1928; Jankowski, 1991; Yablonsky, 1966; Knox, 1993; Block and Niederhoffer, 1958; Short and Strodtbeck, 1965; Spergel, 1967). On the one hand, scholars contend that cultures of organized gangs emerged as a response to the lack of legitimate economic opportunities provided to immigrants. Gangs provided minorities who faced discrimination, especially during harsh economic times, a chance for economic survival. The illegitimate structures found in vice (gambling, prostitution, protection, alcohol) offered those willing to participate in such activities economic wealth that they could not otherwise have attained because of **social stratification**. Moreover, gangs served as support groups for immigrants, who in many cases were seen as inferior (Williams and McShane, 1998). Cultural conflict was saturated in the Zone of Transition, because newly arrived immigrants and migrants settled in the area. Here one could find the ghetto, Chinatown, Little Sicily, and other cultural neighborhoods. These groups lived in close physical proximity to each other with their many cultural differences.

> **social stratification**—The division in society whereby people are ranked or characterized based on the amount of income or economic buying power that they have.

Symbolic Interaction

> **symbolic interactionism**—A theory by Robert Herbert Mead, Charles Horton Cooley, and William Thomas arguing that people interact with each other and communicate both verbally and symbolically. Through a process of communication, people come to develop an identity based on the group's expectations of them. They also learn about the people with whom they interact, and their identity is basically created and sustained by group activity and involvement.

Sociologists at Chicago were also influenced by the work of William Thomas, George Mead, and Charles Cooley on symbolic interactions. They believed that **symbolic interactionism** explained the solidarity among deviant and criminal subcultures that were commonly found in deteriorating neighborhoods. Sociologists have long argued that symbolic interaction occurs within intimate groups and can explain group, as well as individual, behavior. Symbolic interaction posits that in close groups, or cliques, members communicate with each other orally, as well as symbolically. They define who they are based on the expectations that other members have of them. Their personality and behaviors are shaped and molded by what they perceive is valued by the group. They are rewarded and held in high esteem or good standing if they exhibit the qualities that the group values and promotes. Therefore, if a group advocates illegal behavior, those individuals who display such behaviors are highly valued within that subculture. Herbert Blumer (1969) thought that human behavior is a product of social symbols communicated among individuals. He argued that the mind and the self are products of their social environments. In the process of communicating and interacting, people learn to define themselves, as well as others. Blumer postulated that in a clique or group, the symbols that are communicated provide meaning to members. Moreover, he argued that each person selects his or her own self-concept from the perception that he or she feels others have of him or her. Blumer contends that "others" are not necessarily persons we may know, but rather they could be generalized others. We create our own identities based on reflections from others. The logic of symbolic interactionism is that we have a multiplicity of identities based on the social settings and gatherings in which we participate. Each setting demands its own role, behavior, attitude, and its own identity. Therefore, a proper definition of the situation is required in order to respond with the appropriate behavior.

Socioeconomic Structure and Crime

American society is structured, ordered, class based, or stratified. Social stratification is a pattern in which individuals and groups are assigned to different positions in the social order. Social strata are created by unequal distributions of wealth, power, and prestige. Ascription is often based on race, gender, and family. Some positions afford varying amounts of access to desirable goods and services in the society (Julian and Kornblum, 1986). Some scholars contend that in America, stratification decides who gets what and why and addresses attainment capacities. Social stratification can be defined as the complex distribution of power, wealth, and status. To some economists, power signifies a demonstration of natural prowess or a superior display of diligence. Wealth represents the material means of existence, and status means honorable or worthy employment. Power, wealth, and status are highly valued in capitalistic societies, such as the United States (Kerbo, 1983).

A social class is a large number of people who have roughly the same degree of economic well-being. In the United States, people may enter or leave a given class as their economic fortunes change. In fact, it is possible to move from the underclass to the middle class and vice versa, while it is also possible to go from the middle class to the upper class. The United States is primarily composed of three dominant classes: upper, middle, and lower, with a broad range of economic variation (Siegel, 2012). For example, unlike the upper class, the upper-upper class is composed of a very small number of families with ownership of enormous financial and social resources. In fact, a U.S. Census Bureau report reveals that in 2007, among the very rich, or the top 1%, the average family annual income was $1.6 million, but among the elite rich, or the very top 400 highest earning households, the average earnings was $345 million (DeNavas-Walt, Proctor, and Smith, 2012). The report also provides that since 2001, the average income for the elite rich has more than doubled. **Harold Kerbo**

Kerbo, Harold—An international sociologists devoted to the study of social stratification, comparative systems, and economic development and world poverty. He is best known for his works entitled: Sociology: Social Structure and Social Conflict, Social Stratification and Inequality, and WorldPoverty: Global Inequality and the Modern World System. He has been a Fulbright professor in Japan, Thailand, Great Britain, Germany and Switzerland.

(1983) suggests that some wealthy families are considered the corporate or political elite. In most cases, these are the old established families with significant ownership of major corporations, such as the Rockefellers, Du Ponts, Carnegies, Mellons, and Fords.

The middle class signifies those with relatively little property, but high to middle positions of employment (nonmanual labor) and authority. For example, those in the middle class occupy positions characterized as professional, managerial, and entrepreneurial. Some people in this class may acquire access to the upper class (or power elite or the corporate class). Normally, when one thinks of the middle class, one thinks of education, occupation, income, identity, lifestyle, consumption, and status. Distinctions can be made between the middle class and the power elite (fewer corporate managers, doctors, lawyers, and so forth).

> **poverty**—The state of having little or no money, goods, or means of support.

In contrast to the wealthy and middle class, those in the lower class are disproportionately affected by high levels of crime, **poverty**, inadequate housing, community disorganization, gang involvement, unemployment, fatherlessness, drug addiction, teenage pregnancy, fear, and feelings of helplessness and hopelessness. Moreover, they may also disproportionately suffer from low levels of education, high levels of infant mortality, and lack of access to adequate health care and insurance. Crime statistics indicate that the overwhelming majority of the criminal offenders in society (those committing index crimes) have membership in the bottom tier of the economic structure. Moreover, the lower class signifies those individuals with no property who are often unemployed and have no authority (that is, the poor). The working class is composed of skilled, semiskilled, and unskilled workers who face some social problems in their communities, but not to the same extent as those in the underclass.

While the socioeconomic structure of the American system of stratification is a defined social structure, the system is not so rigid that it can be considered a caste system. Simply being born into poverty does not mean that one cannot move within the social structure. For example, individuals can escape poverty and other social problems found in areas that are socially disorganized due to a lack of economic and cultural resources. The United States is referred to as "the land of opportunity" because it is believed that those with the will and determination to work hard can advance themselves and earn a better life for themselves and their families. Indeed, the American culture teaches all to aspire to economic **success**, and in theory promises to make opportunities available to everyone regardless of race, ethnicity, gender, or land of natural origin. This is the hallmark of the American experience. However, the reality is that the social structure may not afford everyone equal access at opportunities to achieve success (Eitzen and Zinn, 1989). Steven Barkan (2006) argues that social class position often determines one's quality of life and life chances.

> **success**—A term used in the United States to mean that a person has reached a certain level of economic independence. It is typically associated with those in the middle and upper classes who enjoy a high standard of living because of educational attainment, occupation, social class position, or the amount of money they have managed to accumulate.

The Underclass

A recent report from the U.S. Census Bureau (DeNavas-Walt, Proctor, and Smith, 2012) finds major economic disparities in the United States that disproportionately affect minorities and the poor. More specifically, the Bureau reports that in 2011, about 15.9% of the U.S. population had income below the poverty level, an increase from 15.3% in 2010. As such, the number of people living in poverty grew from 46.2 million to 48.5 million during the same period. It also reveals that the poverty rate varies by race and ethnicity. For example, the poverty rates for blacks and Hispanics greatly exceed the national average. In 2010, 27.4% of blacks and 26.6% of Hispanics were poor, compared with 9.9% of non-Hispanic whites and 12.1% of Asians. The poverty rate is exacerbated when taking into account families that are headed by single women, especially among blacks and Hispanics.

Economic disparities will continue to have an adverse impact on people living in lower-class communities. This will affect children as well as adult residents. It does not matter if they are among the working poor, or if they subscribe to middle-class values that include acquiring an education and being disciplined. For the sole reason that they often face negative circumstances on a daily basis, they may be prevented from reaching their potential since their goals and dreams can be easily frustrated by life circumstances. For example, many lower-class communities are characterized by random gun violence, teenage pregnancy, drug addiction, family dysfunction, and lack of a social network. Because of these factors, criminologists often argue that many lower-class residents are irreversibly lost to their neighborhood since they may not acquire the social skills or support systems needed to transition into mainstream or conventional society (Warner, 2003).

Child Poverty

Since children are among the most vulnerable members of society, they are also highly exposed to poverty. In fact, a report from the National Poverty Center (2012) finds that children are disproportionately represented among the poor. The report estimates that while children make up 24% of the total U.S. population, they account for 36% of those living in poverty. The Center reports that in 2010, an estimated 16.4 million, or 22%, of the nation's children were living in poverty. The report also pointed out that there are substantial variations with regards to race and ethnicity found among the nation's poor children. More specifically, poverty rates were 12.4% for non-Hispanic whites, 38.2% for blacks, 35% for Hispanics, and 1.36% for Asians, respectively (DeNavas-Walt, Proctor, and Smith, 2012).

The fact that millions of American children are living in poverty should be a matter of national crisis since the effects of poverty are well documented in both health studies and criminological research. More specifically, research is replete with studies documenting the negative and harmful effects of a lack of access to health care, the impacts of poverty on the family, and the impact that poverty has on individual as well as group behavior (Schneider, 2013). For example, it is generally known that children growing up in poverty are less likely to attain academic success and are more likely to drop out of school compared with their affluent counterparts. They are also more likely to suffer emotional and psychological problems that may go undiagnosed owing to a lack of health insurance. Moreover, in some communities, it is taboo to receive treatment for mental health issues. The matter is often never discussed or shared with officials in the health community, family, or neighbors. As such, people with serious mental health issues such as bipolar personality disorder and depression may go untreated and pose a danger to themselves and others. Furthermore, some criminologists argue that people in the lower class who are exposed to extreme poverty either commit or become desensitized to acts of rage, aggressiveness, and violence (Rose and McCain, 2003; Sampson and Wilson, 1995; Phillips, 2002). The lack of treatment for health issues may manifest into serious problems that will eventually impede the developmental processes of the poor.

Minority Groups and Poverty

Public health experts have long warned that health disparities exist in the United States, and they are mostly demographic in nature. These same officials argue that differential access to health care is primarily caused by poverty (Krug et al., 2002; Schneider, 2013). More specifically, research reveals that demographical characteristics such as race, ethnicity, gender, and marital status are consistent measures that influence type of health care received. Health statistics show that in the United States, minority groups experience higher mortality rates due to disease and violence than their white counterparts. Males have higher mortality rates than females in all age groups. People who are married are healthier than those who are single, separated, divorced, or widowed (Schneider, 2013). Despite these indicators, the most compelling factor that explains health disparities is socioeconomic status (SES). SES includes income, education, and occupation. It is the best predictor for determining differences in health by race, ethnicity, gender, and marital status. For example, research finds that blacks and Hispanics are less healthy than whites and have lower SES than their white counterparts. Surprisingly, research finds that even wealthy educated blacks have a mortality rate that is higher than similarly situated whites (Sorlie, Backlund, and Keller, 1995). Public health data reveal that people with the lowest SES have the highest morality rate. This fact is not unique to the United States, but has global significance since other countries also report that poor people are generally unhealthy and have higher rates of deaths related to poverty and a lack of health care (Krug et al., 2002).

Those with lower SES live in poor housing, lack education, have high unemployment rates, and experience other poverty-related conditions. While these factors often have a damaging effect on people in general who are subjected to them, they really disadvantage some young people in areas in particular since they face peer pressure to participate in violence and criminal behavior (Krug et al., 2002). Lower SES may actually produce higher levels of stress due to the adverse physical and social conditions that poor people live under. Some stressors may include finding affordable and reliable child care, getting proper nutrition, paying rent on time, securing reliable transportation, finding employment, and dealing with exposure to racial prejudice (Krug et al., 2002). A study on disparities in annual income found the following average earnings: Asian ($65,469), white ($54,461), Hispanic ($38,039), and black ($32,584), respectively (Evans, Wells, and

Moch, 2003). Of these groups, young black men in particular have historically fared worse than others with regard to being employed. In fact, the U.S. Department of Labor (2010) reports that the unemployment rate for young black males is higher than for their white counterparts. A recent U.S. Census Bureau report shows that while 25% of African Americans and 22% of Hispanics live in poverty, only 8% of non-Hispanic whites and 11% of Asians live in poverty (DeNavas-Walt, Proctor, and Smith, 2012).

From the aforementioned report of annual income, one can surmise that African American and Latino children are more likely to be poor than Asian and white children. Research by the Center for Health Policy (2003) reveals that some minority children start their lives at a social and educational disadvantage since some minority children are four times less likely to have health insurance, and they also face significant disparities in the time spent in structured preschool settings. Unfortunately, lower-class communities lack the social support to assist residents who experience different levels of stress. However, people with higher income and education have the resources needed to help them cope with life's problems, thus protecting their health. The consequence of these disparities is that they take an adverse toll on the poor since they are relegated to inner-city life, where they face continuous income inequality and other race-based forms of discrimination. The whites who live a life of privilege are shielded from various forms of race-based disparities and institutional racism (Velez, Krivo, and Peterson, 2003).

Social Structure Theories

Criminologists use macro-level theories to explain the dynamics of group behavior found throughout the United States. Because of the social conditions that poor people live under, environmental factors found in the social structure are essential to explaining their disproportionate participation in delinquency and crime. Hence, social structure refers to physical features or characteristics found in communities, as well as unequal distributions of resources such as power, wealth, status, and the relationships among groups of people in social class groupings. Some structural theorists argue that inequality is institutionalized throughout stratified societies, and the United States is no exception (Kerbo, 1983).

Negative structural conditions such as poverty, deteriorated communities, crime, race-based discriminatory practices, and overcrowded housing are symptomatic of environmental problems that the poor often endure (Bjerk, 2007; Patchin et al., 2006; Barkan, 2006). These structural conditions are referred to as social forces. These forces greatly influence the behavior and attitudes of community residents and may explain why the urban poor, unlike their affluent counterparts, disproportionately engage in street crime. Since people with higher social status can accumulate greater amounts of goods and services through legitimate means, they do not usually commit crimes of violence or crimes of economic desperation. However, when they do engage in crime, they commit white-collar crimes such as fraud or embezzlement because of their access to opportunities in the legitimate marketplace.

The structural approach provides context for understanding the relationship between crime and the urban poor in the United States. Structural theorists argue that negative social forces affect people when they are young and continue to influence their behavior as they grow into adulthood. Moreover, to the extent that lower-class people are continuously exposed to negative environmental factors, they face a greater likelihood of continuing to engage in crime as adults (Patchin et al., 2006). Unlike affluent members of society, if poor people are troubled by life's stressors, their communities lack the resources to provide help or a safety net to seek legitimate remedies for their ailment. As such, the poor may engage in criminal behavior to seek economic relief from their circumstances. Despite this, criminologists would be remiss if they believed that all poor people respond in similar fashion to poverty and stress. The reality is that the vast majority of poor people do not engage in criminal behavior, but this fact alone does not mitigate the negative impact of living in areas where adverse community factors overwhelm some residents. Criminologists believe the circumstances under which the lower class must live, rather than the people inhabiting these areas, better explain the behaviors that occur in lower-class communities.

While the majority of people in the United States view inequality as unfair, the perception is that the existing social structure is simply the way things are (Kerbo, 1983). This assertion may provide more insight into understanding the plight of young minority males who struggle with the pains of inner-city urban life (Anderson, 1999). In fact, research suggests that much of the destructive crime that occurs in the lower-class environment is committed by youth gangs that are disproportionately composed of underemployed young adults (Wilson, 1985; Wilson, 1987). A recent study reports that the real crime problem is caused by poor youths who are reared in impoverished households. Because of this, the children and young adults inhabiting these areas are at a greater risk of seeking illegal opportunities since their family and community lack the same resources that are available to and even shield many young adults in the middle and upper classes from engaging in crime (Bjerk, 2007).

Social structural theories dismiss the cause of crime as attributable to psychological and biological traits. They also reject the belief that people in lower-class communities freely decide to engage in crime as a matter of choice. After examining crimes committed throughout the social structure (in lower, middle, and upper classes), they conclude that environmental factors in general, but negative social forces in particular, push lower-class people into committing expressive and economic crime. Stated differently, structural theorists consider the impact of poverty, stress, deteriorated and decaying neighborhoods, gangs, unequal distribution of resources and opportunities, and how they influence the attitude and behavior of poor and disadvantaged people. They argue that because street crime is disproportionately committed by the poor in urban areas, there must be forces at work in these environments that generate or produce crime. Social structure theories provide three independent branches of explanation: **social disorganization theory**, strain theory, and subcultural (cultural deviance) theory.

social disorganization—The state in which the informal mechanisms of social control are not working, and crime and delinquency flourish. Socially disorganized communities lack economic and cultural resources, and adults lack the ability to make residents conform their behaviors to standards of the law.

Social Disorganization Theory

Clifford Shaw and **Henry McKay** advanced the tradition of the social ecology of crime. While following Park and Burgess in studying crime and deviance in Chicago, they fully understood and were able to recognize and use concepts such as culture conflict and symbolic interaction. In studying crime and **juvenile delinquency** in Chicago in the context of the zone maps, they were able to show the close relationship between juvenile delinquency and other social problems, such as poverty and slum housing. Shaw and McKay relied on the maps and other sources to safeguard against bias. They examined crime data from local juvenile justice agencies, schools, social service agencies, census data, and police reports. By using a triangulated methodology, Shaw and McKay were able to move beyond relying solely on official police reports (which are known for their biases).

Shaw, Clifford—One of the researchers who studied the zone maps of Robert Park and Ernest Burgess. He helped to coin the phrases "social disorganization" and "cultural transmission of deviance." Many consider him part of the Chicago School of criminology.

McKay, Henry—Researcher who, along with Clifford Shaw, developed social disorganization theory and cultural transmission of deviance theory, based on the five concentric circles.

juvenile delinquency—Illegal or criminal behavior committed by someone who is not in the age of majority and is subjected to the jurisdiction of the juvenile justice system, rather than the adult criminal justice system.

After researching each zone, Shaw and McKay (1931) noticed obvious differences within the city of Chicago with respect to the five zones. For example, they noticed that social problems were saturated in the inner-city area, and as one moved away from the central city, fewer social problems were encountered. Social problems were believed to exist because of poverty, which brings a host of other problems such as crime, joblessness, deteriorated neighborhoods, and gang behavior. Perhaps Shaw and McKay's most important finding was discovered in Zone Two (the Zone in Transition). Community problems, such as crime and delinquency, truancy, infant mortality, mental disorders, and tuberculosis, proliferated in the area (Williams and McShane, 1999). Shaw and McKay were able to show that areas with a high level of such problems were also marked by low educational attainment, a high proportion of families on welfare, low rental value of property, a high percentage of the workforce at low occupational levels, and poor community organization. They argued that these social problems remained constant over time, and regardless of which race or ethnic group occupied the area, the results were the same: the problems of delinquency and crime persisted. According to Shaw and McKay (1931), "It appears to be established, then, that each racial, nativity, and nationality group in Chicago displays widely varying rates of delinquents; that rates for immigrant groups in particular show a wide historical fluctuation; and that diverse racial, nativity, and national groups possess relatively similar rates of delinquents in similar social areas."

Applying concepts of cultural conflict and symbolic interaction, Shaw and McKay argued that in deviant cultures, those people who hold deviant values are able to transmit or pass them down to others. The researchers arrived at this conclusion by making close observations and interviewing delinquents and criminals. Offenders would tell the researchers that they had other associates who either taught them or shared their reasons for violating the law. Once taught, those who accepted the reasons were free to engage in deviant and criminal behavior.

Shaw and McKay reported that because Zone Two lacked resources, it provided no legitimate job prospects or **opportunity structure** for young or older community residents. As a result, criminal structures appeared attractive to some immigrants and migrants who wanted a better life for themselves and their families, but were blocked from participation in the labor force because of race, ethnicity, or tough economic conditions. Criminal gangs and organized criminals served as role models for poor residents to emulate.

> **opportunity structure**—A term used by Richard Cloward and Lloyd Ohlin in their theory of differential opportunity structures. Essentially, an opportunity structure is a path to acquire goals. There are both legitimate and illegitimate opportunity structures.

Negative social conditions, such as the Great Depression (from 1929 to the mid-1930s) and Prohibition (from 1920 to 1933), offered many disenfranchised people lucrative opportunities in the illegitimate structure, especially in bootlegging and other vices. In the process of interaction, criminals taught and passed on techniques, rationale, and definitions to others who lacked legitimate economic avenues. Again, because of symbolic interaction, when new members entered the criminal subculture, they were indoctrinated into the lifestyle and acted accordingly. In the final analysis, Shaw and McKay concluded that communities in Zone Two suffered from social disorganization. They argued that these areas lacked community organization and social networks because they suffered structural problems—namely, a lack of resources. Communities are socially disorganized, they argued, when informal mechanisms of social control are ineffective at controlling or restraining the behaviors of community residents. In such areas, the church, schools, families, associates, and community leaders were too weak to exert control over the behaviors of community residents. Therefore, crime, delinquency, and lawlessness were able to saturate in these areas and sustain themselves over extended periods. In a sense, Shaw and McKay argued that the informal mechanisms that make a community strong were either absent or ineffective.

Socially disorganized communities lack the ability to make residents conform their behaviors to standards of the law. It is also important to note that many of the children of immigrants found in Zone Two were not completely attached to their parents' ways of thinking since they had not been fully socialized in the old world ways of their native country. This was mainly because young children wanted to assimilate into the dominant culture in America. As a result, they did not show much allegiance to the values, customs, and traditions of the European country from which they had immigrated. In fact, history records that many young immigrants were embarrassed and even ashamed of their parents, because they could not quickly grasp the English language. Many of them did not bring American friends home out of fear they would be ridiculed. Some scholars contend that because of culture conflict, many parents in Zone Two lost control of their children (Williams and McShane, 1999).

The Chicago School in the 1920s contributed to our understanding of crime by moving away from discussions of biology and feeblemindedness. Instead, sociologists examined the social ecology of crime by placing academic emphasis on structural conditions that emerged from stratification, in general, but also from the rapid social changes that were taking place in their city. They examined economic disparities and various forms of discrimination and exclusion, gangs, juvenile delinquency, and inner-city decay (see Lilly, Cullen, and Ball, 1995). More specifically, the Chicago scholars studied aspects of urban life that gave rise to crime, poverty, inadequate housing, and broken homes. The sociologists at Chicago found that the diversity of values, customs, and traditions essentially caused a breakdown of social controls and family structure. As a result, some people found cohesion and membership in gangs or subcultures that provided opportunities that were absent from their community. In essence, those scholars at Chicago in the sociology department discovered that cultural diversity breeds competition that adversely affects many, and sometimes the result is that subcultures emerge within the dominant culture that may hold values, norms, and traditions that are repugnant to conventional society.

Resurgence in Social Disorganization Theory

Since the 1980s, there has been renewed interest in social disorganization theory, and sociologists as well as criminologists are rediscovering that the theory is a powerful tool that can be used to explain crime and victimization in urban areas (Bursik, 1988; Krohn, 2000). Barkan (2001) contends that, unlike the early work of Shaw and McKay, which was criticized for its overreliance on official crime data, contemporary investigations use self-report and victimization surveys as well as complex neighborhood-level measures that were not created when Shaw and McKay originally presented the theory. Despite the different methodology used in these investigations, their findings still suggest that both crime and levels of victimization saturate in areas with characteristics such as: (1) low participation in voluntary organizations, (2) few networks of friendship ties, (3) low levels of community supervision of adolescents and other informal control mechanisms, and (4) high degrees of family mobility, population density, single-parent homes, dilapidated housing, and poverty (Peterson, Krivo, and Harris 2000; Sampson, 1997). Moreover, Paul Bellair (1997) found that social interaction among community residents is a central element in controlling community crime. His research reveals that not only does interaction matter, but frequent interaction among community residents is most effective in reducing crime. More specifically, he finds that when residents get together at least once a year, it can help to reduce the numbers of burglaries, motor vehicle thefts, and robberies. Therefore, he suggests that future research on social disorganization theory would benefit more if it closely considered the social dynamics of local network structures. It should focus on the interactions among neighbors since in most urban areas the problems associated with social disorganization could be a function of infrequent interactions among community members.

Contemporary research on the social disorganization theory consistently finds that weak social ties may serve to perpetuate crime because informal social controls are lax or nonexistent (Wilson, 1980, 1987, 1996). Unfortunately, many lower-class neighborhoods are characterized as being socially disorganized. Consequently, when the temptation of delinquency or illegal opportunities are present, informal mechanism of control must be strong or the prospect of preventing delinquency or controlling the behaviors of residents will be unsuccessful. Therefore, a lack of community control or cohesiveness will signal to motivated youths that they are free to seek or join delinquent peers or groups to pursue crime without fear of punishment for their behavior (Warner, 2003; Kelling and Wilson, 1982). Some scholars have suggested that the massive efforts the United States has expended toward incarceration have contributed to further destabilizing many minority communities since they lack both economic and human resources needed to garner control (Mauer, 1999, 2001; Messner and Rosenfeld, 2007). Moreover, the degree of lawlessness in socially disorganized areas is so high that it leaves residents feeling that they are trapped in their own community; the pervasiveness of crime has forced them to literally barricade themselves in their dwellings for self-protection. In fact, they often report feeling helpless that their community cannot help them, and they feel equally hopeless about local law enforcement ability to protect them against gangs and other criminals (Messner and Rosenfeld, 2007). These findings reveal that social disorganization theory is still relevant to the study of crime in contemporary times.

Anomie Theory: Durkheim's Legacy

Merton, Robert King—A sociologist who borrowed from the anomie theory of Émile Durkheim, applying it to the United States' emphasis on economic success, and changed the name to strain theory.

In 1938, anomie theory was introduced in the United States by **Robert King Merton**. The theory is an elaboration of the Durkheimian theory of anomie. However, because the theory emphasizes the pressure imposed on people by the economic structure of society (rather than rapid social change), it is often referred to as strain theory (Empey, 1982; Kornhauser, 1978; Vold and Bernard, 1986). Though introduced in the late 1930s, the theory gained widespread popularity in the 1960s. Merton's work attacked the individualistic explanations regarding the motivation for crime and moved the discussion into the context of the social structure and what occurs when poor disadvantaged people cannot achieve the cultural **aspirations** held out by the broader society.

aspirations—Strong goals and desires that are typically induced by the social culture of a society.

It would be difficult to explain strain without a brief discussion of the American system of stratification and the anomie theory. In the United States, people are divided, or categorized, based on race, gender, family, and ultimately the amount of economic resources they have. As mentioned earlier, people are divided into the underclass, the working class, the middle class, and the upper class, or what some scholars call the power elite. Assignment to any class or group is determined by the amount of accumulated wealth or property owned. For example, the upper class consists of a small number of exceptionally well-to-do families that maintain enormous financial and social resources, while the poor, or underclass, consists of an estimated 46.2 million people who live in poverty (DeNavas-Walt, Proctor, and Smith, 2012).

Membership in a particular class determines the number of opportunities that one may have, and at the same time, it affects one's life chances. For example, in the United States, people in the middle and upper classes are more educated and culturally refined than people in the lower class (Kerbo, 1983). Since the dominant culture is created and fashioned by the former groups rather than the latter, a tremendous amount of emphasis or value is placed on educational and cultural attainment. Those in the middle and upper classes live in communities that are shielded and protected from violent and property crime. Some live in exclusive communities we refer to as the suburbs. Moreover, the parents of children in the middle and upper classes often make plans to send their children to college so that they may continue to enjoy the fruits of the American Dream, or **economic prosperity**. This may not be a reality for those in the working and underclass (Messner and Rosenfield, 1997).

> **economic prosperity**—The notion of being economically independent and living the "good life." It is normally associated with being wealthy.

While the United States does not have a caste system, it is exceedingly difficult for those in the lower, or working class, to escape poverty. As a result, generations of poor continue in the vicious cycle of poverty (Wilson, 1987). Sometimes one can find in housing projects generations upon generations of families that have been relegated to inner-city ghettos. Ghettos are characterized by high rates of crime and violence, inadequate housing, poor health care, drugs, joblessness, high mortality rates, dysfunctional families, poor quality of life, and a bleak prospect for the future of young residents. In his works *The Truly Disadvantaged* (1987) and *When Work Disappears* (1996), Wilson captures the plight of the poor by describing the underclass as being isolated from mainstream society, pointing out that their problems continue to grow, since the global economy means that many jobs are disappearing from urban areas. He contends that many factories and industries are relocating and leaving behind large numbers of unemployed people. This destroys the social bonds that unite communities and weakens the level of community control they would otherwise exercise over residents. Wilson states that the prospect of future employment is so bleak for many inner-city residents that the situation warrants government intervention.

Before presenting Merton's strain theory, a brief review of the concept of anomie is necessary. In his analysis of the evolutionary changes that were occurring in Europe, Durkheim argued that during periods of rapid social change, a condition of normlessness developed. When this occurred, members of society essentially lost or forgot about their shared standards of conduct that regulated behavior and guided all people toward conformity. Normlessness, or anomie, developed because of a process that he referred to as deregulation. Durkheim postulated that when evolutionary changes occur, people do not always know which rules are appropriate to follow. This is a common occurrence when a society experiences evolutionary changes, such as being transformed from a communal (farmlike) society to an industrialized one based primarily on formal structures rather than informalities governing essential aspects of communal life. For example, in the wake of industrial capitalism, many Europeans began to relocate from rural areas, leaving behind the hard life of farming and working the land in search of better opportunities in newly formed urban areas where factory work and productivity was changing the economy and transforming the society. They quickly discovered that those same norms, values, and traditions that regulated life in the rural areas were no longer applicable in the newly developing urban areas. Some scholars argue that because of the population shifts and the diversity that came along with efforts toward migration, the rules that regulated simple living were not applicable in large cities, and as a result, anomie emerged. Some scholars even argue that as technological advances continue to emerge in contemporary society, normlessness or lawlessness will also emerge whereby some people will engage in crime. Notwithstanding, Durkheim argued that when anomie occurred, it invariably led to social isolation and a low degree of social participation for some people. The by-product was typically crime, deviant behavior, and in some cases, even suicide (see Durkheim, 1893/1933, 1897/1951).

The American Dream and Strain Theory

Merton borrowed from Durkheim by taking general principles from the anomie theory and applying them to the social structure in the United States. Merton noticed that the United States placed great emphasis on accumulating material wealth and striving for the American Dream. According to Merton, every American is socialized and indoctrinated with the belief that he or she should aspire to reach the "good life" that is associated with economic success. Merton argued that in America, this essentially means having a life of luxury and being financially independent. He argued that achieving this status does not mean simply being able to pay one's bills or keeping one's head above water, but rather, it means being able to live life abundantly with all the amenities that one desires. The American Dream is exactly what it claims to be, a dream or idea that there should be no limitations placed on one's aspirations, or what can be achieved since America is the "land of opportunity." For many Americans who pursue the dream, if they can conceive it, they can also achieve it. While applying this reasoning, Merton noticed on close observation that America is also a structured society. In the United States, there are different **social class** arrangements, and not everyone is afforded equal opportunities to realize their culturally induced aspiration to achieve economic prosperity. Merton, therefore, thought that achieving the American Dream may not be a viable option for every member of American society. He reasoned that some people would naturally turn to crime to offset the limitations placed on them by structural conditions in American society.

> **social class**—The level of rank at which one is placed in a stratified society. In the United States, the dominant social classes are the lower, middle, and upper. The class in which an individual has membership will ultimately determine his or her life's chances and quality of life.

Figure 6.2 illustrates the relationship between social class position and achieving the American Dream. More specifically, it reveals where people in the lower, middle, and upper classes are situated in the structural hierarchy in the Unites States when it comes to achieving the **cultural goal** of economic success. As indicated by the figure, people in the lower class are further away than other people in reaching the society's dominant cultural goal,

> **cultural goals**—The aspirations that are instilled in everyone living in a particular society.

while people in the middle class have a greater chance of attaining it. People in the upper class are already wealthy. They enjoy the American Dream since they can afford the very best materials that the society has to offer. They enjoy their status and the privilege that comes with their social arrangement. The figure also shows that in the race to reach the dream, some groups start at a disadvantage, while others have more access to reaching the dream. This may become a source of intensive frustration and strain for some people in the lower class.

In 1896, the United States Supreme Court decided a landmark case that epitomized the internal struggle that has gripped American society when trying to resolve the question of race. The case was *Plessy v. Ferguson*. In *Plessy*, the Court held that separate facilities and disparate treatment of minorities by the majority was constitutional. By the time *Brown v. Board of Education* (1954) overturned *Plessy*'s "separate but equal" edict, separatism and exclusion were deeply embedded in the American social structure, as well as the psyche. Furthermore, some legal scholars contend that the legal endorsement of *Plessy* served to institutionalize unequal treatment in all facets of the American experience. *Plessy* went deeply into the American social structure in general, and areas of economic and social opportunities in particular, since the Court's decision institutionalized disparate treatment. *Plessy* was the law of the land until it was overturned by *Brown* in 1954. Therefore, before Merton introduced and discussed anomie theory, many people in America were treated unfairly and excluded from conventional activities. They were held back from

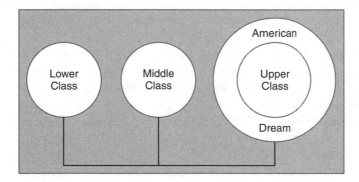

Figure 6.2 Social Class and the American Dream

egalitarian philosophy—Any ideology that promotes equality and fairness with respect to access to opportunities and advancement.

social, political, economic, and educational participation by a society that has always espoused an **egalitarian philosophy** and championed rugged individualism (Messner and Rosenfeld, 2007).

While formulating his theory, Merton believed that the motivation to commit a crime stemmed from the egalitarian philosophy that the United States espoused and the limitations that the social structure placed on groups at the bottom of the structural hierarchy. To Merton, this was a contradiction since the United States was seen throughout the world as the land of opportunity and individual freedom, to be enjoyed by all regardless of race, color, or creed. The presumption has always been that if people are willing to work hard and sacrifice, their dreams and aspirations could be realized. According to Merton, many people in the lower class experienced exclusion and blocked opportunities. In America, not all minorities experienced the same disparate treatment. Despite this, other groups were also discriminated against, but there were different levels of exclusion. Eventually, some groups successfully assimilated into the dominant culture after immigrating from other countries. This has not been an easy reality for other groups. This fact alone makes the promise of equality in America an abstraction at best.

Merton thought that people engaged in crime because of the contradiction found in the American culture (socializing everyone to aspire to reach the American Dream) and the institutionalized (structural) means by which people can achieve the goals of society. The institutionalized means are also called middle-class values, or the Protestant work ethic. Stated another way, in America, not only does the culture socialize everyone into pursuing economic prosperity, but it also teaches everyone the legitimate avenues to achieving that cultural goal. Merton noticed that the culture dictates both the accepted goals (material wealth) and the means to reach those goals. For example, the conventional avenues to reach success in America have always included education, hard work, deferred gratification, and honesty. Needless to say, in the 1930s, not every segment of society was afforded equal opportunities, because many were disenfranchised. Many were denied the right to vote, college admission, jobs, housing, due process, and fundamental fairness because of race, ethnicity, or place of origin. These denials constituted disparate treatment in the United States. Simply put, the United States failed to provide equal access to the structural avenues of success for everyone. Scholars contend that because of institutionalized and government-sanctioned exclusion, not everyone could participate in mainstream activities leading to economic prosperity (Jenkins, 1984).

Merton believed that unequal access to legitimate economic structures was a source of intense strain, rage, and anger for some Americans who were blocked from opportunities. He saw crime as a response by those for whom society failed to provide legitimate access to achieving the American Dream. However, he noticed that not everyone who failed to reach societal goals will engage in crime. For example, some people will drink, use drugs, or suffer mental depression or other types of mental illness (Jenkins, 1984). Despite strain, not everyone living in poverty will turn to a life of crime. Merton argued that because not all persons can be expected to achieve the goals of the culture, it is very important that the culture place a strong emphasis on the institutionalized means and the necessity of following them for their own value. Although strain is experienced by people in other classes, it proliferates in inner-city areas among persons in the lower class.

Figure 6.3 illustrates Merton's **strain theory**. It presents the dominant cultural goal of economic success and the approved institutionalized means. The figure shows that some **institutional means** used to achieve the cultural goal of economic success include: education, hard work, deferred gratification, and honesty. The figure reveals that these avenues are available to members of the middle and upper classes. However, it also illustrates that members of the lower class are blocked out of these avenues. Therefore, they turn to alternative means to acquire the culturally induced goal of economic status. Moreover, people in the middle and upper classes have legitimate access to economic success, while people in the lower class may have to resort to crime as an instrument to acquire economic success or images associated with success.

> **strain theory**—The theory that holds because America is a stratified society and has different social classes, not everyone can compete for success on an equal footing. These disparities in opportunity cause some people to engage in crime to reach the cultural goal of economic success. ⟵
>
> **institutional means**—The acceptable or conventional avenues that a culture or society allows one to use to achieve the goals or aspirations that culture deems worth striving to achieve.

The Cause of Strain

For Merton, strain was caused by the inequities in the American social structure or system of stratification that subjects large segments of people to poverty and a lack of

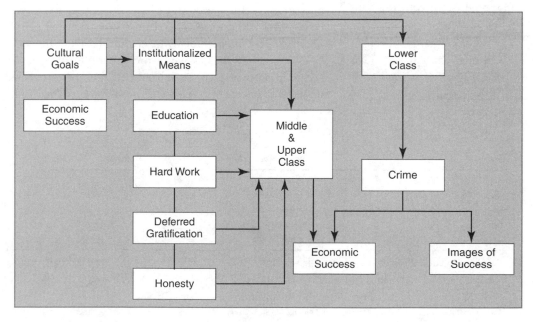

Figure 6.3 The Mertonian Theory of Strain

legitimate opportunities. Merton also argued that the culture places too much emphasis on achieving material or economic prosperity, even among those populations with no realistic chance of achieving it. The goal of economic success is not only dominant in the middle and upper classes, where people have realistic opportunities to achieve it, but also in the lower class, where there is a lack of resources for achieving it. Stated another way, Merton was articulating in the 1930s that because of various forms of discrimination, exclusions, and a lack of resources in the lower-class culture, many residents use crime as a vehicle to reach their cultural goals. More specifically, Merton contended that the economic structure in America was anomic, because it created lower-class conditions and disallowed its residents to have equal access to the nation's wealth. For Merton, crime was an inevitable outcome of the structural conditions in the United States.

> **modes of adaptation**—Mechanisms that are used to either cope with or adapt to a particular state of being. Robert K. Merton provides several strategies that people use to cope with the strain of trying to achieve economic prosperity or the American Dream.

Responding to Strain

When explaining strain theory, Merton created a scale which he appropriately titled the **modes of adaptation**. The scale places the reactions of people into distinct typologies. In essence, the model captures how people in the United States respond to the cultural goals and institutionalized means of the society. The scale also demonstrates the reactions of those who do and others who do not subscribe to the goals and means of society. An interesting point made by Merton is that since the United States is a capitalistic society, the majority of people will naturally choose to pursue the American Dream by trying to accumulate property and economic prosperity. If this were not the case, the society would not be able to sustain itself. Therefore, the majority of people in any society must abide by its economic structure.

> **conformity**—A concept used in the mode of adaptation presented by Robert K. Merton to express that most people in the United States subscribe to the cultural goals and accepted means to achieve those goals.

Conformity occurs when most people in a society accept and practice the socialized cultural norms handed down by that society. Since the United States is a capitalist

Table 6.1 Typology of the Modes of Individual Adaptation

Rejects	Modes of Adaptation	Accepts
	Conformity	✹ ▲
▲	Innovation	✹
✹	Ritualism	▲
✹ ▲	Retreatism	
⟷	Rebellion	

✹ Cultural goals and economic prosperity

▲ Institutional means and middle class values

⟷ Rejection of prevailing values and substitutions with new values

Data from: Merton, R. (1957). "Social Structure and Anomie." In *Social Theory and Social Structure* (Glencoe, IL: Free Press).

society, the cultural norms overwhelmingly stress the goal of acquiring wealth. People in the United States are in constant competition in pursuit of the American Dream. Though most people will not achieve economic prosperity, they still accept it as a legitimate goal and believe that it should be achieved by the accepted structural or institutionalized means such as hard work, education, deferred gratification, and honesty.

Innovation particularly refers to the behavior of people in the United States who accept the cultural goal of success, but reject the institutional means to reaching it. They may resort to deviant and criminal behavior. Merton thought that people who innovated ways to acquire wealth were from the lower class, since they lived in social structures that do not provide viable avenues to achieve the cultural goal of economic success. He argued that their communities lacked legitimate opportunities

> **innovation**—The process by which one creates an illegal way to acquire the cultural goals (economic success) of society. This could entail engaging in drug sales, Ponzi schemes, imbellzement and others. Within the stain theory, Merton argued that innovation occurs when one accepts the cultural goals of society, but lacks the legitimate or institutionalized means to acquire them.

for them to achieve social status, and, as a result, they engaged in criminal enterprises. For many living in the urban ghettos amidst abject poverty, the institutionalized means to achieving status (e.g., education, deferred gratification, hard work, and honesty) are nonexistent or unrealistic. Of all the modes of adaptation, innovation prevents a problem.

Ritualism refers to the behavior of people who do not demonstrate allegiance to the goal of economic prosperity, but are committed to investing in hard work, education, deferred gratification, and being honest. They typically have no desire to be rich or simply do not hold to false hopes of becoming wealthy. They wish to "play it safe." They are not disappointed by failure to achieve their goals, since they have abandoned them. They are considered frightened employees, organizational men and women who commit their lives to retaining and safeguarding their position. They are complacent and comfortable with achieving a minimal level of success through the institutionalized means. The fear of losing what they already have seals their position in the social structure. However, they socialize their children to be hardworking, engage in educational pursuits, and be honest. They may also sacrifice immediate gratification to invest in their children's future.

> **ritualism**—A mode of adaptation that provides that some members of society will reject the cultural goals of society, but accept the institutionalized means to achieve them. These people come to accept contentment from their current lifestyle. They abide by the rules of conventional society that include engaging in hard work, deferred gratification, receiving an education, and being honest, but they have abandoned the idea of reaching the cultural goal of success.

> **retreatism**—A mode of adaptation that provides that some members will either reject or give up on the cultural goals of society and retreat into other arenas such as a drug culture or alcoholism. This mode allows for escape into an unproductive, noncompetitive, or leisurely lifestyle with few if any demands on its participants. Since they reject the cultural goals, they do not accept the institutionalized means of society.

Retreatism refers to the behavior of those who reject both the cultural goals of success and the institutionalized means to achieve these goals. People who retreat from society include psychotics, dropouts, outcasts, vagrants, vagabonds, tramps, chronic drunkards, and drug addicts.

Merton argued that retreatism can occur in people who lack the ability to achieve the cultural goals, but also in people who have a very strong commitment to both the goals and the means, but no real possibility of achieving success. For example, not having the ability to truly compete in a competitive society may make some retreat because of the pressure. This adaptation could also stem from drug use or mental deficiency. While some may retreat voluntarily, others may do so because of forces over which they have no control. The result is the same; they do not achieve the cultural goals of society by using the institutionalized means.

> **rebellion**—A mode of adaptation that provides that some members of society will reject both the cultural goals and institutionalized means and opt to replace them with other goals and means such as creating an alternative scheme for a new social structure. Some people could seek to develop a socialist state or create militias contending they have lost faith or confidence in the legitimacy of the U.S. government.

Rebellion refers to those who engage in behavior that runs counter to the American culture. They may even have opposing ideologies that differ from those of the majority of people. Those who rebel are not interested in the cultural goals of society, especially economic success, nor do they find the institutionalized means helpful. They prefer replacing the existing goals and approved means with different ideas. For example, some rebels have suggested transforming the society from capitalism to socialism or even communism. Since some people believe that the existing arrangement, or the status quo, is unfair to the poor and disenfranchised, they may be inclined to call for redistributions of the nation's wealth. It is also important to note that those who might be inclined to rebel do not necessarily have to be from the lower class. For example, from the mid-1960s and 1970s, many middle-class, as well as lower-class, people protested the direction in which society was headed. Some even called for a move toward socialism. Others who are considered rebels may have an interest in altering their state of consciousness by using illegal substances to transcend reality.

A Reaction to Strain

While many contradictions are found in the American culture and social structure where opportunities are concerned, the society also vigorously advertises and promotes the American Dream by commercializing economic success or the symbols associated with success in America. Some symbols may include acquiring an education from a prestigious university, owning fine or vintage cars (e.g., Mercedes, Lexus, BMW, Cadillac, and others), homes, a business, investments, fine jewelry, designer clothes, and other amenities that symbolize success. Some scholars argue that advertisements can be a source of intense pressure or frustration for those who live in poverty (especially teenagers, who may be reluctant to attend school if they cannot dress in a fashionably correct manner). Advertisement is a constant reminder of commodities that are en vogue and owned by successful people. It is also believed to be a reminder to the poor of their economic failure. People are made to feel inadequate if they do not have lifestyles or clothes similar to characters on television. Therefore, some scholars believe the impetus for many to engage in crime might be feelings of inadequacy that are amplified by the commercialization and commodification of goods and services associated with economic prosperity (Haymes, 1995; Nightingale, 1993). A prevailing attitude among many inner-city youth may be that though they are aware of the poverty that exists in their immediate surroundings, at least they can enjoy the benefit of being dressed like megastar sports athletes. This, of course, means being dressed from head to toe in Nike, Adidas, Reebok, Under Armour, Converse, and other sports apparel. Crime reports indicate that many teenagers engage in criminal behavior to either purchase or steal designer clothing. Again, the image of success may propel some offenders into a life of crime (Haymes, 1995; Nightingale, 1993).

Strain theory has been disproportionately used to explain the behavior of poor people who are out of the mainstream. It seems to do a better job of explaining the poor's participation in economic or property crimes rather than crimes of violence, as a result of the anger and frustration people experience when living in economically challenged areas in one of the richest nations in the world. Strain theory can be used to explain crimes committed by all people in society and not the poor exclusively. On the one hand, the poor may commit crime because of their inability to achieve the cultural aspirations since they face blocked opportunities (real or perceived). On the other hand, the rich may engage in "elite" crimes such as white-collar, corporate, healthcare, or governmental crime for economic reasons. Some suggest that while they are not strained to the same extent as the urban poor, some people in the middle and upper classes may experience "relative" deprivation. This typically occurs when they compare what they have to what others around them have. Because of this pressure, some people in these classes may devise illegal money-making enterprises, which may go undetected for extended periods of time.

Surprisingly strain theory may also be used to explain crime in times of prosperity, as well as in economic recession amidst high levels of unemployment (Siegel, 2000). For example, during periods of economic prosperity, some people may have an increased desire to own more. This can create an intense pressure to achieve the cultural goal of having more economic prosperity. On the other hand, high levels of unemployment and joblessness may either drive some people to a life of crime or convince them that the economy is doing poorly and that their expectations should reflect a declining market. However, as the gap between the rich and poor continues to widen, one can expect the levels of crime committed by each group to increase. However, we can expect a disproportionate number of crimes to be committed by the urban poor, since they are those with the least in a nation that has an abundance of resources (Messner and Rosenfeld, 2007).

The need to engage in economic crime is guided by the cultural emphasis on acquiring wealth when structural lines prevent all from competing for it on an equal footing. Society, through the use of mass media, advertises and markets the American Dream, making those who do not look, dress, or act like characters in commercials feel unsuccessful, and even like losers. Strain is a constant reality, because reminders of success are always present, from childhood through adulthood. For people living in communities with a lack of resources, the strain becomes unbearable and crime becomes a by-product.

Merton suggests that perhaps society should not place as much emphasis on economic success, or should do away with its egalitarian philosophy that everyone has an equal chance to reach the American Dream.

Agnew, Robert—A sociologist who developed general strain theory, which expanded the Mertonian theory of anomie from the macro to the micro level of explanation.

general strain theory—A theory developed by Robert Agnew that proposes that crime and deviance are not necessarily the domain of the lower class, but rather anyone in society can feel strain and, therefore, engage in crime.

General Strain Theory

Unlike the Mertonian theory of strain, which explains the behavior of the lower class on a macro level, **Robert Agnew's general strain theory** (GST) focuses on the micro, or individual, level. It postulates that any person in any social class can commit criminal behavior after experiencing the negative effects of strain (Agnew, 1985). Agnew argues that criminal behavior stems from negative affective states caused by anger, frustration, and adverse emotions that could develop into destructive social rela-

tionships. For Agnew, negative affective states could come from multiple stress-producing sources and not solely those that stem from the lack of economic opportunities to reach the American Dream. More specifically, Agnew argues that strain can be caused by factors such as: (1) failure to achieve positively valued goals (this is strain as discussed by Merton with respect to the lower class being unable to reach the cultural goal of economic success), (2) the disjuncture of expectations and achievements (this explains the criminal behavior of middle- and upper-class people when they engage in crime to either maintain their status or keep up with others around them), (3) the removal of positively valued stimuli from the individual (the loss of a desired promotion could lead to crime), and (4) the presentation of negative stimuli (being terminated from a job or reprimanded by an employer for misbehavior or a lack of productivity).

Agnew believes that strain could cause people to experience negative emotions, such as disappointment, anger, depression, or even fear. He argues that anyone in society could experience strain, and it could take many forms, such as when a love interest refuses to reciprocate, the death of a family member or loved one, a contentious custody battle, a divorce, being reprimanded on a job, failure to reach an anticipated promotion, failure to meet a projected profit margin, a perceived unfair evaluation by a superior, failure to receive a passing score in a high school or college course, and even experiencing either a physical or verbal victimization from an assailant. Agnew (1992) reports that of the different emotions that people experience, anger is very important in the decision to commit a crime, especially if the angry person feels the need for revenge. The person may be compelled to take action if he or she feels retaliation is justified. This typically occurs if the person believes that he or she has been wronged by others. Agnew warns that repetitive strain can trigger delinquency when it creates hostility, suspicion, and an aggressive attitude, especially if it creates a violent reaction. Agnew links crime to negative emotions that could come from multiple sources of stressors. He also believes that when faced with strain, some individuals may display appropriate behavioral responses. However, the strain that leads to crime can affect anyone in any social class.

Institutional Anomie Theory

In the mid-1990s, Steven Messner and Richard Rosenfeld, in their book *Crime and the American Dream,* presented an elaboration of Merton's anomie theory. They referred to their model as institutional anomie theory (IAT). Unlike the works of Merton and Agnew, IAT is a macro-level analysis that posits crime is rooted in cultural and institutional factors that are defining characteristics of capitalist societies. Though their theory is consistent in part with Merton's, in that achieving economic success is a dominant theme in American culture, Messner and Rosenfeld argue that the American Dream involves accumulating material goods and wealth through open-individual competition. They argue that in the United States, capitalism encourages innovation to pursue monetary rewards. However, the structure is anomic because the intense pressure built into the system drives people apart while they selfishly pursue success at any cost. For example, Messner and Rosenfeld argue that all people (regardless of social class position) are willing to take chances and risks to acquire what they desire. These risks could range from investors manipulating the stock market to people taking a five-finger discount at a local shopping center. The win-at-any-cost mentality is pervasive in the United States, and it weakens and compromises the collective sense of community and limits any ambition other than those based on acquiring wealth.

Messner and Rosenfeld argue that crime occurs in the United States, in part, because the culture promotes intense pressure for economic success. Similarly, other research finds that capitalist culture "exerts pressure toward crime by encouraging an anomic cultural environment in which people are encouraged to adapt an anything goes mentality in the pursuit of personal goals. . . . The economic pressures inherited in the American Dream are nourished and sustained by an institutional balance of power dominated by the economy" (Liska and Reed, 1985, p. 553). In fact, IAT posits that because the United States overemphasizes its economy, other social institutions, such as the family, school, church, and polity, are unable to exert their social control function. As such, they have been rendered ineffective. Thus, the value structure of the United States is dominated by economic realities.

This is revealed in a number of ways. Messner and Rosenfeld argue that other social institutions have been undermined for several reasons. First, noneconomic roles and functions have been devalued in contemporary society. For example, any outstanding performance in the family, school, or community is given lower value or priority compared with achieving economic success.

Second, in the presence of conflict, noneconomic roles are relegated to a subordinate status, and must accommodate economic remands. For example, the needs of the workplace typically take priority and dominate family planning, scheduling, and school as well as other aspects of social life. This is highlighted in examples where one is relocated because of a job promotion or transfer. When this occurs, the family moves to a new city, state, or country. The children in such families will be reenrolled at another school. If the family observes and practices religion, a new place of worship will be sought.

Finally, the language of business has penetrated into every aspect of life. For example, business terms such as "bottom line," "partner," "clients," "downsizing," and "outsourcing" have invaded schools, family, churches, and other social institutions (Messner and Rosenfeld, 2007). Because the economy is given such high priority, other social institutions are rendered ineffective. As such, they lack the ability to exert informal social control.

Research on General Strain Theory

In their research, Paul Mazerolle and Jeff Maahs (2000) posed three questions. First, are delinquent behavior and exposure to strain related in a systematic manner? Second, is the conditioning hypothesis of general strain theory supported when focusing on exposure to delinquent peers, the lack of moral constraints against delinquency, a behavioral propensity toward delinquency and deviance, and a combined total risk index of these influences? Third, do the hypothesized conditioning influences vary when examined cross-sectionally and longitudinally?

The research finds both cross-sectional and longitudinal support for strain and delinquency being related. It also finds support for the conditioning hypothesis of GST. Mazerolle and Maahs report that exposure to delinquent peers, a behavioral propensity toward deviance, and a lack of moral beliefs can lead to deviance. They caution that this finding could present a theoretical challenge to GST, since it could have occurred independently of strain. It could leave GST appearing too general. The research of Nicole Piquero and Miriam Sealock (2000) addressed whether GST operates as predicted within a group of delinquent or criminal offenders. They obtained positive support for some negative effects, especially anger, in predicting interpersonal aggression. Moreover, they argued that their research findings are similar to those of Mazerolle and Piquero (1997), who found a crime-specific effect of anger on violent offenses. However, instead of relying on a sample of college students, Piquero and Sealock used a delinquent offender population.

Relative Deprivation Theory

In general, the **relative deprivation theory** contends that the poor are demeaned in competitive societies characterized by the unequal distribution of resources. The motivation to engage in crime is based on perceived humiliation and the legitimate right to humiliate others in return. For example, poor males may both fear and envy people who are affluent if they believe that the rich became wealthy at their expense. Sometimes those who are poor may internalize the idea that if they do not take aggressive action, they will continue to be blocked from achieving economic success (Wilson and Daly, 1997).

In their discussion of relative deprivation theory, **Judith Blau** and **Peter Blau** (1982) integrated concepts

---

relative deprivation theory—The theory that crime is a function of the perception of social injustice with respect to the continued unequal access to power and wealth. The poor become enraged when they see the gap increase between those in society with the most and those with the least. The situation is amplified when they live in close physical proximity to the affluent because they are constantly reminded of their poverty.

Blau, Judith—A sociologist devoted to promoting human rights who argued that efforts should be made to rid the society of inequities that lead to poverty, discrimination, racism, sexism, and imperialism. Some of her scholarship has focused on crime and the underclass, relative deprivation and crime, and human rights violations.

Blau, Peter—A sociologist and theoretician best known for his work in macrosocial structure which examined the systems of organizations, social exchange, social classes, and the structure of societies. He is also one of the founders of the field of organization sociology. His work helped transformed the study of social inequities and mobility.

from anomie and social disorganization theory and concluded that when poor people compare their economic plight and prospects to those of the rich, they become angry and believe that they are unjustly treated. This is especially true if they have minority status in America. Eventually, the poor begin to develop a distrust of the society that has created and sustained their exclusion from economic, as well as political, activities. The feelings of inadequacy that result from their lack of economic success causes repressed feelings of aggression and hostility that could lead to violence.

Moreover, Tomislav Kovandzic, Lynn Vieraitis, and Mark Yeisley (1998) contend that the effects of inequality can be exacerbated when those in poverty believe that they are growing less capable of competing for resources, and that more resources are going to the wealthy. When this occurs, the poor are more likely to search for illegal enterprises in which to engage. Relative deprivation theory essentially argues that crime is sometimes a function of the perception of social injustice with respect to the continued distribution of unequal access to power and wealth. Kovandzic, Vieraitis, and Yeisley argue that such feelings are more likely to manifest when the affluent and poor live in close physical proximity to each other. The poor are constantly reminded of their poverty as they watch the divide increase between themselves and the rich. In cities such as Chicago, Los Angeles, New York, and Boston, there are clear divides separating poor and wealthy areas. Poor residents are constantly reminded of their poverty and grow increasingly frustrated with the existing social arrangement in the United States (Siegel, 2000).

Criticisms of Strain Theory

While strain theory has been instrumental in demonstrating that unequal distributions of economic resources create problems for disenfranchised populations, it has not been effective in terms of explaining the different offending rates among impoverished populations. For example, one theme of strain theory, as well as of other structural theories, is that people engage in crime because of poverty. Therefore, the assumption is made that poverty causes crime. While this assertion may be true to an extent, it comes short of addressing other salient causal factors that push some people into a life of crime. It presupposes that poverty is directly linked to crime. If poverty alone explained crime, everyone living in economically strained communities would engage in crime. Instead, crime is believed to be a function of many factors that could include living in poverty and having deviant, or criminal, associates who might influence one's behavior. Crime could also be a function of poverty and poor family structure (Wilson and Herrnstein, 1985; Gottfredson and Hirschi, 1990), or living in a dysfunctional family. Poverty and dysfunctional parents who exhibit violence could vicariously socialize children into engaging in similar behavior (Bandura, 1973). Some even contend that poverty and drugs or school failure can better explain the relationship between poverty and crime (Brownstein, 2000).

Arrest statistics clearly demonstrate that not everyone who lives in poverty or is economically challenged turns to crime as a result of life circumstances. Some people living in inner-city areas may resist the temptations of crime because of their participation in religious activities. Research demonstrates that those with strong religious connections and/or beliefs are more inclined to stay away from crime and delinquency (Johnson, Larson, DeLi, and Jang, 2000; Larson, Sawyer, and McCullough, 1998; Hirschi, 1969; Benda, 1995; Benda and Corwyn, 1997; Cochran, Wood, and Arneklev, 1994; Elifson, Petersen, and Hadaway, 1983). Stated another way, crime committed in impoverished areas could be a function of socialization, or the quality of one's rearing, especially where religious training is concerned.

Another item for which strain theory has been criticized is its failure to explain why females engage in less crime than their male counterparts. Can one assume that strain affects gender differently? Do females have fewer aspirations than males? Do they not desire equal opportunities and a legitimate chance to obtain the American Dream? While ecological research (examining conditions, such as economic disparities) provides good structural explanations of high crime rates in urban areas, it misses the gender variable. Barkan (2001) contends that most structural explanations fail to demonstrate the effects that inner-city problems have on women. For example, most ecological research neglects questions of how females are affected by dilapidated conditions, economic deprivation, racial prejudice and discrimination, intensive stress, and crime and violence.

There are several explanations that could explain the disparity between male and female offending where structural theory is concerned. First, since males commit more crimes than females, researchers typically rely on samples of male offenders in their analyses of crime, thereby excluding the representation of females. Second, some research suggests that when young females are interviewed by researchers, they report that they perceive having fewer opportunities than their male counterparts. If this assumption is true, their aspirations may be lower, and therefore could present less strain when their goals are not realized. Third, the socialization of females could be vastly different from that of their male counterparts. For example, if females are taught to be less competitive and more passive, while males are socialized into being competitive and aggressive, this could explain why women do not commit as many violent crimes as men. This may also explain the lack of female representation in crime statistics.

> **subculture**—A culture found within a dominant culture. Subcultures are typically secondary groups that provide their own set of values, customs, beliefs, and traditions. Individual solidarity can be strong in either a dominant culture or a subculture.

Subcultural (Cultural Deviance) Theories
What Are Subcultures?

The concept of **subculture** emerged in the 1930s to take its place with other sociological terms, such as social class and roles. These terms served as the foundation of sociology (Arnold, 1970). Essentially, subculture is a concept handed to sociologists by anthropologists (Gordon, 1947). Subcultures are defined as smaller cultures found within dominant cultures. They provide values, norms, and traditions that regulate social life within the context of a given group. Gordon defines subculture as a subdivision of a national culture, composed of a combination of social situations, such as class status, ethnic background, regional and rural or urban residence, and religious affiliation. These social situations have a consuming impact on the individuals who share them. The expectation is that each member will abide by the group's rules. J. Milton Yinger (1960) contends that subcultural norms are unknown to, looked down upon by, or thought of as separating forces by the rest of society. He further argues that all societies have differentiating rules, but only heterogeneous societies have subcultures. Within a subculture, people occupying certain positions are assigned the rights and duties appropriate to those roles. Subcultures can emerge in response to situations or problems. Harold Kerbo (1983) contends that subcultures are the result of social interactions. They represent the dynamic characteristics of the framework within which one is socialized.

When attempting to understand the dynamics of subcultures, one must consider several factors, such as structural position, differential interaction, segment-related subculture, and individual attributes and behavior. First, the structural position in society of the population under study must be examined. Second, those segmented at different levels in the social structure tend to interact more with one another rather than with people in different social class positions. Third, segment-related subculture deals with the subcultures that emerge from the different types of interactions of people sharing the same structural position. Fourth, subcultural membership manifests itself through the behaviors and attributes that emerge from these interactions and associations (Arnold, 1970).

While looking at class subcultures, one must consider the beliefs, worldviews, values, and behaviors associated with those attributes and how they may differ with respect to class position. Subcultures can determine aspects of lifestyle that are more superficial in nature, such as taste, preference, and general styles of living (Arnold, 1970). Lifestyle differences can also be traced to experiences and problems that vary based on class. Subcultures are known to be accepted by everyone who participates in them. However, those who are part of a subculture are also governed by the rules of the dominant culture.

The rules of the dominant culture or mainstream society should supersede those found in subcultures. Sometimes, conventional society defines behaviors that are practiced in subcultures as criminal or deviant. This may occur even if the behaviors are not clearly defined. The only thing that matters is that some group with power perceives that the behavior is deviant or criminal (Becker, 1963). Though many subcultures can be found in the United States, a number of illegal subcultures proliferate in impoverished areas.

Some scholars contend that in societies with unequal distributions of resources and blocked opportunity structures, groups of people come together to serve as support groups for each other. At the same time, these structures may create criminal opportunities for those denied access to legitimate employment. In these areas, gangs exist and may come to view their subculture as the only opportunity they have. Martin Sanchez Jankowski (1991) maintains that conditions in lower socioeconomic communities eliminate legitimate opportunities. As a result, poor ethnic minorities are forced to form illicit opportunity structures for their economic survival. Frederic Thrasher (1928) argued that gangs that emerged from immigration and migration were associated with crime and deviance.

Cloward, Richard—One of the authors of differential opportunity theory. Along with Lloyd Ohlin, he argued that in some lower-class communities, illegal activities could be found that would allow some an avenue to reach cultural success. He argued that three types of groups or gangs could be found in some lower-class neighborhoods.

Ohlin, Lloyd—Co-author of the theory of differential opportunity along with Richard Cloward.

Cohen, Albert—A sociologist who postulated why gangs formulated in lower-class culture. He introduced typologies of gangs that emerge in response to strain.

Miller, Walter—A sociologist who studied communities in Boston using a participant observation technique and formulated the controversial focal concerns theory.

Later studies by **Richard Cloward** and **Lloyd Ohlin** (1960), **Albert Cohen** (1955), Herbert Bloch and Arthur Niederhoffer (1958), Lewis Yablonsky (1959), James Short and Fred Strodtbeck (1965), **Walter Miller** (1958), and Irving Spergel (1967) focused on gangs as a response to poverty and social class in the tradition of strain and subcultural theories instead of immigration and cultural conflict. They found that gangs are complex institutions with distinct structures and organization, including identifiable leadership and division of labor (some members are fighters, others burglars, while some are known as deal-makers). They are governed by rules and rituals. They often have identifiable turf (Jankowski, 1991). According to the symbolic interaction point of view, gang members influence one another's personalities through a process of communication that is verbal and symbolic. In this process, members learn their proper role. They learn what is expected of others, as well as themselves. They learn what is valued by the group, and as a result, they aspire to embody the group's values. When they demonstrate the values of the group, it provides members with status.

Criminological theories of the 1950s and early 1960s disproportionately focused on juvenile delinquency, in general, but on gang behavior, in particular. This occurred because of mounting concerns over criminal and deviant subcultures emerging in many inner cities across the nation. Sociologists grew increasingly concerned about gangs and the lower class. The 1950s were economically prosperous for the dominant U.S. society. However, the wealth was not distributed equally to the lower classes. Researchers who embarked on the study of gangs and deviant subcultures relied on the advances made by the University of Chicago with respect to poverty, social disorganization, and the effects that the social ecology could have on individual or group behavior. The subcultural theories addressed in this chapter include the work of Cohen (1955), Cloward and Ohlin (1960), Miller (1958), and **Marvin Wolfgang** and **Franco Ferracuti** (1967). These subcultural theories are thought of as the dominant theories of the period. They focus on gang research and criminal subcultures. Perhaps the biggest questions posed about subcultures in general, but gangs in particular, have been: (1) Do

Wolfgang, Marvin—A sociologist who conducted longitudinal research using a birth cohort to examine the repeat or chronic offender. He also examined homicides while paying close attention to victim precipitation. He is typically identified as having conducted research with Ferracuti on the subculture of violence theory.

Ferracuti, Franco—One of the writers of a subculture of violence theory who argued that most violent crime in the 1960s occurred in the southern states among people who shared a willingness and readiness to engage in extreme violence.

subcultures refer to a group of people? and (2) Do subcultures refer to the shared ideas of a group of people?

Subculture of Delinquency

In 1955, Albert Cohen published *Delinquent Boys*. Cohen based this work on the scholarship of the sociologists at the University of Chicago. His book was also influenced by the Mertonian theory of strain; Shaw and McKay's work on social disorganization and **cultural transmission of deviance**; and Thomas, Mead, and Cooley's contribution of symbolic interaction. These theoretical developments contributed to the foundation of Cohen's book.

> **cultural transmission of deviance**—A theoretical argument from Clifford Shaw and Henry McKay concerning the continuing of deviance and criminal behavior in the socially disorganized community found in Zone Two of the five concentric circles. They argued that deviance is taught or passed from one community resident to another.

Again, though juvenile delinquency in general was a concern for researchers in the 1950s and 1960s, gang behavior was the main focus. Cohen's work tried to understand why teenagers were attracted to gangs. Cohen noted that delinquency was most often found among lower-class males and that gang delinquency was the most common form (Cohen, 1955). Unlike other researchers during this period, Cohen also conducted research on middle-class delinquency. Cohen observed that when middle-class girls engaged in delinquency, they typically engaged in promiscuous behavior, and middle-class boys stole cars to go joyriding. Both males and females engaged in deviant behavior to rebel against the control their parents had over them. However, Cohen argued that those in the lower classes were more likely to be attracted to gangs. He determined that gang subcultures were characterized by behavior that was non-utilitarian (senseless behavior that does not benefit the gang), malicious (mean spirited), and negativistic (detrimental) (Cohen, 1955).

Cohen argued that juveniles drawn to gangs had no rationale for committing delinquency (not even an economic need because of poverty), but did so to attack middle-class values. He argued that any behavior that was contrary to mainstream society was attractive to lower-class gang members. He concluded that the primary reason gang members engaged in crime was to seek status from their fellow gang members and others in society. Cohen argued that gang members were hedonistic and short-sighted. They did not plan for the future and were concerned only with short-term gratification. They had no real plans for the future, but lived from day to day. They were irresponsible. They resented and took offense to outsiders telling them how to live their lives, and they took a strong delight in causing discomfort to non–gang members (Cohen, 1955).

By integrating concepts from strain theory, Cohen borrowed from Merton. However, instead of positing that children are concerned with economic prosperity (the American Dream), he claimed they were trying to acquire social status. Problems arose because not all children could compete for status on an equal footing. Cohen argued that because of the American system of stratification, juveniles of different classes are positioned differently in the social structure. Poor children lack the ability to compete for status with others in a higher social class; children in the middle and upper classes have both a symbolic and economic advantage over youths in the lower class. It is very difficult, if not impossible, for lower-class youths to acquire status through the educational system, where they compete with students in the other classes who are better educated and have parents who are educated. Middle- and upper-class parents represent success in the educational system; many graduated from high school and college, and some attended professional school. This symbolic advantage signals to their children the benefits of an education. Moreover, if middle-class children need help with homework, their parents can easily provide assistance or hire a tutor. Their economic position affords this luxury. Unfortunately, those in the lower class who face a symbolic and an economic disadvantage do not have the benefit of educated parents. They have no help with homework, and their parents do not serve as positive role models after which to pattern their lives. Because of their position in the social structure, lower-class children are disadvantaged.

Cohen argued that the first major problem of status with which children are confronted occurs in schools during the educational process. Despite the economic and symbolic disadvantages that confront those in the lower class, they must also be evaluated by someone who is part of the middle-class structure, who perhaps identifies more with middle-class families. Cohen contended that in traditional classroom settings, social status is conferred on students by their teachers. When status is conferred, teachers use a **middle-class measuring rod** to bestow recognition for academic achievement, and tend to favor students with the same background as their own. Teachers sometimes inadvertently show middle-class students favor because of the promise they believe the students hold. Those in the lower class may lose interest in the educational process, since they do not see many people in their community benefiting from efforts made via mainstream avenues. According to Cohen, those who desire social status the most suffer **status frustration**. They develop defensive mechanisms to cope with their inability to achieve mainstream recognition or status in the presence of their teachers and peers. Cohen referred to this as an overreaction to the middle-class value system. As a result of their inability to acquire social status, lower-class youths collectively develop a solution (**collective solution**) to the problem of achieving status. They collectively create **new norms** (ones they are capable of accomplishing) that are used to confer status (Cohen, 1955). In a process of cultural transmission and symbolic interaction, lower-class individuals are able to teach one another reasons for accepting deviant and criminal lifestyles, and eventually gangs emerge from the subcultures

middle-class measuring rod—The standards set by middle-class authority figures.

status frustration—A state of dejection caused by the inability to achieve social status in any aspect of life whose value is stressed by the American society.

collective solution—A concept that was coined by Albert Cohen that revealed the actions of lowerclass youths who faced the inability to reach the culturally induced goals of status through the educational system. The collective solution led to the formulation of gangs.

new norms—Behaviors that lowerclass youths decided would be status conferring. According to Albert Cohen, because youths in the lower class could not achieve status via conventional means, they created status-conferring behaviors that they could easily attain.

found in lower-class areas. According to Cohen, gangs confer status on their members when they engage in behaviors that are characterized as malicious, non-utilitarian, and negativistic. The more members engage in these behaviors, the more status they acquire from fellow gang members. Cohen contended that gangs emerged because of society's emphasis on achieving social status and the lack of opportunities afforded people in the lower class.

Cohen's Categories of Subcultures

Cohen argued that several categories of gang subcultures emerged in the lower-class culture in response to middle-class rejection. Some of the groups posed little if any problems for the society, and others were problematic because they engaged in delinquency and crime. To the extent that a lower-class male suffered the problem of status frustration from the desire to achieve social status, it may have served to determine the group in which he sought membership. The groups included: the corner boys, the college boys, and the delinquent boys.

The corner boy category was the most common response to middle-class rejection. Those who became corner boys did not engage in high levels of crime and delinquency. Instead, they engaged in petty offenses. They were very loyal to the group in which they had membership, because the group was seen as a source of motivation, strength, and interest. The values of the group became the values of all members. Corner boys accepted the realization that they would never achieve the American Dream. They retreated to the lower-class community and accepted their fate. They got married, maintained a low-paying job, and remained part of the lower-class structure. Those in this category were seen by some community residents as being too passive because of their willingness to accept their plight.

The college boy category consisted of inner-city young males who embraced the social values of the middle class. They tried to reach the cultural goal of success by using mainstream means. Cohen believed that this group faced a hopeless future, because they were ill prepared academically, socially, and linguistically to achieve the rewards of the middle-class lifestyle. This category was also the most despised in the lower-class community, because of their desire to assimilate into the dominant culture. Many in the lower-class community believed that college boys resented their poverty and were ashamed of their lower-class culture. Because of this, they were viewed by many residents with contempt.

the corner boy—Another type of group typology described by Albert K. Cohen that developed in lower class culture because of unequal distributions of wealth and status. These boys made the most out of their situation. They remained in the community without ever leaving the lower class. They hung out in the neighborhood and spent time engaging in group activities such as gambling and athletics. They did not commit serious crime, but disproportionately engaged in petty offenses. They received support from their peers and were extremely loyal to the group and neighborhood. In the end, they found menial labor and lived a conventional lifestyle.

the college boy—One type of group described by Albert K. Cohen in his book, *Delinquent Boys* (1955). Such group while few in numbers emerge in response to the failure of member of the lower class achieving middle class social status. These boys reject their lower class culture and desperately attempt to assimilate into middle class society by embracing middle class standards. Cohen believed these boys faced a bleak prospect of integrating in the middle class for several reasons, but namely their academic deficiencies.

the delinquent boy—The third of three typologies that Albert K. Cohen described as emerging in the lower class culture and arguably the most troubled and problematic. This group posed a serious threat to the community because it engaged in delinquency as a way of rejecting middle class values. This group initially emerged because of adolescences and teenagers failure to achieve "middle class" status during the educational process owing to a lack of economic and symbolic disadvantages. To deal with middle class rejection, they resulted to reaction formation. Consequently, this group bestowed a different type of status on its members. In this group, social status was conferred on members by other lower class children to the extent that they demonstrated behaviors that were nonutilitarian, malicious, and negativistic. To them, if behaviors were considered inappropriate by middle class society, it was considered appropriate and acceptable by the group. The members were extremely loyal to each other and resisted all efforts by any authority figure to control the group's behavior.

differential opportunity—The theory that people living in lower-class communities can find opportunities of a different kind to reach cultural goals of success.

The delinquent boy category represented a problem population. They were those who had created a way to confer status on the members of their own group. They constantly engaged in behaviors that were repugnant to middle-class values. They participated in hedonistic behavior and celebrated their group's autonomy. They were critical of and resistant to social control and authoritative figures, such as the family, school, church, and outsiders with an interest in changing their behaviors. Status was gained by being good at behaviors that were characterized as non-utilitarian, malicious, and negativistic. In the final analysis, Cohen contended that the greater one's aspirations or desires, the greater the strain or frustration one experiences when goals are not met. Because of their economic and symbolic disadvantages (the lack of resources and positive role models), those in the lower class tend to rebel against conventional society whenever the occasion presents itself (Cohen, 1955).

Differential Opportunity Theory

In creating the theory of **differential opportunity**, Cloward and Ohlin relied on the earlier works of Shaw and McKay, Merton, and scholars at the University of Chicago to theorize about the social ecology of crime and gang formation. Like Cohen's work, Cloward and Ohlin's theory was used to explain the development of gangs. Their theory was inspired by Merton. In fact, it is viewed as a reaction to Merton's strain theory. For example, Merton previously argued that some people in the social structure have legitimate access (such as hard work, education, deferred gratification, and honesty) to pursue the American Dream and others do not. Cloward and Ohlin argued that the cultural aspirations and dreams of lower-class people could be realized through illegitimate structures that may be just as established in some communities, but not in others. To Cloward and Ohlin, criminal opportunities could be just as established in some communities as were legitimate opportunities in other communities.

Cloward and Ohlin argued that while Merton's strain theory contributed much to the understanding of crime, the theory missed a major area of concern. They argued that males in lower socioeconomic structures of society could find opportunities of a different kind. They contended that while strain theory had addressed only conventional economic avenues, disproportionately available to the middle class, other channels for reaching success were available to the poor. Through illegitimate avenues, or criminal enterprises, people in the lower class could succeed, but there was no guarantee that they could even find illegal opportunities.

Relying on observational work from sociologists at Chicago, along with **Solomon Kobrin's** work on **integrated communities**, Cloward and Ohlin were able to determine why illegal enterprises emerged and sustained themselves over extended periods of time. According to Kobrin's discussion of integrated communities, these were areas characterized by having high levels of control over the behaviors of their residents. They argued that in lower-class communities, illegitimate activities provided residents with alternative means by which they could reach their cultural aspirations. To some, the illegal enterprises offered mobility; they could start as street-level gang members and work their way up to becoming organized crime (mafia) members. Criminal structures also afforded some people the opportunity to move laterally into legitimate business. However, illegal opportunity structures were contingent upon the degree of integration (social control) that existed in one's community (Kobrin, 1951). A criminal activity such as organized crime could not sustain itself if it offended the wishes of the community. When community residents are aware that they face unequal opportunities, they may be inclined to allow for such activities if violence is held to a minimum. Cloward and Ohlin discussed three types of gangs that emerged from the lower-class culture they studied: criminal gangs, retreatist gangs, and conflict gangs.

Criminal gangs were found in fully integrated communities. In these communities, residents exercised a tremendous amount of social control over the behaviors of those participating in illegal activities. These gang members occupy the role of apprentices to organized crime gangs. They concentrated on making money, and violence was used only when necessary. Because these gang members were conducting business instead of engaging in random acts of violence, they were provided with an avenue to reach the conventional aspiration of economic success. Criminal gangs were successful because the community allowed them to operate over time.

Kobrin, Solomon—A contributor to the Chicago School with his study of communities and the degree of integration or social organization that they have. Kobrin argued that degree of integration determines whether criminal activities will flourish in lower-class communities.

integrated communities—Areas of the city in which residents exercise a high level of social control. The term refers to areas that approve and allow criminal enterprises to sustain themselves over time.

criminal gangs—One of three gang typologies discussed by Richard Cloward and Lloyd Ohin in their book, *Delinquency and Opportunity* (1960) that emerged in response to the lower class culture and a lack of legitimate opportunities. They were found in stable slum areas that had connections among adolescence, young adults and adult criminals. The areas provided an environment for successful criminal enterprises. Unlike the other two gangs (conflict and retreatist), these gang members served as apprentices. They were taught a criminal trade and were primarily recruited to learn how to make money. They were also trained to not jeopardize criminal operations by keeping violence at a minimum. They were often able to transition into organized crime. These gangs were often found in socially organized communities.

retreatist gangs—One of three gang typologies discussed by Richard Cloward and Lloyd Ohin in their book, *Delinquency and Opportunity* (1960) that emerged in response to lower class culture and a lack of legitimate or illegitimate opportunities. Unlike the other two gangs (conflict and criminal), these gang members were considered as double failures since they were unable to succeed through legitimate avenues and unwilling to do so through illegal means. Some members tried but failed at a life of crime either because of weakness, clumsiness, or fear. Some may have even been viewed by gang members as unacceptable members. They then retreated to the fringes of society where they searched for ways to alter their state of mind with alcohol, pot, heroin or engaging in unusual sexual experiences. Despite this, they were best known for selling and using drugs. Because they could not succeed in either the conventional or lower class structure, they were referred to as two time losers.

conflict gangs—One of three gang typologies discussed by Richard Cloward and Lloyd Ohin in their book, *Delinquency and Opportunity* (1960) that emerged in response to lower class culture and a lack of legitimate or illegitimate opportunities. Unlike the other two gangs (criminal and retreatist), these gang members were typically found in socially disorganized communities where they engaged in violence against community residents as well as rival gangs in order to win a reputation. This allowed them to acquire status, a self-image, and access to scarce resources in impoverished areas.

focal concerns—A subcultural explanation given by Walter Miller of the behaviors of lower-class gang members. According to Miller, focal concerns replaced conventional values and traditions. Moreover, adherence to the focal concerns was status conferring.

Retreatist gangs, were located in integrated communities, but members of these gangs lacked access to either criminal or conventional opportunity structures. They were concerned with buying and selling drugs. In these gangs, participants were seen as two-time losers, because they had no legitimate avenues to succeed and were unsuccessful when engaging in criminal activities. This could be because they were afraid or simply did not have what it takes to be a criminal. Although criminal gangs were located in integrated communities, many youths were not allowed to participate in them, because they were not trusted by the gangs or organized crime groups; therefore, they became part of retreatist gangs. Research suggests that since members of organized crime lived in the same communities, the older organized crime members may have deemed some youths unacceptable for gang membership.

Conflict gangs were disproportionately found in nonintegrated communities. These communities lacked a well-organized structure and exercised very weak community control over juveniles. These gangs exhibited unrestrained criminal behavior. Communities characterized as having poor or no social control over the behavior of residents were viewed as violent places, because gang members would attack and intimidate residents, as well as fight rival gangs. Crime proliferated because no one controlled the gang members' behaviors.

Cloward and Ohlin researched the reaction of lower-class youths to a social structure based on inequities. They concluded that gang formation was a reaction to the strain of not having access to conventional means to reach the cultural goal of economic success. With the realization that their position in the social structure essentially meant their exclusion from success, lower-class residents simply sought "differential opportunities," or opportunities of a different kind, to achieve their aspirations, rather than abandoning the idea of economic prosperity. Both subcultural theories by Cohen, and Cloward and Ohlin, are considered extensions of Merton's strain theory.

Focal Concerns Theory

In 1958, Walter Miller published his controversial work on the lower class, positing a theory that he referred to as **focal concerns**. Focal concerns is essentially a grounded theory that resulted from observational, or field, research. The research consisted of daily contacts for nearly 13 months with participants who composed 21 corner group units in a "slum" district of Boston (Miller, 1958). Data were collected using a triangulated method that relied on contact reports, participant observation reports, and direct tape recordings of group activities and discussions.

Focal concerns theory is based on firsthand observations made by Miller and his research team while interacting with groups of Negroes, whites, males, and females in their early, middle, and late adolescence, as described in the report. Miller approached this undertaking without any preconceived notions about the subjects in the community he selected for research. As such, he had no biases from the beginning of the project. However, as the study unfolded, Miller developed a grounded theory that explains the social reality confronted by those living in the lower-class culture. He discovered the meaning of the social experiences of people who occupy the bottom tier of the social structure.

Of the subcultural theories that were dominant in the 1960s, Miller's is considered the most controversial. He argues that the people in the subculture he investigated were not concerned about the dominant cultural values or conventional goals of society, but rather they had created a value system that was unique to their own experiences and was a dominant theme in their subculture. Stated another way, Miller reports that the people in the lower class he studied were not concerned about hard work, deferred gratification, education, being honest, or traditional middle-class values, but rather they had essentially replaced mainstream values with their own. These values Miller called focal concerns. According to Miller, all community residents adhered to and accepted these informal values.

Before discussing focal concerns, it is important to note that in the lower-class cultures Miller studied, many households were headed by a single parent, most often a woman. Many of the male figures were absent either because they could not sustain a workable relationship with the mothers of their children or because they were in prison. As a result, women were faced with the responsibility of rearing young males to become men. Many young males resented this because of their concerns over masculinity. Young men in these communities had few positive male role models to emulate, and for that reason, they were forced to socialize one another into what they considered appropriate adult male behavior. Moreover, unemployment and joblessness were pervasive.

Miller's focal concerns include: trouble, toughness, smartness, excitement, fate, and autonomy. **Trouble** was a dominant theme found in the lower class. Most males in the lower-class subculture displayed a tremendous potential for staying in trouble. They exhibited trouble with people in the community, as well as with informal and formal authority. Trouble in the community was seen as something that was unavoidable, and even expected of lower-class males. Because getting into and staying in trouble was so common in the lower class, it was deeply entrenched in the subculture.

Toughness was seen as a good trait to have in the lower-class community. This concept was associated with manliness. Because in many homes the male figure was

trouble—A unavoidable theme that is common to lower class subculture that helps to assess one's suitability and standings in the lower class milieu.

toughness—A dominant theme or value that is commonly found in lower class subculture due to a lack of fatherly figures who are absent from the family. It holds that part of the male socialization in lower class culture was to overly emphasize measures of masculinity.

absent, there were widespread concerns in the community that some males were not strong or "macho" enough. As a result, any display of toughness was highly valued. For example, if one had good athletic skills, a reputation as a good fighter, a history of rebellion against maternal authority, or a reputation for having made many sexual conquests, one would be held in high esteem by male peers. In these communities, toughness was synonymous with physical prowess, skill, fearlessness, bravery, and daring behavior.

smartness—A dominant theme or value that is commonly found in the lower class subculture and highly praised that holds some residents are gifted with the ability to con others into getting what they want from them by using mental agility instead of having to work or engage in physical labor to acquire what they desire.

excitement—A dominant theme or value common to lower class subculture that posits that on the weekends, large numbers of poor community residents go uptown in search of thrills such as drinking, dancing, fighting, and fulfilling sexual pleasures.

Smartness was the most valued of all focal concerns. Within the lower-class subculture, smartness had nothing to do with one's academic ability, but instead rested on using mental agility to acquire some desired commodity. Those with the ability to outsmart or "con" others were highly regarded by people in the subculture. Lower-class children actually practiced their conning skills to take advantage of unsuspecting people. Those gang members who were considered smart by the rest of the group had established themselves as people who were unwilling to gain money the traditional way and were good at conning others to acquire that they wanted.

Excitement was a major goal for underclass people. Miller reported that people in the lower class looked forward to going "uptown" to celebrate and party at end of each week. He argued that they would stage an exodus from the ghetto to seek excitement and pleasure. They went searching for a drink, dance, fight, or other behaviors they associated with having a good time, even if it brought disadvantageous consequences. This also meant going from bar to bar in search of fun, excitement, and danger. Miller argued that men often went looking for women who would entertain their sexual desires, and conversely, women looked to entertain the sexual fantasies of their male counterparts. In the lower-class community, excitement was synonymous with thrill, risk, change, and activity.

fate—A theme that is common to lower class subculture that holds that many residents of urban ghettos are superstitious and often make life decisions about their futures based on unsubstantiated beliefs.

autonomy—A dominant theme or value common to lower class subculture that suggests people covertly express a desire to function independently of state authority but often contradict this by engaging in overt behavior that will bring them into the criminal justice system.

Fate was what people in the lower class believed would dictate a certain outcome. Miller argued the lower-class people he encountered were superstitious and believed that if they experienced strange occurrences during the early part of a day, the rest of the day would somehow end in disaster. They believed that forces existed over which they had no control.

Autonomy was what the poor claimed to have wanted, but acted in a manner that revealed contrary behavior. Miller thought that people in the lower class embodied contradictions, in that, while they overtly argued one position, they covertly desired something entirely different.

For example, he argued that while the males in the lower class often displayed the need to be free and independent of state authority and control, they often re-engaged in crime after release from jail or prison, which meant that they would once again come under the control of the criminal justice system.

Miller and Street Corner Gangs

Miller reported that young men in the lower class always spent time on street corners. Spending time with other young men who were similarly situated allowed these young men time to come together and share their experiences with others. The street corner was the place where many would be socialized into the value system shared by other young men. It represented more than just a place to meet; those who frequented the corner were part of a special group. For boys reared in female-headed households, the corner group provided an opportunity to learn essential aspects of the male role with peers facing similar problems of gender-role identification. In order to obtain status in the group, Miller argued, these young men would have to display a commitment to the focal concerns that served as the values in the lower-class culture. Those males who displayed toughness, smartness, autonomy, and a commitment to resisting authority were held in high regard and maintained good standings in the group. The street group served as a symbol of belonging and standing for its participants. The extent to which youth belonged to the gang was determined by the degree to which they engaged in the group's activities. For example, engaging in illegal behaviors was seen as a rite of passage from adolescence to adulthood (Miller, 1958).

Subculture of Violence Theory

In 1967, Marvin Wolfgang and Franco Ferracuti introduced the last of the dominant subcultural theories. Their theory, referred to as the **subculture of violence**, was different from others in that it took on a much larger focus than gangs or street corner groups. It attempted to explain the behaviors of entire subcultures. Wolfgang and Ferracuti postulated that in subcultures of violence,

> **subculture of violence**—A subculture, generally in a lower-income urban area, where violence is more used and tolerated by community residents. Because violence is so pervasive, many residents are desensitized to it.

the environment may directly or indirectly socialize residents into accepting and participating in criminal and violent behavior. They argued that after being exposed to such an environment, community residents become desensitized to the vicious nature of crime and violence that proliferate in these areas. Moreover, since they are part of the culture that engage in these behaviors, they are socialized into thinking that these behaviors are acceptable and even expected as normal occurrences given that certain actions have already transpired.

In creating the theory, the authors relied on the work of many criminological traditions and combined them in their explanation of criminal behavior. The subculture of violence theory integrates concepts from cultural conflict, symbolic interaction, and learning theories. The theory argues that members of the subculture may have values that are conducive to criminal behavior because they are confronted with social maladies early in the socialization process. These values may remain with them for extended periods of time, depending on whether they remain in a violent subculture. When those exposed to violence in the subculture are guilty of such behavior themselves, it is because they are the product of negative environmental surroundings. However, people who engage in violence and criminal behavior without being exposed to a subculture of violence, Wolfgang and Ferracuti argued, tend to be more pathological than people subjected to violence at an early age.

> **structured action theory**—A theory developed by sociologist James W. Messerschmidt that addresses the gendered nature of crime. In *Crime as Structured Action*, he looks at relations between gender and crime by examining how people in specific settings can use crime to construct social relations, social situations, and how social structures and setting helps to produce and reproduce different types of masculinities and femininities.

Structured Action Theory

In 1997, James Messerschmidt presented the **structured action theory** to conceptualize the gendered nature of crime in western industrialized societies. In his book *Crime as Structured Action: Gender, Race, Class, and Crime in the Making*, Messerschmidt argues that the social settings in which people find themselves account for different constructions of masculinities and femininities that can serve as a resource for doing crime. He believes that crime is a masculine enterprise since men are disproportionately found among all arrest statistics. He also notes that masculinities and femininities can be understood as fluid, relational, and structured constructs. Within these settings, people construct social relations and social structures that direct and place constraints on their behavior. Messerschmidt argues that to understand crime, one must know how gender, crime, and class relations exist together, rather than separately.

Structured action helps to contextualize how people "do" gender, race, class, and crime. With regard to "doing" gender, race, class, and crime, each is given meaning and expression in specific social relations. For example, the social situation in which people find themselves may require a different type of gender, race, class, or even crime. Stated differently, through social practices in specific settings, people do gender, race, and class. As such, gender, race, and class can vary by social situations and circumstances. Messerschmidt (1997), for example, argues that "gender, race, and class are accomplished systematically not imposed on people or settled before hand, and is never static or finished products. Rather, people construct gender, race, and class in specific social situations" (p. 5).

To the extent that people "do" gender, race, and class (differently) is determined by the social structural constraints they encounter. People can use innovation to influence the structures where they engage in social relations or have membership. Moreover, where people are positioned, in the social structure in general and their social relations in particular, determines the specific forms of gender, race, and class that are available to them.

For example, poor people do gender, race, and class differently than their middle- and upper-class counterparts. They also construct masculinity and femininity differently (this could mean that some forms may run oppositional to others, but they are still masculine and feminine; the social setting may demand that they be accomplished differently). More to the point, robbery is considered a masculine crime by someone in the lower class who is constrained by its limitations, yet masculinity is received by the offender if he successfully commits this offense. A wealthy offender would feel masculine if he was able to successfully manipulate the stock market without detection. Both offenders by virtue of their position in the social structure are doing different types of gender, race, and class. Messerschmidt contends that gender, race, and class must be viewed as structured action. In a classic example of structured action theory by Messerschmidt, he uses the life-history approach to reveal how Malcolm Little (an adolescent from Nebraska), Detroit Red (robber, drug dealer, pimp), and Malcolm X (religious and political leader) were able to construct masculinity differently as they changed social settings and social structures (Messerschmidt, 1997).

Summary

Social structure theories argue that unlike biological or psychological explanations used to explain the high rates of crime among the poor, environmental factors greatly impact their behavior. These theories consider poverty, community decay, unequal distributions of resources and how they impact different segments of society. Structural or environmental explanations are rooted in the early writings of Adolf Quetelet and Émile Durkheim, who documented the effects of negative social forces and population shifts and how they influenced crime and delinquency.

However, sociologists at the University of Chicago capitalized on the social forces and structural changes that were occurring in the United States in general, but in Chicago in particular, to advance studies of the social ecology of crime. More specifically, they studied how negative environmental factors affected people, as well as their respective communities. In doing so, they transformed the discipline of sociology and the study of crime by de-emphasizing biology and psychology as primary causes of crime and instead focused on how the social environment and the social structure of society influenced criminal decision making. Sociologists affiliated with the university argued that crime was a function of where people lived and where they were positioned in the social structure. Moreover, the research legacy of the "Chicago School" eventually influenced others who believed that environmental factors could explain the high crime rates of the poor and disadvantaged.

Those who find merit in the fact that environmental factors influence crime are referred to as social structure theorists. Social structure theories are divided into three separate branches of theory that include social disorganization, strain, and subcultural (cultural deviance) theory. Social disorganization theory holds that because of a lack of resources, poor communities exert low if any control over the behaviors of community residents; thus, this accounts for the high rates of crime and lawlessness found in these areas. Strain theory in general holds that because of social stratification, or the structure of society, people in the lower class are unable to acquire the materials or lifestyles that the culture prescribes as measures of success or the American Dream. Those who feel strained the most are likely to use crime as an avenue to achieve what they are not allowed by the structural means in society. Subcultural theories have been used to explain how gangs emerged in society in general, but among inner-city poor in particular. The commonality that structural theories share is that the effects of poverty and unequal access to material resources serve to create crime in general, and in many cases gangs in particular, since people often become innovative in pursuit of materials of success. Despite these dominant structural theories, others have also emerged, including the institutional anomie theory as well as structured action theory.

Shortcomings of the Theories

1. Strain theories do a poor job of explaining offending disparities between males and females living under similar economic and social conditions.

2. Structural theories fail to explain why some people who face the same challenges found in disorganized and deteriorated communities refrain from engaging in crime.

3. Traditional strain theory fails to provide a comprehensive discussion of the social institutions in society.

4. Many structural theories do not advocate social reform efforts to make the system of stratification more equitable.

5. Many of the subcultural theories do not explain why boys are more attracted to subcultures than girls.

Discussion Questions

1. What are some common problems associated with the lower class?

2. What is the general position of social structural theory?

3. How are the urban poor and racial minorities impacted by poverty and other forms of inequality?

4. What is the primary difference between Merton's anomie theory and Agnew's general strain theory?

5. How does the economy undermine other social institutions in the United States?

6. According to the structured action theory, what allows people to reproduce gender, race, and class?

References

Agnew, R. (1985). A Revised Strain Theory of Delinquency. *Social Forces, 64,* 151–67.

Agnew, R. (1992). Foundations for a General Strain Theory of Crime and Delinquency. *Criminology, 30,* 47–87.

Akers, R. L. (1994). *Criminological Theories: Introduction and Evaluation.* Los Angeles, CA: Roxbury.

Anderson, E. (1999). *Code of the Street: Decency, Violence, and the Moral Life of the Inner City.* New York, NY: W. W. Norton & Company.

Arnold, D. O. (1970). *The Sociology of Subcultures.* Santa Barbara, CA: Glendessary Press.

Bandura, A. (1973). *Aggression: A Social Learning Analysis.* Englewood Cliffs, NJ: Prentice-Hall.

Barkan, S. E. (2001). *Criminology: A Sociological Understanding* (2nd ed.). Upper Saddle River, NJ: Prentice-Hall.

Barkan, S. E. (2006). *Criminology: A Sociological Understanding* (3rd ed.). Upper Saddle River, NJ: Prentice-Hall.

Becker, H. S. (1963). *Outsiders: Studies in the Sociology of Deviance.* New York, NY: Free Press.

Bellair, P. E. (1997). Social Interaction and Community Crime: Explaining the Importance of Neighbor Networks. *Criminology, 35*(4), 677–701.

Benda, B. B. (1995). An Examination of a Reciprocal Relationship Between Religiosity and Different Forms of Delinquency Within a Theoretical Model. *Journal of Research in Crime and Delinquency, 34,* 163–86.

Benda, B. B., and Corwyn, R. F. (1997). Religion and Delinquency: The Relationship After Considering Family and Peer Influence. *Journal for the Scientific Study of Religion, 36,* 81–92.

Bjerk, D. (2007). Measuring the Relationship Between Youth Criminal Participation and Household Economic Resources. *Journal of Quantitative Criminology, 23,* 23–39.

Blau, J., and Blau, P. (1982). The Cost of Inequality: Metropolitan Structure and Violent Crime. *American Sociological Review, 147,* 114–29.

Bloch, H. A., and Niederhoffer, A. (1958). *The Gang: A Study in Adolescent Behavior.* New York, NY: Philosophical Library.

Blumer, H. (1969). *Symbolic Interactionism: Perspectives and Methods.* Englewood Cliffs, NJ: Prentice-Hall.

Brownstein, H. H. (2000). *The Social Reality of Violence and Violent Crime.* Needham Heights, MA: Allyn and Bacon.

Burgess, E. W. (1926). *The Urban Community.* Chicago, IL: University of Chicago Press.

Bursik, R. J. (1988). Social Disorganization and Theories of Crime and Delinquency: Problems and Prospect. *Criminology, 26,* 519–51.

Cavan, R. S. (1969). *Juvenile Delinquency* (2nd ed.). New York, NY: J. B. Lippincott Company.

Center for Health Policy Research, University of California at Los Angeles (2003). *The Health of Young Children in California: Findings from the 2001 California Health Interview Survey.* Los Angeles, CA: Author.

Cloward, R. A., and Ohlin, L. E. (1960). *Delinquency and Opportunity: A Theory of Delinquent Gangs.* New York, NY: Free Press.

Cochran, J. K., Wood, P. B., and Arneklev, B. J. (1994). Is the Religiosity–Delinquency Relationship Spurious? A Test of Arousal and Social Control Theories. *Journal of Research on Crime and Delinquency, 31*(1), 92–123.

Cohen, A. K. (1955). *Delinquent Boys: The Culture of the Gang.* New York, NY: Free Press.

DeNavas-Walt, C., Proctor, B. D., and Smith, J. C., for the U.S. Census Bureau (2012). *Income, Poverty, and Health Insurance Coverage in the United States: 2011.* Current Population Reports, P60-243. Washington, DC: U.S. Government Printing Office.

Durkheim, E. (1893/1933). *The Division of Labor in Society*. Trans. George Simpson. New York, NY: Macmillan.

Durkheim, E. (1893/1951). *Suicide*. Glencoe, IL: Free Press.

Durkheim, E. (1895/1982). *The Rules of Sociological Method*. New York: Free Press.

Durkheim, E. (1897/1951). *Suicide: A Study in Sociology*. Trans. John A. Spaulding and George Simpson. New York: Free Press.Egley, A., and Ritz, C. E. (2006). *Highlights of the 2004 National Youth Gang Survey*. Washington, DC: Office of Juvenile Justice and Delinquency Prevention.

Eitzen, D. S., and Zinn, M. B. (1989). *Social Problems* (4th ed.). Boston, MA: Allyn and Bacon.

Elifson, K. W., Petersen, D. M., and Hadaway, C. K. (1983). Religiosity and Delinquency. *Criminology, 21,* 505–27.

Empey, L. (1982). *American Delinquency: Its Meaning and Construction* (Rev. ed.). Homewood, IL: Dorsey.

Evans, G., Wells, N., and Moch, A. (2003). Housing and Mental Health: A review of the Evidence and a Methodological and Conceptual Critique. *Journal of Social Issues, 59,* 475–501.

Gibbons, D. C. (1979). *The Criminological Enterprise: Theories and Perspectives*. Englewood Cliffs, NJ: Prentice-Hall.

Gordon, M. (1947, October). The Concept of the Subculture and Its Application. *Social Forces, 26,* 40–42.

Gottfredson, M., and Hirschi, R. (1990). *A General Theory of Crime*. Stanford, CA: Stanford University Press.

Haymes, S. N. (1995). *Race, Culture, and the City: A Pedagogy for Black Urban Struggle*. Albany, NY: State University of New York Press.

Hirschi, T. (1969). *Causes of Delinquency*. Berkeley, CA: University of California Press.

Jacoby, J. E. (1979). *Classics of Criminology*. Prospect Heights, IL. Waveland.

Jankowski, M. S. (1991). *Islands in the Streets: Gangs and American Urban Society*. Berkeley, CA: University of California Press.

Jenkins, P. (1984). *Crime and Justice: Issues and Ideas*. Pacific Grove, CA: Brooks/Cole.

Johnson, B. R., Larson, D. R., DeLi, S., and Jang, S. J. (2000). Escaping from the Crime of Inner Cities: Church Attendance and Religious Salience Among Disadvantaged Youth. *Justice Quarterly, 17*(2), 377–91.

Julian, J., and Kornblum, J. (1986). *Social Problems* (5th ed.). Englewood Cliffs, NJ: Prentice-Hall.

Kelling, G. L., and Wilson, J. Q. (1982, March 1). Broken Windows: The Police and Neighborhood Safety. *The Atlantic*.

Kerbo, H. R. (1983). *Social Stratification and Inequality: Class Conflict in the United States*. New York, NY: McGraw-Hall.

Klein, M.W., and Maxson, C. L. (2006). *Street Gang Patterns and Policies*. New York: Oxford University Press.

Knox, G. (1993). *An Introduction to Gangs*. Buchanan, MI: Vande Vere.

Kobrin, S. (1951). The Conflict of Values in Delinquency Areas. *American Sociological Review, 16,* 653–61.

Kornhauser, R. R. (1978). *Social Sources of Delinquency: An Appraisal of Analytic Models*. Chicago, IL: University of Chicago Press.

Kovandzic, T., Vieratis, L., and Yeisley, M. (1998). The Structural Covariates of Urban Homicide: Reassessing the Impact of Income Inequality and Poverty in the Post-Reagan Era. *Criminology, 36,* 369–600.

Krohn, M. (2000). Sources of Criminality: Control and Deterrence Theories. In J. F. Sheley (Ed.), *Criminology: A Contemporary Handbook* (pp. 373–99). Belmont, CA: Wadsworth.

Krug, E. G., Dahlberg, L. L., Mercy, J. A., Zwi, A. B., and Lozano, R. (2002). *World Report on Violence and Health.* Geneva: World Health Organization.

Larson, D. B., Sawyer, J. P., and McCullough, M. E. (1998). *Scientific Research on Spirituality and Health: A Consensus Report.* Rockville, MD: National Institute for Healthcare Research.

Lilly, J. R., Cullen, F. T., and Ball, R. A. (1995). *Criminological Theory: Context and Consequences* (2nd ed.). Thousand Oaks, CA: Sage Publications.

Liska, A. E., and Reed, M. D. (1985). Ties to Conventional Institutions and Delinquency: Estimating Reciprocal Effects. *American Sociological Review, 50,* 547–60.

Mauer, M. (1999). *Race to Incarceration: The Sentencing Project.* New York, NY: New Press.

Mauer, M. (2001). Causes and Consequences of Prison Growth in the United States. *Punishment & Society, 3,* 9–20.

Mazerolle, P., and Maahs, J. (2000). General Strain and Delinquency: An Alternative Examination of Conditioning Influences. *Justice Quarterly, 17*(4), 753–73.

Mazerolle, P., and Piquero, A. (1997). Violent Responses to Situations of Strain: A Structural Examination of Conditioning Effects. *Violence and Victims, 12,* 323–44.

Merton, R. K. (1938). Social Structure and Anomie. *American Sociological Review, 3,* 672–82.

Merton, R. K. (1968). *Social Theory and Social Structure.* New York, NY: Free Press.

Messerschmidt, J. W. (1997). *Crime as Structured Action: Gender, Race, Class, and Crime in the Making.* Thousand Oaks, CA: Sage.

Messner, S. F., and Rosenfeld, R. (1997). *Crime and the American Dream* (2nd ed.). Belmont, CA: Wadsworth.

Messner, S. F., and Rosenfeld, R. (2007). *Crime and the American Dream* (4th ed.). Belmont, CA: Wadsworth.

Miller, W. B. (1958). Lower-Class Culture as a Generating Milieu of Gang Delinquency. *Journal of Social Issues, 14,* 5–19.

National Gang Center (2013). *National Youth Gang Survey Analysis.* Washington, DC: Office of Juvenile Justice and Delinquency Prevention.

National Gang Intelligence Center (2010). Washington, D.C.: U.S. Department of Justice.

National Poverty Center (2012). "The Well Being of Families and Children as Measured by Consumption Behavior." http://www.npc.umich.edu/research/npc_research/consumption/

News One for Black America. (2012). "Warzone 2012: Chicago Devastated by Gangs, Murder." http://www.newsone.com

Nightingale, C.,H. (1993). *On the Edge: A History of Poor Black Children and Their American Dreams.* New York, NY: Basic Books.

Palen, J. J. (1981). *The Urban World* (3rd ed.). New York, NY: McGraw-Hill.

Park, R. E. (1936, April). Succession: An Ecological Concept. *American Sociological Review, 1,* 171–79.

Park, R. E., and Burgess, E. (Eds.). (1924). *The City.* Chicago, IL: University of Chicago Press.

Patchin, J., Huebner, B., McCluskey, J., Varano, S., and Bynum, T. (2006). Exposure to Community Violence and Childhood Delinquency. *Crime and Delinquency, 52,* 307–32.

Peterson, R. D., Krivo, L. J., and Harris, M. A. (2000). Disadvantage and Neighborhood Violent Crime: Do Local Institutions Matter? *Journal of Research on Crime and Delinquency, 37,* 31–63.

Pfohl, S. J. (1985). *Images of Deviance and Social Control: A Sociological History.* New York, NY: McGraw-Hill.

Phillips, J. A. (2002). White, Blacks, and Latino Homicide Rates: Why the Difference? *Social Problems, 49,* 349–74.

Piquero, N. L., and Sealock, M. D. (2000). Generalizing General Strain Theory: An Examination of an Offending Population. *Justice Quarterly, 17*(3), 449–78.

Quetelet, A. (1831/1984). *Research on the Propensity for Crime at Different Ages*. Trans. Sawyer F. Sylvester. Cincinnati, OH: Anderson.

Rose, H. M., and McCain, P.D. (2003). Homicide Risk and Level of Victimization in Two Concentrated Poverty Enclaves: A Black/Hispanic Comparison. In D. F. Hawkins (Ed.), *Violent Crime: Assessing Race and Ethnic Differences* (pp. 3–21). Cambridge, UK: Cambridge University Press.

Sampson, R. J. (1997). Neighborhoods and Violent Crime: A Multilevel Study of Collective Efficacy. *Science, 277*, 918–24.

Sampson, R. J., and Wilson, W. J. (1995). Toward a Theory of Race, Crime, and Urban Inequality. In J. Hagan and R. D. Peterson (Eds.), *Crime and Inequality* (pp. 37–56). Stanford, CA: Stanford University Press.

Schneider, M. J. (2013). *Introduction to Public Health*. 4th ed. Gaithersburg, MD: Aspen.

Sellin, T. (1938). *Culture Conflict and Crime*. New York, NY: Social Science Research Council.Shaw, C. R., and McKay, H. D. (1931). *Social Factors in Juvenile Delinquency*. Report No. 13, Vol. 2, National Commission on Law Observance and Enforcement. Washington, DC: U.S. Government Printing Office.

Short, J. F., and Strodtbeck, F. L. (1965). *Group Process and Gang Delinquency*. Chicago, IL: University of Chicago Press.

Siegel, L. (2000). *Criminology* (7th ed.). Belmont, CA: Wadsworth/Thompson Learning.

Siegel, L. (2012). *Criminology* (11th ed.). Belmont, CA: Wadsworth/Cengage Learning.

Sorlie, P. D., Backlund, E., and Keller, J. B. (1995). U.S. mortality by economic, demographic, and social characteristics: The National Longitudinal Mortality Study. *American Journal of Public Health, 85*, 949–56.

Spergel, I. A. (1967). *Street Gang Work: Theory and Practice*. Garden City, NY: Anchor Books.

Thrasher, F. (1928). *The Gang: A Study of 1303 Gangs in Chicago*. Chicago, IL: University of Chicago Press.

Trojanowicz, R. C., and Morash, M. (1987). *Juvenile Delinquency: Concepts and Control* (4th ed.). Englewood Cliffs, NJ: Prentice-Hall.

U.S. Department of Labor, Division of Labor Force Statistics (2010). *Employment and Unemployment in Families by Race and Hispanic or Latino Ethnicity, 2008–09 Annual Averages*. Washington, DC: U.S. Department of Labor.

Velez, M., Krivo, L., and Peterson, R. (2003). Structural Inequality and Homicide: An Assessment of the Black–White Gap in Killings. *Criminology, 41*, 645–72.

Vold, G. B., and Bernard, T. J. (1986). *Theoretical Criminology* (3rd ed.). New York, NY: Oxford University Press.

Warner, B. (2003). The Role of Attenuated Culture in Social Disorganization Theory. *Criminology, 41*, 73–97.

Whitehead, J. T., and Lab, S. T. (1990). *Juvenile Justice: An Introduction*. Cincinnati, OH: Anderson.

Williams, F. P., and McShane, M. D. (1998). *Criminology Theory: Selected Classic Readings* (2nd ed.). Cincinnati, OH: Anderson.

Williams, F. P., and McShane, M. D. (1999). *Criminological Theory* (3rd ed.). Upper Saddle River, NJ: Prentice-Hall.

Wilson, W. J. (1980). *The Declining Significance of Race: Blacks and Changing American Institutions* (2nd ed.). Chicago: University of Chicago Press.

Wilson, W. J. (1985, December). Cycles of Deprivation and the Underclass Debate. *Social Service Review, 59*, 541–59.

Wilson, W. J. (1987). *The Truly Disadvantaged: The Inner City, the Underclass, and Public Policy*. Chicago, IL: University of Chicago Press.

Wilson, W. J. (1996). *When Work Disappears: The World of the New Urban Poor*. New York, NY: Alfred A. Knopf.

Wilson, J. Q., and Herrnstein, R. T. (1985). *Crime and Human Nature: The Definitive Study of the Causes of Crime*. New York, NY: Simon & Schuster.

Wilson, M., and Daly, M. (1997). Life Expectancy, Economic Inequality, Homicide and Reproductive Timing in Chicago Neighborhoods. *British Journal of Medicine, 314,* 1271–74.

Wolfgang, M. E., and Ferracuti, F. (1967). *The Subculture of Violence: Towards an Integrated Theory of Criminology*. London, UK: Travistock.

Yablonsky, L. (1966). The Delinquent Gang as a Near-Group. *Social Problems, 7,* 108–17.

Yinger, J. M. (1960). Contraculture and Subculture. *American Sociological Review, 25,* 625–35.

Cases Cited

Brown v. Board of Education, 347 U.S. 483 (1954).

Plessy v. Ferguson, 186 U.S. 537 (1896).

Chapter 7

Social Processing Theories: Emphasis on Socialization

Chapter Outline

- Socialization and Crime
- Toward a Social Processing Explanation
- Learning Theories
- Control Theories
- Theories of Personal and Social Controls
- Labeling Theories
- Theory Integration
- Summary
- Shortcomings of the Theories
- Discussion Questions

Kenny Parker was a standout football player at Blount High School in Prichard, Alabama. Many players, coaches, and scouts considered him to be one of the best running backs from the state of Alabama in the past three decades. In fact, many teams in the South-eastern Conference (SEC) and other conferences throughout the United States wanted to recruit him. Kenny's parents were both present and active in the home. They were devout in their religious beliefs. They introduced Kenny to religion and insisted that he regularly attend church and that he keep his sports success in perspective while he managed other aspects of his life. His parents fully supported him on and off the field. When he played in local games, they always attended. When games were scheduled out of town, they rearranged their work schedules to support Kenny's efforts. Though they were pleased with Kenny's athletic prowess displayed on the football field, they were more impressed and proud of his academic accomplishment in the classroom, since Kenny was also an academic all-American with a GPA of 3.89. In fact, it was commonly known throughout the city that several colleges had been trying to convince Kenny to matriculate at their respective schools.

On the night of his high school graduation, Kenny and his friends attended a series of parties hosted by fellow graduates. It was a night that everyone had been looking forward to since it would be the last time they would be together before going in different directions. On this night, Kenny and several other football players attended one particular party where alcohol and drugs were available to anyone who wanted them. Though Kenny's classmates were aware that he did not use drugs or drink alcohol, they offered him both, telling him that since graduation was over, he needed to "relax a bit" and "blow off steam." He took their advice and joined them in having a good time. At some point during the evening, he was told by a teammate to go upstairs and join in some fun with other football players. Kenny did as he was told. When he entered the room, he observed several athletes having sex with two girls he recognized from high school. Three of his teammates encouraged him to have his turn, so he had sexual intercourse with one of the girls. Afterward, he returned downstairs, stayed until the party was over, and he went home. The next morning, Kenny and his family were awakened by loud knocks on the door. Police officers had a warrant for Kenny's arrest in connection with having sex with a minor who claimed she had been raped by Kenny and other athletes. He was handcuffed and taken into custody. When the news was reported by the local and national media, Kenny's life was turned upside down, and his dreams of receiving a scholarship to college disappeared before his eyes. But, Kenny's troubles were just beginning, since he and several other teammates were subsequently found guilty of raping a minor and sentenced to 20 years. They are also required by law to register as sex offenders for the rest of their lives.

Kenny's example is the exception rather than the rule. It is disturbing and shocking since it defies what most people expect from someone from a healthy family background. Kenny's story is tragic since he had everything going in his favor, such as being a talented athlete, being academically gifted, and having two loving and supportive parents who made sacrifices to provide him with a nurturing environment. In fact, one could surmise that his family did everything that it was required to do to properly rear Kenny to becoming a responsible and productive member of society, and had it not been for peer pressure from his fellow teammates, he may have avoided this negative outcome and instead received a scholarship to one of the SEC schools or another college and had a productive career as a student athlete. After receiving a college degree, he may have made positive contributions to society. But because his life took a different trajectory, he received an extended prison sentence and a label that will redefine who he is and alter his life course forever. This chapter examines how people are socialized and how it impacts their behavior.

The **elements of socialization** that are responsible for molding individuals into law-abiding and conforming citizens are the informal mechanisms of **social control**. They should instill mainstream values and beliefs into the young in hope that what they learn early in life will carry over into adulthood. They are responsible for teaching individuals the proper cultural goals, aspirations, expec-

> **elements of socialization**—The family, peers, school, church, and other institutions that are essential to social processing.
>
> **social control**—That which makes people conform their behaviors to standards of the law.

tations, and respect for the laws that should generate conformity to group norms and values. Socializing institutions are one's family, peers, school, church, and other significant institutions. These institutions provide individuals with structure and profoundly affect the way people live their lives. They establish the context and realities in which one lives. They invariably determine how people spend time, and eventually mold people into what they become (Henslin, 1991).

Socialization and Crime

Influenced by sociologists in the 1930s and 1940s who focused on the social–psychological components of criminal behavior, social process theorists attribute criminal behavior to human interaction and relationships that are developed and nurtured for better or worse in the **socialization** process that each person experiences. They are also concerned with the dynamics that occur within the context of those interactions (Siegel, 2012). This position holds that individual relationships with the family, school, peers,

> **socialization**—The process by which people are taught conventional or delinquent behavior while interacting with the family, peer, schools, and significant others.

and others can provide a better understanding of human behavior. Not everyone who lives in poverty or experiences negative social forces will engage in delinquency and crime, since the relationship between class and crime is tenuous at best. In fact, the majority of criminologists have not agreed that a class–crime relationship exists (Barkan, 2012). Today, over 40 million Americans live in poverty. Are we to assume that everyone who lives in this condition will engage in crime? The answer is absolutely not. **Social processing** theorists argue that there must be other factors that can explain why those not affected by negative economic factors will commit crime.

> **social processing**—The branch of theories that contains learning, labeling, and social control, and that argues that the quality of interactions that people have with socializing institutions and significant others will determine their future behaviors.

Researchers find that children who are reared in unhealthy households where conflict is a dominant theme, attend substandard schools, and associate with deviant peers are more likely to be influenced by these negative exposures and interactions. In fact, social processing theorists believe they greatly impact behavior. To these scholars, human socialization that begins at childhood and continues into adulthood will more likely determine individual behavior. More specifically, these scholars argue that human socialization or those interactions that people have with important institutions and processes will have more influence on them than their structural position. For these scholars, social processing can explain the behavior of people found throughout the society and not only those who are disadvantaged. They argue that the quality of socialization process with the family, the educational system, peer associations, and agents of the justice system will determine the types of behavior in which individuals are likely to engage. For example, through healthy socialization with the family, the school system, and peers, one should learn respect for societal rules and authority figures such as parents, teachers, community leaders, coaches, and law enforcement. However, people with negative experiences with the family, schools, and peers can teach us how they are linked to delinquency and crime. Criminologists study institutions such as the family, school, and peers to determine their impact on crime.

Family Relations

The importance of the family relationship has an established presence in the criminological literature (Glueck and Glueck, 1950). The family is the most important institution in the socialization process. It should teach individuals respect for the law, self, and others. The family fosters healthy personality development by providing love, warmth, support, and encouragement. Parents are supposed to lead by example while acting as positive role models. They should provide supervision, monitoring, and discipline when appropriate (Gottfredson and Hirschi, 1990). In fact, the family's goal is to ensure children's health and safety, prepare them for a life of productivity as adults, and transmit cultural values. Experts argue that a quality parent–child relationship is essential for healthy development. As such, researchers find that in the socialization process, the family is the most significant institution since it is a major determinant of behavior. Unlike youths reared in healthy families, those who are exposed to destructive relationships and behavior such as violence, alcohol abuse, drugs, and emotional and psychological abuse are more likely to engage in crime. Some experts argue that children who are socialized in households that lack love and support are at a higher risk of developing poor emotional well-being, externalizing problems, and participating in antisocial behavior (Cui and Conger, 2008). Conversely, children living in poverty and high crime areas that receive love and support from parents who serve as positive role models are better able to navigate the lures of pressures and vice found in poor areas. Despite this, children reared in situations where the family functions poorly and unhealthily are at a greater risk of delinquency (Cui and Conger, 2008).

Family structure is also important to child development and behavioral outcome. Family structure presents a concern in the United States. In fact, sociologists and social workers argue that the problem is pervasive since an estimated 32% of all children live in single-family homes (Siegel, 2012). Child experts also express concerns that life in a single-parent household can be stressful for children as well as adults. Research suggests that over the past 20 years, single-parent families have become more common than the "nuclear family." The relationship between family structure and crime is critical when considering the rates of divorce (Siegel, 2012). Divorce or family disruption has a negative effect on children. Research reveals that children reared in homes where one or both parents are absent are more likely to participate in delinquency (Sourander et al., 2006). Moreover, there is also a pronounced relationship between arrest rates and single-parent households (Savolainen, 2000).

Research finds that divorce may contribute to delinquency because a single parent is typically unable to provide adequate supervision, or the parent may expose children to negative effects of antisocial friends (Rebellion, 2002). Exposure to such situations could lead some children to act impulsively and impair their ability to exercise self-control or lead them to seek out undesirable friends for association who may be similarly situated. Research also reveals that the effect of a family breakup could lead to negative school performance and peer relationships. Conversely, children who are reared in two-parent households receive more supervision and more encouragement, and they tend to perform better academically. They are also more likely than their counterparts to attend college. Other studies have found a significant relationship between parental deviance and crime and the likelihood that children reared by them will also engage in crime. More specifically, research reveals that parental deviance is a powerful influence on children's future behavior since children want to model their parents. In fact, a significant number of delinquents have criminal fathers. Research suggests that this effect is intergenerational (Shaw, 2003). Some experts argue the family is the most important socializing institution because of the amounts of time children spend in the home and the degree to which they are exposed to family members' behaviors. Experts contend that if the family fails, the result could be failed and dysfunctional children (Wallace, 1999; Tower, 1996).

Educational Experiences

The educational process has also been linked to delinquency and crime. The education process is important because there is an established relationship between educational success and conventional behavior. The educational process teaches civil duties and provides one with the skills needed to be functional and competitive in a progressive society. Moreover, because individuals spend large amounts of time in school each day, it is expected they will come to respect the ideas and values of teachers who promote middle-class socialization. A demonstration of success in the educational process could mean later success in conventional society. However, educational failure could mean that youths may experience a life of delinquency and later crime (Jenkins, 1997; Prothrow-Stith, 1991).

Studies reveal that nationally, inmates serving time in jails, state, and federal prisons report having completed only a 10th-grade education. However, other studies reveal that children who perform poorly in school, who lack academic motivation, and who feel alienated are more likely to engage in crime. Moreover, education has a prominent place among those arrested in general, but also among those who committed violent crime in particular. Research suggests that children who commit serious crime are likely to continue into adulthood (Jussim, 1989).

Some research finds that when children are labeled troublemakers in school, the educational system may do them a grave disservice by labeling them since negative labels are linked to continued delinquency and crime. These researchers argue that "negative tracking" systems stigmatize some students whose identities may become compromised or transformed by the label. For example, students who are labeled slow or less intelligent than others may receive less help or attention from teachers and other students. Unfortunately, students who are labeled may accept the label as true. Thus, the labeling itself could lead to underachievement as well as prompting some students to leave school early by dropping out entirely (Oakes, 1985). Dropping out is a major problem in the United States. In fact, educational experts view this issue as a national crisis for a number of reasons; chief among them is that it threatens domestic security.

It is estimated that three out of 10 high school students do not graduate on time, and the numbers are more alarming in minority communities. For example, research estimates that nationally nearly 50% of African Americans and 40% of Latino youths attend high schools where dropping out is the norm. Statistics indicate that dropouts are 3.5 times more likely to be arrested than teenagers who finish high school. They are also eight times more likely to be incarcerated. Some experts argue that increasing the graduation rates by 10 percentage points would prevent over 3,000 murders and nearly 175,000 aggravated assaults annually (School Library Journal, 2008). Despite this, research in this area provides mixed results. For example, some research suggests school dropouts face a greater risk of entering a criminal career, while other studies have not been able to support that finding (Sweeten, Bushman, and Paternoster, 2009). Nevertheless, most research concludes that dropping out of school is related to poor school performance, and leaving school without an education sets students up for failure since they will face a bleak prospect of finding work that pays decent wages.

Peer Relationships

Peer groups have always had a significant impact on individual behavior. Whether by choice or pressure, the influence is undeniable. The presence of this relationship is well established and documented throughout the criminological literature. Peers are a very important part of the socialization process. Adolescents between the ages of 8 and 14 actively seek out friends or cliques as they mature. At this point, some experts contend that the relationships children have with friends may be stronger and more binding than the influence their parents have on them. Children, at this juncture in life, often desire popularity and social acceptance. Moreover, they may be more comfortable discussing personal issues with friends than parents. At this stage, children's behavior can be influenced by peers for better or worse, since they are impressionable. For example, if children associate with delinquent peers, they may begin engaging in delinquent behavior. On the contrary, if they associate with law-abiding friends, who are committed to conventional behavior, they may develop similar ambitions. It is important to note that delinquent and criminal peers can undermine years of healthy child rearing practices.

Some researchers report that peer influence is found in almost every culture, and the influence is universal (Antonaccio et al., 2010). Peer acceptance represents having status or popularity within a group (Yu, Tepper, and Russell, 2009). When peer group experiences are healthy, they can contribute to positive self-image, social competence, and achievement. They may also protect members against the influence of negative family functions. Young people who have a difficult time developing healthy relationships with peers are more likely to be aggressive, lonely, and experience depression (Yu et al., 2009). Moreover, peer relations often occur out of reach from parental supervision. Therefore, there are opportunities for peers to share both constructive and destructive behavior. The latter could lead to delinquency and crime (Anderson and Hughes, 2009).

While children and young adults are not immune from the negative influences of their peers, research suggests that some youth are more susceptible to negative peer influence than others. For example, studies show that children who lack popularity and are unaccepted by their peers, or even those who experience rejection, are more inclined to display violence and aggression that includes bullying and other forms of antisocial behavior (Elliott, Huizinga, and Ageton, 1985). Other studies report that the more antisocial the group, the greater the likelihood that its members will engage in delinquency (Battin et al., 1998). Still other research finds that children who engage in delinquency are five times more likely than nonoffenders to associate with delinquent friends (Battin et al., 1998). Studies on delinquency have reported several interesting findings; for example, at-risk children often choose to associate with older peers. Researchers believe this is the case because these children feel better protected and secure with older friends who they believe are tough enough to intervene on their behalf if needed. Another fact revealed by research is that older peers do not cause children who are otherwise nondelinquent to misbehave. However, research suggests that they do increase the likelihood that their younger peers will participate in antisocial behaviors. Finally, research shows that the loyalty delinquents express toward their peers often outweighs the fear of punishment that they can receive (Harding, 2009; Deptula and Cohen, 2004; Matthews and Agnew, 2008).

Religion

Research supports the belief that religion can prevent offenders from engaging in delinquency and crime (Johnson, 2011). More specifically, some research finds that youths who are more religious are less likely to participate in delinquent acts such as drinking alcohol, using drugs, and engaging in sexual behavior compared with their counterparts (Petts, 2009; Wallace et al., 2007). If religion can influence the behavior of teenagers or young adults, does it have the same effect on adult behavior? Studies of adult behavior also reveal that those who report having religious faith also report engaging in reduced amounts of criminality (Evans et al., 1995; Petts, 2009). Moreover, national studies suggest that religiosity helps to reduce premarital sex among adults who have never been married. Other research has reported similar results. For example, Lee (2006) reported that violent crimes occur less often in rural areas where there are more churches per capita than those with fewer churches. Despite these findings, researchers who examine the relationship between religion and delinquency speak of the difficulty in examining this relationship. They argue that with teenagers, it is difficult to fully understand their behavior; since most teens desire excitement, they easily tire of religion. As such, some are less religious and are more likely to engage in delinquency. Because of this, some researchers argue that the relationship between delinquency and religion is partially spurious (Cochran, Wood, and Arneklev, 1994). However, others present contradictory research from a national longitudinal study that found religion had a nonspurious effect on delinquency because it increased disapproval of delinquency and the proportion of law-abiding friends (Johnson et al, 2001; Barkan, 2012, p. 200).

The church as a socializing institution applies to those who believe in the existence of God or a higher power. Parents with religious faith often instill faith in their children. It serves as an internal mechanism of social control, forcing compliance to the laws of society and those of a higher power. Religion teaches peace and conformity to groups and societal expectations, and at the same time forces moral adherence (Cochran, Wood, and Arneklev, 1994; Brenda, 1997; Stark and Bainbridge, 1996). Experts argue that those with high levels of religiosity who regularly attend church are less likely to violate the law than people who are atheists or agnostics.

Significant Others

Significant others can be sources of informal control when they are actively involved in the socialization process. They are usually community leaders, respected people in the community, coaches, law-abiding relatives, and those involved in youth groups and their development. They often supervise teenagers and spend productive time with them. For some, employers and coworkers may serve this function (Henslin, 1991). Many people who are important in the lives of children act as positive role models. Significant others are sometimes aware that they function in this capacity, while others may be completely unaware that juveniles hold them in high regard (Henslin, 1991).

The socialization process is supposed to teach children and young adults the approved cultural norms of the broader society. To the extent that they are successful, people display law-abiding behavior. To the extent that they fail, people engage in crime and deviant behavior. Despite the arrangement of importance, when one element of the socialization process breaks down, it is possible for others to be strong or influential enough to negate a life of crime or delinquency. For example, if children are reared in a broken home (headed by a single parent) or a household characterized by poor or destructive forces (conflict, violence, abuse), the educational process, peers, church, or significant others can serve as a buffer to the ineptness of the family. However, in most cases when these mechanisms fail, the criminal justice system (police, prosecution, court, and corrections) or the formal mechanisms of control are activated. To the extent that social structure theories are influenced by the tradition of the Chicago School, so too are social processing theories.

Toward a Social Processing Explanation

Since many people doubt that poverty and **economic inequality** alone cause crime, experts have looked to social processing theories to provide an explanation for deviant and criminal behavior. Many argue that if poverty alone produced crime, then everyone (females included) living in the ghetto and slum areas would be a criminal, without exception. The reality is that many law-abiding and hard-working Americans can be found in lower economic structures of society. Therefore, critics contend that crime is a product of social processing—that is to say, crime can be attributed to the socialization processes to which individuals are subjected from childhood, and which carries over into their adult lives (Siegel, 2012). The socialization process consists of those interactions that one has with important socializing institutions, such as the family, peers, schools, church, and significant others. To the extent that interactions and relationships are healthy and nurturing, individual behavior should conform to mainstream values, such as hard work, being law-abiding, acquiring an education, and raising a family. However, if one's socializing institutions in society (family, peers, education, church) are ineffective or inept, this could mean failed socialization, with the consequence of deviant and criminal behavior. A very strong point in social processing explanations is that they can be used to explain the behaviors of all people in America regardless of race, gender, or social class. Social processing theories include learning, as well as control and labeling.

> **economic inequality**—Unequal distribution of monetary resources and access to employment opportunities.

Learning Theories

Social learning theories postulate that all behaviors (whether deviant or confirming) are learned through the socialization process. More specifically, learning theorists argue that crime is a product of learning the norms, values, and behaviors associated with criminal activity. Because of their circumstance, some people learn behaviors that are unlawful and prohibited by the broader society. This may explain why people reared in urban areas where street crime is saturated will typically engage in similar behavior. The same argument can be made for people from the middle and upper classes. They engage in behaviors and crimes that commonly occur in their respective communities. It has been argued that criminals model their behavior and motivations after those of other offenders (Reid, 2012).

Social learning theories provide context with regard to how people adapt their views about the acceptability of committing crime. In addition to learning the necessary attitudes and values, criminals also learn the proper techniques associated with the crime, such as the mechanics involved, as well as the psychological aspects, including how to neutralize their feelings or to suppress the guilt and shame of committing crime. While there are differences found among proponents of the **learning theory**, they all agree that delinquency and crime is a consequence of negative socialization. This section addresses several learning theories, including those regarded as the most prominent.

> **learning theory**—Theory that posits that human behavior is learned in the social environment from interactions with the family, friends, school, media, community, and the broader society. To extent that one has destructive or negative interactions with important people and institutions, it could determine impact his or her behavior.

> **Tarde, Gabriel**—A French sociologist and criminologist whose work in the area of imitation is considered the forerunner to the Differential Association Theory. His work on imitation contradicted early biological positivism.
>
> **imitation theory**—The theory that we learn through imitating the behavior of others.

Imitation Theory

In 1890, **Gabriel Tarde** (1843–1904) presented the **imitation theory**. He is arguably the first person to attempt to use social learning or modeling to explain criminal behavior. This theory is viewed as the forerunner of contemporary imitation theory (Reid, 2012). Tarde rejected Cesare Lombroso's work on biological determinism and argued that people are not born criminal, but rather they become criminal because of social factors. He did not subscribe to social determinism, since he believed that people had some choice over their behavior. To explain criminal behavior, Tarde introduced the theory of imitation, which was composed of three laws. The theory reflects the belief that all acts in life are carried out after observing a previous occurrence. This latter statement notwithstanding, the first law states that people imitate one another in proportion to the amount of contact they have with each other. The second law suggests that inferior people imitate superiors. The third law posits that when two fashions come together, one will substitute for the other.

As for the first law, Tarde observed that in cities, where life was exciting and active, people had close contact and imitated one another's behavior. He argued that fashions, for example, were imitated behavior. However, in families or stable groups disproportionately found in rural areas, life was less exciting and active. In these rural areas, people had less contact with one another. People in these areas tended to have more customs. According to Tarde, customs could become fashions, but not as quickly as they would in cities. In terms of the second law, Tarde also noticed that when crimes were committed by people in the aristocracy, those crimes would later become fashionable and be imitated by people in the lower class. Some examples of these crimes, according to Tarde, were drunkenness, vagabondage, death by poisoning, and murder. Again, he thought the actions of superiors were imitated by inferiors. Tarde referred to the third law as insertion. Insertion occurs when two crimes are introduced, and one becomes fashionable and replaces the other crime (Wilson-Vine, 1954).

> **Sutherland, Edwin**—Researcher who proposed the theory of differential association and was the first to coin the phrase "whitecollar crime." Sutherland argued that crime, like any other behavior, is learned in a process of association and interacting with others. He also argued that crime "in the suites" was just as worthy of sociological attention as crime on the streets.

Differential Association Theory

Social learning theory is generally traced to the work of prominent criminologist **Edwin Sutherland**, who is considered by many scholars as the most important criminologist of the 20th century (Akers and Sellers, 2009). In 1939, Sutherland wrote the first edition of his renowned book *Criminology*, in which he presented the theory of differential association. He argued that criminal behavior is learned the same way as any other behavior is learned.

Not completely satisfied with the theory, he revised it with the help of Donald Cressey, reintroducing it in 1947. There were many factors that influenced the theory: the work of Thorsten Sellin on culture conflict, Clifford Shaw and Henry McKay's contribution of social disorganization and cultural transmission of deviance, and the ecological work of those at the University of Chicago. Sutherland attempted to set forth a theory with great explanatory power that went beyond lower-class subcultures to explaining all criminal behavior. Sutherland was of the opinion that crimes committed "in the suites" were just as worthy of sociological attention as crimes committed on the streets. Therefore, Sutherland used his theory to explain crimes committed by the wealthy as well as the poor. As such, differential association is the first theory that addressed white-collar crime.

With the introduction of differential association, Sutherland rejected many commonly held beliefs about crime and people in the lower class. During this time, a popularly held view was that crime was caused by biological or psychological impairments, and those who engaged in it were of inferior stock. Criminals were thought of as people who were biologically different from law-abiding people or who suffered from feeblemindedness. Sutherland's work refuted these popular notions and ultimately included people in every social class as having the propensity to engage in crime. Sutherland argued that crime was not genetically or psychologically passed down from one person to the next, but rather was learned in a way similar to any other behavior from intimate others in a process of close communication.

Sutherland's theory was based on several observations; in particular, he considered the Great Depression, Prohibition, and known criminals. First, Sutherland noticed that during the Great Depression, which occurred with the collapse of the stock market in 1929, many respectable business people, who had not previously known or associated with any criminals, began to take advantage of their positions to manipulate banks and stocks. As a result of the Depression, they turned to crime and criminal behavior as a way to sustain their lifestyles. Second, Sutherland looked at the Prohibition period of the 1920s, a confusing period that revealed that the social climate can be controlled by the law; behaviors can be legal at one time, then criminalized at the request of the government. This occurs whether the behavior in question is actually harmful. Prohibition effectively created economic opportunities for many disenfranchised people who took advantage of the demand for the illegal distribution of alcohol. Many of these people had not been criminals before Prohibition, although a substantial number had been involved in some aspects of organized crime (prostitution, gambling, drugs, and protection rackets).

In addition to his finding that people in the middle class also engaged in crime, Sutherland noticed that many people who were attracted to crime were poor immigrants for whom it offered economic opportunities that they would otherwise not have had. In making this point, Sutherland discussed culture conflict. He argued that in America, people could have allegiance to both a subculture and the dominant culture. When it came to deciding whether to engage in crime, the individual had to choose between the values of the subculture and the laws of the dominant culture. Sutherland contended that what would eventually determine the decision to either violate societal rules or follow the

> **differential association**—A theory that argues that criminal behavior is learned in a process of communication with intimate others who provide reasons favorable to violating the law.
>
> **Conwell, Chic**—The pseudonym given to a main character (and real-life criminal) in Edwin Sutherland's book *The Professional Thief.*

law would be one's **differential association**. Differential association is an association of a different kind with people who have favorable reasons for engaging in law violations. This not only applies to poor people, but extends to those among the wealthiest segments of society.

A third factor that convinced Sutherland that crime was a learned behavior was the time he spent with real-life thief **Chic Conwell**, based on which he wrote *The Professional Thief*. By relying on observational techniques used by the Chicago School, Sutherland was able to follow Conwell and witness firsthand many of the activities in which he engaged. In addition, he conducted extensive interviews with Conwell, who related to him that he had been taught his craft. Sutherland was convinced that learning criminal behavior was similar to learning any other behavior. Sutherland presented nine propositions based on the theory of differential association.

1. "Criminal behavior is learned." In this proposition, Sutherland argued that criminal behavior was not a product of biological or psychological degeneracy, but rather, it was learned behavior.

2. "Criminal behavior is learned in interactions with other persons in a process of communication." Sutherland argued that the learning process requires both personal and verbal interactions.

3. "The principle part of the learning of criminal behavior occurs within intimate personal groups." Sutherland did not believe that learning was influenced by the media. This belief must be taken within the context of 1939.

4. "When criminal behavior is learned, the learning includes (a) techniques of committing the crime, which are sometimes very complicated, sometimes very simple; and (b) the specific direction of motives, drives, rationalizations, and attitudes." In this proposition, Sutherland suggests that to learn to commit crime, one must master how to commit the crime as well as the attitudes needed to justify the act.

5. "The specific direction of motives and drives is learned from definitions of the legal code as favorable or unfavorable." In this proposition, Sutherland suggests that criminals must learn to decide whether the law is worth following.

6. "A person becomes delinquent because of an excess of definitions favorable to violation of law over definitions unfavorable to violation of law." To Sutherland, this principle was essential since it means that people will more likely break the law if they have more reasons to do so than not to break the law.

7. "Differential association may vary in frequency, duration, priority, and intensity." This statement is at the heart of the theory since it means that the association with criminals and noncriminals varies with regards to frequency, duration, priority, and intensity. He referred to *frequency* as how often one spends with friends. *Duration* means how much time one spends during each association with friends. *Priority* refers to how early in life the associations occur, and *intensity* means how much importance or prestige one

attaches to friends. Perhaps the more frequent and longstanding these relationships, the more loyalty friends have for one another.

8. "The process of learning criminal behavior by association with criminals and anti-criminal patterns involves all of the mechanisms that are involved in any other learning." Sutherland suggests that the social process for crime is the same for learning law-abiding behavior.

9. "While criminal behavior is an expression of general needs and values, it is not explained by those general needs and values, since non-criminal behavior is an expression of the same needs and values." Sutherland explains that the motivations are not sufficient to explain crime.

Essentially, the theory of differential association argues that people learn to commit crime and develop deviant behaviors from others in a process of communication. During this process, intimate others (a relationship must exist) provide reasons favorable to violating the law. This is established in a process of symbolic interaction in which individuals learn about themselves and others from their associations. Moreover, they learn what is expected of them and others with whom they interact. Individuals are taught how to commit criminal behavior. Perhaps the most important thing determining the intensity of the association is the frequency (how often meetings with the group occur), duration (how long meetings with the group last), priority (at what age the association begins), and intensity (the importance of the person in association). With these in combination, a person may be compelled to violate the law, especially if his or her reasons outweigh a commitment to conventional behavior and values.

Sutherland's theory has profoundly impacted the study of crime since it propelled criminological theory from biological and psychological theories to environmental factors that influenced crime. Differential association links crime and learning to socialization, which allows for explanation of variations in offending among people who experience similar structural conditions. As such, the theory has been used to explain white-collar crime, gang criminality, drug use, and other forms of deviant and criminal behavior. Despite this, many researchers have encountered problems with the theory (Bernard, Snipes, and Gerould, 2010). Some criticisms charged against differential association have included the problems with testing, the causal ordering of learned behavior, the effect of television on learned behavior, criminals often acting alone, and the fact that new friends can also influence behavior.

Social Modeling Theory

In 1969, psychologist **Albert Bandura** developed his **social modeling theory**. He rejected the notion that people are born aggressive and argued instead that aggression is a

Bandura, Albert—A learning theorist who developed social modeling theory, the idea that aggressive behavior is often modeled behavior.

social modeling theory—A branch of social learning theory that is traced to the work of psychologist Albert Bandura who conducted extensive research in the areas of aggression, media, and imitation. It is also referred to as imitation theory.

modeling theory—Posited by Albert Bandura, a theoretical argument that posits that offenders learn to engage in crime by modeling the behaviors of those who have committed crime. A relationship does not have to exist between people since modeling can be learned from television or books.

learned behavior. Bandura argued that we may witness friends and parents acting in aggressive manners, and we may also view aggressive and violent media productions. More specifically, he noted that early in life, children may witness family members engaging in aggressive behavior and may also be accustomed to seeing aggressive behavior on television. From this, children may learn to accept aggressive behavior as normal. According to the theory of modeling, and unlike Sutherland's differential association theory, criminal behavior is not a condition of social learning, but rather people are influenced by watching the behavior of others. This can take the form of personal observations of people, watching a movie, or reading a book. If people are rewarded for engaging in a particular behavior, those watching can be vicariously rewarded or reinforced to engaging in similar behavior. People can also learn to model their behavior after others when there are no observed consequences for their behavior (Bandura, 1969, 1973). In developing this theory, Bandura relied on the contributions of operant conditioning. He was also one of the first psychologists to examine the effect that violence in the media has on violent behavior in the broader society.

Operant Learning Conditioning

Some experts argue that operant conditioning is essential to learning. It is concerned with the effects that an individual has on his or her environment and the subsequent effects the environment has on the individual. **Operant learning** argues that people are the products of their social environment, and the behavior in which they engage may be predicated on past experiences. In fact, operant learning contends that behavior is shaped and maintained by its consequences. Behaviors are typically reinforced or punished. Reinforcements are actions following the behavior that increase the behavior. Punishments are sometimes called aversive stimuli; they reduce the behavior that they follow. The more people are reinforced after engaging in behavior, the more likely they are to continue the behavior. However, if people are punished after engaging in behavior, the punishment may offset the desire to continue in the behavior. In other words, the way society reacts to deviant or criminal behavior will determine whether that behavior increases or decreases (Nye, 1996).

> **operant learning**—Concerned with the impact that the individual has on the environment and, likewise, the impact that the environment has on the individual.

Six Principles of Operant Learning

Burrhus Frederic Skinner (1953) introduced six principles of operant learning conditioning. Skinner believed that behavior operates on the environment, and the environment consequently affects behavior. He argued that operant behavior is produced by an organism in the absence of any easily identifiable stimuli, and therefore is controlled by its consequences. Moreover, Skinner argued that operant behavior constitutes the most significant responses that define individuals. To him, reinforcements were the most important determinant of continued behavior, since reinforcements would

> **Skinner, Burrhus Federic**—Researcher who provided the six principles of operant learning: positive reinforcement, negative reinforcement, positive punishment, negative punishment, discriminative stimuli, and schedules.

actually strengthen behavior (Nye, 1996). B. F. Skinner's six principles of operant learning conditioning were positive reinforcement, negative reinforcement, positive punishment, negative punishment, discriminative stimuli, and schedules.

Positive reinforcement increases the behavior they follow. People will continue their behavior if it is followed by rewards or positive reinforcement (approval or promotion). *Negative reinforcement* increases the behavior if something undesirable that follows the behavior is removed. Removing something that is undesirable to a person who engages in crime will not prevent the behavior. *Positive punishment* uses aversive stimuli (punishment) to reduce a desired behavior. This punishment is significant enough to prevent future engagement in the behavior. *Negative punishment* involves taking something desirable away from someone in order to reduce the occurrence of a particular behavior. Punishment that is not punitive enough or severe enough will not deter the undesirable behavior. *Discriminative stimuli* signal whether reinforcements or punishments are forthcoming. Such stimuli could be friends. The stimuli are used to control behavior. They can be present either before or as the behavior occurs. They are the moral components of behavior that are learned by the individual. Discriminative stimuli work two ways. First, after learning what is expected from a subculture, one knows that if he or she violates something that is highly valued by the group, that behavior is likely to bring punishment. Second, expressions of disapproval or disappointment from members of a clique for behavior should serve as discriminative stimuli. Finally, *schedules* indicate the probability that a particular consequence will occur after the behavior. It could be either a reinforcement or punishment (Nye, 1996).

Differential Reinforcement Theory

In 1966, **Robert Burgess** and **Ronald Akers** presented their **differential reinforcement** theory. Burgess and Akers argued that criminal behavior and attitudes are learned through a process of receiving reinforcements and rewards for engaging in the behavior. These typically come from friends, family, or both. More specifically, they argued that when the rewards for committing criminal behavior outweighed the rewards for alternative behavior (conformity), differential reinforcement occurs, and criminal behavior is learned. As such, differential reinforcement theory is based on the anticipated consequences of the behavior in which one has engaged. For example, will the behavior be followed by rewards or punishment after it is committed? Furthermore, whether an offender will refrain from or continue criminal behavior is solely a product of past experience and anticipation of what the behavior will bring with respect to rewards or punishments. Akers contended that if individuals engage

Burgess, Robert—A sociologist best known for his work with Ronald Akers that elaborated on Edwin Sutherland's theory of differential association. Along with the help of Akers, they presented the differential reinforcement theory that addressed many elements that were not addressed by Sutherland, but were salient to learning and the continuation of deviant and criminal behavior.

Akers, Ronald—A social learning theorist who argued that behaviors are learned and sustained via a process of reinforcements.

differential reinforcement—A theory that argues that behaviors persist or desist to the extent that they are rewarded or punished.

in crime and are provided positive reinforcements, such as peer approval, money, food, or any feeling that is favorable, the likelihood is increased that they will continue in a life of crime. Akers argued that people learn to evaluate their behavior from their interacting with significant others and the groups with which they associate. These groups control sources of reinforcements since they define what is right or wrong and provide behaviors that can be modeled from observational learning. At the same time, if an individual is able to avoid being brought to justice for criminal behavior, that experience can sustain his or her involvement in crime. However, Akers argued, if the behavior is met with punishment, the offender may desist from engaging in such behavior in the future. As a rule, Akers thought that the greater the reinforcement, the greater the likelihood that the behavior would be repeated (Akers, 1985).

While learning can occur without physical contact, Akers argued that the social environment was the most important reinforcement for behavior. He believed that most people learned deviant and criminal behavior from human exchanges. For example, a drug subculture provides teenagers an environment that encourages and rewards using drugs. Within the context of such groups, teenagers are provided many opportunities to observe others use drugs, and they typically learn from these experiences. While interacting with others, people learned from words, responses, and presence. Furthermore, the presence of people provides reinforcement and a social setting for such reinforcement (Akers, 1994). Akers's social learning theory contends that whether deviant and criminal behavior is begun or persists depends on the degree to which it has been rewarded or punished, and the rewards or punishments attached to other alternatives. The more an individual views his or her behavior as correct or at least justified, the more likely the individual will continue to engage in crime. Further elaborations were made to the theory. In a later study, Christine Sellers and Ronald Akers (2006, p. 90) state:

1. "*Differential reinforcement* refers to the balance of actual or anticipated rewards and costs, both social and nonsocial, that follow a behavior."

2. "*Imitation* refers to engagement in behavior after observing similar behavior in others who have meaning to the individual."

3. "*Definitions* refer to one's own attitudes that define the commission of an act as right or wrong, justified or unjustified."

4. "*Differential association* refers to direct and indirect exposure, via associations with others, to patterns of behavior as well as to patterns of norms and values."

Control Theories

Control theories consider human nature (Williams and McShane, 1998). They assume that all people are naturally selfish, evil, and capable of committing delinquency and crime. Unlike other criminological theories, control theories are concerned about why people conform to the rules and standards of society. Social control scholars argue that people who obey the law are responding to appropriate controls that they received during the socialization process. In contrast, those who violate the law lack social control, or their bonds to law-abiding people are not strong enough to make them adhere to the requirements of the law. Furthermore, their socialization process may have been so unhealthy that they never developed bonds with law-abiding people. Therefore, control theorists view criminals as people who live in the wrong areas or neighborhoods where social control is either absent or ineffective. They also argue that criminals can engage in unrestrained behavior because they lack self- and social controls.

Control theories devote attention to two important areas: personal controls and social controls. First, personal controls are those found within the individual. They include an individual's conscience, commitment to law, and positive self-concept. Second, social control is established and maintained through attachments and involvement with conventional institutions found in the socialization process, including family, school and teachers, peers, religion, and significant others (Barkan, 2001). Scholars argue that weak personal controls are the result of ineffective social control. As a general rule, control theorists believe that a positive self-concept and other personal controls combined with strong attachments to conventional social institutions can prevent individuals from engaging in a life of delinquency and crime. However, when either personal or social control is weakened, the individual is free to engage in antisocial behavior.

Theories of Personal and Social Controls

In 1951, **Albert Reiss** presented his work "Delinquency as the Failure of Personal and Social Controls." He argued that delinquency occurred in juveniles as a result of personal and social failures. More specifically, he argued that delinquency was caused by the failure of the family to instill social control in the individual, and at the same time it was the failure of social groups or institutions

> **Reiss, Albert**—Researcher who made contributions to control theory by arguing that delinquency results from a lack of proper internal development, a breakdown of internal controls, and an absence of social rules provided by an important social group.

to restrain the child from engaging in delinquent behaviors. Reiss felt that delinquency occurred when there was an absence of internalized norms within individuals and when there was a breakdown in previously established controls and or relative absence of or conflict in social rules preventing individuals from engaging in delinquency or even punishing them after the behavior (Reiss, 1951, p. 196). Stated differently, Reiss believed that delinquency would occur as a result of any of the following: (1) a lack of proper internal controls developed during childhood, (2) a breakdown of internal controls, and (3) an absence of or conflict in social rules provided by the family, schools, and significant others.

In 1958, **Ivan Nye** presented *Family Relationships and Delinquent Behavior* to elaborate on social control theory. Nye's work focused on the family as a source of control. He introduced three categories of social control that he believed would prevent juvenile delinquency. These were

> **Nye, Ivan**—Researcher who contributed to control theory by suggesting that juveniles engage in delinquency because the family fails to provide direct control.

internal controls—Selfcontrol to restrain from engaging in crime and delinquency.

direct control, indirect control, and **internal control**. Of the elements found in the socialization process, Nye believed that the family was the most important and could provide each level of control that juveniles needed, especially instilling internal control and providing juveniles with direct control. He felt that the family could directly control youths in a number of ways that included applying direct constraints that would limit opportunities they would have to commit delinquency. The family could also provide rewards and punishments when appropriate. Moreover, if the family was effective, youths' behavior would be constrained even when they were free from direct control of parents since they could anticipate parental disapproval (indirect control) or develop a conscience. More specifically, indirect controls would induce feelings of guilt and shame one would anticipate from engaging in delinquency (Nye, 1958). The last category of control, indirect control, would be provided by formal agencies of social control. Nye reasoned that juveniles engaged in delinquency because they failed to receive the attention and affection they needed from home. Nye argued that delinquency stemmed from the failure of the family to meet the needs of juveniles. If families were functional, providing direct and indirect controls, delinquency could be prevented. Nye suggested that when the family failed, delinquency would be an inevitable consequence. Nye's work was a radical departure from other scholarship at the time that focused on structural explanation. He brought the family under criminological inspection. The concepts from Reiss's and Nye's work became essential precursors of the formulation of control theory.

Reckless, Walter—Researcher who developed the containment theory while making contributions to the social control tradition.

containment theory—The theory that one can experience inner pushes and outer pulls that may induce crime.

external controls—Family, community, schools, and other informal mechanisms of social control.

Containment Theory

In the 1960s, **Walter Reckless** elaborated on Reiss's and Nye's work by presenting his **containment theory**, which held that there are inner and outer forces of containment that restrain people from committing crime. While engaging in research, Reckless studied a group of nondelinquent boys who lived in a high-delinquent neighborhood. He was interested in why they did not engage in delinquency and crime. Reckless's containment theory is based on the assumption that internal and **external controls** exist. According to Reckless, pushes from within the individual, such as resentment, hostility, and anger, along with outer pulls, such as poverty, discrimination, and associating with delinquents or gang members, may induce a person toward criminal behavior. Unless inner and outer containments are present to offset or neutralize those desires, the individual will probably engage in delinquent or criminal activities. He argued that inner forces stem from moral and religious beliefs, as well as from personal sense of right and wrong. Moreover, he believed that each person has a self-concept typically formed early in life, and with a strong self-concept, a person could live in a criminogenic community without participating in delinquency or crime. Reckless argued that if the self-concept, or self-esteem, is strong enough, it can counteract internal pushes, external pressures, and external pulls. However, if the self-concept is weak, one is likely to give in to pressures and engage in delinquency or crime.

Reckless believed that one's self-concept was developed and nurtured by the family during the socialization process. He added that those outer containments that could help the child resist delinquency and crime could be parents, teachers, supervision, discipline, strong group cohesion, and significant others. Again, he argued that delinquency and crime could be prevented by inner containments, such as a good moral conscience or a good self-concept. Reckless felt that either form of containment could negate one from being induced into crime and delinquency. To Reckless, the effectiveness of containment forces could be influenced by external factors, such as effective supervision, and internal factors, such as a good self-concept. Reckless argued that more inner controls are needed to match outer controls to ensure that delinquency will not occur. He also believed that a good self-concept could insulate one from personal and social forces that could lead to delinquency and crime.

Techniques of Neutralization and Drift Theory

In 1957, **Gresham Sykes** and **David Matza** introduced the **techniques of neutralization theory**, and Matza later elaborated on the idea of neutralization and **drift theory**. Some scholars argue that their work was in response to Albert Cohen's *Delinquent Boys* thesis, and others claim that their work addressed why potential offenders were more likely to remain law-abiding instead of committing delinquency and risk being caught. To this end, Sykes and Matza argued that delinquency carries a certain amount of guilt and shame if one is caught. Moreover, they believed the feelings of guilt and shame could be so intense and compelling for some would-be offenders that it may convince them not to engage in certain behaviors and run the risk of being caught. Because of this, they felt that potential offenders need to create one of five techniques to neutralize any guilt and shame before they engage in delinquency. These techniques enable them to rationalize, or justify, violating the law. They provide relief from moral constraints and allow otherwise law-abiding people to drift in and out of delinquency and crime. They precede all acts and are consistent with Sutherland's definitions favorable to violating the law. When juveniles master these techniques, they are no longer committed to law-abiding behavior. Sykes and Matza identified five techniques that juveniles use to drift in and out of conformity: denial of responsibility, denial of injury, denial of the victim, condemnation of the condemners, and appeal to higher loyalties.

Sykes, Gresham—Coauthor of the techniques of neutralization theory with David Matza.

Matza, David—Researcher who worked with Gresham Sykes to contribute to the formulation of the techniques of neutralization theory.

techniques of neutralization—Strategies used by delinquents to excuse or justify drifting in and out of conforming behavior. The techniques were created by Gresham Sykes and David Matza as a reaction to Albert Cohen's suggestion that lower-class youths completely reject middle-class values.

drift theory—A theory that refers to the ability to shift in and out of conforming behavior.

First, *denial of responsibility* occurs when individuals argue that delinquency occurs because of circumstances beyond their control. For example, offenders may suggest that because they were reared in a dysfunctional family, or their father was never present, or they were under the influence of a mind-altering drug at the time of the act, they bear no responsibility for committing delinquency or crime.

Second, *denial of injury* occurs when people argue that no one suffers or is hurt as a result of their crime. For example, they argue that the property they stole was insured, or the company will recoup the loss from theft by passing the cost on to consumers by increasing the prices of goods. The accused may believe that no real harm results from stealing because businesses have ways to protect themselves financially.

Third, *denial of the victim* occurs when people argue that the victims got what they deserved. This is a way of diminishing the personhood of the victim. For example, when people participate in gay bashing or other hate crimes, they reason that the victims are "asking for it" with their public displays of affection or by simply being in the wrong place at the wrong time.

Fourth, *condemnation of the condemners* occurs when people charged with committing a crime argue that other people, including agents of the criminal justice system, also engage in questionable or illegal behavior. Therefore, they wonder why everyone is making such a big deal of their crime. These individuals argue that police are on the take, lawyers are unethical, and that judges sometimes accept bribes. These people practice deflection because they quickly focus on or shift to what others may be capable of doing instead of examining their own behavior.

Fifth, *appeal to higher loyalties* occurs when people view the motivation of their criminal behavior as being greater than it appears. Offenders view themselves as making a sacrifice for the entire group or clique of which they are a part. This is especially true of gang members, or even drug-addicted prostitutes who claim they turn tricks for their children when the real motive is to support their drug habit. To them, the act is justified and the level of punishment should be diminished, because the behavior was brought on not by selfishness, but rather by utilitarian impulses.

Social Bonding Theory

social bonding theory—A theory developed by Travis Hirschi that argues that when juveniles have weakened or broken bonds to society, the stage is set for delinquent behavior.

In 1969, Travis Hirschi elaborated on control theory by presenting his **social bonding theory**. He argued that we need to place more emphasis on understanding why people conform to the rule of society and less on delinquent behavior. To this end, he wanted to know why, with the pressures and opportunities in society to commit crime, most people turn from those opportunities and make the right decision to remain law-abiding. Is it because they care about their family? Is it because they do not want to be disgraced? Is it because they want to retain their status and standing in their community? Is it because of their religious convictions? Is it because they fear going to prison? Is it because they want to be around to raise their children and see them grow up? Hirschi argued that there are certain social bonds that guide individuals toward conformity and conventional behavior. However, when those bonds are weakened or broken, people are free to engage in delinquency.

Hirschi's control theory takes a negative view of human nature. It argues that all individuals naturally have the potential to break the law, but some are restrained from doing so by the fear that they may disrupt important relationships with significant others, such as family, peers, teachers, community, and prospective employers. Hirschi argued that some relationships are so valued and important to people that they are not willing to risk damaging those relationships. Furthermore, if people lack strong social bonds, mechanisms of social control do not compel them to conform to societal rules, including the law.

Major Social Bonds Ensuring Conformity

Figure 7.1 illustrates the effect of strong, weakened, and broken bonds that are presented in Travis Hirschi's social bonding theory. Hirschi argues that if the bonds an individual has to conventional society are strong, the person will conform to the rules of society. However, if the bonds are weakened or broken, it is likely that the individual will engage in delinquency or even criminal behavior. The strength of these bonds is contingent upon how significant the people are with whom one interacts.

This determines whether the individual will comply with societal rules, as well as obey the law. He notes that the elements are interrelated and if one of them is weakened or broken, it will affect the other bonds in an adverse way. Hirschi argues that the elements in the social bonding process include: attachment, commitment, involvement, and belief.

attachment—One of four elements found in Travis Hirschi's social bonding theory that posits that strong attachments or ties to conventional institutions of society such as the family, school, church, and peers will bind individuals toward conformity. To the extent that one's attachments to important people and institutions are weaken or broken, the individual is free to engage in delinquency.

Attachment refers to the feelings we have toward others. Moreover, conformity occurs when individuals establish and maintain ties with significant others such as

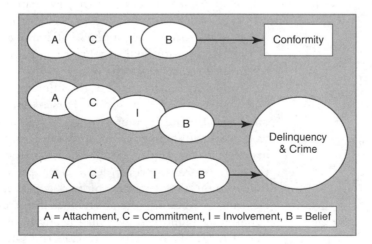

Figure 7.1 Strong, Weakened, and Broken Social Bonds

parents, peers, school, and social institutions. Hirschi argues that the attachment element is the most important of all because of the amount of time children spend with parents and teachers. Parents should instill in their children proper values and respect for others and for law and order. Children also spend a large amount of time in school, where they are generally provided an education that emphasizes mainstream values. Hirschi thought that parents and teachers have the greatest influence on children because of the amount of time children spend with them. Children seek the approval of parents and teachers and learn to respect their opinions. Hirschi contends that the attachment bond is developed further when adolescents spend time with teachers, and with family members engaging in conventional activities. Hirschi also stressed that attachment to peers may also prevent delinquency. Attachment is important, and the lack of it is conducive to delinquency.

commitment—One of four elements found in Travis Hirschi's social bonding theory that involves the amount of time, energy and effort an individual spends engaging in conventional activities such as acquiring an education, maintaining a job, or saving money. To the extent that a person invests in conventional activities, he or she has too much to lose by engaging in delinquency. A commitment to conventional activities is believed to strengthen one's social bonds to society.

Commitment refers to the investment an individual has in a set of conventional activities. Hirschi argues that in the United States, people typically invest in education, the accumulation of property, and establishing a good reputation. He reasoned that people who invest in these activities are more reluctant to engage in crime than others, because they have too much to lose if they are caught violating the law. They have a stake in conformity. People without such investments are more likely to engage in crime since they do not have as much to lose. Students working assiduously in school and adhering to expectations of their parents and teachers have established bonds that are stronger than those who do not make such investments. A business owner who is paying a mortgage and saving for his children's college education also has more to lose than someone who lacks similar investments. Hirschi argues that the law-abiding conform to the law because of their awareness of their investments. He asserts that in order for conventional society to maintain itself, it must constantly recognize deviation and conformity, and punish and reward these behaviors, respectively.

involvement—One of four elements found in Travis Hirschi's social bonding theory that argues that the degree of participation that one has in conventional activities will strengthen his or her bond toward conformity. To the extent that one is busy spending time with the family, school, extracurricular activities, or working a job, he or she would likely not have time to transgress by engaging in delinquency. The more teenagers are busy engaging in constructive activities, it reduces the time they have to engage in destructive activities.

Involvement refers to the degree of participation that one has in conventional society. Hirschi contends that one's social bonds become stronger if one spends time participating in family activities, studying, and engaging in extracurricular activities. Individuals who spend time in these productive and constructive behaviors simply lack time to transgress. The more often they partake in these behaviors with family, peers, and teachers, the stronger their bonds and commitment become to conventional society. The element of involvement teaches the value of hard work. It is believed to negate the impulsiveness and desire for immediate gratification that are linked to deviant and criminal behavior. Hirschi also argued that if juveniles are busy engaging in conventional activities, they lack the time to engage in delinquency or crime.

Belief refers to the individual accepting conventional values and norms as correct and worthy of being followed. A belief that the values and norms are acceptable intensifies the obligation to conform. However, if the individual does not believe that rules and norms are fair or sensitive, the bond to conformity is weakened or broken. As a result, the individual would be free to engage in criminality or other antisocial behavior.

Scholars argue that in the past 25 years, the social bonding theory has been the most dominant criminological theory. Unlike other theories, control theory, especially social bonding theory, asks why people conform their behaviors to standards of the law. Some scholars argue that it is the most frequently discussed and tested of all criminological theories (Stitt and Giacopassi, 1992).

belief—One of four elements found in Travis Hirschi's social bonding theory that holds that some individuals are socialized to accept moral values and beliefs as truth. Therefore, they create an obligation on them to follow. To the extent that people believe that they are following rules that are just and fair, they will engage in conformity since they have stronger bonds than those who do not agree with or accept conventional behaviors. If belief is absent, individuals will have weaker bonds to society and will engage in delinquent behavior.

Self-Control Theory

In 1990, **Michael Gottfredson** and **Travis Hirschi** presented their work entitled *A General Theory of Crime*. In the book, they elaborate on the social bonding theory with a general theory of crime by postulating that criminal and analogous behaviors are caused by low self-control. Their **self-control theory** integrates concepts of Hirschi's social bonding theory with rational choice theory and argues it is necessary to separate the criminal act from the offender. According to Akers (1994), Gottfredson and Hirschi's general theory sets out to explain all individuals' propensity to commit or abstain from criminal and analogous activities. A general theory of crime attempts to explain all forms of crime and analogous behavior, and addresses age and gender variables.

Gottfredson, Michael—With Travis Hirschi, argued that criminal and analogous behaviors are caused by low selfcontrol.

Hirschi, Travis—Theoretician who developed control theory, especially social bonding. In 1969, he introduced his book *Causes of Delinquency*. He later coauthored the book *A General Theory of Crime*.

self-control theory—A theory by Michael Gottfredson and Travis Hirschi that argues that criminal offenders have low self-control, leading to risk taking and impulsive behavior.

Gottfredson and Hirschi argue that individuals who lack self-control are more inclined to be criminal than others who exhibit a strong commitment to self-control. They characterize people with low self-control as impulsive, insensitive, risk-taking, shortsighted, and nonverbal. Because of their impulsiveness and "here and now" attitude, they are likely to have unstable relationships with family members and intimate others, high levels of unemployment, and low levels of education. They are likely to engage in crime and unearned sexual relations. However, this does not mean that everyone who lacks self-control will engage in crime and deviant behavior. Gottfredson and Hirschi contend that certain circumstances must be in place before low self-control can produce crime. These include having the opportunity to engage in crime and analogous behavior.

Gottfredson and Hirschi contend that low self-control is caused by ineffective or improper socialization during the early childhood years. They argue that adolescents with low or no self-control have parents who suffer from the same shortcoming. In contrast, parents who are attached to their children are attentive to their needs. They provide them with supervision and discipline when needed. Gottfredson and Hirschi argue that punishing a child helps to correct deviant behavior and teach self-control. This, they contend, prevents juveniles from becoming delinquents while young and criminals when they reach adulthood. Gottfredson and Hirschi postulate that discipline from a parent is perhaps the most important negative sanction demonstrating disapproval of undesirable behavior. Surprisingly, they argue that peers are not important in the development of self-control; since it is formed during childhood, it is not likely to change over time.

Research Supporting the Low-Self-Control Theory

Anita Mak (1990) tested Gottfredson and Hirschi's low self-control theory and found support for their contentions. Mak discovered that 793 adolescent students who reported a lack of commitment, attachment, and belief in social institutions scored high on measures of impulsiveness and apathy toward fellow students and others who were likely to engage in delinquent behaviors. Mak (1990) argues that it is possible that a chain of events flows in the following manner: (1) impulsive personality, (2) lack of self-control, (3) the weakening of social bonds, and (4) crime and delinquency. Similarly, Carl Keane, Paul Maxim, and James Teevan (1993) examined low self-control and drunk driving offenses and concluded that offenders who reported they used alcohol weeks before being arrested for drinking and driving exhibited low self-control. Akers (1994) counters this finding, claiming that it offers an indirect measurement of the theory, creates mixed signals, and tells nothing, because it claims that drinking alcohol is related to getting arrested and receiving a charge of driving under the influence (DUI). According to Akers, this conclusion says nothing about self-control that cannot be assumed based on the DUI charge alone. He contends it perpetuates the **tautological problem** (Akers, 1991, 1994). Other indirect measures with mixed results include research conducted by Daniel Nagin and Raymond Paternoster (1991) and Nagin and David Farrington (1992).

tautological problem—Circular reasoning or circular logic that is common to some theoretical arguments.

Bruce Arneklev and colleagues (1993) examined low self-control by using three imprudent behaviors: gambling, drinking, and smoking. Although Arneklev and his colleagues found significant correlations between drinking, gambling, and smoking and low-self control, the findings were mixed. Robert Agnew applied the theories of social control, strain, and differential association/social learning to data from the Youth in Transition Survey and the National Youth Survey and argued that intervening processes cause delinquency in adolescents. Agnew (1993) contends that low attachment, commitment, and belief increase anger and frustration and foster delinquent peer associations. Increases in anger and frustration may be attributed to social processes that create low self-control. The increase in association with delinquent peers may be caused by increased freedom stemming from low self-control. Therefore, frustration and association with delinquent peers cannot be a function of attachment, commitment, and belief. Agnew claims delinquent behavior may be affected more by strain theory than low self-control.

John Cochran, Peter Wood, and Bruce Arneklev (1994) conducted research exploring the religiosity of racial and ethnic adolescents and the prevalence of substance use and delinquency. They used both the arousal theory (thrill-seeking, impulsive, and risk-taking behaviors) and social control theory to assess whether or not the relationship is spurious (Ellis, 1987; Elifson, Petterson, and Hadaway, 1983). The authors did not test control theory, but instead examined the general influence of control on delinquency, borrowing from control theory common measures of self- and social control. They used three sources of control: (1) internalized control (self-esteem and socialization), (2) parental control (parental supervision and broken-home status), and (3) institutional control (school attachment and commitment). Cochran and colleagues applied the arousal and control theories, and found that a spurious relationship exists between religiosity and delinquency when controlling for assault, vandalism, illicit drug use, and truancy. However, they noted that in cases concerning alcohol and tobacco use, significant negative effects were constant when adolescents participated in religion (Cochran, Wood, and Arneklev, 1994).

Labeling Theories

Like learning and control theories, **labeling theory** is another branch of the social processing approach. The labeling theory is important since it is concerned with how society reacts and responds to people who are deviant and criminal. Because of this, it is appropriately referred to as the **societal reaction school**. Labeling is of interest to criminologists and sociologists because it may adversely affect those who are labeled, even if the intended purpose is to divert the target from a certain path. For example, some scholars contend that one of the main reasons the juvenile justice system was created was to divert "wayward" youths from a life of crime and the adult criminal justice system (Whitehead and Lab, 1990; Trojanowicz and Morash, 1987; Cavan, 1969). The reality is that labeling did more harm than good, because after being labeled a juvenile delinquent, many people in the reacting audience, as well as people in the free community, failed to recognize troubled kids, but rather focused on the label given to them. As a result, more juveniles labeled as delinquent were processed in the adult system.

labeling theory—First postulated by Frank Tannenbaum in 1938, the theory that criminal career continuity was a result of the "dramatization of evil" in which the subject is singled out from his peers and treated as a criminal. In essence, this theory explains criminal behavior as a reaction to having been labeled as a delinquent. Often, when subjects are stigmatized as delinquents, they are driven to a self-fulfilling prophecy. Thus, labeling pushes violators onto a course of further deviance. Labeling theorists assert that those in power place labels on the powerless that cannot be removed. Also known as societal reaction school.

societal reaction school—Another name used to refer to label theory since it addresses how stigma effects people who receive labels and its consequences.

A major concern of labeling is that negative evaluations become part of a permanent file that may follow a person for the rest of his or her life. This evidence of prior trouble could discourage any chance of advancement (Siegel, 2010, 2012). The focus of labeling theory is not on the initial act or what leads someone to be officially labeled. Instead, the theory focuses on the consequences of being labeled.

Labeling theory stresses that whether a given behavior is considered deviant depends on the circumstances under which it takes place. The labeling theory was the first critical perspective of the 1960s, and it paved the way for conflict theories that followed in the 1960s and 1970s. Lundman (1993) contends that the labeling theory led to the "diversion" movement of the 1970s that kept many juveniles out of juvenile courts and youth centers. It also led to the decarceration movement (Einstadter and Henry, 1995). The labeling theory essentially addresses three primary issues. Steven Barkan (2001, 2012) reports these issues as follows:

1. The definitions of deviance and crime are relativistic in that nothing about a given behavior automatically makes it deviant.

2. It is possible that discrimination occurs in the application of official labeling and sanction because some people and behaviors are more likely than others to be labeled deviant.

3. Labeling affects continued criminality because many people who are labeled deviant develop a deviant self-image and are more likely to commit other deviant behavior.

The labeling approach to deviance can be divided into two areas: (1) the problem of explaining how and why certain individuals are labeled, and (2) the effect the label has on subsequent deviant behavior. The labeling approach is critical because the process of labeling offenders early in life could have the unintended effect of creating and sustaining a permanent underclass of youths. For example, when the label is successfully applied to individuals, they may be denied legitimate opportunities to engage in conventional activities that could allow them social mobility to escape a life of poverty. The labeling theory is influenced by symbolic interactionism, or **interactionist theory**, which argues that once individuals have been labeled and shunned by mainstream society, they may turn to each other for support and understanding. The label, combined with being barred from legitimate occupations, could form the basis for a delinquent or even a criminal subculture (Braithwaite, 1989).

interactionist theory—One of the three major sociological paradigms. Symbolic interactionists assert that symbols—things to which we attach meaning—are the basis of social life. They further assert that people do not interact with the world directly, but rather indirectly, based on the meaning they perceive for the entity in question.

Labeling is pervasive in social processing (those interactions that we have with institutions of socialization). Children are often labeled by family members (especially parents) for better or worse. Sometimes parents evaluate their children and make them aware of their strengths and weaknesses. This practice may challenge some adolescents to work harder for parental praise and approval, but it may cause others to rebel against the family if they feel the criticisms are destructive. This often occurs when children cannot meet the expectations that parents place on them. Another institution that labels children is the school system. Unfortunately, the educational process labels children as either academically sophisticated or intellectually deficient. More specifically, because of tracking systems used by many school systems in the United States, children who lack motivation or those in need of more attention may be placed in special education programs and may never evolve beyond this level. This is not intended to suggest that some students do not need special education programs; however, evidence suggests that many students in special education programs have behavioral (disciplinary) problems and could perhaps be better served with counseling. Unfortunately, placement into such programs can have the unintended effect of negating a child's potential for growth and competition before giving him or her a legitimate chance to meet certain standards.

As a result of special education programs, many students are mocked, ostracized, and ridiculed by other students. Many passively accept their label, and others may opt to leave school altogether by dropping out. What happens to those who are processed with this negative label? The overwhelming majority are "cut off" from conventional avenues of success, such as pursuing a college education or technical training, receiving state and federal employment, or pursuing a career in the armed forces. Because they are not challenged and are socialized into thinking that they are different and educationally inferior, they come to accept the label, and their lives are forever altered. There are some exceptions, but the rule is that the negative effects of labeling are first encountered during the educational process. Perhaps one of the biggest dangers of labeling is that it could be a "self-fulfilling prophecy." This is of major concern because there is an established association between school failure and crime (Siegel, 2008).

The labeling theory was once viewed as a safe theoretical argument. Those who subscribed to the negative aspects of labeling saw many problems associated with it. They paid particular attention to how lower-class people in general, but those without social power and influence in particular, were easy targets of the criminal justice system. They were intrigued with how these groups of people disproportionately came under the control of the justice agencies. Those involved in this movement were instrumental in getting others to see the unequal treatment that existed in society in general, but the criminal justice system in particular, especially where the lower classes were concerned. Labeling theories eventually paved the way for the conflict theories that were popular during the mid-1960s and 1970s (Lilly, Cullen, and Ball, 1994). The labeling theory alerted the social audience to the disparate treatment and social reaction given to certain groups in society, but came short of attacking the many forms of inequality found in the social structure of society. Several theoreticians made contributions to studies in labeling.

Dramatization of Evil and Tagging

In 1938, **Frank Tannenbaum** presented his book *Crime and the Community*. He argued that criminality lay in society's inability to accept deviation from what is viewed as

Tannenbaum, Frank—Researcher associated with the labeling perspective who examined the negative effects of applying labels to juveniles.

normal. He felt that what the society considered normal was merely passing moral judgments on its own habits and way of life. In fact, Tannenbaum (1938) argued that society excludes and sets the deviant apart from the group to ensure that order is not compromised. He presented the labeling theory in response to his study of juvenile street gangs, in which he argued that the process of defining deviant behavior as different among juvenile delinquents and conventional society causes mainstream society to "tag" juveniles as delinquent. Moreover, the stigma that comes from "tagging" causes delinquents to fall deeper into nonconformity (Pfohl, 1994).

Tannenbaum's research also focused on how juveniles failed to adjust to community standards, but instead adjusted to different social groups within the community whose rules and norms were at odds with conventional society. Two different views of acceptable behavior existed. As such, when teenagers were caught engaging in behavior that was repugnant to the community, they would be "tagged" as juvenile delinquents and treated accordingly. During this process, community residents would no longer see the juvenile, but rather would come to view the teenager solely as a delinquent. Stated another way, the tag identified the child as a deviant. It depersonalized the juvenile, and was of chief concern to those with the power to attach a label. Moreover, if the teenager was not strong, the tagging could affect his or her self-esteem, or self-concept, and exacerbate the possibility that he or she would reengage in delinquency. For Tannenbaum, the tag had the unintended effect of changing the child's self-image, which could produce more delinquency and crime and cause people to react to the tag, not the child. Tannenbaum argued that the process of "tagging" itself created deviants and criminals. His work inspired others who believed crime was created by social reaction.

Moral Indignation and Degradation Ceremonies

In 1956, Harold Garfinkel presented his work entitled *Conditions of Successful Degradation Ceremonies*. His work addressed the use of degradation ceremonies to transform the identity of people who are considered lower in the relevant group's scheme of social types. Garfinkel argued that the structural conditions of moral indignation and shame and the conditions of status degradation are not unique to the United States, but rather they are found in every society. In the United States, however, they are found in the law in general, but in the courts in particular, where degradation ceremonies are carried out in a public forum by professional degraders such as lawyers, judges, and police officers as a matter of occupational routine. According to Garfinkel (1956), the process of status degradation must meet eight conditions to be successful. However, degradation ceremonies leading to identity transformation can be achieved by four key criteria. First, the specific event and perpetrator are (a) viewed as identical, and (b) made to stand out as deviant. Second, this deviance is constructed to a morally required dialectical encounter. Third, the perpetrator's immoral choice is denounced (a) by a public figure, (b) in the name of supra-personal values, and (c) by an entity legitimated with the right to speak of these values. Finally, the perpetrator is (a) socially in a position apart from the witnesses and denouncer, then (b) actually separated from a place in the legitimate order. When the conditions of the status degradation ceremony are met, the accused individual is typically removed from society. To the accusers, the degraded person is irrevocably and irreversibly transformed to a lower status.

Of the early labeling theorists, Garfinkel was the most critical of labeling by the justice system. To that end, he argued that the people who were disproportionately arrested were typically from lower-class, urban areas. In his model, he argued the greater the social distance between those with the power to label (accusers) and those being labeled (accused), the greater the likelihood that labeling (degradation ceremonies) will take place. Furthermore, he argued that the societal reaction is greater if the group being labeled is socially isolated, is less powerful, and has different values than the dominant society. Because of this, Garfinkel concluded that certain groups of people came to the attention of the justice agencies more often than others. It is commonly agreed among scholars that Garfinkel's position is closer to the arguments of conflict theories (Williams and McShane, 1999).

Moral Entrepreneurs and Outsiders

In 1963, **Howard Becker** presented *Outsiders: Studies in the Sociology of Deviance*. He argued that a label of deviance effectively creates social groups and does not reflect a real concern about the quality of the behavior being expressed. He felt that studying the act or behavior of the individual is unimportant because deviance is simply rule-breaking

> **Becker, Howard**—A sociologist who argued that those whose labels successfully attach are referred to as outsiders. He also argued that not everyone who is labeled takes on a deviant identity.

behavior that is labeled deviant by those having the power to define behavior as deviant. More specifically, Becker believed that people in positions of power and authority make and enforce the rules. He argued that rules are created by moral entrepreneurs who may be guided by the need to crusade for a rule that would right a societal wrong. Moral entrepreneurs believe they better appreciate rules and the moral code. The moral entrepreneur's motive may be to elevate the social status of people in society that are positioned lower than him- or herself. They think that with the enforcement of the moral code or the creation of new laws that protect morality, people in general, but the lower class in particular will be made better, saved, or even elevated morally. Sometimes, the unintended consequence of their good intensions is labeling. To the extent that they are successful means the creation of new groups of outsiders and a new responsibility of control agencies. According to Becker (1963), members of the rule-breaking society may label rule-breaking behavior deviant depending on the degree of reaction over time. Moreover, he felt that people who break the rules are different from the rule-abiding members of society. He uses the term *outsiders* to refer to a labeled rule breaker or deviant who has accepted the label. They are also those who have come to view themselves as different from others in conventional society. Deviants may consider themselves more "outside" than others who have been labeled, but have not accepted the label. At the same time, deviant outsiders may view those rule-abiding members of society as outsiders of their social group. Thus, Becker believed that because members of different social groups have different definitions of what is appropriate behavior given certain situations, deviance is in the eyes of the beholder. He argued that before deviance can occur, there must be a reaction to the behavior by some opposing group that does not agree with the appropriateness of the behavior. Those people in the social audience making observations and imposing their moral judgments usually set themselves apart from the group being judged with rules, circumstances, and other characteristics. They have the power to label others' behavior as deviant or troublesome. Becker argued that what is most interesting about this process is that the behavior in and of itself need not be deviant to get the label (since the act is sometimes unimportant), but rather, if those in the social audience or community believe the behavior to be deviant, it is therefore deviant. Becker argues that the reaction to the behavior actually creates the behavior.

> **amplification of deviance**—A concept used in labeling theory that refers to the likelihood of a labeled person to receive more attention from the labeling audience which causes them to continue labeling people already known as a delinquent or criminal.

Amplification of Deviance

In 1967, Leslie Wilkins presented his work entitled *Social Deviance*. He argued that small deviations can spiral into increasing significance through processes of labeling or over reaction. The process of labeling individuals leads to an **amplification of deviance**. Interested in how deviant identities become integrated into daily life, Wilkins provided two categories explaining how a label becomes amplified. First, the label catches the attention of the labeling audience, causing them to watch and continue to label the individual. If the label is internalized by the individual, this could lead to the acceptance of a deviant self-concept. This means that once labeled, the individual may be unable to remove the label or get beyond the way it defines him or her. For example, after spending time in a place of confinement and paying one's debt to society, one would expect, upon release, to get one's life back, but society can be unforgiving. Those who have served time in jail or prison are almost always referred to as ex-cons, criminals, parolees, or probationers. Not only may they be denied access to employment opportunities, but others may be afraid to work with them, especially if they were incarcerated for a violent crime. Second, among the problems that a label creates is a subsequent reaction. Those who have been labeled are more conspicuous to others, especially when others know about a person's criminal history. Those labeled become more visible, because people are more aware of them. This awareness often means that those who have been labeled are watched more closely than others. Wilkins also discussed the internalization of the label. He argued that an acceptance of being labeled may lead to the erosion of one's self-esteem, which could lead offenders into continued criminal behavior. This is contingent on how often the labeling occurs and the strength of the individual who has been labeled (Wilkins, 1965; Williams and McShane, 1999).

> **Lemert, Edwin**—Part of the labeling tradition who argued that primary deviance could lead to secondary deviance if the individual is labeled and relabeled.

Primary and Secondary Deviance

In 1951, **Edwin Lemert** presented his work *Human Deviance, Social Problems, and Social Control*. In it, he discussed primary and secondary deviance as they relate to labeling. He argued that offenders are affected by the reactions of the labeling audience. According to Lemert, when individuals engage in an initial act of **primary deviance**, it does not affect their self-esteem, or self-concept. In fact, it has little impact on their personality, and the matter can quickly be forgotten. For example, a college student experiments with marijuana only once. She successfully graduates from college, attends medical school, and becomes a heart surgeon. Because her one-time marijuana use went undetected, it was an unimportant event that did not impact her future. In contrast, **secondary deviance** occurs when deviance comes to the attention of significant others or social control agencies that have already labeled someone. Lemert argued that secondary deviance is a reaction to the label since someone who has already been labeled may come to accept or internalize his or her

> **primary deviance**—A term used by Edwin Lemert to explain the initial act of deviance or crime committed by a person. Unless reprimand for the behavior, the initial act does not cause any harm to the person's identity or personality.
>
> **secondary deviance**—A term used by Edwin Lemert to explain the continuance of deviant and criminal behavior. When society reacts by punishing behavior, it could have the unintended effect of producing or causing more of the same behavior (secondary deviance), especially if the person internalizes the label given to him or her.

behavior and personality after committing the original deviant act. For example, the student who was a one-time marijuana user is caught by a resident adviser in her dormitory and was subsequently expelled from college. She is shunned by friends, family, and prospective employers. Because of the treatment she receives from others, she grows to share their feelings and commits petty crimes until she graduates into serious crime and receives an extended prison sentence. Labeling scholars argue that secondary deviance involves a process of re-socialization into a deviant role (Siegel, 2012). This could be because some are mentally and emotionally stronger than others. Therefore, levels of vulnerability may vary. For example, if a person is not strong and has a weak self-concept, the process of labeling could lead to more deviance. The more often a person is labeled, the more this process of change takes place. As a result, secondary deviance is caused by a process of labeling and re-labeling until the labeled person finally accepts the label as his or her real identity. Lemert contended that deviance is created by a continuous labeling process that leads to an identity transformation (Lemert, 1951).

Master Status and Retrospective Interpretation

Everett Hughes and Howard Becker expanded upon the labeling theory by generating a discussion of an individual's dominant or **master status** and **retrospective interpretation**. They argued that each person has a central identity trait that shadows other aspects or characteristics that he or she may possess. Hughes and Becker referred to an individual's dominant trait as his or her master status. They contended that an individual's master status is usually his or her gender or job, or the type of deviance or crime that person has committed (e.g., rape, murder, or a sexual offense committed against children). For example,

> **master status**—A concept used in labeling theory to express the dominant feature of one who has been successfully labeled a certain type of deviant or criminal offender. This status dominates other qualities the labelled person possesses.
>
> **retrospective interpretation**—A concept used in labeling theory by Edwin Schur that posits once a person is labeled a criminal; one can reexamine or deconstruct past events and behavior to fit the new label given to that person.

if an otherwise upstanding citizen in the community engages in an act of child molestation, that act becomes his defining trait, or master status, and blinds society to all the
other activities in which he may be involved. Other behavior and characteristics take a
secondary role, and emphasis is placed solely on the act that is his or her master status.
As such, if the former law-abiding citizen were a banker, a Sunday school teacher, a
father, and a husband, society would still see only a pedophile; the person's other characteristics and roles would be overshadowed and rendered unimportant. Hughes and Becker
argued that once a person has been labeled a criminal, it is hard for others to see him or
her as someone who may be worthy of a second chance. The same holds true even if the
criminal offense is a one-time occurrence. Moreover, labeling is so powerful that when we
reflect on the encounters that we have with people who have been labeled, we essentially
reconstruct reality to fit the label given to them by society. This is called retrospective
interpretation. For example, when we examine the past behavior of someone given an
official label, we always see the master status of a criminal. In the case of the pedophile, we
may remember the person working with youths, volunteering to babysit, or even serving
as Boy Scout leader. We reflect on the number of times we remember the pedophile interacting with children, perhaps to win their confidence and trust, and it makes sense that
the person would eventually commit the crime (Hughes, 1945; Becker, 1963).

Life Course Theory

Life course or developmental theory is concerned with the dynamics of problem behaviors
and offending with age. It focuses on identifying causal factors that precede behavioral
development and determining how they impact behavior (Loeber and LeBlanc, 1990,
p. 377). It also embraces the use of labeling to determine its lasting impact throughout the
life course of individual offenders. Robert Sampson and John Laub (1990) presented their
developmental model after reanalyzing Sheldon and Eleanor Glueck's work entitled *Unraveling Juvenile Delinquency*. Their model postulated that some people who develop strong
conventional bonds as children may later have these bonds attenuated and be placed on a
path to criminal behavior. However, the trajectory for some individuals could change. For
example, some people may emerge from childhood with weak bonds, but they may have
positive experiences in life with conventional peers or at school or in a community setting
that will strengthen their bonds and set them on a noncriminal path. They contend that
the same sequence can be initiated at any point during the life span, even after adolescents
have engaged in delinquency. A person may experience serious difficulties during adolescence, but later manages to transition into prosocial roles and develop strong social bonds
(such as employment and marriage), and is therefore likely to desist from involvement in
delinquency or criminal behavior. The developmental approach has allowed criminologists
to explain why most delinquents desist from participating in crime during their early adult
years and why a significant number of adult criminals do not have past records of delinquency (Sampson and Laub, 1993; Bartusch et al., 1997; Paternoster and Brame, 1997).

In later research, Sampson and Laub (1997) argued that people who receive labels
also experience cumulative disadvantages in future opportunities. As such, the lives of

delinquents and criminal offenders are changed after receiving the label since they will not be allowed many legitimate opportunities to participate in conventional activities, such as finding employment. Sampson and Laub (1997) argued that the cumulative disadvantages that offenders will experience are because of the negative consequences of criminal offending and official sanction. The life course theory suggests that juvenile offenders may actually forfeit any opportunities that they would otherwise have in the future after engaging in delinquency and crime since official processing (such as arrest, official labeling, and incarceration) will exclude them from obtaining certain types of employment as well as educational opportunities. Research in the area of life course views criminality as a dynamic process that is influenced by a variety of factors that includes individual characteristics, traits, and social experiences. Criminologists who use this approach focus their attention on criminal careers. They argue that life course research has led to a better understanding of life course view, latent trait view, and trajectory view.

Current Research on Labeling

Most tests of labeling theory focus on the effects of race, social class, and gender on the chances of being labeled, with the argument that official labeling discriminates against people of color, the poor, and women. Moreover, the discretion used at every level of the criminal justice system works to the detriment of minorities, including African Americans, Latinos, Asian Americans, and Native Americans (Siegel, 2012; Bontrager, Bales, and Chiricos, 2007; Western, 2006; Steen, Engen, and Gainey, 2005). Research conducted by Daniel Curran and Claire Renzetti (1994) finds that nonwhites, the poor, and women are more likely to be officially labeled. Akers (1997) provides that "differential processing" sometimes occurs, but concludes that legal factors (the weight of the evidence and the seriousness of the crime) matter more than extralegal ones such as class and race (Wooldredge, 2007). Mixed findings such as these have led many critics to dismiss labeling theory, contending that most people who are officially labeled have committed the behavior for which they are labeled.

As mentioned earlier, labeling theory is viewed as one of the first attempts to point out the biased treatment and injustice some people experience in the justice system. Notably, people from the lower class, with a different culture, and without power capture the attention of the criminal justice system. Labeling is important as a social processing theory, because it argues that negative social processing in general, but labeling in particular, could have the unintended effect of putting juveniles, especially those in the lower class, on a destructive path that they may be unable to escape. While early legal intervention in the lives of juveniles may have been done with good intentions, the reality is that it may have served only to process young individuals from one system to another. Statistics and research show that many inmates in adult correctional facilities were also processed in and out of the juvenile justice system. The labeling theory is also instrumental in discussions of creating and sustaining a permanent underclass, because early labeling could mean later exclusion from legitimate career opportunities. Therefore, the labeling theory is credited with having paved the way for conflict theories that would not only address unequal justice with respect to social, political, and economic power, but would also attack the prevailing power structure and attempt to demystify law, ideology, and justice in the capitalist state.

Negative Consequences of Labeling

Childhood experts advise parents to praise their children in order to enhance their self-esteem and self-confidence, and they caution against rebuking children too often, lest they become defensive and lacking in self-esteem (Barkan, 2001, 2012). In a classical experiment that illustrates the powerful effects of negative labels, Robert Rosenthal and Lenore Jacobson (1968) tested children at the beginning of the school year. The students' teachers informed them which were designated as "bright" and which were designated as "dull." At the end of the year, the children were tested again, and their scores were compared with their earlier test scores. The "bright" students learned more than the "dull" students. Because of such findings, scholars such as Robert K. Merton and others have claimed that labeling is a "self-fulfilling prophecy," in that a label could have the unintended effect of transforming the individual into the opposite of what society wants him or her to become. There are several critiques of the labeling theory:

1. Empirical research fails to consistently support its arguments on the influence of extralegal factors on labeling and the effect of labeling on continued deviance.

2. The theory fails to explain primary deviance and thus ignores the effect of family, peers, teachers, and other significant elements found in the socialization process.

3. The theory may imply that a life of crime or secondary deviance will not occur unless official labeling first occurs.

4. Critics also disagree with the labeling theory's position on how to reduce crime and delinquency. The position is not to use official processing, such as arrests and imprisonment, to fight crime except for the most serious offenders.

5. Proponents of the labeling theory have called for "radical nonintervention." Critics contend that such a policy would increase rather than reduce crime and delinquency (Barkan, 2001, 2012).

Future of the Labeling Theory

Recent research on labeling theory has begun to return the theory to its roots in symbolic interaction. It addresses the negative effects of informal labeling by social networks of friends, relatives, and loved ones (Wellford and Triplett, 1993). At the same time, Ross Matsueda (1992) argued that formal labeling can result in negative consequences, such as resentment, a deviant self-image, and continued deviance. The main focus of recent research, however, is to establish that unofficial labeling may underscore how the informal processing of children by parents, schools, peers, and others could lead to deviance and crime. Research conducted by John Braithwaite (1989) on crime, shame, and reintegration holds promise. With respect to labeling, he distinguishes between disintegrative and reintegrative shaming. Disintegrative or stigmatizing shaming occurs when offenders of crime are treated by a community as outcasts, are not forgiven for the crimes that they have committed, and are not provided ceremonies of forgiveness to return them to the community. This, Braithwaite contends, could lead to continued deviance, because it serves to humiliate and anger offenders. Furthermore, because they are now labeled as offenders, they are denied access to legitimate employment opportunities that could assist them in becoming law-abiding. Conversely, reintegrative shaming helps to negate the negative impact of a criminal or deviant label. Braithwaite argues that reintegrative shaming focuses on welcoming the offender back into the community. In this process, the offender gets the opportunity to feel ashamed for engaging in crime. Such ceremonies are designed to make the offender view himself or herself as a good person who made a poor decision. Stated another way, the process reassures the offender that his or her actions were evil, but he or she is a good person nonetheless. It is believed that this type of shaming reduces deviance. Braithwaite argues that while this type of shaming could be used in the United States, it is most commonly found in Japan, Australia, and New Zealand and other communitarian societies.

Theory Integration

The idea of **theory integration** appears to be a logical stage in the evolution of theoretical development. Theory integration or **integrated theory** is the process by which parts of different theories are brought together to serve as a whole. More specifically, several closely related theories are combined into one. But why integrate several theories into one? Perhaps the best rationale comes from David Wagner and Joseph Berger (1985), who contend that theoretical integration is best viewed as one strategy for developing more cogent explanations and for promoting theoretical growth. The logic of their argument is twofold. First, scholars feel that some theories come short of fully explaining the social phenomenon called crime. Second, theory integration can be used as a tool to further the growth of past criminological theories. For example, Margaret Farnworth (1989) argues that the primary goal of theory integration is to produce better theory. She defines theoretical integration as the combination of two or more preexisting theories, selected on the basis of their perceived commonalities, into a single reformulated theoretical model with greater comprehension and explanatory value than any one of its component theories. To Farnworth the process of integrating two theories gives the sum total of the theory more predictive and explanatory power than either of the individual theories had prior to being integrated.

The appeal of theory integration may be driven by the idea that crime is so complex that there cannot be a single cause, but instead there must be several reasons explaining why people engage in such behavior (Elliott, 1985; Huizinga, Esbensen, and Weiher, 1991; Simons et al., 1994) or opposing trajectories for criminal typologies (Moffitt, Lyam, and

theory integration—The process by which two or more theories are combined to provide greater explanatory power.

integrated theory—The combining of components of traditional paradigms in order to broaden the comprehensive understanding of criminal behavior. Integrated theory represents an attempt to combine existing theory for greater explanatory power.

Silva, 1994; Nagin, Farrington, and Moffitt, 1995). For example, social structural theories posit that strain, social disorganization, and subcultural explanations can be used to explain the criminal and deviant behavior committed by people who are influenced by poverty and other economic disadvantages (Siegel, 2008). These theories (found within the social structure tradition) almost invariably fail to explain why females living in the same impoverished, deteriorating, and disorganized communities as their male counterparts tend to commit less crime. Additionally, these theories come short of demonstrating why some people living under adverse economic conditions do not resort to a life of crime, and why some people in the middle and upper classes commit crime. Perhaps there is no simple linear relationship between poverty and crime that has a single explanation.

Theories in the social processing tradition include social learning, social control, and labeling (Siegel, 2008). These theories focus on the socialization process of everyone in society, ignore poverty, and contend that the interactions that people have with important institutions (family, peers, schools, etc.) in society will determine whether they become criminal or law-abiding. These theories argue that anyone, regardless of race, class, or gender, has the potential to engage in crime. Despite their logic, these theories ignore a salient point: the social class in which one has membership will invariably determine his or her quality of socialization. For example, if a poor person living in an inner-city housing project is properly socialized, this background could easily be negated by external influences, such as drugs, gun availability, delinquent or criminal peers, or a lack of legitimate opportunities.

While some critics charge that theory integration emerged because of a lack of growth in the discipline of criminology, others believe it may have come about because of theory competition. Theory competition postulates that theories compete for survival. Theory competition requires verification of theories, which involves the derivation of test implications and the evaluation of these implications with empirical observations. The important thing to remember is that the acceptability of a theory increases as it successfully survives more tests (Hempel, 1966). Allen Liska, Marvin Krohn, and Steve Messner (1989) provide an example of a study conducted by Lawrence Sherman and Richard Berk. They argue that the researchers applied two contradictory hypotheses about the effect of making a formal arrest in domestic violence cases. They relied on the theories of deterrence and labeling. Deterrence theory posits that formal punishments will reduce the probability that punished behavior will be repeated, while the labeling position is that the stigma from being labeled an arrestee or criminal may actually produce more crime. In contrast to the latter claim, Sherman and Berk found decreases in the number of domestic violence cases that followed a formal arrest. This, they argued, gave support to the deterrence theory and made them question the assumptions of labeling theory.

Proponents of Theory Integration

Despite the logic of testing and verifying the acceptability of theories, the competition approach has come under attack. For example, Delbert Elliott, though he advocates the process of theory integration, attacks the argument of theory competition on three fronts.

First, he argues that while testing is appealing, classical theories that focus on crime and deviance do not always lend themselves to hypothesis testing. Second, the results from testing are not always definitive because of methodological problems, such as the measurement of variables and concepts. Elliott is also concerned about the idea of accepting one theory and rejecting another. Finally, he contends that the amount of explanatory power found in theories that hold up to rigorous testing can be weak at best. He argues that the main reason that classical theories perform poorly is that they typically involve a single explanatory variable (Elliott, 1985). He therefore suggests that in order to fully understand crime and deviance, with their complicated nature, it is necessary to integrate different theories to achieve the full range of causal explanations. Elliott (1985) contends that theory competition discourages this activity by requiring unproductive choices among theories, and as a result, prohibits rather than encourages theory development.

Liska, Krohn, and Messner (1989) have concerns over Elliott's defense of classical theories. For example, they argue that if the classical school is entrenched with ambiguous hypotheses, this illustrates a need for greater precision. Addressing Elliott's second concern, Liska, Krohn, and Messner agree that crucial tests of theories of crime and deviance are not always definitive. However, they contend, this criticism can be made of any field of study. Relying on a discussion from Hempel (1966), Liska, Krohn, and Messner agree that "even the most extensive tests can neither disprove one of two hypotheses nor prove the others" (1989, p. 4). They criticize Elliott for expecting definitive results in any aspect of hypothesis testing, and charge that the lack of definitive results in competitive approaches does not in itself call for the adoption of an alternative strategy for theorizing. Finally, they argue that Elliott overstates that classical theories of crime and deviance involve single explanatory variables. Theoreticians can construct complex interconnections of variables to explain the complex nature of crime and deviance.

Opponents of Theory Integration

Critics argue that integration essentially creates a "theoretical mush" by serving to dilute the characteristics and assumptions of independent theories, reducing their individual explanatory powers (Akers, 1989). Travis Hirschi (1989) argues that in the process of integrating theories, many important differences among theories typically get ignored. Hirschi claims that many attempts at integration serve only to take a particular side in a theoretical argument. Hirschi argues that the only time theory integration can be achieved is when the theories are almost identical. He argues that attempts at theory integration without compatibility are useless; theories must have overlap. Steven Brown, Finn-Aage Esbensen, and Gilbert Geis (1998) point out that some criminologists claim that integration of distinct theories fails to generate new theoretical insights, much less a distinct paradigm. Other critics charge that the process of integrating theories is hopeless, because many theories are incompatible, with contradictory assumptions about the causes of behavior.

Another interesting observation about the opposition to theory integration is that a number of theorists are reluctant to discuss and participate in the creation of new theories at the expense of having the theory that they formulated lose any of its acclaim. This simply means that theoreticians may become unobjective, and even biased, and allow their egos to hinder theoretical development and growth. They dismiss the argument that theory integration is possible by insisting that original concepts and variables are measured differently, and for that reason alone, one cannot deconstruct and reconstruct existing theories. This, they contend, is the equivalent of "pouring old wine into new bottles." They argue that such a practice is an exercise in futility.

Side-by-Side (Horizontal) Integration

> **up-and-down integration**—Identifies levels of abstraction that incorporate conceptualizations from constituent theories.
>
> **horizontal integration**—Partitions the causes of deviance and crime by theories that best explain the behavior. Also referred to as side-by-side integration.

Liska, Krohn, and Messner (1989) argue that there are several types of theoretical integration, including side-by-side, end-to-end, and **up-and-down integration**. Side-by-side, or **horizontal integration**, is considered the easiest of all forms of theory integration. It partitions the causes of deviance and crime by theories that best explain the behavior. When partitioning occurs, theoreticians must consider the subject matter and link it to the scope of the theory since it must state the conditions that a theory applies. For example, Charles Tittle (1975) used labeling and deterrence theory. Deterrence theory postulates that as punishment increases, crime should decrease. The argument of labeling theory is that as one gets labeled and relabeled, the likelihood of criminal behavior increases. The two theories can be equated because as one is increasingly punished, a label soon attaches, and as one is labeled it becomes punishing. While some critics would argue that these theories cannot be integrated because they are inconsistent, Tittle (1975) argues that these theories have different scopes and their conditions do not necessarily overlap. For example, the process of deterrence may operate, yet the process of labeling may not, and vice versa. If the labeling process outweighs the deterrence process, the end result could be more deviance. Stated another way, deterrence may work for some crimes, while labeling may be more significantly related to other crimes. Tittle (1975) uses the examples of prostitution and shoplifting. He argues that labeling a woman a prostitute may prevent her from, and even close her access to, engaging in legitimate relationships. Such labeling could actually foster a criminal career. On the other hand, if a person is convicted of shoplifting, this could limit his or her opportunities for continuing the craft, but not completely remove opportunities for conventional work. According to the side-by-side integration model, there must be agreement on the criteria that partition the subject matter. This allows alternative theories to explain different behaviors. Moreover, this approach may link theories by recognizing that they partially overlap, but sometimes diverge to account for different behavior and typologies of criminals (Liska, Krohn, and Messner, 1989).

End-to-End (Sequential) Integration

> **sequential integration**—Conceptualizes a dependent variable in a theory as if it was an independent variable. Also known as end-to-end integration.

Sequential integration is recommended when conditions can be ordered on a continuum for immediate and remote causes. Immediate causal conditions act quickly and without much direction with respect to crime and deviance. Remote causal conditions act indirectly or via connecting conditions with respect to crime and deviance. Sequential integration involves conceptualizing a dependent variable in a theory as if it were an independent variable, and likewise treating an independent variable as if it were a dependent variable. According to Richard and Shirley Jessor (1973), the efforts are not mediated by other conditions. A theory that focuses on immediate cause is differential association. It provides that definitions of right and wrong behavior are learned from day-to-day experiences with friends. A theory that focuses on remote causes is social disorganization. It relies on conditions of beliefs, values, perceptions, and daily experiences to explain deviance and crime.

An established example of end-to-end integration is combining the concepts found in differential association as proximate causes and social control theory as remote causes (see Liska, Krohn, and Messner, 1989). In an end-to-end integrated model, variables taken from social control theory do not affect deviance, but rather they influence variables from differential association theory, which explains deviance. Some argue that such integration may not truly integrate secondary (constituent) theories in a meaningful way (Hirschi, 1989), and may be a form of theory elaboration.

Up-and-Down Integration

Up-and-down theory integration is considered the classical form of integration. It is concerned with identifying certain levels of abstraction that incorporate conceptualizations from constituent theories. Consider two existing theories. If Theory One is more abstract than Theory Two, the central parts of Theory Two can be accommodated within the structure of Theory One (Liska, Krohn, and Messner, 1989). This process is referred to as theoretical reduction. Theoretical reduction is applied in cases of homogenous integration, whereby two theories use the same terms to explain different realities. Problems typical of up-and-down integration occur when the characteristics of one theory are very different from the characteristics of another, especially when there are conceptual differences (heterogeneous reduction). Liska, Krohn, and Messner (1989) contended that the problem of reduction is increased when one theory is used for micro-level (individual) explanations and the other is used for macro-level (group) explanations. These types of theory integration have generated the most controversy and debate because they attack the conceptualization component of independent theories. Many scholars view theoretical reductionism as a negative activity and think of it as "revisionist takeover" (Taylor, Walton, and Young, 1973). Moreover, up-and-down integration involves increasing the level of abstraction of one theory so that its proposition may follow from the conceptually broader theory (Bernard and Snipes, 1996).

Summary

Unlike structural theories that attribute delinquency and crime to poverty and other destructive forces in the environment, social processing theories such as learning, control, and labeling disagree, postulating that the majority of poor people are law-abiding. These theories view the socialization process as essential to understanding why deviant behavior may start during the adolescent years and continue throughout adulthood.

When interactions with significant people and important institutions such as the family, school, religion, and the justice system are healthy, people are more likely to abstain from delinquency and crime. However, when these relationships and interactions are dysfunctional, people typically turn to crime. Stated differently, when people experience healthy socialization and maintain strong relationships with family, peers, teachers, and significant others, they bind them toward conformity. This may explain the difference between delinquents and nondelinquents. Moreover, correctional research is replete with evidence showing that the vast majority of inmates and prisoners experienced negative and destructive relationships prior to incarceration.

As far as the individual theories are concerned, research reveals that people who associate with cliques or groups and are taught deviant and criminal values and lifestyles are more likely to model their behavior even if it means participating in delinquency and crime. Conversely, people who have been instilled with healthy values and taught the difference between right and wrong, and have a positive self-image, may actually possess inner and outer controls that will help them avoid potential trouble. However, those who are labeled and stigmatized by family, school, peers, and other institutions in society may develop a negative self-image and pursue delinquency and crime. These negative influences are not limited to the lower-class culture; they can influence anyone regardless of socioeconomic status.

The idea of theory integration seems like a logical conclusion since researchers point out similarities in theories as well as their strengths and weaknesses. Despite this, some researchers are optimistic about the idea, while others shun the notion of combining theories they claimed may have been created or operationalized for different purposes other than what some researchers intend. Nevertheless, while some people may question processing theories, hardly anyone argues that destructive relationships and socialization put people on the wrong path.

Shortcomings of the Theories

1. Differential association fails to consider that new friends can have an impact on behaviors more than former associates.

2. Control theories do not explain why some people engage in delinquency and crime while young, but become law-abiding adults later.

3. Control theories fail to properly explain why children in the middle and upper classes engage in delinquency and crime.

4. The labeling theory does not do a good job of explaining why people engage in delinquency and crime.

Discussion Questions

1. To what do social processing explanations attribute crime?

2. According to Ronald Akers, what causes crime?

3. What is the most important element found in the social bonding process?

4. What is the commonality shared by all social processing theories?

5. What is the difference between personal and social control?

6. How do degradation ceremonies transform one's identity?

References

Agnew, R. (1993). Why Do They Do It? An Examination of the Intervening Mechanisms Between "Social Control" Variables and Delinquency. *Journal of Research in Crime and Delinquency, 30,* 245–65.

Akers, R. L. (1985). *Deviant Behavior: A Social Learning Approach* (3rd ed.). Belmont, CA: Wadsworth.

Akers, R. (1989). A Social Behaviorist's Perspective on Integration of Theories of Crime and Deviance. In S. F. Messner, M. D. Krohn, and A. E. Liska (Eds.), *Theoretical Integration in the Study of Deviance and Crime: Problems and Prospects* (pp. 23–36). Albany, NY: State University of New York Press.

Akers, R. (1991). Self-Control as a General Theory of Crime. *Journal of Quantitative Criminology, 7,* 201–11.

Akers, R. L. (1994). *Criminological Theories: Introduction and Evaluation.* Los Angeles, CA: Roxbury.

Akers, R. L. (1996). *Criminological Theories: Introduction and Evaluation.* (2nd ed.). Los Angeles, CA: Roxbury.

Akers, R. L., and Sellers, C. S. (2009). *Criminological Theories: Introduction, Evaluation, and Application* (5th ed.). New York, NY: Oxford University Press.

Anderson, A., and Hughes, L. (2009). Exposure to Situations Conducive to Delinquent Behavior: The Effects of Time Use, Income, and Transportation. *Journal of Research in Crime and Delinquency, 46,* 5–34.

Antonaccio, O., Tittle, C., Botchkovar, E., and Kranidioti, M. (2010). The Correlates of Crime and Delinquency: Additional Evidence. *Journal of Research in Crime and Delinquency, 47*(3), 297–328.

Arneklev, B. L., Grasmick, H. G., Tittle, C. R., and Bursik, R. (1993). Low Self-Control and Imprudent Behavior. *Journal of Quantitative Criminology, 9,* 225–47.

Bandura, A. (1969). *Principles of Behavior Modification.* New York, NY: Holt, Rinehart and Winston.

Bandura, A. (1973). *Aggression: A Social Learning Analysis.* Englewood Cliffs, NJ: Prentice-Hall.

Barkan, S. E. (2001). *Criminology: A Sociological Understanding* (2nd ed.). Upper Saddle River, NJ: Prentice-Hall.

Barkan, S. E. (2006). Religiosity and Premarital Sex Dating During Adulthood. *Journal for the Scientific Study of Religion, 45,* 407–17.

Barkan, S. E. (2012). *Criminology: A Sociological Understanding* (5th ed.). Upper Saddle River, NJ: Prentice-Hall.

Bartusch, D. J., Lynam, D. R., Moffitt, T. E., and Silva, P. A. (1997). Is Age Important? Testing a General Versus a Developmental Theory of Antisocial Behavior. *Criminology, 35,* 13–48.

Battin, S., Hill, K., Abbott, R., Catalano, R., and Hawkins, D. J. (1998). The Contribution of Gang Membership to Delinquency Beyond Delinquent Friends. *Criminology, 36,* 93–116.

Becker, H. S. (1963). *Outsiders: Studies in the Sociology of Deviance.* New York, NY: Free Press.

Bernard, T. J., and Snipes, J. B. (1996). Theoretical Integration in Criminology. In M. Tonry (Ed.), *Crime and Justice: A Review of Research* (Vol. 20). Chicago: University of Chicago Press.

Bernard, T. J., Snipes, J. B., and Gerould, A. L. (2010). *Vold's Theoretical Criminology* (6th ed.). New York, NY: Oxford University Press.

Blomberg, T. G., and Cohen, S. (1995). *Punishment and Social Control.* New York, NY: Aldine De Gruyter.

Bontrager, S., Bales, W., and Chirios, T. (2005). Race, Ethnicity, Threat and the Labeling of Convicted Felons. *Criminology, 43,* 589–622.

Braithwaite, J. (1989). *Crime, Shame and Reintegrative Shaming.* Cambridge: Cambridge University Press.

Brenda, B. B. (1997). An Examination of a Reciprocal Relationship Between Religiosity and Different Forms of Delinquency Within a Theoretical Model. *Journal of Research in Crime and Delinquency, 34,* 163–86.

Brown, S. E., Esbensen, F. A., and Geis, G. (1998). *Criminology: Explaining Crime and Its Context* (3rd ed.). Cincinnati, OH: Anderson.

Cavan, R. S. (1969). *Juvenile Delinquency: Development Treatment Control* (2nd ed.). New York, NY: J. B. Lippincott Company.

Cochran, J. K., Wood, P. B., and Arneklev, B. J. (1994). Is the Religiosity-Delinquency Relationship Spurious? A Test of Arousal and Social Control Theories. *Journal of Research in Crime and Delinquency, 31,* 92–123.

Cohen, A. (1955). *Delinquent Boys: The Culture of the Gang.* New York, NY: Free Press.

Cohen, S. (1985). *Visions of Social Control: Crime, Punishment, and Classification.* New York, NY: Polity Press.

Cui, M., and Conger, R. D. (2008). Parenting Behavior as Mediator and Moderator of the Association Between Marital Problems and Adolescent Maladjustment. *Journal of Research on Adolescence, 18*(2), 261–84.

Curran, D. J., and Renzetti, C. M. (1994). *Theories of Crime.* Boston, MA: Allyn and Bacon.

Deptula, D., and Cohen, R. (2004). Aggressive, Rejected, and Delinquent Children and Adolescents: A Comparison of Their Friendships. *Aggression and Violent Behavior, 9,* 75–104.

Durkheim, E. (1893/1933). *The Division of Labor in Society.* Trans. George Simpson. New York, NY: Macmillan.

Einstadter, W., and Henry, S. (1995). *Criminological Theory: An Analysis of its Underlying Assumptions.* Fort Worth, TX: Harcourt Brace College Publishers.

Elifson, K., Petterson, D. M., and Hadaway, C. K. (1983). Religiosity and Delinquency: A Contextual Analysis. *Criminology, 21,* 505–32.

Elliott, D. (1985). The Assumption That Theories Can Be Combined with Increased Explanatory Power: Theoretical Integration. In R. F. Meier (Ed.), *Theoretical Methods in Criminology.* Beverly Hills, CA: Sage.

Elliott, D. S., Huizinga, D., and Ageton, S. S. (1985). *Explaining Delinquency and Drug Use.* Beverly Hills, CA: Sage.

Ellis, L. (1987). Religiosity and Criminality from the Perspective of Arousal Theory. *Journal of Research in Crime and Delinquency, 24,* 215–32.

Evans, T. D., Cullen, F. T., Dunaway, G., and Burton, V. (1995). Religion and Crime Reexamined: The Impact of Religion, Secular Controls, and Social Ecology on Adult Criminality. *Criminology, 33,* 195–224.

Farnworth, M. (1989). Theory Integration Versus Model Building. In S. F. Messner, M. D. Krohn, and A. E. Liska (Eds.), *Theoretical Integration in the Study of Deviance and Crime: Problems and Prospects* (pp. 93–100). New York, NY: State University of New York Press.

Garfinkel, H. (1956). Conditions of Successful Degradation Ceremonies. *American Journal of Sociology, 61,* 420–24.

Glueck, S., and Glueck, E. (1950). *Unraveling Juvenile Delinquency.* Cambridge, MA: Harvard University Press.

Gottfredson, M. R., and Hirschi, T. (1990). *A General Theory of Crime.* Stanford, CA: Stanford University Press.

Harding, D. (2009). Violence, Older Peers, and the Socialization of Adolescent Boys in Disadvantaged Neighborhoods. *American Sociological Review, 74,* 445–64.

Hempel, C. (1966). *Philosophy of Natural Science*. Englewood Cliffs, NJ: Prentice-Hall.

Henslin, J. M. (1991). *Down to Earth Sociology: Introductory Readings* (7th ed.). New York: Free Press.

Hirschi, T. (1969). *Causes of Delinquency*. Berkeley, CA: University of California Press.

Hirschi, T. (1989). "Exploring Alternatives to Integrated Theory." In S. F. Messner, M. D. Krohn, and A. E. Liska (Eds.), *Theoretical Integration in the Study of Deviance and Crime* (pp. 37–49). Albany, NY: State University of New York Press.

Horowitz, A. V. (1990). *The Logic of Social Control*. New York: Plenum Press.

Hughes, E. C. (1945). Dilemmas and Contradictions of Status. *American Journal of Sociology, 50,* 353–59.

Huizinga, D., Esbensen, F., and Weiher, A. W. (1991). Are There Multiple Paths to Delinquency? *Journal of Criminal Law and Criminology, 82*(1), 83–118.

Jeffery, C. R. (1965). Criminal Behavior and Learning Theory. *Journal of Criminal Law, Criminology, and Police Science, 56,* 294–300.

Jenkins, P. H. (1997). School Delinquency and the School Social Bond. *Journal of Research in Crime and Delinquency, 34,* 337–67.

Jessor, R., and Jessor, S. (1973). The Perceived Environment in Behavioral Science: Some Conceptual Issues and Some Illustrative Data. *American Behavioral Scientist, 16,* 801–28.

Johnson, B. R. (2011). *More God, Less Crime: Why Faith Matters and How It Could Matter More*. West Conshohocken, PA: Templeton Press.

Johnson, B. R., Sung, J. J., Larson, D. B., and Spencer, D. L. (2001). Does Adolescent Religious Commitment Matter? A Reexamination of the Effects of Religiosity on Delinquency. *Journal of Research in Crime and Delinquency, 38,* 22–44.

Jussim, L. (1989). Teachers Expectations: Self-Fulfilling Prophecies, Perceptual Biases, and Accuracy. *Journal of Personality and Social Psychology, 59,* 469–80.

Keane, C., Maxim, P. C., and Teevan, J. J. (1993). Drinking and Driving, Self-Control, and Gender: Testing a General Theory of Crime. *Journal of Research in Crime and Delinquency, 30,* 30–46.

Lee, M. (2006). The Religious Institutional Base and Violence Crime in Rural Areas. Revisiting the Southern Subculture of Violence. *Journal of the Scientific Study of Religion, 45,* 309–24.

Lemert, E. M. (1951). *Human Deviance, Social Problems and Social Control*. Englewood Cliffs, NJ: Prentice-Hall.

Lilly, J. R., Cullen, F. T., and Ball, R. A. (1989). *Criminological Theory: Context and Consequences*. Thousand Oaks, CA: Sage.

Lilly, J. R., Cullen, F. T., and Ball, R. A. (1994). *Criminological Theory: Context and Consequences* (2nd ed.). Thousand Oaks, CA: Sage.

Liska, A. E., Krohn, M. D., and Messner, S. F. (1989). Theory Integration Versus Model Building. In S. F. Messner, M. D. Krohn, and A. E. Liska (Eds.) *Theoretical Integration in the Study of Deviance and Crime: Problems and Prospects* (pp. 1–19). Albany, NY: State University of New York Press.

Loeber, R., and LeBlanc, M. (1990). Toward a Developmental Criminology. In M. Tonry and Morris, N. (Ed.). *Crime and Justice* (Vol. 12.). Chicago, IL: University of Chicago Press.

Lundman, R. L. (1993). *Prevention and Control of Juvenile Delinquency*. New York, NY: Oxford University Press.

Mak, A. (1990). Testing A Psychological Control Theory of Delinquency. *Criminal Justice and Behavior, 17,* 215–30.

Matsueda, R. L. (1992). Reflected Appraisals, Parental Labeling, and Delinquency: Specifying a Symbolic Interactionist Theory. *American Journal of Sociology, 97,* 1577–1611.

Matthews, S. K., and Agnew, R. (2008). Extending Deterrence Theory: Do Delinquent Peers Condition the Relationship Between Perceptions of Getting Caught and Offending? *Journal of Research in Crime and Delinquency, 45,* 91–118.

Moffitt, T. E., Lyam, D. R., and Silva, P. A. (1994). Neuropsychological Tests Predicting Persistent Male Delinquency. *Criminology, 32*(2), 277–300.

Nagin, D., and Farrington, D. (1992). The Onset and Persistence of Offending. *Criminology, 30,* 235–60.

Nagin, D. S., Farrington, D. F., and Moffitt, T. E. (1995). Life-Course Trajectories of Different Types of Offenders. *Criminology, 30*(1), 111–39.

Nagin, D., and Paternoster, R. (1991). On the Relationship of Past to Future Participation in Delinquency. *Criminology, 29,* 163–89.

Nye, I. F. (1958). *Family Relationships and Delinquent Behavior.* Westport, CT: Greenwood Press.

Nye, R. D. (1996). *Three Psychologies: Perspectives from Freud, Skinner, and Rogers* (5th ed.). New York, NY: Brooks/Cole.

Oakes, J. (1985). *Keeping Track: How Schools Structure Inequality.* New Haven, CT: Yale University Press.

Paternoster, R., and Brame, R. (1997). Multiple Paths to Delinquency: A Test of Developmental and General Theories of Crime. *Criminology, 35,* 49–84.

Petts, R. J. (2009). Family and Religious Characteristics' Influence on Delinquency Trajectories from Adolescence to Young Adulthood. *American Sociological Review, 74*(3), 465–83.

Pfohl, S. J. (1994). *Images of Deviance and Social Control: A Sociological History* (2nd ed.). New York, NY: McGraw-Hill.

Prothrow-Stith, D. (1991). *Deadly Consequences: How Violence Is Destroying Our Teenage Population and a Plan to Begin Solving the Problem.* New York, NY: Harper Perennial.

Rebellion, C. (2002). Reconstructing the Broken Homes/Delinquency Relationship and Exploring Its Mediating Factors. *Criminology, 40,* 103–36.

Reckless, W. C. (1955). *The Crime Problem.* New York, NY: Appleton-Century-Crofts.

Reid, S. T. (2012). *Crime and Criminology* (13th ed.). New York, NY: Oxford University Press.

Reiss, A. J. (1951). Delinquency as the Failure of Personal and Social Controls. *American Sociological Review, 16,* 196–207.

Rosenthal, R., and Jacobson, L. (1968). *Pygmalion in the Classroom.* New York, NY: Holt.

Sampson, R. J., and Laub, J. H. (1990). Crime and Deviance over the Life Course: The Salience of Adult Social Bonds. *American Sociological Review, 55,* 609–27.

Sampson, R. J., and Laub, J. H. (1997). A Life Course Theory of Cumulative Disadvantage and the Stability of Delinquency. In Thornberry, T. P. (Ed.)., *Advances in Criminological Theory: Developmental Theories of Crime and Delinquency* (Vol. 7). New Brunswick, NJ: Transaction.

Savolainen, J. (2000). Relative Cohort Size and Age-Specific Arrest Rates: A Conditional Interpretation of the Easterlin Effect. *Criminology, 38,* 117–36.

School Library Journal (2008). "Crime Linked to Dropout Rates, Report Says." http://www.slj.com

Sellers, C. S., and Akers, R. L. (2006). Social Learning Theory: Correcting Misconceptions. In S. Henry and M. M. Lanier (Eds.), *The Essential Criminology Reader* (pp. 89–99). Boulder, CO: Westview.

Shaw, D. (2003). Advancing Our Understanding of Intergenerational Continuity in Antisocial Behavior. *Journal of Abnormal Child Psychology, 31,* 193–99.

Sherman, L., and Berk, R. (1984). The Specific Deterrent Effects of Arrests for Domestic Assault." *American Sociological Review* 49:261-72.

Siegel, L. J. (2008. *Criminology: The Core* (3rd ed.). Belmont, CA: Thomson Wadsworth.

Siegel, L. J. (2010. *Criminology: Theories, Patterns, and Typologies* (10th ed.). Belmont, CA: Wadsworth/ Cengage Learning.

Siegel, L. J. (2012). *Criminology* (11th ed.). Belmont, CA: Wadsworth/Cengage Learning.

Simons, R. L., Wu, C., Conger, R. D., Lorenz, F. O. (1994). Two Routes to Delinquency: Differences Between Early and Late Starters in the Impact of Parenting and Deviant Peers. *Criminology, 32*(2), 247–76.

Skinner, B. F. (1953). *Science and Human Behavior*. New York, NY: Macmillan.

Sourander, A., Elonheimo, H., Niemela, S., Nuutila, A. M., Helenius, H., Sillanmaki, L., . . . Almovist, F. (2006). Childhood Predictors of Male Criminality: A Prospective Population-Based Follow-Up Study From age 8 to Late Adolescence. *Journal of the American Academy of Child and Adolescent Psychiatry, 45,* 578–86.

Stark, R., and Bainbridge, W. S. (1996). *Religion, Deviance, and Social Control*. New York, NY: Routledge.

Stitt, B. G., and Giacopassi, D. J. (1992). Trends in the Connectivity of Theory and Research in Criminology. *The Criminologist, 17,* 1, 3–6.

Sutherland, E. H., and Cressey, D. R. (1978). *Principles of Criminology* (10th ed.) Philadelphia, PA: Lippincott.

Steen, S., Engen, R., and Gainey, R. (2005). Images of Danger and Culpability: Racial Stereotyping, Case Processing, and Criminal Sentencing. *Criminology, 43,* 435–68.

Sweeten, G., Bushway, S. D., and Paternoster, R. (2009). Does Dropping Out of School Mean Dropping into Delinquency? *Criminology, 47,* 47–91.

Sykes, G. M., and Matza, D. (1957). Techniques of Neutralization: A Theory of Delinquency. *American Sociological Review, 22,* 664–70.

Tannenbaum, F. (1938). *Crime and the Community*. Boston, MA: Ginn and Company.

Taylor, I., Walton, P., and Young, J. (1973). *The New Criminology: For a Social Theory of Deviance*. New York, NY: Harper and Row.

Tittle, C. (1975). Crime Rates and Police Behavior: A Test of Two Hypotheses. *Social Forces, 54*(2), 441–51.

Toby, J. (1957). Social Disorganization and Stake in Conformity: Complementary Factors in the Predatory Behavior of Hoodlums. *Journal of Criminal Law, Criminology, and Police Science, 48,* 12–17.

Tower, C. C. (1996). *Child Abuse and Neglect* (3rd ed.). Needham Heights, MA: Allyn and Bacon.

Trojanowicz, R. C., and Morash, M. (1987). *Juvenile Delinquency: Concepts and Control* (4th ed.). Englewood Cliffs, NJ: Prentice-Hall.

Wagner, D. G., and Berger, J. (1985). Do Sociological Theories Grow? *American Journal of Sociology, 90,* 697–728.

Wallace, H. (1999). *Family Violence: Legal, Medical, and Social Perspectives*. Needham Heights, MA: Allyn and Bacon.

Wallace, H., Yamaguchi, R., Bachman, J. G., O' Malley, P. M., Schulenberg, J. E., and Johnston, L. D. (2007). Religiosity and Adolescent Substance Use: The Role of Individual and Contextual Influences. *Social Problems, 54,* 308–27.

Wellford, C. F., and Triplett, R. A. (1993). The Future of Labeling Theory: Foundations and Promises. In F. Adler and W. S. Laufer (Eds.), *New Directions in Criminological Theory* (pp. 1–22). New Brunswick, NJ: Transaction.

Western, B. (2006). *Punishment and Inequality in America*. New York, NY: Russell Sage Foundation.

Whitehead, J. T., and Lab, S. P. (1990). *Juvenile Justice: An Introduction*. Cincinnati, OH: Anderson.

Wilkins, L. T. (1965). *Social Deviance: Social Policy, Action, and Research*. Englewood Cliffs, NJ: Prentice-Hall.

Williams, F. P., and McShane, M. D. (1988). *Criminological Theory*. Englewood Cliffs, CA: Prentice-Hall.

Williams, F. P., and McShane, M. D. (1998). *Criminological Theory* (2nd ed.). Upper Saddle River, NJ: Prentice-Hall.

Williams, F. P., and McShane, M. D. (1999). *Criminological Theory* (3rd ed.) Upper Saddle River, NJ: Prentice-Hall.

Wilson-Vine, M. (1954). Gabriel Tarde: 1843–1904. In H. Mannheim (Ed.), *Pioneers in Criminology* (2nd ed.). Montclair, NJ: Patterson-Smith.

Wooldredge, J. (2007). Neighborhood Effects on Felony Sentencing. *Journal of Research in Crime and Delinquency, 44,* 238–63.

Yu, J.J., Tepper, H., and Russell, S.T. (2009). "Peer Relationship and Friendship." http://calscf.calsnet .arizona.edu/fcs/bpy/content.cfm?content=peer_rel

Chapter 8

Conflict Theories

© vs148/ShutterStock, Inc.

Chapter Outline

The Occupy Movement

The Occupy movement is a relatively new protest movement that has both national and international presence. It uses social media networking to mobilize and inform its members and the general public about its activities. The first Occupy movement, known as Occupy Wall Street, started in September 2011 in Zuccotti Park, near the Wall Street financial district in New York City. Members were protesting injustices perpetrated by the economic and political elite, including those responsible for the crash of the housing market that caused millions of homeowners' mortgages to go underwater. The Occupy movement uses nonviolent civil disobedience to call attention to social and economic inequality, greed, corruption, and the perception of undue influence of corporations on government (Chomsky, 2012). Occupy activists stage demonstrations and protests at banks, corporate headquarters, board meetings, colleges and universities, and other places they deem appropriate. While protesting, its members often use the slogan "We Are the 99%," which refers to the inequalities of income and wealth distribution in the United States between the wealthiest 1% and the rest of the population. During these demonstrations, activists are often arrested, and many of them have violent confrontations with police officers. More alarming is the fact that documents have been obtained through the Freedom of Information Act revealing that from its inception, the Federal Bureau of Investigation (FBI), the Department of Homeland Security, and local law enforcement agencies have engaged in widespread domestic surveillance on Occupy activists. Moreover, their meetings have been infiltrated, and members have been tracked online. Matthew Rothschild (2013) reports that the government has treated the Occupy movement as a potential terrorist threat to the social order. He also reports that although law enforcement agencies acknowledge that Occupy activists engage in peaceful protests and do not use violence during demonstrations, federal, state, and local agencies continue to collect counterintelligence information on Occupy activists. Research also shows that the efforts of law enforcement to spy on Occupy members have been coordinated with the private sector or in cooperation with Wall Street firms and other companies the protesters have criticized and targeted for scrutiny. There is even evidence that suggests personal information collected by law enforcement on Occupy activists has been turned over to financial institutions (Rothschild, 2013).

Criminologists view conflict as an evitable part of life. Those who consider themselves conflict criminologists often go by many names, such as leftist, Marxist, conflict, radical, critical, and others. Their scholarship is devoted to addressing the inequalities that exist among the different social classes. They believe that conflict occurs because of **class struggles** over limited social, political, and economic resources. They argue that those who control the resources in society also control the mechanisms of social control. For example, conflict criminologists view the justice system as a mechanism to control the lower class and maintain the status quo rather than as a means of dispensing fair and equal justice. The

class struggle—A condition found in stratified societies where people are grouped based on economic class, leading to struggles over social, political, and economic resources. Class struggles are based on the struggle to dominate other groups.

mechanisms of control include: police, courts, corrections, criminal law, armies, and civil service agencies (Buchholz et al., 1974). These instruments are used to maintain the existing arrangements. Furthermore, those in positions of power use their influence to create laws that promote their interests at the expense of other groups in society. For example, Raymond Michalowski and Edward Bohlander (1976) argue that those in power will never bring their own behaviors under the rule of criminal law, but instead the rich will disproportionately use the law to criminalize the behaviors of powerless groups in society. Conflict theorists hold that in the United States, law enforcement agencies (an estimated 17,000) spend the overwhelming majority of their time trying to prevent the criminal behavior of powerless people (Reiman, 1990).

The behavior of the rich and powerful (people in positions of respectability), if it comes under the rule of law, is controlled by regulatory agencies, such as the Food and Drug Administration, the Environmental Protection Agency, the American Medical Association, the Occupational Safety and Health Administration, and the Securities and Exchange Commission. To conflict criminologists, these agencies do not work with the same sense of urgency and vigor as do police departments devoted to fighting street crime committed by lower-class offenders. Moreover, some argue that people in positions of power have engaged in crime for decades, including murder and injury for profit, and have rarely, if ever, been brought to justice. Some of the crimes in which they engage include writing unnecessary prescriptions and performing unnecessary surgery, costing large sums of money and causing premature deaths. Other types of crime in which the rich engage are improper emergency room care, subjecting employees to workplace disease and accidents, pollution, and injuries and deaths caused by products (e.g., the tobacco industry). Despite the undeniable harm that comes from these behaviors, the law does not reflect their seriousness (Inlander, Levin, and Weiner, 1988; Elias, 1986). Conflict scholars argue that if we focused on these crimes, we would target a different type of criminal offender, the wealthy and property owners (Lynch and Groves, 1986).

Conflict criminologists view the pursuit of Occupy activists as an effort by the government to protect the interests of corporate conglomerates and to closely monitor what it believes is left-wing activism from members of Occupy who are merely exercising their constitutional rights (Rothschild, 2013). In fact, some conflict criminologists see an alliance between big business and the government to maintain the existing social arrangement. Therefore, they argue that because the society is unjust, there is a need for groups such as Occupy to demand accountability and social justice. They understand that staging demonstrations against capitalist institutions may mean that activists will be subjected to surveillance, arrested, and even subjected to violence by police and other governmental officials who could have an interest in defending the status quo. Nevertheless, as a political group committed to reclaiming its mortgaged future, Occupy activists support the democratic process by advocating several principles of solidarity, which include: (1) engaging in direct and transparent participatory democracy; (2) exercising personal and collective responsibility; (3) recognizing individuals' inherent privilege and the influence it has on all interactions; (4) redefining how labor is valued, (5) protecting the sanctity of individual privacy; (6) accepting the belief that education is a human right; (7) making technologies, knowledge, and culture open to all to freely access, create, modify, and distribute.

Historical Development of Critical Criminology

Marx, Karl—Wrote the *Communist Manifesto* and other important works. He is mostly associated with the Communist Party and his critiques of the economy, including his work challenging the inequalities that exist in capitalist societies. It is argued that all conflict theories can be traced to the work of Marx.

capitalism—An economic system based on private ownership of property and the accumulation of material goods and services; investments in the private ownership of the means of production, distribution, and exchange of wealth.

mode of production—The economic structure that underlies all producing societies.

Conflict theories have their intellectual roots in the work of **Karl Marx**. While Marx said little about crime, scholars have taken his analysis of the economic structure of society and applied it to discussions of crime. Marx believed that with the inherent inequalities built into **capitalism**, class struggles between the "haves" and "have nots" are inevitable. Further, he argued that the **mode of production** in any society served to regulate all aspects of human life. It essentially had three parts: first, the elements of production; second, the relationship of production; third, the dominant consciousness. Marx thought that the mode of production shaped both the characteristics of individuals and the elements of the state law. The characteristics of individuals shaped the behavior of the individuals. The behavior of the individuals would either conform to or violate the law. At the same time, the elements found in the mode of production would serve to define and control the behavior of the individual. The elements of state law disproportionately protect private property and the owners of property (Michalowski, 1985). An examination of the list of index crimes reveals that they disproportionately reflect interests in preserving property, rather than in protecting individuals' lives.

bourgeois—A person who is in the middle class and shares the values of those in this group.

proletarians—Those people who make up the poor working class and are exploited by the owners of the means of production.

Marx argued that under capitalism, people entered into relationships. Those who owned the means of production were called the **bourgeoisie** (middle class or industrialists, merchants, bankers), and those who sold their labor for wages were referred to as the **proletarians** (working class or poor). These relationships were characterized by conflict and disagreement over working conditions and whether profit earnings would be distributed in an equitable manner (Michalowski, 1985). For example, from the materials supplied by property owners, the poor produced commodities whose value exceeded the wages they earned. Marx believed that the profits made from commodities rightfully belonged to the working class (Del Rio, 1974). The poor, however, were constantly exploited by the ruling class, given very low wages, and made to work 10 to 12 hours each day.

surplus population—In Marxist analysis, the concept refers to large segments of people who are without work and who contribute nothing to capitalist society.

Marx observed that capitalism also required a surplus labor population to be successful. He believed that the **surplus population** helped to sustain exploitation and allowed wages to remain low. Working-class people would be more inclined to suffer exploitation because they had no bargaining power; if they protested the insufferable working conditions, they would be terminated and become part of the surplus population (Lynch and Groves, 1986). Marx discussed class struggles and how people were motivated to pursue selfish interests by the social class in which they had membership. The class to which they belonged would invariably shape their interest and **ideology**. For example, those who represented the ruling class were trying to find better ways to control lower-class groups (Jenkins, 1984).

> **ideology**—The philosophy or doctrine that a group of people accepts and incorporates in its core values. According to Marx, a person's action is consistent with his or her ideology.

Marxist Criminology

While many are not receptive to the ideas of Marx, his influence is deeply embedded in the structure of society. It can be seen in social security, pensions, paid holidays, unions, conflict resolution, affirmative action, civil rights legislation, collective bargaining, and scholarships (Del Rio, 1974). Despite this, those who consider themselves Marxist criminologists view crime as the primary function of the capitalist mode of production. They believe that in a capitalist society, those who hold political power also determine the definition of crime and control who should be processed through the criminal justice system. Marxists view crimes such as rape, murder, theft, and mugging as disproportionately committed by the poor. On the other hand, crimes such as cheating on one's taxes and actions such as racism, sexism, classism, and profiteering are disproportionately engaged in by the middle and upper classes (Jenkins, 1984; Michalowski, 1985). Essentially, Marxist criminology posits: (1) crime and criminal justice must be viewed in a historical, social, and economic context, (2) crime is a political concept created to protect the interests of the powerful and to secure the power base of the elite at the expense of other members of society, (3) capitalism produces high levels of crime and violence, and (4) the only real way to reduce crime and criminality is to restructure society and end the social conditions that create and produce crime.

The Creation of Critical Criminology

Initially developed by scholars at the University of California at Berkeley, conflict theories were widely used in academia to make sense of the social reality of the 1960s. **Conflict theory** as a model of crime argues that (the) criminal justice system is used by the ruling class to control the lower class. By the late 1960s through the early 1970s, conflict theories were beginning to influence criminological studies. Because of the works of Willem Bonger, Ralf Dahrendorf, George Vold, and Richard Quinney, many mainstream scholars abandoned their previous theoretical paradigms and embraced conflict arguments. Bonger's arguments embraced Marx's analysis of competitive capitalism. Bonger believed that capitalism makes people selfish and more concerned with acquiring economic resources than with the plight of others, even if it means committing

> **conflict theory**—The theory that the chaos in society exists because of different groups and classes of people who have different interests and power struggles.

crime. Dahrendorf created a conflict theory of human behavior that proved useful in the development of modern conflict criminology. Vold argued that conflict is related to intergroup clashes. Vold viewed society as a collection of diverse groups with their own interests. Some groups come together if they have common interests to better serve the collective. He argued that the more groups fight for common interests, the more the ties between united groups are strengthened. This can also be used as a powerful tool for state manipulation.

Another conflict theorist who contributed significantly was Richard Quinney. In *The Social Reality of Crime* (1970), he noted the importance of power in the law-making process. He viewed crime as a product of social definition, supporting his contention with the following six propositions: (1) crime is a definition of human conduct that is created by authorized agents in a political organized society; (2) criminal definitions describe behaviors that conflict with the interests of the segments of society that have power to shape political policy; (3) criminal definitions are applied by the segments of society that have the power to shape the enforcement and administration of criminal law; (4) behavior patterns are structured in segmentally organized society in relations to criminal definitions, and within this context persons engage in actions that have relative probabilities of being defined as criminal; (5) conceptions of crime are constructed and diffused in the segments of society by various means of communication; and (6) the social reality of crime is constructed by the formulation and application of criminal definitions, the development and behavior patterns related to criminal definitions, and the conception of criminal conceptions.

Quinney argued that in stratified social systems, a group's behavior becomes judged and condemned by another dominant and more powerful group. Political power is necessary to label criminal behavior. He also argued that even violent crime is the result of the brutal conditions under which the working class poor must live. Though there are different varieties of conflict theories, some of the most popular are: radical criminology, the **new criminology**, left realism, peacemaking criminology, the phenomenological school, **feminist criminology**, and **postmodernism**.

The 1960s and 1970s were turbulent times in American history. Almost every aspect of life was affected by social conflict between individuals, groups, and even the government. For this reason, many of the theories used to explain the social events and movements of the time are referred to as conflict theories. The various social and political movements of this period would invariably transform the structure of the American society. Some of the most

new criminology—A branch of conflict theory that was developed in 1973 by British scholars Ian Taylor, Paul Walton, and Jock Young that critiqued existing methods of criminology and advocated the development of new methods of analyses and critiques that were critical of the status quo.

feminist criminology—A branch of criminology that examines issues related to women's participation in crime in the context of male dominance. It argues that what is needed to understand women's participation in crime is a gender-based criminology that takes into account the experiences of women, instead of generalizations drawn from studies of male criminals.

postmodernism—The school of thought that contemporary theories have failed to explain or prevent the continuing of criminal behavior and have also failed to adequately influence justice policies to alleviate the conditions of the poor. It argues that objectivity does not exist.

important movements and events of the time included: the protest against the Vietnam war, the civil rights struggle, the counterculture movement, political assassinations, the women's rights movement, the Red Scare, the gay and lesbian movement, the prostitutes' struggle for equality, the invasion of Cambodia, and the Watergate scandal. While there were many other important social and political movements occurring within this time-frame, these were seen as the most significant, because of their undeniable impact on the social fabric of American society. The social and political movements that changed society were linked by a common thread—that is, they all demanded social justice.

Social justice is defined as having equality and fairness under the law, including equitable distributions of social, political, and economic resources regardless of one's race, ethnicity, or socioeconomic status. Those critical of the American arrangement argued that social justice should be dispensed to everyone and not only to wealthy people. Critics examining the events of the time concluded that poor and minority groups were given disparate treatment by the establishment (government) in general, but by the agencies of social control (police, courts, corrections) in particular. Observers of the time saw police officers use brutality against certain segments of society. More specifically, instead of properly managing crowds that engaged in legal and organized protests, police routinely incited crowds into violence. Observers also noticed that in courts and places of confinement, the poor were often denied justice primarily because of who they were. Furthermore, critics charged, society exerted too much control over the lives of citizens by subjecting them to an oppressive system of government that demanded unquestioned obedience without allowing autonomy and independent thinking. As a result, segments of American society began to question, and even challenge, many conventional practices. Acts such as demonstrations, protests, and civil disobedience placed many citizens in direct opposition to state authority (Jenkins, 1984). Therefore, as conflict theories became prominent, conflict criminologists started to: (1) identify "real" crimes in the United States, (2) evaluate how the criminal law was used as a mechanism of social control, and (3) focus on inequalities in the United States (Lynch and Groves, 1986).

Movements and Events That Influenced Critical Criminology

The Vietnam War claimed the lives of 58,000 Americans. Fought in Southeast Asia, it was a war that very few Americans, including the soldiers, understood. America got involved to help South Vietnam resist the communist influence of Ho Chi Minh. Despite the U.S. government quickly realizing that the war was unwinnable, it routinely deceived the American public and escalated the fighting. After spending hundreds of millions of dollars and risking the lives of hundreds of thousands of soldiers, the U.S. government sought a body count of the Viet Cong and Northern Vietnam soldiers to compensate for a war it could not win. Because of misinformation and widespread deception, the war divided Americans and served to increase the distrust of government (Dye, 1994; *Dictionary of World History*, 1994).

The struggle for civil rights was characterized by widespread protests and acts of civil disobedience whereby blacks, Hispanics, and others protested and petitioned the

214 ■ Chapter 8 Conflict Theories

government to recognize all Americans as citizens entitled to the same constitutional rights and protections as the white majority, especially with respect to the 14th Amendment (which provides due process and equal protection under the law). Though the law, in theory, had given people of color equal rights, many state and local jurisdictions refused to implement or embrace the spirit of the law. During the turbulent 1960s, demonstrators who exercised their constitutional right to petition the government for a redress of grievances were routinely harassed and violently beaten by police officers, National Guard soldiers, and other agents of state authority. Thousands of protesters were arrested. It was not uncommon for officers of state authority to turn dogs on protesters, to spray nonviolent marchers with fire hoses, and even to escalate peaceful demonstrations into violence. Powerless groups also challenged the status quo for access to educational opportunities, employment, housing, and public accommodations. During this period, the FBI infiltrated many organizations, such as the Southern Christian Leadership Conference, the National Association for the Advancement of Colored People, the Black Panther Party, the Student Nonviolent Coordinating Committee, the Nation of Islam, the Organization of Afro-American Unity, and others for the purpose of dismantling and agitating (Blackstock, 1988; Dye, 1994; *Dictionary of World History*, 1994).

The counterculture movement can be traced to the "people's park" in California, where students at the University of California at Berkeley along with street people, other students, hippies, and local poor people came together and fought the city for a three-acre plot owned by the University of California. Its members had spent thousands of dollars and many hours planting and putting up swings so that people in the community would have access to a local park. The university disapproved and sent bulldozers and 250 police officers to destroy the park. The efforts of the police did not go unchallenged: the students and others who built the park threw stones, and the police returned fire with shotguns loaded with bird shot. More than 60 people were shot and hospitalized, and one bystander was killed. Despite this, the fighting continued, and then-Governor Ronald Reagan mobilized more than 2,000 National Guards who, with the help of helicopters, sprayed the crowd with tear gas. Reports indicate that 150 people were hurt, including police, and 9,000 arrests were made (Dye, 1994; *Dictionary of World History*, 1994).

As the decade continued, the civil rights movement and anti-Vietnam clashes radicalized young people. Many Americans began to question the legitimacy of the government and why certain orders were given. Many people became disenchanted with the system. They saw it as unjust, autocratic, brutal, and mindless. Moreover, those who were part of the counterculture viewed conventional society as the "establishment," which was morally corrupt and guilty of oppression. While initially excited about the prospect of President L. B. Johnson's "Great Society," many young Americans quickly saw funding that had been earmarked to fight the "War on Poverty" funneled to the war effort. This, coupled with the assassinations (of President John F. Kennedy, Dr. Martin Luther King Jr., Medgar Evers, Attorney General Robert Kennedy, and Malcolm X), made those already dissatisfied with government come to realize how violent America had become. In reaction, they formed a counterculture. Their message was a simple one: "Spread love and peace, not war." The new culture rejected many values of the conventional society. Its members started a cultural revolution that challenged mainstream values regarding economic success, marriage, sexuality, drug use, racial prejudices, and religion. Those behaviors that defied conventional practices were acceptable. The movement created a sexual revolution for both men and women. People who were part of the counterculture, and others in the broader society, questioned and abandoned traditional socialized roles and engaged in freedom of expression. Sometimes this included experimenting with illegal drugs, such as marijuana, speed, LSD, and other hallucinogenic or mind-altering drugs. It also meant exploring unconventional lifestyles (Dye, 1994; *Dictionary of World History*, 1994).

The campaign for the rights of women included the struggle for social, political, and economic equality. Early European campaigners of the 17th and 19th centuries fought for women's right to own property, have access to higher education, and vote. Once women's suffrage was achieved in the 20th century, the emphasis of the movement shifted to the goals of equity in social and economic opportunities, including equal pay for the same work. The women's movement gained widespread momentum after World War II, and in 1966, the National Organization of Women was founded in New York (Sommers, 1994; *Dictionary of World History*, 1994).

The Cold War created ideological, political, and economic tensions between the Soviet Union/Eastern Europe and the United States/Western Europe, lasting from 1945 to 1990. It was exacerbated by propaganda, covert activity by intelligence agencies, and economic sanctions. The Cold War intensified conflict everywhere in the world. Arms-reduction agreements between the United States and the Soviet Union in the late 1980s, and a diminution of Soviet influence in Eastern Europe, symbolized by the opening of the Berlin Wall in 1989, led to a reassessment of positions, and the "war" officially ended in 1990 (Dye, 1994; *Dictionary of World History*, 1994).

While the sexual revolution was under way, homosexuals began "coming out of the closet." They demanded social, political, and economic equality. They also insisted that they had a right to reject heterosexuality. In 1967, Columbia University became the first to recognize a gay organization on campus. By 1969, Greenwich Village in New York City was full of gay bars. The 1960s gave homosexuals the opportunity to pursue their own lifestyle openly (*Dictionary of World History*, 1994).

Many prostitutes engaged in protests to alert the general public to the plight of those in the world's oldest profession. They argued that since women are treated as second-class citizens where economic opportunities are concerned, many of them participate in prostitution to earn a living. They also protested the criminalization of prostitution and the treatment prostitutes received at the hands of law enforcement officers. These feminists strongly argued that the free choice of women to engage in prostitution is an expression of women's status as equals and not a symptom of subjugation. During this period, prostitutes also petitioned the government for social security benefits and a retirement plan. Needless to say, these goals were not realized, because prostitution is viewed as morally wrong by many people in America's mainstream (Siegel, 2000).

In 1972, members of the Republican Committee to Re-elect the President were caught after breaking into the Watergate Hotel with complex electronic surveillance equipment. Investigations implicated the White House in the break-in, and revealed that it kept a "slush fund" to finance unethical activities. In August 1974, President Richard M. Nixon was forced by the U.S. Supreme Court to surrender to Congress tape recordings of conversations he had had with administration officials that revealed his involvement in a cover-up. President Nixon resigned rather than face impeachment on charges of obstruction of justice and other crimes. The Watergate scandal was sobering to many Americans who already believed that the United States was facing moral decline. With the other social and political protests that were occurring in the United States, corruption in the Oval Office was the final signal that much was wrong in America. This was compelling evidence to those who already distrusted the government (Dye, 1994; *Dictionary of World History*, 1994).

Instrumental and Structural Marxism

instrumental Marxism—The belief that the law and justice system are instruments used by the powerful elite to control the poor or the surplus populations.

state—The central political insitutions of a given society.

While there are many variations of Marxist ideology, perhaps the most popular where the study of crime is concerned are instrumental and structural explanations. First, **instrumental Marxism** contends that criminal law and the criminal justice system exist as instruments used solely for controlling the poor. It argues that the **state** is the instrument used by those in power to control everyone. Moreover, instrumental Marxists contend that capitalist justice is designed solely to serve the interests of powerful and rich people. The instrument of the law and other mechanisms of social control were created by them and for them to instill and impose their brand of morality and standards on the rest of society. In the book *Law, Order, and Power,* William Chambliss and Robert Seidman (1982) discuss how the justice system operates to protect the rich and powerful. In *The Social Reality of Crime* (1970), Richard Quinney argues that criminal definitions are generally formulated by those with power and influence. To Quinney, the formulation of a definition is based on four factors: (1) changing social conditions; (2) emerging interests; (3) increasing demands that political, economic, and religious interests be protected; and (4) changing concepts of public interests. Quinney argues that criminal definitions are constantly changing and reflects the political organizations of society and their reliance on power.

structural Marxism—A branch of social conflict theory that holds that the law is designed to support and sustain the continuance of capitalism and will punish anyone who threatens the system.

Structural Marxism disagrees with the position held by instrumentalists. Quinney attempted to develop a social theory that advanced a socialist society that would provide "knowledge and politics for the working class, rather than knowledge for the survival of the capitalist class" (Reid, 2012, p. 131). In fact, advocates such as Chambliss and Siedman (1982) argued that the instrumental Marxist position is too limited since it is too focused on economics and is incorrect in its views that all law is the created to advance the interests of the ruling class to the detriment of the powerless. They argue that laws aid the capitalists, but do not necessarily work in the interests of the ruling class. For example, laws regulate trade and commerce, employment discrimination, working conditions, wages, and consumer laws. Structural Marxism does not view the law as the exclusive domain of the powerful and rich. Instead, it believes that the law is used to maintain the long-term interests of the capitalist system. Therefore, structural Marxists contend that the law and criminal justice system are in place to control members of any class who pose a threat to the continuance of capitalism and its productive forces. Moreover, structural Marxists look to the underlying forces that shape law. They believe that these forces often create conflict between capitalism in general, and any particular capitalist (Reid, 2012).

Power Threat Theory

In 1967, Hubert Blalock presented his **power threat theory**. It is arguably an extension of the instrumental Marxist prospective. Blalock argues that when minorities presenting a threat to the status quo begin to become powerbrokers or real stakeholders, the establishment will defend its power base by eliminating those who pose a

> **power threat theory**—A theory that holds that as minority group's increase in economic or political power, majority groups will subject them to greater amounts of social control.

threat to its dominance. More specifically, the theory holds that the majority population will impose punitive sanctions on its minority population when it believes that minorities have developed into a threat to the status quo or existing social arrangement, especially in the areas of social, political, and economic power. For example, the theory argues that an emerging minority group will demand redistributions, or reallocations of resources that were typically held by the majority population. Consequently, the system will either engage in preemptive strikes to prevent the newly emerging powerbroker or stakeholder from becoming a force or concede to surrendering more equality and a fair playing field. The theory holds that when the minority population (such as blacks and Latinos) increases to the level that the majority (whites) have to compete for economic and political control, the majority will use punitive sanctions (as an instrument of social control) to shift the balance of power back to its advantage. Some mechanisms have historically been used by the criminal justice system to control threatening populations of minorities. They included jails, prisons, courts, disparate sentencing guidelines, and discriminatory drug laws (Bodapati, Anderson, and Brinson, 2008).

While some people may question whether the power threat theory has merit, the 2012 presidential election showed how important a minority vote can be. Were it not for President Barack Obama receiving the lion's share of votes from Latinos, African Americans, women, and other minority groups, it is probable that the Republican Party would have succeeded in winning the White House. While both parties were aware of the need to win the Latino vote, the Democratic platform embraced them and supported immigration reform through the idea of a pathway to citizenship and passage of the Development, Relief, and Education for Alien Minors (DREAM) Act. The Democrats also publicly challenged the discriminatory practices that were designed to profile Latino-speaking people and discourage them from participating in the election. Conversely, the Republican position on immigration reform included voting against the DREAM Act, encouraging self-deportation for illegal immigrants, providing tighter border controls, promoting random identification "stops" by law enforcement officers to verify immigration status, and advocating longer waiting periods at voting booths (to make it more difficult for minorities to vote).

Power threat theory suggests that a large number of minority voters represent a power base that can threaten the existing arrangement since it could represent a noticeable shift in power from the majority with respect to having a direct impact on how elections will be decided, the number of representatives from each district, and ultimately to redistributing economic and political resources that will likely benefit minorities. The surge in the number of minorities can be attributed to rapid and dramatic demographic changes that have occurred in the United States in the past decade, especially among racial and ethnic minorities, who account for 85% of the nation's population growth.

Radical Criminology

Radical criminology was developed at the National Deviancy Conference. It is critical of positivistic criminology. At the conference, there was a split between the interactionists' labeling paradigm and those who held to Marxist ideology. However, after Ian Taylor, Paul Walton, and Jock Young published *The New Criminology*, **radical theory** quickly gained a powerful academic boost (Barkan, 2001). Radical criminology is the brand of criminology that emphasizes that wealthy and powerful groups control poor members of society. It argues that crime is defined by those in political and economic power in such a way as to control those in the lower socioeconomic classes (Quinney, 1977). Despite this, both groups are influenced by the capitalist society, but the criminal law is designed to protect the interests of the property owners and is largely focused on behaviors committed by the powerless. One only needs to examine the criminal law or the index crimes and see that they disproportionately protect the ownership of power. They tend to emphasize protecting the property of those in society who own the most. Radical scholars view the behaviors committed by the state, or formal government, as being more criminal than those committed by marginalized people who are disenfranchised from conventional opportunities. They argue that abuses of the criminal law can be seen as violations of human rights that ultimately promote racism, sexism, and imperialism (Schwendinger and Schwendinger, 1970). Steven Spitzer (1975) argued that when capitalism produces surplus populations that guarantee that wages will be low, serious problems result among disenfranchised segments. Spitzer argued that this produces five types of problem populations: (1) the poor who steal from the rich, (2) those who refuse to work, (3) those who retreat to drugs (social junk), (4) those who refuse schooling or do not believe in the benefit of family life, and (5) those who actively pursue a noncapitalist society. He referred to the latter group as social dynamite and

> **radical theory**—A branch of conflict theory that focuses on the political nature of the definition of crime and the oppressive use of the criminal law and the criminal justice system.

warned that the criminal justice system would be used to control this problem population. Radical theory argues that crime is the result of a struggle for power and resources between owners of capital and workers. Moreover, radical theory demands that capitalism be overthrown. The theory postulates that socialism can reduce the crime rate (Quinney, 1974).

The New Criminology

The New Criminology, published in 1973 by Ian Taylor, Paul Walton, and Jock Young, attacked positivism. An important argument the book makes is that scientific neutrality is a myth and that there is no consensus in society, but instead all groups, including experts, are more likely to work for the interests of the group in which they have membership. The book also attacked biological and psychological theories that were commonly accepted in the 1960s and 1970s, and concluded that even the concept of "normality" is defined with regard to class. For example, if one accepts middle- and upper-class values, one is seen as normal; if not, one is thought of as either insane or a social deviant. This movement placed emphasis on social theories and ideas of conflict. It argued that the medical model commonly used in the 1960s and 1970s was a myth coming from a seizure of power by the medical profession in the late 19th century. The new criminologists argued that the problem of deviance is a problem for society as a whole, and that in a just society, there would not be a need to create deviance. "The task is to create a society in which the facts of human diversity, whether personal, organic or social, are not subject to the power to criminalize" (Jenkins, 1984, p. 11).

Those who embraced the new criminology were critical of the aforementioned radical scholars. They charged that radicals were more political than objective and were more concerned with promoting their own personal agendas than with humanitarian motivations (Toby, 1979). Scholars who aligned themselves with the new criminology rejected the radical view that the government was always "evil" and offenders were the "innocent" victims of oppression and governmental brutality. These scholars accused radicals of being unrealistic in their search for a utopian society in which the material wealth of the United States would be distributed equally among its population. The new criminologists believed that many crime problems, as well as societal problems, could be corrected by working within the system for greater social change.

Left Realism

Another radical approach to criminology is left realist theory. The movement called **left realism** was started by Jock Young and other British criminologists in the late 1980s (Young, 1987). Some contend that the movement was a reaction or even an objection to the idealism held by instrumental Marxists (Lea and Young, 1984). More specifically, left realism emerged because of the scant attention given to street crime by those on the radical left, the instrumental Marxists. Left realists argued that too much emphasis

> **left realism**—A movement staged by conservative realists accusing instrumental Marxists of downplaying the seriousness of street crimes committed by the underclass against one another.

was placed on crimes committed by the powerful members of society, while scant attention was given to street crime. Instrumental Marxism viewed crimes committed by powerless groups (composed mainly of cultural minorities) as a result of the conditions under which the victims of capitalism lived or as a political rebellion created by hostility and alienation (Quinney, 1974). In so doing, they downplayed the seriousness of many crimes, chief among them domestic violence, rape, and sexual harassment and assaults (Barkan, 2001). This ignited criticisms from some criminologists who argued that instrumental Marxists appeared unconcerned about the plight of poor people in general, but about poor women in particular who were subjected to physical violence. The left realist movement also emerged as a reaction against the conservative law-and-order approach, which advocated long-term imprisonment and harsh treatment of juveniles.

Left realists argue that street crime is a serious problem for the lower and working classes (Lea and Young, 1984). They argue that index crimes such as rape, burglary, assault, robbery, and theft are serious forms of antisocial behavior that have a negative impact on the lives of people who are affected by them. They hold that most of the perpetrators of these crimes are men in the lower class who are responsible for most of the criminal treatment of women and minorities. Left realists argue that most people who understand and recognize these facts are conservatives (DeKeseredy and Schwartz, 2006). At the same time, left realists view crimes committed by powerful elites as a major concern because those crimes, like index crimes, have a great impact on powerless groups of people. They argue that crimes such as industrial waste, unsafe working conditions, unsafe products, and poor medical care are also detrimental to lower-class people (Pearce 1992; DeKeseredy and Goff, 1992). Left realists believe that the more vulnerable people are politically and economically, the more likely they will be victimized from all directions, due to forces like white-collar crime, street crime, unemployment, and poverty (Schwartz and DeKeseredy, 1991). In fact, left realists believe that extreme poverty in high-crime areas cannot explain criminal behavior because all poor people do not engage in crime. As such, they hold to the belief of relative deprivation, arguing that it can occur at any socioeconomic level. However, because of the social structure, those at the bottom tier of society are more exposed to a lack of jobs and hopelessness. Consequently, subcultures emerge in these areas that may support delinquency and crime. In terms of public policy, this movement advocates that the poor be provided with jobs, decent and affordable housing, and day-care services (DeKeseredy and Schwartz, 2006). Advocates of left realism contend that this could bring optimism, hope, and opportunities to individuals and empowerment to the community.

Those scholars on the radical left view left realism as a Trojan horse. They contend that while some of its arguments are justified, its policy implications do not go far enough, because they do not call for changes in the social structure that create the conditions that generate crime. Furthermore, scholars on the left see left realism as saturated with contradictions. For example, they argue that while left realism accepts theories such as strain, subculture, and relative deprivation, it stops short of observing the theories' policy implications. To scholars on the radical left, the policy implications of left realism would do more harm than good by replacing one form of social control with another, thus serving to create more crime.

Peacemaking Criminology

Started by Richard Quinney and Hal Pepinsky, **peacemaking criminology** searches for peaceful conflict resolutions and restorative justice instead of official punishments. It advocates a compassionate criminology, or a criminology of nonviolence, and posits that compassion, wisdom, and love are essential for understanding human suffering. They defined peacemaking as "the art and science of transforming violent relations [power plays that some inflict on others] into safe, trustworthy, mutually respectful, balanced relations" (Pepinsky and Quinney, 1991, p. 279). Moreover, acts such as murder, discrimination, and war are examples of power play by people, groups, and government. Unsafe working conditions are also included as examples of power play inflicted on people in society. Peacemaking criminology argues that criminologists should examine all cases of violence and not only those that appear to be of a one-on-one or personal nature such as rape or murder. This view holds that any type of violence breeds more violence, including the use of capital punishment to execute the criminally convicted (Pepinsky and Quinney, 1991). This approach argues that crime control agencies and the citizens they serve should work together to alleviate social problems and human suffering, reducing crime through their united efforts. Moreover, official agents of social control need to work with both victims and offenders to achieve a new world order that is more equitable and just for everyone. They argue that society should strive to make peace and not war. Peacemaking criminologists endeavor to find humanistic solutions to social problems and crime rather than punishment and imprisonment. Peacemakers view the efforts of the state to punish and control as crime-encouraging and therefore counterproductive. This approach seeks to transform violent relations into good, constructive, and beautiful human relations (Pepinsky, 2006).

> **peacemaking criminology**—The brand of criminology that promotes love and peace, not war. It argues for less formal intervention from the criminal justice system and promotes informal responses to crime, such as compassionate resolutions between victim and offender when reconciliation is possible.

The Phenomenological School

The phenomenological school is greatly influenced by symbolic interaction. The pioneers of this school are Stuart Henry and Dragon Milovanovic. The school posits that crime and victims are both socially constructed. Crime is the product of an active process of creation and interpretation of agreed-upon definitions by the broader society. This school also contends that crime is knowable only to the actors who participate, both criminals and victims. For example, scholars who advanced symbolic interactionism, such as William Thomas and George Mead, took the position that the importance of any behavior is relative to the intentions behind it and to the situation in which it is interpreted. Humans create "an ideology of crime" that gives crime meaning and sustains it as a concrete reality. Those in the phenomenological school view crime and its control as social constructions

> **phenomenological criminology—** Argues that criminal behavior is knowable only to the people who engage in it, and that society socially constructs behavior that becomes what the consensus believes.

produced through a process in which offenders, victims, and society are involved. **Phenomenological criminology** focuses on the social process by which crime and criminology become cultural reality. The phenomenological school avoids discussion of causality, thereby offering few or no solutions or treatment for crime and offenders.

Feminist Criminology

Feminism is the struggle of women to free themselves from male discrimination, exploitation, and oppression while advancing gender identity and social, political, and economic equality. Some contend that this is achieved only when women can free themselves from

> **Marxist feminist—**One who views gender inequality as stemming from the unequal distribution of power in a capitalist society. According to Marxist feminists, women are exploited by patriarchal societies.
>
> **radical feminism—**A branch of conflict theory that views the problem of gender inequality and the subordination of women to male power as caused by the problem of patriarchy.

being sexual commodities (Daly, 1973). While there are different varieties of feminist criminology, the two most common types are **Marxist feminist** and **radical feminist**. On the one hand, Marxist feminists view gender inequality as stemming from unequal distributions of power and prestige in capitalist society. They view gender inequality as a function of the exploitation of females by their male counterparts. This, they contend, includes fathers and husbands. They also argue that because women do not fare well in capitalist societies, their powerlessness increases the likelihood that they will become the targets of violence. Unlike Marxist feminist scholars, radical feminists view crime as

stemming from the onset of male supremacy and the subsequent subordination of women. Radical feminists see women as being controlled by male aggression, and the efforts of men to control women sexually as a cause of women continuing in a life of crime (Barkan, 2001).

A central problem of the feminist movement has been its lack of consensus on an acceptable definition of feminism (some wanting social reform, others wanting to eradicate domination and elitism in all human relationships) and its lack of a sound foundation on which to construct theory or engage in meaningful praxis (Hooks, 1984). Feminists are criticized because of the different factions within their ranks. Criticisms include: (1) not all women share the same ideas about what equality means, and (2) some feminists fail to consider the impact of race and class as factors that lead to exploitation and oppression. Stated another way, some feminists do not advocate the interests of women of color or those who are in the working class or poor (Hooks, 1987).

During the 1970s, early feminist-crime scholars, such as Freda Adler and Rita Simon, conducted research to examine women's lack of participation in crime. They researched why there was gender disparity in the number of crimes committed. They argued that women tended not to engage in crime to the same extent as men because women lacked the same opportunities as men to engage in crime. However, they argued that there were reported increases in violent crimes committed by women. In their books, *Sisters in Crime* and *Women in Crime*, Alder and Simon argued that more women were beginning to engage in crimes that were traditionally considered male rather than female crime. They argued that women were becoming murderers, muggers, bank robbers, and even members of organized crime (Adler, 1975; Simon, 1975). They also argued that since men participated in the labor market, they left home each day to work. This provided men with greater access and opportunities to engage in crime, while women were relegated to a life of domesticity rearing children, cleaning the home, and being accommodating to the needs of their spouse. They had fewer opportunities to commit crime. While some criminologists embraced the argument of Adler and Simon, others criticized them, claiming that the gender differences in reported levels of crime were probably due to methodological problems in the data collection and analysis (Steffensmeier, 1983).

Early feminist-crime scholars argued that women offended at lower rates than men because of the socialization process. They reported that men were taught to be aggressive and competitive, while women were taught to be supportive and submissive. Men were taught to have higher aspirations than their female counterparts. Women suffered more inequities because they lived in a patriarchal society and were viewed as less than equal. These scholars argued that as equality increases, so too will convergence between the rates at which women and men participate in crime. The logic of the feminist argument is that as women become emancipated from domestic life and join the labor force, they will encounter more opportunities to engage in law violations. Contradictory to this prediction, women have received a tremendous amount of social, economic, and political power since the 1970s, and yet their crime rates still remain lower than those of their male counterparts. Some experts are doubtful that convergence will ever occur.

Contemporary feminist scholars take a different position. For example, Kathleen Daly and Meda Chesney-Lind argue that the early works of Adler and Simon were inadequate in explaining female criminality, and what is needed is a "gender-aware" criminology that applies feminist thinking to criminological analysis. These feminists contend that a gender-aware criminology should challenge traditional criminology, because all criminological theories were constructed and researched with males in mind. Women were considered the generalized other. Contemporary feminists argue that studies that use male samples cannot explain the behaviors of women because women's experiences are not the same. Feminist scholars argue that what is needed in the development of feminist theory is contributions from males and females that explain female crime, and not sole contributions made by women. Moreover, criminological theories are needed that test samples of females to explain the behavior of women. Feminists believe research should address gender-related issues. They argue that anything short of this misses the point, because women are different from men, and so are their experiences.

Today, feminist scholars examine the dominance of men over women in patriarchal society and closely analyze the impact that it has on crimes against women. They place the focus on differential amounts of power that one gender has over the other (Reid, 2012). Feminist scholars desire to go beyond explaining female crime. They also examine female victimization and the amount of attention and treatment it receives from the criminal justice system. Because of this, feminists have conducted extensive research in the area of gender and delinquency and female victims of rape and other sexual assaults.

Power–Control Theory

power–control theory—A theory by sociologist John Hagan that holds that power relations in the household and workplace conditions patterns of parental control of children in two parent families resulting in gender differences in rates of delinquency.

In 1985, John Hagan and colleagues presented the **power–control theory**, a feminist argument regarding gender differences and the onset of criminal behavior (Hagan, Gillis, and Simpson, 1985). Accordingly, the theory postulated that delinquency and crime are influenced by class position (power) and family function (control). They argued that these two variables are linked, in that within the family, parents reproduce the power relationship they participate in the workplace. As such, a parent who occupies a position of power or dominance at work typically exerts the same degree of control in the home. Because of power relative to the workplace, class position can influence the criminality of children (Hagan, McCarthy, and Foster, 2002).

Power–control theory discusses two types of families: paternalistic families and egalitarian families. In paternalistic families, fathers occupy the traditional role of breadwinner or provider, while mothers remain in the home performing domestic duties, or they may hold low-wage jobs. Consequently, mothers are expected to supervise and control the behaviors of their daughters, while allowing their sons freedom to roam and explore. In the paternal home, the parent–daughter relationship is characterized as socialization in "domesticity." This decreases the likelihood that girls will become involved in delinquent behavior. At the same time this is occurring, the opposite effect is taking place with boys, because they are not under their mothers' direct supervision and control. Moreover, girls who are reared in patriarchal families are socialized to fear legal sanctions, while boys are not to the same degree. Therefore, boys in paternalistic families commit more delinquency and have greater opportunities to participate in adult behaviors such as having transportation or a part-time job. Hagan, McCarthy, and Foster argue that these outlets of expression are not equally available to girls. Therefore, those girls who are unhappy or dissatisfied with their perceived unequal status may either run away or consider suicide (Hagan, McCarthy, and Foster, 2002).

In egalitarian families, where there are no power differences between husband and wife in the home or workplace, daughters experience freedom that reflects reduced parental controls. The amount of reported delinquency within these families is similar for brothers and sisters. This is likely because girls have greater opportunities from their freedom to engage in legitimate adult status behaviors. As such, they may not desire to create deviate outlets to protest or express themselves (Blackwell, Sellers, and Schlaupitz, 2002).

Researchers examining the relationship between power and control have asked whether these relationships exist in nontraditional families or in those where one parent is absent. For example, is a child's criminal behavior influenced by a single parent's position in the workplace? The researchers reported that when fathers and mothers held equal managerial positions, the amount of delinquency committed by their sons and daughters was strikingly similar. From the power–control theory, we can infer that in middle-class homes, girls are more likely to engage in delinquency because they receive less supervision and control compared with their lower-class counterparts (since high levels of unemployment may place parents at home to supervise and control their daughters). However, in homes where both parents share similar amounts of power there and in the workplace, we can expect to see similar rates of delinquency between sisters and brothers because girls will also share similar expectations about having a career. As such, both siblings will probably be reared to take risks and participate in other behavior related to delinquency (Hagan, McCathy, and Foster, 2002).

Postmodern Criminology

Another variation of critical criminology examines how meaning is conveyed in language. It is referred to as postmodernism. Postmodernism is a criminological approach that announces truths about how crime, justice, law, social control, punishment, and deviance are embodied in speech and regulate our lives. Moreover, it discusses how people take for granted that language often has one objective or standard meaning (Arrigo, 1995). The theory asks, whose values and whose interests are represented by the writings we accept, since all writing is subjective? This approach looks at the meaning of words that may be used by people in power to impose their own values onto others. This, postmodernists contend, is so because the precise meaning and content are not clear in what we say and write. There is often an abundance of subtext concealed in communication, or a hidden meaning behind the surface meaning. Postmodernists strive to demystify hidden values, explore their meaning, and find a more complete meaning or understanding about the underlying aspects of social life. This position in criminology analyzes the hidden power of words (Arrigo, 1995). Because of this, postmodernists view themselves as being in search of truth, knowledge, and understanding (Henry and Milovanovic, 1996). Some contend that they are part of a new revolution in academia.

Postmodern criminology draws attention to the violence perpetrated through speech production, whether it is written or verbal (Arrigo, 1995). Postmodernists argue that offenders, as well as victims, are often forced to suppress their thoughts and expressions and simply comply with the commonly held values of mainstream society. To postmodernists, such a practice does violence to participants in the criminal justice system. For example, the words or labels *criminal* and *victim* carry a negative connotation or meaning. They suggest that one is a predator and the other is in need of help, protection, or assistance. The word *victim* even suggests that one is vulnerable. Both words are different from being seen as a nonvictim or noncriminal. Postmodernists argue that maintaining a code of acceptable or agreed-upon speech essentially requires one to surrender a portion of oneself. Failure to do so, however, could mean that the criminal justice system punishes the nonconformist. Again, postmodernism examines language to determine how powerful people use it to control and demean those who are powerless (Reid, 2012).

Postmodernists argue that past criminological theories have failed to realistically unmask the true causes of crime and have therefore failed to provide viable strategies to prevent crime from occurring. They reject the methodologies used in past criminological studies and challenge all assumptions of objective truth. Postmodernism rejects epistemological assumptions, refutes methodological conventions, resists knowledge claims, obscures all truths, and dismisses policy recommendations (Rosenau, 1992). Furthermore, postmodernism argues that some theories may have been effective in the past, but have outlived their usefulness in contemporary society. Postmodern criminology challenges and debunks conventional thought, as well as existing theories of crime, by engaging in a process of deconstruction (Henry and Milovanovic, 1996).

> **deconstructionist**—A theoretician who believes there is no objective reality and who attacks traditional theories without the intent to rebuild them.

Deconstruction tears a text apart, revealing its contradictions, assumptions, and intent (Rosenau, 1992). A scholar who follows this tradition is often referred to as a **deconstructionist.** While they provide viable approaches to deconstructing existing theories, they rarely discuss how to properly reconstruct theories so that they may have better explanatory power. Pauline Rosenau (1992) contends that deconstructionists make no attempts to improve, revise, or offer a better version of the text. The contention is that postmodernists yield a negative or fatalistic reality. Many wonder if postmodernists can arrive at the truth or an absolute understanding about social reality (Arrigo and Bernard, 1997; Henry and Milovanovic, 1996). Critics argue that if postmodernists can demystify one reality only to create a new reality, to what extent should it be believed, since there is latent meaning found beneath all surface meaning? Because of this fatal flaw, some contend that any attempt at deconstruction without reconstruction may lead to anarchy.

Cultural Criminology

> **cultural criminology**—The study of crime within the frameworks of experiential dynamics of illicit subcultures, the symbolic criminalization of popular cultural forms, the mediated construction of crime, and crime-control issues.

Cultural criminology emerged in the mid-1990s with its roots established in the works of interactionist, subcultural, and naturalistic ideas of the scholars from the University of Chicago and the politically charged theoretical framework of Marxist and critical criminology (Ferrell and Hamm, 1998). This critical perspective emerged in 1995 when Jeff Ferrell and Clint Sanders edited the first collection of works under the guise of "cultural criminology." This new brand of scholarship focused on imagery, meaning, and representation between crime and crime control. Cultural criminology advances the idea of understanding crime within the frameworks of experiential dynamics of illicit subcultures, the symbolic criminalization of popular cultural forms, the mediated construction of crime, and crime control issues. Stated differently, cultural criminology is a theoretical, methodological, and interactionist approach to the study of crime that relies on culture as a major social product that contextualizes crime and the agencies of social control as creative social constructs that are constantly changing (Ferrell, 1999).

One major theme of the 1995 collection of essays is living-on-the-edge practices, such as abortion violence, base jumping, fast motorcycle riding, binge drinking, drug dealing, music, fashion, and style (Beirne and Messerschmidt, 2011). Some scholars argue that the conceptual focus of edgework is in the excitement from risk taking in a world dominated by boredom and the pointless drudgery of late modernity (Lyng, 2005; Milovanovic, 2006). Furthermore, edgework finds patterns of power and excitement and harm in diverse places that include back alleys, garbage dumps, cliff tops, and corporate boardrooms (Williams, 2007). Cultural criminologists are often critical of mainstream data collections and research designs that are stale or dated. They are especially critical and suspicious of quantitative criminology in general, and survey research in particular, as a method of gathering and analyzing data. Instead, cultural criminologists emphasize the use of edgework, meaning, and the complex efforts of globalization on everyday life (Beirne and Messerschmidt, 2011). They argue that rather than having a single best method of research or having each method compete for supremacy, cultural criminology embraces a plurality of methodical techniques in its analysis of crime and culture (Ferrell and Sanders, 1995, p. 305).

Cultural criminologists study the effects of media and cultural presentation in movies and television shows such as *Carlito's Way*, *Boyz n the Hood*, *Menace II Society*, *Goodfellas*, *The Sopranos,* and others to determine whether they construct negative or stereotypical images of people. More specifically, they are concerned that some people, by virtue of their social class status, race, or ethnicity, may be treated more suspiciously than others because of how they are portrayed in the popular culture. They often ask, after mediated constructions, how do people in society perceive and react to people who resemble Hollywood's depictions of "gangstas" and "thugs"? Images and meaning that are attached to changing constructs are mediated and present the interplay of crime and crime control policy (Farrell, 1999). Cultural criminology addresses the effects of popular culture, media, and subcultures on criminal behavior. This theoretical tradition studies how criminals and their subcultures are portrayed by pop culture and presented in the media. Stated differently, cultural criminology focuses on the representation that the popular culture and media gives to different groups of people and the corresponding reaction they receive from the broader society.

Green Criminology

Green criminology was introduced in the early 1990s by Michael Lynch. While it is the newest member of the critical criminology community, green criminology does not solely focus on crimes committed by powerless people, and it starts by rejecting the state or mainstream definitions

> **green criminology**—The study of crime that focuses on harm and damage inflicted on the environment that impacts people, animals, and the natural materials. It investigates devastation caused by air pollution, oil spills, global warming, forest fires, illegal dumping of chemical waste, and other types of damage to the earth's resources.

of harm and crime (Beirne and Messerschmidt, 2011). Green criminology focuses on harm done to the natural environment. In fact, some scholars argue that the theory combines the theoretical insights of two movements: the leftist/liberal environmental movement and the animal rights movement (Brisman and South, 2012; Beirne and Messerschmidt, 2011). More specifically, green criminologists bring together criminology and environmental issues such as damage that could be intentionally caused by individuals or corporate greed or neglect (Potter, 2010). These criminologists are concerned with all types of harm inflicted on the environment even when the victims are not humans. For example, they study oil spills, global warming, forest fires, illegal dumping of chemical waste, and any other type of devastation, including pollution to the earth's resources that adversely impacts the quality of life for people, animals, and the natural environment (Beirne and Messerschmidt, 2011; Carrabine et al., 2009). Similarly, researchers report that some major areas of emphasis of green criminology include corporate and state criminality with environmental effects, workplace health and safety where breaches cause governmental harm, illegal disposal of toxic waste, and acts leading to harmful effects on the water supply and air quality (Brisman and South, 2012; Lynch and Stretesky, 2003).

In the absence of traditional laws, green criminologists view any harm to the environment as a crime, and consequently, they seek to understand the nature and extent of these victimizations by studying how, when, why, and where they occur. More importantly, they are interested in knowing who suffers when ecological crimes are committed. One approach that green criminologists use to study **environmental crime** is to divide green crimes into two categories: primary and secondary (Carrabine et al., 2014). Primary crimes result directly from the destruction and devastation of the earth's resources—for example, pollution of the oceans, abuse of animals, and deforestation. Secondary crimes are categorized as harm that is symbolic or dependent on destruction and efforts made to regulate or prevent it. This typically stems from the exploitation of conditions that emerge after an environmental crisis. Such crimes may include illegal sales of food, medicine, water or others in violation of rules that attempt to regulate environmental harm (Brisman and South, 2012).

> **environmental crime**—Criminal activity that leads to the destruction of the natural environment—for example, dumping hazardous waste and engaging trade in of products such as endangered species or ozone-depleting substances.

In responding to environmental harm, many green criminologists rely on traditional methods of crime prevention that include policing and punishment (Potter, 2010). Others believe that reforms can be made through protest movements and changing the culture of consumption (Lynch, 2013). A recent environmental crime that received national attention from the media was the BP oil spill that occurred in Mobile, Alabama, in 2010. Experts estimate that 170 million gallons of oil flooded into the gulf after the explosion of BP's Deepwater Horizon oil rig, causing devastation to coastal beaches, the death of birds and other wildlife, decreased fish and wildlife populations, pollutants that could cause cancer, and a decline in tourism to Mobile Bay, which adversely impacts its local economy. While attempting to calculate the amount of devastation to the Gulf Coast area, green criminologists and other experts cite the Exxon Valdez oil spill that occurred 20 years earlier, reporting that the long-term impact of the spill is still unknown.

Green criminologists desire to develop social, environmental, and ecological justice to stop the destruction of the environment, even when it means holding offenders socially, civilly, and criminally responsible for their wrongdoings (Lynch and Stretesky, 2003). While the popularity of green criminology continues to grow, some scholars suggest that green criminologists should seek new ways of confronting critically the intersection of culture, crime, justice, and the environment. They also contend that because there are many similarities between cultural criminology and green criminology (both are interdisciplinary and intellectually liberal), efforts should be made to link them for their mutual benefit (Brisman and South, 2012). Despite this, some criminologists debate whether green criminology is a theory of perspective (White, 2008).

Summary

Conflict and radical theories view crime as a function of the conflict that exists in capitalist society. They argue that those with power not only control social, political, and economic resources, but also get to define criminal behavior. Conflict theorists argue that those in power use the law to protect their interest, to the detriment of the poor. Moreover, to maintain their dominance, those in power also use the law to control powerless groups. To conflict criminologists, the definition of crime has political undertones, since powerful people rarely bring their own behavior under criminal inspection. As such, they argue that the law, the police, the courts, and the corrections system target poor and marginalized people. They also believe that the justice system and the capitalist structure are in place to protect and advance the economic and political interests of the wealthy.

While conflict theory continues to influence criminological studies, it emerged within the backdrop of social changes that were occurring during the 1960s and 1970s, especially events such as the civil rights movement, the Vietnam war, the counterculture movement, political assassinations, protests and riots, the sexual revolution, and other historical events that characterized the turmoil that defined the struggle for equality and human dignity. To understand this chaotic period, scholars began to examine Karl Marx's analysis of the economic structure of society in general, and power relations in particular, and the work of such scholars as Bonger, Dahrendorf, and Vold to explain conflict.

Eventually, several varieties of conflict theory developed, including instrumental Marxism and structural Marxism. Other theories included radical, left realism, peacemaking, phenomenological, power threat, feminist, and power-control theory. All of these theories are critical of the economic structure of the United States because it creates inequalities that many scholars believe cause violence and street crime. Conflict theorists point out that criminals who engage in elite crime are not treated as harshly as common criminals. In fact, they attempt to expose the relationship between social class and differential processing in the justice system.

Of the conflict theories, feminist research focuses on the gendered nature of criminal behavior, especially women's participation in crime. Feminist theory focuses on how power relations affect women in regard to victimization, differences in criminal offending, and treatment in the criminal justice system. While some feminists believe that traditional criminological theory can help us understand crime, others argue that in order to develop feminist theory, we need a gender-aware criminology that explains the gender differences in crime variation. As such, some examine studies in masculinities and femininities to explain differences. Cultural criminology has emerged to focus on social constructs that are created through imagery, meaning, and media presentations. Green criminology is the newest conflict theory. It emphasizes preventing harm done to the natural environment.

Shortcomings of the Theories

1. The theories fail to objectively establish that a conspiracy exists among the rich to subordinate and exploit the poor.

2. Despite the efforts of Hagan and others, it may be difficult to incorporate the conflict theory on the micro level to explain the dynamics occurring within the context of the home in general, and the family in particular.

3. The theory ignores that work in capitalist societies may eventually empower some individuals and groups. For example, certain types of work can be both economically as well as spiritually liberating to people who are oppressed by an unjust structural arrangement.

4. Though a historical and economic theory, conflict theory fails to consider the importance of race, ethnicity, gender, disability, age, and other factors when it comes to people's desire to identify themselves and how they may choose to organize the world. This failure often leads people to overlook the reality that inequality is based on more than just where one is situated in the social structure.

Discussion Questions

1. What do instrumental Marxists believe cause crime?

2. Why did conflict theories become popular in the United States?

3. What are some issues that feminist scholars are concerned about?

4. What is the relationship between power and the definition of crime?

5. What do radical scholars believe to be the solution to the crime problem?

6. What is the relationship between crime and the economic structure of society?

References

Arrigo, B. (1995). The Peripheral Core of Law and Criminology: On Postmodern Social Theory and Conceptual Integration. *Justice Quarterly, 12*(3), 447–72.

Arrigo, B., and Bernard, T. (1997). Postmodern Criminology in Relations to Radical and Conflict Theory: A Preliminary Explication. *Critical Criminology: An International Journal, 8*(2):39–60.

Barkan, S. E. (2001). *Criminology: A Sociological Understanding* (2nd ed.). Upper Saddle River, NJ: Prentice-Hall.

Beirne, P., and Messerschmidt, J. W. (2011). *Criminology: A Sociological Approach.* (5th ed.). New York, NY: Oxford University Press.

Blackstock, N. (1988). *COINTELPRO: The FBI's Secret War on Political Freedom*. New York, NY: Pathfinder.

Blackwell, B. S., Sellers, C., and Schlaupitz, S. (2002). A Power-Control Theory of Vulnerability to Crime and Adolescent Role Exits—Revisited. *Canadian Review of Sociology and Anthropology, 39*, 199–219.

Bodapati, M., Anderson, J. F., and Brinson, T. E. (2008). Revisiting Hubert Blalock's Power Threat Theory to Determine its Effect on Court Workgroup Behavior as it Concerns Structured Sentencing. *Criminal Justice Studies: A Critical Journal of Crime, Law, and Society, 21*(2), 109–34.

Brisman, A., and South, N. (2012). A Green-Cultural Criminology: An Exploratory Outline. *Crime Media Culture, 9*(2), 115–35.

Buchholz, E., Hartmann, R., Lekschas, J., and Stiller, G. (1974). *Socialist Criminology: Theoretical and Methodical Foundations*. Lexington, MA: Saxon House.

Carrabine, E., Cox, P., Hobbs, D., Thiel, D., Turton, J. and South, N. (2014). *Criminology: A Sociological Introduction* (3rd ed.). London: Routledge.

Carrabine, E., Cox, P., Lee, M., Plummer, K., and South, N. (2009). *Criminology: A Sociological Introduction* (2nd ed.). London: Routledge.

Chambliss, W. J., and Seidman, R. (1982). *Law, Order, and Power* (2nd ed.). Reading, MA: Addison-Wesley.

Chomsky, N. (2012). *Occupy*. Occupied Media Pamphlet Series. Brooklyn, NY: Zuccotti Park Press.

Daly, M. (1973). *Beyond God the Father*. Boston, MA: Beacon Press.

Daly, K., and Chesney-Lind, M. (1988). "Feminism and criminology." *Justice Quarterly* 5(4):497–538.

DeKeseredy, W., and Goff, C. (1992). Corporate Violence Against Canadian Women: Assessing Left-Realist Research and Policy. *Journal of Human Justice, 4*, 55–70.

DeKeseredy, W., and Schwartz, M. D. (2006). Left Realist Theory. In S. Henry and M. M. Lanier (Eds.), *The Essential Criminology Reader*. Boulder, CO: Westview.

Del Rio, E. (1974). *Marx for Beginners*. New York, NY: Pantheon Books.

Dictionary of World History. (1994). London: Brockhampton Press.

Dye, T. R. (1994). *Politics in States and Communities* (8th ed.). Englewood Cliffs, NJ: Prentice-Hall.

Elias, R. (1986). *The Politics of Victimization: Victims, Victimology and Human Rights*. New York, NY: Oxford University Press.

Ferrell, J. (1997). Against the Law: Anarchist Criminology. In B. D. Maclean and D. Milovanovic (Eds.), *Thinking Critically About Crime* (pp. 146–54). Vancouver, BC: Collective Press.

Ferrell, J. (1999). "Cultural Criminology." *Annual Review of Sociology* 25:395–418.

Ferrell, J., and Hamm, M. S. (1998). *Ethnography at the Edge: Crime, Deviance, and Field Research*. Boston, MA: Northeastern University Press.

Ferrell, J., and Sanders, C. R. (1995). *Cultural Criminology*. Boston, MA: Northeastern University Press.

Hagan, J., Gillis, A. R., and Simpson, J. (1985). The Class Structure and Delinquency: Toward a Power-Control Theory of Common Delinquent Behavior. *American Journal of Sociology, 90*, 1151–78.

Hagan, J., McCarthy, B., and Foster, H. (2002). A General Theory of Delinquency and Despair in the Life Course. *Acta Sociologica, 45*, 37–47.

Henry, S., and Milovanovic, D. (1996). *Constitutive Criminology: Beyond Postmodernism*. London: Sage.

Hooks, B. (1984). *Feminist Theory: From Margin to Center*. Boston, MA: South End Press.

Hooks, B. (1987). Feminism: A Movement to End Sexist Oppression. In A. Phillips (Ed.), *Feminism and Equality* (pp. 62–76). New York, NY: New York University Press.

Inlander, C. B., Levin, L. S., and Weiner, E. (1988). *Medicine on Trial: The Appalling Story of Ineptitude, Malfeasance, Neglect, and Arrogance*. New York, NY: Prentice-Hall.

Jenkins, P. (1984). *Crime and Justice: Issues and Ideas*. Pacific Grove, CA: Brooks/Cole.

Lea, J., and Young, J. (1984). *What Is to Be Done About Law and Order?* New York: Penguin.

Lynch, M. J. (2013). Reflections on Green Criminology and Its Boundaries: Comparing Environ-mental and Criminal Victimizations and Considering Crime from an Eco-City Perspective. In N. South and A. Brisman (Eds.), *The Routledge International Handbook of Green Criminology*. London: Routledge.

Lynch, M. J., and Groves, W. B. (1986). *A Primer in Radical Criminology*. New York, NY: Harrow and Heston.

Lynch, M. J., and Stretesky, P. (2003). The Meaning of Green: Contrasting Criminological Perspec-tives. *Theoretical Criminology, 7*(2), 217–38.

Lyng, S. (2005). *Edgework: The Sociology of Risk Taking*. New York, NY: Routledge.

Michalowski, R. J. (1985). *Order, Law, and Crime: An Introduction to Criminology*. New York, NY: Random House.

Michalowski, R. J., and Bohlander, E. W. (1976). Repression and Criminal Justice in Capitalist America. *Sociological Inquiry, 46*, 95–106.

Milovanovic, D. (2006). Edgework: Negotiating Boundaries. In S. Henry and M. Lanier (Eds.), *The Essential Criminology Reader* (pp. 234–46). New York, NY: Westview.

Pearce, F. (1992). The Contribution of Left Realism to the Study of Commercial Crime. In J. Lowman and B. MacLean (Eds.), *Realist Criminology: Crime Control and Policing in the 1990s* (pp. 313–35). Toronto: University of Toronto Press.

Pepinsky, H. (2006). Peacemaking. In S. Henry and M. M. Lanier (Eds.), *The Essential Criminology Reader*. Boulder, CO: Westview.

Pepinsky, H., and Quinney, R. (1991). *Criminology as Peacemaking*. Bloomington, IN: Indiana Univer-sity Press.

Potter, G. (2010). What Is Green Criminology? *Sociology Review, 20*(2):8–12.

Quinney, R. (1970). *The Social Reality of Crime*. Boston, MA: Little, Brown.

Quinney, R. (1974). *Critique of Legal Order: Crime Control in Capitalist Society*. Boston, MA: Little, Brown.

Quinney, R. (1977). *Class State and Crime: On the Theory and Practice of Criminal Justice*. New York, NY: Longman.

Reid, S., T. (2012). *Crime and Criminology* (13th ed.). New York, NY: Oxford University Press.

Reiman, J. (1990). *The Rich Get Richer and the Poor Get Prison: Ideology, Crime, and Criminal Justice*. Needham Heights, MA: Allyn and Bacon.

Rosenau, P. M. (1992). *Postmodernism and the Social Sciences: Insights, Inroads, and Intrusions*. Princeton, NY: Princeton University Press.

Rothschild, M. (2013, May 20). Spying on Occupy Activists. *The Progressive*.

Schwartz, M., and DeKeseredy, W. (1991). Left Realist Criminology: Strengths, Weaknesses and the Feminist Critique. *Crime, Law and Social Change, 15*, 51–72.

Schwendinger, H., and Schwendinger, J. (1970). Defenders of Order or Guardians of Human Rights? *Issues in Criminology, 7*, 72–81.

Sellin, T. (1938). *Culture Conflict and Crime*. New York, NY: Social Science Research Council.

Siegel, L. (2000). *Criminology* (7th ed.). Belmont, CA: Wadsworth/Thompson Learning.

Simon, R. J. (1975). *Women and Crime*. Lexington, MA: Lexington Books.

Sommers, C. H. (1994). *Who Stole Feminism: How Women Have Betrayed Women*. New York, NY: Simon & Schuster.

Spitzer, S. (1975). Towards a Marxian Theory of Deviance. *Social Problems, 22*, 638–51.

Steffensmeier, D. (1983). Flawed Arrests Rates and Overlooked Reliability Problems in UCR Arrest Statistics: A Comment on Wilson's *The Masculinity of Violent Crime*—Some Second Thoughts. *Journal of Criminal Justice, 11*, 167–71.

Taylor, I. R., Walton, P., and Young, J. (1973). *The New Criminology: For a Social Theory of Deviance.* London: Routledge and Kegan Paul.

Toby, J. (1979). The New Criminology Is the Old Sentimentality. *Criminology, 16,* 516–26.

White, R. (2008). *Crimes Against Nature: Environmental Criminology and Ecological Justice.* Cullompton, UK: Willan.

Williams, C. (2007). Potential Spaces of Crime: The Playful, the Destructive and the Distinctively Human. *Crime, Media, Culture, 3*(1), 49–66.

Young, J. (1987). The Tasks Facing a Realist Criminology. *Contemporary Crisis, 11,* 337–57.

Chapter 9

The Future of Criminological Theory

When criminology was developed in the 18th century, it postulated that offenders engaged in deviant and criminal behavior after exercising rational thinking and free will. While there have been many criminological advances leading into the 21st century, rational choice remains a dominant theme in the criminal justice system, especially where crime control policies are concerned. It seems that the more things change, the more they stay the same.

But what does the future hold for criminology? An extensive review of the five leading criminological theory textbooks provides no directional map of where the discipline is headed. What reasons can criminologists provide to explain such neglect? After decades of theorizing about crime, have criminologists and sociologists suddenly lost their way? Why are they reluctant to make recommendations on the type of research the discipline should prioritize? The easy answer is that criminologists have the freedom to select the subject matter that they choose to address. The difficult answer is that they should study criminal behavior that continues to pose a threat to public safety. For some criminologists, this may include intimate personal violence, crime and the life course, feminist research, sexual offenders, domestic and international terrorism, and human trafficking, since these are domestic as well as global concerns. Criminologists are free to research what they choose, but what does the future hold for criminological theory?

While criminology appears to have a promising future demonstrated by the growth of criminal justice, as well as of criminology programs around the country, some experts are not as optimistic as others are about its future. For example, Leanne Tuck argues that effective crime control policy cannot be influenced by a single criminological theory since there are contradictions and opposing views held by criminologists. There is little agreement on the part of criminologists about the causation of deviant and criminal behavior. This is probably due in part to the different ideological traditions that at one time or another have dominated the discipline (e.g., crime is caused by poverty, social disorganization, low self-control, negative socialization, capitalism). It seems that because of the different theories, objectivity and neutrality are absent or even compromised. **Joan Petersilia** (1987) argues that criminologists should engage in research that will have an effect on crime by addressing policy implications. While this endeavor is important, research should not be the final say where policy is concerned. She contends that, above everything, the goal of criminology should be to make valid predictions about crime and to influence public policy that is designed to prevent and deter criminal behavior. Ultimately, criminal justice policies should improve the human condition.

> **Petersilia, Joan**—A professor in the Department of Criminology, Law, and Sociology at the University of California, Irvine. She has published extensively on crime prevention and justice for persons with disabilities, parole and prisoner reintegration, and sentencing. One of her recent publications is *Criminal Justice Policy*.

A question that has challenged the effectiveness of criminology is: If the experts cannot agree among themselves, how can anyone reasonably expect policy makers to embrace their research findings? Others argue that criminology has yet to fully recover from the attacks it suffered during the late 1970s, when liberal crime control policies were criticized for failing to reduce crime and improve the adverse social conditions of the poor. The conservative movement of the mid-1970s was successful in ending many of the liberal social programs and the "War on Poverty" that was part of the Great Society effort to make America inclusive of everyone, including people who had historically been disenfranchised from participation in conventional activities. Despite conservative efforts, what was even more damaging to liberal policy was the groundbreaking research conducted by correctional experts perpetuating the notion that nothing worked to rehabilitate or modify the behavior of criminal offenders. History also reveals that conservative crime policies of the 1980s were also unsuccessful (Messner and Rosenfeld, 2007).

A valid criticism of criminological theory is that it has spent many years explaining crime delinquency committed by the powerless (Barkan, 2012). However, with the exception of a few theories, such as differential association and strain, the discipline has survived mainly by conducting research and theorizing about deviant and criminal behavior committed by the poor and desperate. Moreover, criminology has largely ignored the experiences of girls and women, and crimes committed by powerful people. While conflict theorists of the 1960s and 1970s attacked the "establishment" and questioned conservative criminology by examining state criminality, it now appears that scholars have abandoned their critical orientation by changing their focus to issues such as homelessness, the death penalty, and the relationship between the media and crime. Perhaps they believe that justice and equality have been achieved. Notwithstanding, whatever happened to the abundance of scholarship that exposed crimes committed by wealthy people, such as corporate and factory owners, medical professionals, stockbrokers, insurance companies, the auto industry, and pharmaceutical companies that rush new drugs to market without clinical trials and Food and Drug Administration approval in an attempt to maximize profits at the expense of consumer safety? Furthermore, criminologists and criminal justice experts have also been remiss when it comes to equally measuring crimes committed by powerful offenders. For example, there are no uniform crime reports, self-report surveys, or national victimization surveys for the criminal elite. As stated earlier, crimes committed by the criminal elite largely go unreported unless independent researchers investigate them or the media report that many people have been injured or died as a consequence of using unsafe products. Criminologists should create a national clearinghouse database on elite crime.

Much contemporary research in the area of criminal justice and criminology is guided by grant-awarding agencies. The agencies that award funds for research are setting the agenda for what they believe is important to the discipline and public policy. Many criminologists who enter the field may do so because of their concerns about crime and social justice. However, they are often forced to abandon their research interests to follow grant-funding opportunities. They are also pressured to pursue federal funding that could advance their career by bringing job security and recognition from the broader scientific community. This activity is largely fueled by colleges and universities that pressure faculty members to procure external funding as a condition of continued employment. This forces educators to reassess their research interests and redirect them to areas where funding is available. For example, the National Institute of Justice, the Office of Juvenile Justice Delinquency Prevention, and similar institutions allocate millions of dollars each year to research directed at examining aspects of the criminal justice system (i.e., police, court, and corrections), as well as the juvenile justice system. Therefore, federal funding could have an undue influence over academic researchers who are willing to allow these agencies to set their research agendas. What if funding agencies agendas never include an examination of behaviors that have serious social consequences, and may actually be an attempt to divert scrutiny from the most injurious actions that take the greater toll on society? This state of affairs has led critics to argue that many criminologists and social science researchers have compromised the discipline in exchange for grant sponsorship.

The visionary Émile Durkheim argued that crime and deviance emerge during periods of rapid social change. He argued that when society experiences changes in technological advances, the by-product could be deviance and crime. Today, criminologists are deeply indebted to Durkheim. Many crimes and emerging problems are linked to computers and cyberspace. Crimes caused by technological advancements will continue to challenge criminology. For example, identify theft, fraud, cyber-stalking, and online chat rooms used as recruiting grounds for hate groups, terrorists, and sexual predators are of major concern to criminologists as well as the law enforcement community. If criminology is to determine causes and preventions of high-tech crimes, academic programs that offer advanced degrees in criminal justice and criminology must modify their respective curriculums to provide training to students so that they may offer expert opinions and commentaries on the motivation of such behavior. High-tech crimes could prove devastating to the economy, since millions of people invest in the stock market and investment firms invest the retirement funds of millions of people. Computer hackers can conceivably bring companies and people to financial ruin. Currently, computer scientists and officials at the U.S. Department of Justice are aggressively trying to detect and prevent crimes from being committed in cyberspace. If criminology is to remain a force in the study of crime, it must address this concern in the near future.

After years of exposing how the tobacco industry made billions of dollars while subjecting its customers to a cancer-causing product, critical criminologists are witnessing this corporate giant being brought to justice. The late 1990s saw the once invincible industry face civil litigations that amounted to billions of dollars awarded to smokers who suffered poor health after years of using an unsafe product. Despite the tobacco industry's having suppressed decades of research revealing the long-term health risks associated with smoking, several class action lawsuits have revealed juries' ability to discern fiction from the realities of addictive additives knowingly used in cigarettes. Some conflict criminologists, along with consumer advocates, had argued for years that the tobacco industry routinely engaged in death and injury for profits. Though justice for the victims was a long time coming, experts believe that the same strategy can be used to bring gun manufacturers to justice. For example, each year guns are responsible for the deaths of many Americans. Recently, a number of random shootings have occurred that have highlighted the degree of senselessness associated with these killings. They have occurred in public places such as movie theaters, political rallies, and schools where shooters use semiautomatic weapons to indiscriminately fire at anyone. As these deaths occur, gun manufacturers continue to gross billions of dollars annually from gun sales. When victims without insurance are killed or injured by handguns or semiautomatic weapons, an economic burden is placed on the public health system in the state where shootings occur, since someone has to defray the cost of surgical and hospital expenses. Some criminologists argue that like the tobacco industry, gun manufacturers should also be responsible for the consequences of their products. These criminologists argue that the gun manufacturers should be sued in a class action suit under a product liability claim. This is another area some criminologists may consider exploring in the future.

Over the years, the United States has experienced a decrease in crime. What accounts for the reduction in crime? Many scholars attribute this to a relatively healthy economy for almost everyone, including those living in poverty; punitive criminal justice policies, such as mandatory sentences for certain felonies; and a former presidential commitment to placing thousands of police officers on the streets of America to foster better protection and police–community relations. While many criminologists are reluctant to point to any one factor that might account for lower rates of crime, some argue that these factors in combination may explain the reductions. Though these policies appear to have had a positive impact on crime in America, they have come at an expensive price. For example, though the crime rates have been declining since the early 1990s, incarceration rates of offenders in jails and prisons have never been higher. In fact, some correctional experts estimate that there are more than 2 million people in places of confinement and over 5.1 million people under some form of community supervision (Bureau of Justice Statistics, 2008). This is due to strict incarceration policies. More specifically, mandatory sentences, such as mandatory minimums and maximums, including "three strikes" policies, may have the unintended effect of being too costly for some states experiencing strained correctional budgets. In many cases, offenders who were prosecuted under these sentencing guidelines were disproportionately minority and relatively young—which means long periods of time behind bars at the expense of taxpayers. These policies can also be dangerous to law enforcement personnel attempting to bring offenders to justice, especially if offenders are aware of the punishment they are likely to receive if they are apprehended. Alternative strategies of dealing with offenders must be sought. This will present a future challenge for criminologists.

One reliable measure that criminologists have historically used to explain crime has been the age distribution of the population. Because teenagers commit a disproportionate number of crimes relative to their numbers in the general population, criminologists are able to make valid predictions about the number of crimes that adolescents will commit in the future. The general argument is that as the birth rate in society experiences tremendous growth, when children are in their teenage years, the crime rate should reflect the number of young males in the population. Another challenge for criminal justice and criminology is to ensure that measures are taken to reduce the number of crimes committed by future generations of Americans. Criminologists have long argued that reducing the number of social problems in economically and culturally challenged areas will help facilitate lower crime rates. If the poor are afforded better educational opportunities, meaningful jobs, safe housing, and access to medical care, the need for many of them to engage in crime may be eliminated. While these items have never served as a panacea for crime, they could help to reduce crime-generating factors.

Domestic terrorism continues to increase to the extent that hate groups and others are growing in numbers. Terrorism from within the nation is just as dangerous as international terrorism. For example, on April 15, 2013, brothers Dzhokhar Tsarnaev and Tamerlan Tsarnaev ignited bombs at the finish line of a Boston marathon that claimed the lives of three people and injured 260 others. Though not as disturbing as the terrorist attack in New York on September 11, 2001, it, too, is a tragedy that is etched in the minds of many Americans. Whether terrorist crimes are committed by antigovernment militias, individuals, separatist groups, or international terrorists, these crimes threaten the national security of the nation and the American way of life. They are committed for the sole purposes of creating destruction, fear, and terror in those who survive or witness it. Other types of domestic terrorism stem from militias that have declared war on the American government. Sometimes these groups bomb federal and state buildings. Other times, they may target symbols of a nation's strength. Perhaps the most common kind of terrorism occurs when nationalists or religious zealots from other parts of the world attack the United States. A review of current criminology and criminal justice programs reveals that many programs around the nation are beginning to offer courses in homeland security, domestic and international terrorism, and counterintelligence studies. Federal grant funding is also being earmarked for research devoted to understanding and preventing acts of terrorism.

Some criminologists argue that in the future there will also be a movement toward peacemaking criminology. Under this direction, the justice system and others will embrace a restorative justice model that rejects punitive justice practices and policies. It promotes informally resolving conflicts, such as property and violent crimes, through noncoercive means, such as victim–offender reconciliation programs. Such programs rely on a mediator to facilitate face-to-face encounters between victims and attackers. Today, more than 120 of these programs exist in the United States. They serve as a diversion from a traditional court system to an informal setting where a neutral arbitrator listens to claims from both victims and offenders to search for a peaceful conflict resolution. Not only are these programs of help to the participants, but they also reduce the caseloads that come before traditional courts. Some common problems that are found among mediation programs include logistical matters and resources, and before they can be used, victims and offenders must agree to settle their complaint informally.

References

Barkan, S. E. (2012). *Criminology: A Sociological Understanding* (5th ed.). Upper Saddle River, New Jersey: Pearson-Prentice-Hall.

Bureau of Justice Statistics. (2008). One in Every 31 U.S. Adults Was in a Prison or Jail or on Probation or Parole at the End of Last Year. Available at www.ojp.usdoj.gov/bjs/pub/press *-/p06ppus06pr.htm.

Messner, S. F., and Rosenfeld, R. (2007). *Crime and the American Dream* (4th ed.). Belmont, CA: Thomson Higher Education.

Petersilia, J. (1987). *The Influence of Criminal Justice Research* (Santa Monica, CA: Rand Corporation).

Tuck, M. (1989). Is Criminology Any Use? *Research Bulletin, 26,* 5–8.

Glossary

active precipitation theory. A victimization theory that holds that victims of crime are often responsible for the injury or harm they sustain because they are usually the instigator of an event that ends in their victimization. The theory suggests that victims often initiate crime by being the first to either use an insult, rebuke, or physical violence that ends in them becoming a victim.

Age of Enlightenment. Often referred to as the Renaissance. It was a period of intellectual movement and growth, occurring between the 14th and 17th centuries and flourishing in western Europe. The age encouraged the growth of skepticism and free thought, and there were major contributions made in the arts and sciences.

aggravated assault. An unlawful attack by one person on another with the intent to inflict severe bodily harm or injury or the attempt or threat of same behavior.

aggregate data research. Studies that rely on existing statistics or numbers about social behavior.

Agnew, Robert. A sociologist who developed general strain theory, which expanded the Mertonian theory of anomie from the macro to the micro level of explanation.

Akers, Ronald. A social learning theorist who argued that behaviors are learned and sustained via a process of reinforcements.

American Dream. A term that refers to both a cultural goal and process in American society. As a goal, it is concerned with achieving abundant economic wealth or material goods and services. As a process, it entails being socialized into wanting to achieve un- limited monetary success and believing that it is attainable.

amplification of deviance. A concept used in labeling theory that refers to the likelihood of a labeled person to receive more attention from the labeling audience which causes them to continue labeling people already known as a delinquent or criminal.

anomie. A state of normlessness or deregulation brought on by rapid social change. Émile Durkheim used the term to explain how a breakdown or collapse in collective normative behavior could cause deviant and criminal behavior.

arson. Any intentional, malicious burning or attempt to burn with the purpose to defraud a house, building, motor vehicle, aircraft, or the personal property of another.

aspirations. Strong goals and desires that are typically induced by the social culture of a society.

atavistic anomaly. A condition discussed by Cesare Lombroso; refers to the idea that offenders are biologically different from law-abiding people.

attachment. One of four elements found in Travis Hirschi's social bonding theory that posits that strong attachments or ties to conventional institutions of society such as the family, school, church, and peers will bind individuals toward conformity. To the extent that one's attachments to important people and institutions are weaken or broken, the individual is free to engage in delinquency.

autonomy. A dominant theme or value common to lower class subculture that suggests people covertly express a desire to function independently of state authority but often contradict this by engaging in overt behavior that will bring them into the criminal justice system.

Bandura, Albert. A learning theorist who developed social modeling theory, the idea that aggressive behavior is often modeled behavior.

Beccaria, Cesare. One of the founders of the classical school of criminology. He advocated major overhauls to the administration of justice and the use of punishment (only) if it had a deterrent effect.

Becker, Howard. A sociologist who argued that those whose labels successfully attach are referred to as outsiders. He also argued that not everyone who is labeled takes on a deviant identity.

belief. One of four elements found in Travis Hirschi's social bonding theory that holds that some individuals are socialized to accept moral values and beliefs as truth. Therefore, they create an obligation on them to follow. To the extent that people believe that they are following rules that are just and fair, they will engage in conformity since they have stronger bonds than those who do not agree with or accept conventional behaviors. If belief is absent, individuals will have weaker bonds to society and will engage in delinquent behavior.

Bentham, Jeremy. One of the founders of the classical school of criminology; he thought that crime could be deterred only if punishment is great enough to offset the desire to continue crime, and is swift, certain, and severe.

Blau, Judith. A sociologist devoted to promoting human rights who argued that efforts should be made to rid the society of inequities that lead to poverty, discrimination, racism, sexism, and imperialism. Some of her scholarship has focused on crime and the underclass, relative deprivation and crime, and human rights violations.

Blau, Peter. A sociologist and theoretician best known for his work in macrosocial structure which examined the systems of organizations, social exchange, social classes, and the structure of societies. He is also one of the founders of the field of organization sociology. His work helped transformed the study of social inequities and mobility.

bourgeois. A person who is in the middle class and shares the values of those in this group.

Burgess, Ernest. A sociologist at the University of Chicago who helped to design the five concentric circles.

Burgess, Robert. A sociologist best known for his work with Ronald Akers that elaborated on Edwin Sutherland's theory of differential association. Along with the help of Akers, they presented the differential reinforcement theory that addressed many elements that were not addressed by Sutherland, but were salient to learning and the continuation of deviant and criminal behavior.

burglary. Unlawful entry into a building or structure to commit a felony or theft.

capitalism. An economic system based on private ownership of property and the accumulation of material goods and services; investments in the private ownership of the means of production, distribution, and exchange of wealth.

Chicago School. Sociologists at the University of Chicago who studied crime in the city in its natural environment. They were instrumental in shifting the focus of criminological studies from the Germans and Italians and giving sociology in the United States more credibility by discussing the social ecology of crime. This school successfully moved away from "armchair" theorizing and embarked on the use of statistics and empirical observations by using anthropological techniques.

class struggle. A condition found in stratified societies where people are grouped based on economic class, leading to struggles over social, political, and economic resources. Class struggles are based on the struggle to dominate other groups.

classical criminology. The branch of criminological theory considered to be the genesis of the study of crime. This school was instrumental in advancing the idea that criminals were not motivated by demonic or satanic forces, but they engage in crime after exercising free will and a rational thinking process.

Cloward, Richard. One of the authors of differential opportunity theory. Along with Lloyd Ohlin, he argued that in some lower-class communities, illegal activities could be found that would allow some an avenue to reach cultural success. He argued that three types of groups or gangs could be found in some lower-class neighborhoods.

Code of Hammurabi. A biblical code that is commonly referred to as the lex talons, or "an eye for an eye and a tooth for a tooth." Though this code is controversial, many believe that it serves the interests of equal justice or equality of the law.

Cohen, Albert. A sociologist who postulated why gangs formulated in lower-class culture. He introduced typologies of gangs that emerge in response to strain.

collective solution. A concept that was coined by Albert Cohen that revealed the actions of lower-class youths who faced the inability to reach the culturally induced goals of status through the educational system. The collective solution led to the formulation of gangs.

commitment. One of four elements found in Travis Hirschi's social bonding theory that involves the amount of time, energy and effort an individual spends engaging in conventional activities such as acquiring an education, maintaining a job, or saving money. To the extent that a person invests in conventional activities, he or she has too much to lose by engaging in delinquency. A commitment to conventional activities is believed to strengthen one's social bonds to society.

Comte, August. Considered, with Émile Durkheim, to be the founder of sociology.

conflict gangs. One of three gang typologies discussed by Richard Cloward and Lloyd Ohin in their book, *Delinquency and Opportunity* (1960) that emerged in response to lower class culture and a lack of legitimate or illegitimate opportunities. Unlike the other two gangs (criminal and retreatist), these gang members were typically found in socially disorganized communities where they engaged in violence against community residents as well as rival gangs in order to win a reputation. This allowed

them to acquire status, a self-image, and access to scarce resources in impoverished areas.

conflict theory. The theory that the chaos in society exists because of different groups and classes of people who have different interests and power struggles.

conformity. A concept used in the mode of adaptation presented by Robert K. Merton to express that most people in the United States subscribe to the cultural goals and accepted means to achieve those goals.

containment theory. The theory that one can experience inner pushes and outer pulls that may induce crime.

Conwell, Chic. The pseudonym given to a main character (and real-life criminal) in Edwin Sutherland's book *The Professional Thief.*

corporate crime. Crime committed by people in positions of respectability in the course of their occupation. Corporate crime is also referred to as white-collar crime. Some examples of corporate crime are price fixing, fraudulent stock manipulation, insider trading, and the establishment of junk bonds. The purpose of such crime is usually to advance one's personal fortune or the company of one's employment.

criminal gangs. One of three gang typologies discussed by Richard Cloward and Lloyd Ohin in their book, *Delinquency and Opportunity* (1960) that emerged in response to the lower class culture and a lack of legitimate opportunities. They were found in stable slum areas that had connections among adolescence, young adults and adult criminals. The areas provided an environment for successful criminal enterprises. Unlike the other two gangs (conflict and retreatist), these gang members served as apprentices. They were taught a criminal trade and were primarily recruited to learn how to make money. They were also trained to not jeopardize criminal operations by keeping violence at a minimum. They were often able to transition into organized crime. These gangs were often found in socially organized communities.

crisis intervention. One of the services provided to the victims of crime. It is the immediate help or assistance that victims need to help them get through their criminal victimization. Crimes such as domestic violence and rape typically require crisis intervention programs.

cross-section. A representation of an entire community or data collected at one point in time.

culture conflict. A state in which people of different cultural backgrounds clash with one another. This typically occurs when one cultural group is subjected to the culture of another group.

cultural criminology. The study of crime within the frameworks of experiential dynamics of illicit subcultures, the symbolic criminalization of popular cultural forms, the mediated construction of crime, and crime-control issues.

cultural goals. The aspirations that are instilled in everyone living in a particular society.

cultural transmission of deviance. A theoretical argument from Clifford Shaw and Henry McKay concerning the continuing of deviance and criminal behavior in the socially disorganized community found in Zone Two of the five concentric circles. They argued that deviance is taught or passed from one community resident to another.

"dangerous" classes. Those who were not part of the aristocracy and who were disproportionately paupers. Traditionally, poor people, especially those who are criminals, were considered as belonging to the "dangerous" classes.

"dark figures" of crime. Crimes that are hidden from official statistics because they are unreported.

Darwin, Charles. An English naturalist who lived from 1809 to 1882. His work discussing the evolution of man was instrumental in influencing the early biological work of the positivistic school.

Darwinism. The theory that argues that species are derived by descent through the natural selection of those best adapted to survive in the struggle of existence.

deconstructionist. A theoretician who believes there is no objective reality and who attacks traditional theories without the intent to rebuild them.

demonic possession. The state of being controlled by evil forces or the devil and his angels. During the Middle Ages, this was thought to be common among social deviants, sinners, and adulterers. Those who were labeled as being demonically possessed were typically put to death through trial by ordeal.

deterrence. Actions used to prevent crime from occurring by threatening the potential offender with punishment. Deterrence usually has two forms: general and specific. Some experts argue that the criminal justice system acts as a threat system and some do not commit crime because they fear being apprehended and punished.

differential association. A theory that argues that criminal behavior is learned in a process of communication with intimate others who provide reasons favorable to violating the law.

differential opportunity. The theory that people living in lower-class communities can find opportunities of a different kind to reach cultural goals of success.

differential reinforcement. A theory that argues that behaviors persist or desist to the extent that they are rewarded or punished.

dominant culture. The conventional value system of a given society.

drift theory. A theory that refers to the ability to shift in and out of conforming behavior.

Durkheim, Émile. Considered, with August Comte, to be the founder of sociology.

ecological fallacy. A logical error that results when one attempts to make conclusions about individuals based on group data.

economic inequality. Unequal distribution of monetary resources and access to employment opportunities.

economic prosperity. The notion of being economically independent and living the "good life." It is normally associated with being wealthy.

egalitarian philosophy. Any ideology that promotes equality and fairness with respect to access to opportunities and advancement.

elements of socialization. The family, peers, school, church, and other institutions that are essential to social processing.

end-to-end integration. Refers to conceptualizing a dependent variable and in one theory as an independent variable in another or an independent variable in one theory and a dependent variable in another or both. This type of integration is better used when causal conditions can be ordered on a continuum of immediate to remote causes. Also known as sequential integration.

environmental crime. Criminal activity that leads to the destruction of the natural environment—for example, dumping hazardous waste and engaging trade in of products such as endangered species or ozone-depleting substances.

equivalent group hypothesis. A theory of victimization that argues that victims and offenders are essentially the same, since many offenders were once the victim of crime.

ethics. What is morally right or wrong as agreed to by a group or profession.

excitement. A dominant theme or value common to lower class subculture that posits that on the weekends, large numbers of poor community residents go uptown in search of thrills such as drinking, dancing, fighting, and fulfilling sexual pleasures.

experimental design. A study that attempts to approximate laboratory conditions. Experiments include two groups, control and experimental. The experimental group is exposed to a treatment, or independent variable, and the control group is not exposed to the treatment; it is used to compare to the experimental group. The purpose of this research is to determine cause and effect.

external controls. Family, community, schools, and other informal mechanisms of social control.

fate. A theme that is common to lower class subculture that holds that many residents of urban ghettos are superstitious and often make life decisions about their futures based on unsubstantiated beliefs.

feminist criminology. A branch of criminology that examines issues related to women's participation in crime in the context of male dominance. It argues that what is needed to understand women's participation in crime is a gender-based criminology that takes into account the experiences of women, instead of generalizations drawn from studies of male criminals.

Ferracuti, Franco. One of the writers of a subculture of violence theory who argued that most violent crime in the 1960s occurred in the southern states among people who shared a willingness and readiness to engage in extreme violence.

Ferri, Enrico. A theoretician who asserted that free will had no place in criminological theory; he believed crime was caused by three factors: anthropological, physical, and social.

five concentric circles. A layout of the city of Chicago that divided the community into different sections, as delineated by Robert Park and Ernest Burgess; also referred to as zone maps.

focal concerns. A subcultural explanation given by Walter Miller of the behaviors of lower-class gang members. According to Miller, focal concerns replaced conventional values and traditions. Moreover, adherence to the focal concerns was status conferring.

forcible rape. Sexual intercourse with a person forcibly and against his or her will. It also refers to assaults or attempts to commit rape by force or threat of force.

free will. The ability to choose a course of action without external influences. For example, where crime is concerned, it means that the offender voluntarily chooses to engage in crime on his or her own accord.

Freud, Sigmund. The originator of the psychoanalytic perspective. Freud asserted that most human behavior is motivated by unconscious thoughts and memories.

Gall, Franz. An early phrenologist who advocated that people with unusually shaped skulls have a propensity to engage in criminal behavior.

gangs. Groups of people with an identifiable organizational structure that come together to pursue their economic interests. They have identifiable colors and symbols, and occupy an area of a city that is referred to as their turf. They typically engage in criminal activities, such as selling drugs, engaging in prostitution, and dealing in stolen merchandise.

Garofalo, Rafael. A contemporary of Cesare Lombroso and Enrico Ferri who also advocated the early tradition of a biological basis to criminal behavior. He further argued that criminals should be sterilized.

general deterrence. Action used by the justice system to prevent potential offenders from engaging in crime. For example, it is hoped that the spread of information about an offender receiving punishment for having committed a crime will have a deterrent effect on others.

general strain theory. A theory developed by Robert Agnew that proposes that crime and deviance are not necessarily the domain of the lower class, but rather anyone in society can feel strain and, therefore, engage in crime.

genetics. In criminology, the idea that crime is inheritable and can be transmitted to families. The most famous studies used to demonstrate this line of thinking involve two families, the Jukes and the Kallikaks, who were believed to perpetuate criminality via the inheritance of genes.

Gottfredson, Michael. With Travis Hirschi, argued that criminal and analogous behaviors are caused by low self-control.

governmental crime. Also referred to as state crime consists of central political insitutions of a given society. Its major institutions of the government: the legal system, the military, police, management of public health, and administrative branches.

green criminology. The study of crime that focuses on harm and damage inflicted on the environment that impacts people, animals, and the natural materials. It investigates devastation caused by air pollution, oil spills, global warming, forest fires, illegal dumping of chemical waste, and other types of damage to the earth's resources.

healthcare crime. A catchall phrase for any crime committed by medical doctors and others associated with the medical profession in the course of their occupation. Such crimes include ordering unnecessary surgery and prescriptions, defrauding insurance companies to advance one's wealth, or diluting a patient's medication.

Hirschi, Travis. Theoretician who developed control theory, especially social bonding. In 1969, he introduced his book *Causes of Delinquency.* He later coauthored the book *A General Theory of Crime.*

Hooton, Earnest Albert. A Harvard University physical anthropologist who asserted that criminals were organically inferior and that crime was a result of physiological conditions inherent in the criminal.

horizontal integration. Partitions the causes of deviance and crime by theories that best explain the behavior. Also referred to as side-by-side integration.

hypothesis. A tentative theory that predicts a relationship that exists between variables. More specifically, it states the expected relationship between an independent variable and a dependent variable.

id. A Freudian concept designed to explain that part of the personality from which urges and desires emanate. It is concerned with primitive instinctual desires and demands for immediate gratification.

ideology. The philosophy or doctrine that a group of people accepts and incorporates in its core values. According to Marx, a person's action is consistent with his or her ideology.

imitation theory. The theory that we learn through imitating the behavior of others.

index crime. The eight criminal offenses collected by the Federal Bureau of Investigation to be used in its compilation of the Uniform Crime Reports (UCR). These crimes include homicide, rape, robbery, burglary, aggravated assaults, theft, motor vehicle theft, and arson.

innovation. The process by which one creates an illegal way to acquire the cultural goals (economic success) of society. This could entail engaging in drug sales, Ponzi schemes, imbellzement and others. Within the stain theory, Merton argued that innovation occurs when one accepts the cultural goals of society, but lacks the legitimate or institutionalized means to acquire them.

institutional means. The acceptable or conventional avenues that a culture or society allows one to use to achieve the goals or aspirations that culture deems worth striving to achieve.

instrumental Marxism. The belief that the law and justice system are instruments used by the powerful elite to control the poor or the surplus populations.

integrated communities. Areas of the city in which residents exercise a high level of social control. The term refers to areas that approve and allow criminal enterprises to sustain themselves over time.

integrated theory. The combining of components of traditional paradigms in order to broaden the comprehensive understanding of criminal behavior. Integrated theory represents an attempt to combine existing theory for greater explanatory power.

interactionist theory. One of the three major sociological paradigms. Symbolic interactionists assert that symbols—things to which we attach meaning—are the basis of social life. They further assert that people do not interact with the world directly, but rather indirectly, based on the meaning they perceive for the entity in question.

internal control. Self-control to restrain from engaging in crime and delinquency.

involvement. One of four elements found in Travis Hirschi's social bonding theory that argues that the degree of participation that one has in conventional activities will strengthen his or her bond toward conformity. To the extent that one is busy spending time with the family, school, extracurricular activities, or working a job, he or she would likely not have time to transgress by engaging in delinquency. The more teenagers are busy engaging in constructive activities, it reduces the time they have to engage in destructive activities.

Juke family. A family studied by Robert Dugdale; he believed this family showed that heredity is a source of criminal conduct.

juvenile delinquency. Illegal or criminal behavior committed by someone who is not in the age of majority and is subjected to the jurisdiction of the juvenile justice system, rather than the adult criminal justice system.

Kallikak family. The fictitious name of a family studied by Henry Goddard in the early 1900s. He was quite impressed with Sir Francis Galton's assertions that intelligence was hereditary. From this line of thinking he contended that delinquency was also transmitted through lines of heredity. In this text, published in 1912, the author asserted that his analysis showed that heredity could be a cause of criminal behavior.

Kerbo, Harold. An international sociologists devoted to the study of social stratification, comparative systems, and economic development and world poverty. He is best known for his works entitled: Sociology: Social Structure and Social Conflict, Social Stratification and Inequality, and WorldPoverty: Global Inequality and the Modern World System. He has been a Fulbright professor in Japan, Thailand, Great Britain, Germany and Switzerland.

Kobrin, Solomon. A contributor to the Chicago School with his study of communities and the degree of integration or social organization that they have. Kobrin argued that degree of integration determines whether criminal activities will flourish in lower-class communities.

labeling theory. First postulated by Frank Tannenbaum in 1938, the theory that criminal career continuity was a result of the "dramatization of evil" in which the subject is singled out from his peers and treated as a criminal. In essence, this theory explains criminal behavior as a reaction to having been labeled as a delinquent. Often, when subjects are stigmatized as delinquents, they are driven to a self-fulfilling prophecy. Thus, labeling pushes violators onto a course of further deviance. Labeling theorists assert that those in power place labels on the powerless that cannot be removed. Also known as societal reaction school.

larceny. Unlawful taking and carrying away of the personal property of another with the intent to permanently deprive them of possessions; includes shoplifting, theft of accessories, pocket picking or thefts from motor vehicles.

learning theory. Theory that posits that human behavior is learned in the social environment from interactions with the family, friends, school, media, community, and the broader society. To extent that one has destructive or negative interactions with important people and institutions, it could determine impact his or her behavior.

left realism. A movement staged by conservative realists accusing instrumental Marxists of downplaying the seriousness of street crimes committed by the underclass against one another.

Lemert, Edwin. Part of the labeling tradition who argued that primary deviance could lead to secondary deviance if the individual is labeled and relabeled.

lifestyle theory. A victimization theory that posits that some people have certain behavior patterns and lifestyles that increase the likelihood that they will become the victims of crime. They are typically those who frequent public places where the criminal element is found—usually places where alcohol is used. The risk of victimization is increased if a person frequents public places during crime peak hours.

Lombroso, Cesare. Considered to be the father of criminology. An Italian physician and professor of psychiatry at the University of Turin, he studied the cadavers of criminals in order to determine scientifically whether they were different physically from people with more conventional behaviors and attitudes. Lombrosian theory can be outlined in two simple steps. First, Lombroso believed that serious criminal conduct was inherited: criminals were compelled to commit criminal acts. Second, Lombroso asserted that born criminals were atavistic throwbacks from primitive times.

longitudinal design. A study that is conducted over time to determine what causes change. These studies typically use a group of subjects who share similar characteristics (a cohort).

macro-level theory. A theoretical explanation that has an extensive explanatory power, and can be used to explain group behavior. Theories that examine poverty and socialization are typically macro in their level of explanation.

mala in se. Crimes that are inherently evil by their nature, such as murder, rape, and robbery.

mala prohibita. Crimes that offend the sensibility of some people's morality. They are crimes because statutes are in place to prevent them. Such crimes include prostitution, drug sales, drug use, and gambling.

Marx, Karl. Wrote the *Communist Manifesto* and other important works. He is mostly associated with the Communist Party and his critiques of the economy, including his work challenging the inequalities that exist in capitalist societies. It is argued that all conflict theories can be traced to the work of Marx.

Marxist feminist. One who views gender inequality as stemming from the unequal distribution of power in a capitalist society. According to Marxist feminists, women are exploited by patriarchal societies.

Marxist theory. A theory in which criminal conduct is viewed as a function of the capitalist mode of production. Capitalism is made up of the haves and the have-nots, each participating in a unique type of criminality. Marx asserts that the mode of production shapes all social life. Because economic success above all else is the basis of capitalism, competition increases, causing conflict and instability in the social institutions of life. Furthermore, Marxian theorists assert that in a capitalist society, the political elite control the definition of crime, the courts, prisons, and law enforcement personnel. As a result, the proletariat (poor) engage in the only crimes available to them—street crimes, which are severely sanctioned. Members of the upper classes engage in petty theft and fraud—crimes that are less severely punished.

master status. A concept used in labeling theory to express the dominant feature of one who has been successfully labeled a certain type of deviant or criminal offender. This status dominates other qualities the labelled person possesses.

Matza, David. Researcher who worked with Gresham Sykes to contribute to the formulation of the techniques of neutralization theory.

McKay, Henry. Researcher who, along with Clifford Shaw, developed social disorganization theory and cultural transmission of deviance theory, based on the five concentric circles.

mechanical society. Society characterized by remedial divisions of labor. It is commonly a close-knit community that is not technologically developed and where informalities govern all aspects of social life.

Merton, Robert King. A sociologist who borrowed from the anomie theory of Émile Durkheim, applying it to the United States' emphasis on economic success, and changed the name to strain theory.

mesomorph. One of the three body types developed by William Sheldon. Sheldon believed in somatotyping and that criminals displayed body builds that made them more prone to criminal behavior. The mesomorph was described as a muscular and aggressive type. This individual was assertive and confident in his exploits.

micro-level theory. Theoretical explanation that has very limited explanatory power—for instance, to explain the behavior of a single individual. In the study of crime, micro-level theories are primarily biological and psychological.

Middle Ages. Referred to as the Dark Ages by some because it is believed that during this period, there were no contributions made in the arts and sciences. The period extended from the 14th through the 17th centuries.

middle-class measuring rod. The standards set by middle-class authority figures.

Miller, Walter. A sociologist who studied communities in Boston using a participant observation technique and formulated the controversial focal concerns theory.

mode of production. The economic structure that underlies all producing societies.

modeling theory. Posited by Albert Bandura, a theoretical argument that posits that offenders learn to engage in crime by modeling the behaviors of those who have committed crime. A relationship does not have to exist between people since modeling can be learned from television or books.

modes of adaptation. Mechanisms that are used to either cope with or adapt to a particular state of being. Robert K. Merton provides several strategies that people use to cope with the strain of trying to achieve economic prosperity or the American Dream.

motor vehicle theft. Stealing or attempting to steal an automobile or any other mode of transportation that is powered by gasoline or diesel fuel such as trucks, buses, snowmobile, or motor cycles.

murder. Intentionally causing the death of another person with malice aforethought or causing the death of another while committing or attempting to commit a crime.

National Crime Victimization Survey. Survey used to supplement the Uniform Crime

Reports by helping to arrive at an accurate measure of the nature and extent of crime and victimization.

National Incident-Based Reporting System (NIBRS). A crime index created to address the many shortcomings found in the UCR. It includes traditional index crimes, firearms violations, public order crimes, and information on the relationships between victims and offenders.

National Institute of Justice. The research component of the U.S. Department of Justice concerned with funding criminal justice projects and investigations of the elements of the justice system such as police, courts, corrections, and juvenile justice.

National Youth Survey. An important instrument used to collect data on adolescents. It allows researchers to test integrated sociological and psychological theory.

native. A term used in observational research that denotes the researcher has lost objectivity and has overidentified with the subjects of the investigation. The term is also used to refer to a subject who has overidentified with his role in a research project.

neighborhood anticrime campaigns. These are initiatives used by community residents across the country to take an active role in reducing crime and fear. These programs encourage citizens to report suspicious behavior to local law enforcement and not take enforcement matters into their own hands. Such programs work better when they are part of a comprehensive effort to transcend the quality of life for community residents.

new criminology. A branch of conflict theory that was developed in 1973 by British scholars Ian Taylor, Paul Walton, and Jock Young that critiqued existing methods of criminology and advocated the development of new methods of analyses and critiques that were critical of the status quo.

new norms. Behaviors that lower-class youths decided would be status conferring. According to Albert Cohen, because youths in the lower class could not achieve status via conventional means, they created

status-conferring behaviors that they could easily attain.

Nye, Ivan. Researcher who contributed to control theory by suggesting that juveniles engage in delinquency because the family fails to provide direct control.

observational research. A research design whereby the investigator collects data by interacting with the subjects of the research in their natural setting to understand what their experiences mean to them. This approach renders a grounded theory when the research is completed.

Ohlin, Lloyd. Co-author of the theory of differential opportunity along with Richard Cloward.

operant learning. Concerned with the impact that the individual has on the environment and, likewise, the impact that the environment has on the individual.

operationalize. The process of defining variables that represent specific concepts, or portions of concepts, that will be collected from the study subjects. Researchers operationalize by imposing their ideas about how a concept should be measured in the study situation.

opportunity structure. A term used by Richard Cloward and Lloyd Ohlin in their theory of differential opportunity structures. Essentially, an opportunity structure is a path to acquire goals. There are both legitimate and illegitimate opportunity structures.

organic society. Characterized as being technologically advanced with a sophisticated division or labor. In these types of societies, formal laws and regulations govern all aspects of social life.

organized crime. Criminal structures that are involved in the management and coordination of providing illegal goods and services that are desired by many people in society. Such goods and services may include pornography, gambling, prostitution, drugs, and high-interest loans.

Park, Robert. A sociologist who shaped the Chicago School, symbolic interactionism, and much of sociology. He advocated going into the field, or the "real world," and making observations and analyses of social life. This would become the hallmark of the Chicago School. He was also one of the developers of the five concentric circles.

passive precipitation theory. A controversial victimization theory that contends that one can sustain victimization after he or she unknowingly becomes a threat to another's power base. The theory is used to explain rape in the workplace and social, political, and economic situations where the victims unknowingly are perceived as a threat from their attackers.

peacemaking criminology. The brand of criminology that promotes love and peace, not war. It argues for less formal intervention from the criminal justice system and promotes informal responses to crime, such as compassionate resolutions between victim and offender when reconciliation is possible.

peer informants. Refers to a technique used in self-report surveys or studies to validate claims.

Petersilia, Joan. A professor in the Department of Criminology, Law, and Sociology at the University of California, Irvine. She has published extensively on crime prevention and justice for persons with disabilities, parole and prisoner reintegration, and sentencing. One of her recent publications is *Criminal Justice Policy*.

phenomenological criminology. Argues that criminal behavior is knowable only to the people who engage in it, and that society socially constructs behavior that becomes what the consensus believes.

phrenology. One of the first branches of positivistic theories, it examined the shape and size of the human skull as an indicator of propensity to commit crime.

political crime. Illegal activities that can be committed on the city, county, state, and national levels. When they occur on the state level, they may entail state corruption and repression. When they are committed on the international level, they may entail violating an international law or even domestic actions perpetrated against a nation's own people, such as genocide. Also referred to as governmental crime.

Ponzi scheme. A fraudulent investment that pays returns to investors from existing or new capital that comes from new investors instead of from monies earned by the individual or institution.

positivistic criminology. The branch of criminology that began in the 19th century and extended into the 1950s. This school of thought rejected the arguments of free will and rational choice and embraced arguments of biological and psychological determinism. It held that criminals are predestined to be criminals. The school rejected punishing offenders and advocated rehabilitation and treatment.

positivists. Criminologists who attribute crime causation to internal and external forces such as biology, psychology, and the social environment.

postmodernism. The school of thought that contemporary theories have failed to explain or prevent the continuing of criminal behavior and have also failed to adequately influence justice policies to alleviate the conditions of the poor. It argues that objectivity does not exist.

poverty. The state of having little or no money, goods, or means of support.

power–control theory. A theory by sociologist John Hagan that holds that power relations in the household and workplace conditions patterns of parental control of children in two parent families resulting in gender differences in rates of delinquency.

power threat theory. A theory that holds that as minority group's increase in economic or political power, majority groups will subject them to greater amounts of social control.

primary deviance. A term used by Edwin Lemert to explain the initial act of deviance or crime committed by a person. Unless reprimand for the behavior, the initial act does not cause any harm to the person's identity or personality.

proletarians. Those people who make up the poor working class and are exploited by the owners of the means of production.

proportionate sentencing. A punishment in the form of a sentence given by a judge or magistrate that is equal to the gravity or the social injury of the crime.

proximity hypothesis. A victimization theory that argues that if people live in criminogenic communities, they face a greater chance of being the victim of crime than others who live in a crime-free neighborhood. The theory posits that even if a person practiced a law-abiding and healthy lifestyle in such an area, there would be no guarantee that he or she would not experience victimization. Victimization may be an inevitable consequence of living among the criminal element.

punishment. Just deserts for engaging in law-violative behavior. There are many ways to punish offenders, such as incarceration, rehabilitation, retribution, and deterrence.

Quetelet, Adolf. Belgian mathematician who applied mathematics to the study of crime. He examined the role that social forces play in influencing the crime rate. He argued that there is a correlation between crime and season, climate, population density, and alcohol.

radical feminism. A branch of conflict theory that views the problem of gender inequality and the subordination of women to male power as caused by the problem of patriarchy.

radical theory. A branch of conflict theory that focuses on the political nature of the definition of crime and the oppressive use of the criminal law and the criminal justice system.

rational choice. The theory that offenders engage in crime with knowledge of the law and an awareness of the prospect of punishment. They weigh the advantages and disadvantages before they engage in criminal behavior. If they feel that they can successfully engage in crime without apprehension, they will do so.

rebellion. A mode of adaptation that provides that some members of society will reject both the cultural goals and institutionalized means and opt to replace them with other goals and means such as creating an alternative scheme for a new social structure. Some people could seek to develop a socialist state or create militias contending they have lost faith or confidence in the legitimacy of the U.S. government.

Reckless, Walter. Researcher who developed the containment theory while making contributions to the social control tradition.

Reiss, Albert. Researcher who made contributions to control theory by arguing that delinquency results from a lack of proper internal development, a breakdown of internal controls, and an absence of social rules provided by an important social group.

relative deprivation theory. The theory that crime is a function of the perception of social injustice with respect to the continued unequal access to power and wealth. The poor become enraged when they see the gap increase between those in society with the most and those with the least. The situation is amplified when they live in close physical proximity to the affluent because they are constantly reminded of their poverty.

reliability. A consistent or repeated measure. It allows for replication in research.

research. An investigation that employs the use of the scientific method. It is considered as a systematic investigation of phenomena, behavior, or processes that relies on empirical data and logical study and analysis.

retreatism. A mode of adaptation that provides that some members will either reject or give up on the cultural goals of society and retreat into other arenas such as a drug culture or alcoholism. This mode allows for escape into an unproductive, noncompetitive, or leisurely lifestyle with few if any demands on its participants. Since they reject the cultural goals, they do not accept the institutionalized means of society.

retreatist gangs. One of three gang typologies discussed by Richard Cloward and Lloyd Ohin in their book, *Delinquency and Opportunity* (1960) that emerged in response to lower class culture and a lack of legitimate or illegitimate opportunities. Unlike the other two gangs (conflict and criminal), these gang members were considered as double failures since they were unable to succeed through legitimate avenues and unwilling to do so through illegal means. Some members tried but failed at a life of crime either because of weakness, clumsiness, or fear. Some may have even been viewed by gang members as unacceptable members. They then retreated to the fringes of society where they searched for ways to alter their state of mind with alcohol, pot, heroin or engaging in unusual sexual experiences. Despite this, they were best known for selling and using drugs. Because they could not succeed in either the conventional or lower class structure, they were referred to as two time losers.

retrospective interpretation. A concept used in labeling theory by Edwin Schur that posits once a person is labeled a criminal; one can reexamine or deconstruct past events and behavior to fit the new label given to that person.

ritualism. A mode of adaptation that provides that some members of society will reject the cultural goals of society, but accept the institutionalized means to achieve them. These people come to accept contentment from their current lifestyle. They abide by the rules of conventional society that include engaging in hard work, deferred gratification, receiving an education, and being honest, but they have abandoned the idea of reaching the cultural goal of success.

robbery. The taking or attempt to take from another any goods, monies, items, or anything of value through the use of force, violence, or fear.

routine activity theory. Theory introduced by Lawrence Cohen and Marcus Felson, who argued that victimization is greater when there is an availability of suitable targets, an absence of capable guardians, and motivated offenders. These elements, they contend, will not guarantee that crime will occur, but they will increase its likelihood.

sample. A smaller number of individuals taken from a population for the purpose of generalizing to the whole. If the sample is conducted in a random fashion, it should reflect the population.

scientific method. An objective strategy used by natural and social scientists to conduct research. The process entails formulating a hypothesis, collecting data, creating theories, and testing the validity of theories in order to disprove them.

secondary deviance. A term used by Edwin Lemert to explain the continuance of deviant and criminal behavior. When society reacts by punishing behavior, it could have the unintended effect of producing or causing more of the same behavior (secondary deviance), especially if the person internalizes the label given to him or her.

self-control theory. A theory by Michael Gottfredson and Travis Hirschi that argues that criminal offenders have low self-control, leading to risk taking and impulsive behavior.

self-report surveys. A type of research disproportionately conducted by independent researchers. These studies involve asking people to what extent have they violated the law without it having been reported. These surveys help get to the "dark figures" of crime. Conducting this type of research requires interviewing people, such as offenders, inmates, prisoners, judges, prosecutors, thieves, and prostitutes. These surveys allow researchers to measure the association between social variables (e.g., education, family structure, income) and crime.

Sellin, Thorsten. Contributor to studies on the social ecology of crime who posited the existence of culture conflict. He argued that diversity brings with it different cultural values, traditions, and mores that sometimes clash with those of the dominant culture. He also argued that cultural conflict is primary and secondary in nature, and that it could lead to the formation of gangs.

sequential integration. Conceptualizes a dependent variable in a theory as if it was an independent variable. Also known as end-to-end integration.

Shaw, Clifford. One of the researchers who studied the zone maps of Robert Park and Ernest Burgess. He helped to coin the phrases "social disorganization" and "cultural transmission of deviance." Many consider him part of the Chicago School of criminology.

Sheldon, William Herbert. An American psychologist and naturalist who developed the field of somatology and its relationship to delinquent and criminal behavior.

side-by-side integration. Partitions the causes of deviance and crime by theories that best explain the behavior. Also referred to as horizontal integration.

Skinner, Burrhus Federic. Researcher who provided the six principles of operant learning: positive reinforcement, negative reinforcement, positive punishment, negative punishment, discriminative stimuli, and schedules.

social bonding theory. A theory developed by Travis Hirschi that argues that when juveniles have weakened or broken bonds to society, the stage is set for delinquent behavior.

social class. The level of rank at which one is placed in a stratified society. In the United States, the dominant social classes are the lower, middle, and upper. The class in which an individual has membership will ultimately determine his or her life's chances and quality of life.

social control. That which makes people conform their behaviors to standards of the law.

social disorganization. The state in which the informal mechanisms of social control are not working, and crime and delinquency flourish. Socially disorganized communities lack economic and cultural resources, and adults lack the ability to make residents conform their behaviors to standards of the law.

social ecology. Examines the influence that one's community or neighborhood has on the behavior of crime. The argument is that one's neighborhood and surroundings might propel one into a life of crime.

socialization. The process by which people are taught conventional or delinquent behavior while interacting with the family, peer, schools, and significant others.

social modeling theory. A branch of social learning theory that is traced to the work of psychologist Albert Bandura who conducted extensive research in the areas of aggression, media, and imitation. It is also referred to as imitation theory.

social processing. The branch of theories that contains learning, labeling, and social control, and that argues that the quality of interactions that people have with socializing institutions and significant others will determine their future behaviors.

social solidarity. That which binds people and communities together.

social stratification. The division in society whereby people are ranked or characterized based on the amount of income or economic buying power that they have.

societal reaction school. Another name used to refer to label theory since it addresses how stigma affects people who receive labels and its consequences.

sociology. The study of society and what transpires when people interact with each other. It also encompasses the study of the origins and development of social institutions.

smartness. A dominant theme or value that is commonly found in the lower class subculture and highly praised that holds some residents are gifted with the ability to con others into getting what they want from them by using mental agility instead of having to work or engage in physical labor to acquire what they desire.

specific deterrence. Action used by the criminal justice system to prevent a punished offender from recidivating or re-engaging in crime.

Spurzheim, Johann Gaspar. One of the earlier positivists who advocated the tradition of phrenology.

state. The central political insitutions of a given society.

status frustration. A state of dejection caused by the inability to achieve social status in any aspect of life whose value is stressed by the American society.

strain theory. The theory that holds because America is a stratified society and has different social classes, not everyone can compete for success on an equal footing. These disparities in opportunity cause some people to engage in crime to reach the cultural goal of economic success.

structural Marxism. A branch of social conflict theory that holds that the law is designed to support and sustain the continuance of capitalism and will punish anyone who threatens the system.

structured action theory. A theory developed by sociologist James W. Messerschmidt that addresses the gendered nature of crime. In Crime as Structured Action, he looks at relations between gender and crime by examining how people in specific settings can use crime to construct social relations, social situations, and how social structures and setting helps to produce and reproduce different types of masculinities and femininities.

subculture. A culture found within a dominant culture. Subcultures are typically secondary groups that provide their own set of values, customs, beliefs, and traditions. Individual solidarity can be strong in either a dominant culture or a subculture.

subculture of violence. A subculture, generally in a lower-income urban area, where violence is more used and tolerated by community residents. Because violence is so pervasive, many residents are desensitized to it.

success. A term used in the United States to mean that a person has reached a certain level of economic independence. It is typically associated with those in the middle and upper classes who enjoy a high standard of living because of educational attainment, occupation, social class position, or the amount of money they have managed to accumulate.

surplus population. In Marxist analysis, the concept refers to large segments of people who are without work and who contribute nothing to capitalist society.

survey. An instrument used by social scientists to measure attitudes, behaviors, beliefs, and preferences of respondents.

Sutherland, Edwin. Researcher who proposed the theory of differential association and was the first to coin the phrase "white-collar crime." Sutherland argued that crime, like any other behavior, is learned in a process of association and interacting with others. He also argued that crime "in the suites" was just as worthy of sociological attention as crime on the streets.

Sykes, Gresham. Co-author of the techniques of neutralization theory with David Matza.

symbolic interactionism. A theory by Robert Herbert Mead, Charles Horton Cooley, and William Thomas arguing that people interact with each other and communicate both verbally and symbolically. Through a process of communication, people come to develop an identity based on the group's expectations of them. They also learn about the people with whom they interact, and their identity is basically created and sustained by group activity and involvement.

Tannenbaum, Frank. Researcher associated with the labeling perspective who examined the negative effects of applying labels to juveniles.

Tarde, Gabriel. A French sociologist and criminologist whose work in the area of imitation is considered the forerunner to the Differential Association Theory. His work on imitation contradicted early biological positivism.

tautological problem. Circular reasoning or circular logic that is common to some theoretical arguments.

techniques of neutralization. Strategies used by delinquents to excuse or justify drifting in and out of conforming behavior. The techniques were created by Gresham Sykes and David Matza as a reaction to Albert Cohen's suggestion that lower-class youths completely reject middle-class values.

Ten Commandments. Mosaic code given to the Israelites by God as instructions by which to live.

testability. Where research is concerned, one criteria of a good theory is that it must be tested. If it can be tested, it has the potential of making for good theory.

the college boy. One type of group described by Albert K. Cohen in his book, *Delinquent Boys* (1955). Such group while few in numbers emerge in response to the failure of member of the lower class achieving middle class social status. These boys reject their lower class culture and desperately attempt to assimilate into middle class society by embracing middle class standards. Cohen believed these boys faced a bleak prospect of integrating in the middle class for several reasons, but namely their academic deficiencies.

the corner boy. Another type of group typology described by Albert K. Cohen that developed in lower class culture because of unequal distributions of wealth and status. These boys made the most out of their situation. They remained in the community without ever leaving the lower class. They hung out in the neighborhood and spent time engaging in group activities such as gambling and athletics. They did not commit serious crime, but disproportionately engaged in petty offenses. They received support from their peers and were extremely loyal to the group and neighborhood. In the end, they found menial labor and lived a conventional lifestyle.

the delinquent boy. The third of three typologies that Albert K. Cohen described as emerging in the lower class culture and arguably the most troubled and problematic. This group posed a serious threat to the community because it engaged in delinquency as a way of rejecting middle class values. This group initially emerged because of adolescences and teenagers failure to achieve "middle class" status during the educational process owing to a lack of economic and symbolic disadvantages. To deal with middle class rejection, they resulted to reaction formation. Consequently, this group bestowed a different type of status on its members. In this group, social status was conferred on members by other lower class children to the extent that they demonstrated behaviors that were nonutilitarian, malicious, and negativistic. To them, if behaviors were considered inappropriate by middle class society, it was considered appropriate and acceptable by the group. The members were extremely loyal to each other and resisted all efforts by any authority figure to control the group's behavior.

theoretical reduction. The process by which some researchers and theoreticians move from the general to the specific with theoretical argument.

theory. A speculation about how phenomena, behavior, or processes are caused and what takes place after the cause is determined.

theory integration. The process by which two or more theories are combined to provide greater explanatory power.

time series design. A research method that refers to the analysis of a single variable at several successive time periods with a measure taken before treatment and several observations after treatment.

toughness. A dominant theme or value that is commonly found in lower class subculture due to a lack of fatherly figures who are absent from the family. It holds that part of the male socialization in lower class culture was to overly emphasize measures of masculinity.

trial by ordeal. A trial used by "courts" during the Middle Ages. Offenders accused of being witches or demonically possessed were challenged to prove their innocence by showing that God would intervene on their behalf. Ordeals, such as walking on water and holding burning coal, allowed that opportunity. If an offender failed at the ordeal, he or she would be put to death.

triangulation. A research technique that relies on several methodologies to measure the same subject matter.

trouble. A unavoidable theme that is common to lower class subculture that helps to assess one's suitability and standings in the lower class milieu.

Twelve Tables. Also referred to as the Roman Twelve Tables. This set of laws is believed to have provided noble Romans with their rights.

typologies. The different types of theories used to explain criminal behavior.

Uniform Crime Reports (UCR). An annual publication by the Federal Bureau of Investigation of all reported Part I and Part II index crimes provided by over 17,000 police agencies. Compilation focuses mainly on violent and economic crimes. This source is relied on by many practicing criminal justice experts and criminologists. In 1988, the UCR switched to the National Incident-Based Reporting System.

up-and-down integration. Identifies levels of abstraction that incorporate conceptualizations from constituent theories.

utilitarianism. A concept that refers to the greatest good for the greatest number of people. In criminal justice, the utilitarian purpose of the system is to protect the broader society from offenders who prey on law-abiding citizens.

validity. The accuracy or exactness of measurement in research investigations.

victim. Any person who has sustained an injurious action at the hands of another or an object.

victim compensation. One of many programs designed to assist the victims of crime. Applications for victim compensation are given to the victim-turned-witness to a crime to help reimburse or defray the cost of victimization sustained during a criminal episode of violence. In most states, the amount of money one can receive is contingent on the amount available in the state reserve. Typically, it is the job of the local prosecutor to inform the victim-turned-witness about victim compensation applications.

victim impact statements. A device used to garner greater participation of victims or surviving family members in the criminal justice process. In some cases, statements are written by victims and submitted to a judge as part of the investigation before sentence is imposed on the defendant. In others, victims or their surviving family members are allowed to stand before the judge and jury and speak to how the victimization affected the lives of family members. Yet in others, victims sometimes appear before parole hearings to discuss the impact of their victimization. This is believed to affect the board's decision to release the petitioner. To some, the process is heavily weighted against the accused. To others, it allows the victims a sense of closure.

victim precipitation theory. A theory on victimization that argues that victims are responsible and may even cause the harm that they receive by the way they act. The theory argues that if victims act in an aggressive manner by attacking first with physical action, threats, or fighting words, they are believed responsible if someone reacts to their initial behavior.

victimization. The process by which people get victimized.

victimologist. A professional trained to use the scientific method to study crime victims. Victimologists study crime victims to create typologies of victimization, to examine trends and patterns associated with victimization, and to determine how society reacts and responds to the victims of crime. By studying crime victims, they can assess whether crime rates are increasing or decreasing.

victimology. The scientific study of crime victims and the dynamics that exist between victims and offenders. The discipline is also concerned with victim typologies, victimization theories as well as victims experiences in the criminal justice system.

white-collar crime. Typically associated with people in positions of respectability in society who take advantage of their social class positions by engaging in crime. The term was initially coined by Edwin Sutherland in 1939 when he argued that crimes committed "in the suites" are just as worthy of sociological attention as crimes committed on the streets. Commonly referred to as corporate crime.

Wolfgang, Marvin. A sociologist who conducted longitudinal research using a birth cohort to examine the repeat or chronic offender. He also examined homicides while paying close attention to victim precipitation. He is typically identified as having conducted research with Ferracuti on the subculture of violence theory.

Index

Note: Page numbers followed by *f* and *t* indicate material in figures and tables, respectively.